THE LIFE OF JOHN MARSHALL

VOLUME II

JOHN MARSHALL AS CHIEF JUSTICE
From the portrait by Jarvis

THE LIFE
OF
JOHN MARSHALL

BY

ALBERT J. BEVERIDGE

VOLUME II

POLITICIAN, DIPLOMATIST
STATESMAN

1789 — 1801

BOSTON AND NEW YORK

HOUGHTON MIFFLIN COMPANY

The Riverside Press Cambridge

1919

Published October 1916

CONTENTS

shall savagely — Marshall answers his assailants — They make in-
sinuations against his character: the Fairfax purchase, the story of
Marshall's heavy drinking — The Republicans win on their opposi-
tion to Neutrality — Great Britain becomes more hostile than ever
— Washington resolves to try for a treaty in order to prevent war —
Jay negotiates the famous compact bearing his name — Terrific
popular resentment follows: Washington abused, Hamilton stoned,
Jay burned in effigy, many of Washington's friends desert him —
Toast drank in Virginia "to the speedy death of General Washing-
ton" — Jefferson assails the treaty — Hamilton writes "Camillus"
— Marshall stands by Washington — Jefferson names him as the
leading Federalist in Virginia.

Marshall becomes the chief defender of Washington in Virginia —
The President urges him to accept the office of Attorney-General —
He declines — Washington depends upon Marshall's judgment in
Virginia politics — Vicious opposition to the Jay Treaty in Virginia
— John Thompson's brilliant speech expresses popular sentiment
— He couples the Jay Treaty with Neutrality: "a sullen neutrality
between freemen and despots" — The Federalists elect Marshall to
the Legislature — Washington is anxious over its proceedings —
Carrington makes absurdly optimistic forecast — The Republicans
in the Legislature attack the Jay Treaty — Marshall defends it with
great adroitness — Must the new House of Representatives be consulted about treaties? — Carrington writes Washington that Marshall's argument was a demonstration — Randolph reports to Jefferson that Marshall's speech was tricky and ineffectual — Marshall
defeated — Amazing attack on Washington and stout defense of
him led by Marshall — Washington's friends beaten — Legislature
refuses to vote that Washington has "wisdom" — Jefferson denounces Marshall: "His lax, lounging manners and profound hypocrisy" — Washington recalls Monroe from France and tenders the
French mission to Marshall, who declines — The Fauchet dispatch
is intercepted and Randolph is disgraced — Washington forces him
to resign as Secretary of State — The President considers Marshall
for the head of his Cabinet — The opposition to the Jay Treaty
grows in intensity — Marshall arranges a public meeting in Richmond — The debate lasts all day — The reports as to the effect of his
speeches contradictory — Marshall describes situation — The Republicans make charges and Marshall makes counter-charges —
The national Federalist leaders depend on Marshall — They commission him to sound Henry on the Presidency as the successor of
Washington — Washington's second Administration closes — He is
savagely abused by the Republicans—The fight in the Legislature
over the address to him—Marshall leads the Administration forces
and is beaten—The House of Delegates refuse to vote that Washington is wise, brave, or even patriotic—Washington goes out of the

Presidency amid storms of popular hatred — The "Aurora's" denunciation of him — His own description of the abuse: "indecent terms that could scarcely be applied to a Nero, a defaulter, or a common pickpocket" — Jefferson is now the popular hero — All this makes a deep and permanent impression on Marshall.

An old planter refuses to employ Marshall as his lawyer because of his shabby and unimpressive appearance — He changes his mind after hearing Marshall address the court — Marshall is conscious of his superiority over other men — Wirt describes Marshall's physical appearance — He practices law as steadily as his political activities permit — He builds a fine house adjacent to those of his powerful brothers-in-law — Richmond becomes a flourishing town — Marshall is childishly negligent of his personal concerns: the Beaumarchais mortgage; but he is extreme in his solicitude for the welfare of his relatives: the letter on the love-affair of his sister; and he is very careful of the business entrusted to him by others — He is an enthusiastic Free Mason and becomes Grand Master of that order in Virginia — He has peculiar methods at the bar: cites few authorities, always closes in argument, and is notably honest with the court: "The law is correctly stated by opposing counsel" — Gustavus Schmidt describes Marshall — He is employed in the historic case of Ware *vs.* Hylton — His argument in the lower court so satisfactory to his clients that they select him to conduct their case in the Supreme Court of the United States — Marshall makes a tremendous and lasting impression by his effort in Philadelphia — Rufus King pays him high tribute — After twenty-four years William Wirt remembers Marshall's address and describes it — Wirt advises his son-in-law to imitate Marshall — Francis Walker Gilmer writes, from personal observation, a brilliant and accurate analysis of Marshall as lawyer and orator — The Federalist leaders at the Capital court Marshall — He has business dealings with Robert Morris — The Marshall syndicate purchases the Fairfax estate — Marshall's brother marries Hester Morris — The old financier makes desperate efforts to raise money for the Fairfax purchase — Marshall compromises with the Legislature of Virginia — His brother finally negotiates a loan in Antwerp on Morris's real estate and pays half of the contract price — Robert Morris becomes bankrupt and the burden of the Fairfax debt falls on Marshall — He is in desperate financial embarrassment — President Adams asks him to go to France as a member of the mission to that country — The offer a "God-send" to Marshall, who accepts it in order to save the Fairfax estate.

CONTENTS

CONTENTS

Court which Marshall was to exercise totally unsuspected by anybody — Failure of friend and foe to estimate properly his courage
and determination.

ILLUSTRATIONS

LIST OF ABBREVIATED TITLES MOST
FREQUENTLY CITED

All references here are to the List of Authorities at the end of this volume.

Am. St. Prs. *See* American State Papers.

Beard: *Econ. I. C.* *See* Beard, Charles A. Economic Interpretation
of the Constitution of the United States.

Beard: *Econ. O. J. D.* *See* Beard, Charles A. Economic Origins of
Jeffersonian Democracy.

Cor. Rev.: Sparks. *See* Sparks, Jared. Correspondence of the Revolution.

Cunningham Letters. *See* Adams, John. Correspondence with William Cunningham.

Letters: Ford. *See* Vans Murray, William. Letters to John Quincy
Adams. Edited by Worthington Chauncey Ford.

Monroe's *Writings:* Hamilton. *See* Monroe, James. Writings. Edited
by Stanislaus Murray Hamilton.

Old Family Letters. *See* Adams, John. Old Family Letters. Edited
by Alexander Biddle.

Works: Adams. *See* Adams, John. Works. Edited by Charles Francis
Adams.

Works: Ames. *See* Ames, Fisher. Works. Edited by Seth Ames.

Works: Ford. *See* Jefferson, Thomas. Works. Federal Edition. Edited
by Paul Leicester Ford.

Works: Hamilton. *See* Hamilton, Alexander. Works. Edited by John
C. Hamilton.

Works: Lodge. *See* Hamilton, Alexander. Works. Federal Edition.
Edited by Henry Cabot Lodge.

Writings: Conway. *See* Paine, Thomas. Writings. Edited by Moncure Daniel Conway.

Writings: Ford. *See* Washington, George. Writings. Edited by
Worthington Chauncey Ford.

Writings: Hunt. *See* Madison, James. Writings. Edited by Gaillard
Hunt.

Writings, J. Q. A.: Ford. *See* Adams, John Quincy. Writings. Edited
by Worthington Chauncey Ford.

THE LIFE OF JOHN MARSHALL

THE LIFE OF JOHN MARSHALL

CHAPTER I.

INFLUENCE OF THE FRENCH REVOLUTION ON AMERICA

Were there but an Adam and an Eve left in every country, and left free, it would be better than it now is. (Jefferson.)

That malignant philosophy which can coolly and deliberately pursue, through oceans of blood, abstract systems for the attainment of some fancied untried good. (Marshall.)

The only genuine liberty consists in a mean equally distant from the despotism of an individual and a million. ("Publicola": J. Q. Adams, 1792.)

THE decision of the French King, Louis XVI, on the advice of his Ministers, to weaken Great Britain by aiding the Americans in their War for Independence, while it accomplished its purpose, was fatal to himself and to the Monarchy of France. As a result, Great Britain lost America, but Louis lost his head. Had not the Bourbon Government sent troops, fleets, munitions, and money to the support of the failing and desperate American fortunes, it is probable that Washington would not have prevailed; and the fires of the French holocaust which flamed throughout the world surely would not have been lit so soon.

The success of the American patriots in their armed resistance to the rule of George III, although brought about by the aid of the French Crown, was, nevertheless, the shining and dramatic example which Frenchmen imitated in beginning that vast and elemental upheaval called the French Revolution.[1] Thus the unnatural alliance in 1778 between French Royalty and American Liberty was one of the great and decisive events of human history.

In the same year, 1789, that the American Republic began its career under the forms of a National Government, the curtain rose in France on that tremendous drama which will forever engage the interest of mankind. And just as the American Revolution vitally influenced French opinion, so the French Revolution profoundly affected American thought; and, definitely, helped to shape those contending forces in American life that are still waging their conflict.

While the economic issue, so sharp in the adoption of the Constitution, became still keener, as will appear, after the National Government was established, it was given a higher temper in the forge of the French Revolution. American history, especially

[1] "That the principles of America opened the Bastille is not to be doubted." (Thomas Paine to Washington, May 1, 1790; *Cor. Rev.*[2]: Sparks, iv, 328.) "The principles of it [the French Revolution] were copied from America." (Paine to Citizens of the United States, Nov. 15, 1802; *Writings:* Conway, iii, 381.)

"Did not the American Revolution produce the French Revolution? And did not the French Revolution produce all the Calamities and Desolations to the human Race and the whole Globe ever since?" (Adams to Rush, Aug. 28, 1811; *Old Family Letters*, 352.)

"Many of . . . the leaders [of the French Revolution] have imbibed their principles in America, and all have been fired by our example." (Gouverneur Morris to Washington, Paris, April 29, 1789; *Cor. Rev.*: Sparks, iv, 256.)

"All the friends of freedom on this side the Atlantic are now rejoicing for an event which . . . has been accelerated by the American Revolution. . . . You have been the means of raising that spirit in Europe which . . . will . . . extinguish every remain of that barbarous servitude under which all the European nations, in a less . . . degree, have so long been subject." (Catharine M. Graham to Washington, Berks (England), Oct. 1789; *ib.*, 284; and see Cobbett, i, 97.)

of the period now under consideration, can be read correctly only by the lights that shine from that titanic smithy; can be understood only by considering the effect upon the people, the thinkers, and the statesmen of America, of the deeds done and words spoken in France during those inspiring if monstrous years.

The naturally conservative or radical temperaments of men in America were hardened by every episode of the French convulsion. The events in France, at this time, operated upon men like Hamilton on the one hand, and Jefferson on the other hand, in a fashion as deep and lasting as it was antagonistic and antipodal; and the intellectual and moral phenomena, manifested in picturesque guise among the people in America, impressed those who already were, and those who were to become, the leaders of American opinion, as much as the events of the Gallic cataclysm itself.

George Washington at the summit of his fame, and John Marshall just beginning his ascent, were alike confirmed in that non-popular tendency of thought and feeling which both avowed in the dark years between our War for Independence and the adoption of our Constitution.[1] In reviewing all the situations, not otherwise to be fully understood, that arose from the time Washington became President until Marshall took his seat as Chief Justice, we must have always before our eyes the extraordinary scenes and consider the delirious emotions which the French Revolution produced in America. It

[1] See vol. I, chap. VIII, of this work.

must be constantly borne in mind that Americans of
the period now under discussion did not and could
not look upon it with present-day knowledge, perspective, or calmness. What is here set down is,
therefore, an attempt to portray the effects of that
volcanic eruption of human forces upon the minds
and hearts of those who witnessed, from across the
ocean, its flames mounting to the heavens and its
lava pouring over the whole earth.

Unless this portrayal is given, a blank must be left
in a recital of the development of American radical
and conservative sentiment and of the formation of
the first of American political parties. Certainly for
the purposes of the present work, an outline, at least,
of the effect of the French Revolution on American
thought and feeling is indispensable. Just as the
careers of Marshall and Jefferson are inseparably
intertwined, and as neither can be fully understood
without considering the other, so the American by-
products of the French Revolution must be examined
if we would comprehend either of these great protag-
onists of hostile theories of democratic government.

At first everybody in America heartily approved
the French reform movement. Marshall describes
for us this unanimous approbation. "A great revolution had commenced in that country," he writes,
"the first stage of which was completed by limiting
the powers of the monarch, and by the establishment of a popular assembly. In no part of the
globe was this revolution hailed with more joy
than in America. The influence it would have on
the affairs of the world was not then distinctly

foreseen; and the philanthropist, without becoming a political partisan, rejoiced in the event. On this subject, therefore, but one sentiment existed." [1]

Jefferson had written from Paris, a short time before leaving for America: "A complete revolution in this [French] government, has been effected merely by the force of public opinion; . . . and this revolution has not cost a single life." [2] So little did his glowing mind then understand the forces which he had helped set in motion. A little later he advises Madison of the danger threatening the reformed French Government, but adds, reassuringly, that though "the lees . . . of the patriotic party [the French radical party] of wicked principles & desperate fortunes" led by Mirabeau who "is the chief . . . may produce a temporary confusion . . . they cannot have success ultimately. The King, the mass of the substantial people of the whole country, the army, and the influential part of the clergy, form a firm phalanx which must prevail." [3]

So, in the beginning, all American newspapers, now more numerous, were exultant. "Liberty will have another feather in her cap. . . . The ensuing winter [1789] will be the commencement of a Golden Age," [4] was the glowing prophecy of an enthusiastic Boston journal. Those two sentences of the New

---

[1] Marshall, ii, 155. "The mad harangues of the [French] National Convention were all translated and circulated through the States. The enthusiasm they excited it is impossible for me to describe." (Cobbett in "Summary View"; Cobbett, i, 98.)

[2] Jefferson to Humphreys, March 18, 1789; *Works :* Ford, v, 467.

[3] Jefferson to Madison, Aug. 28, 1789; *ib.*, 490.

[4] *Boston Gazette*, Sept. 7 and Nov. 30, 1789; as quoted in Hazen; and see Hazen, 142–43.

England editor accurately stated the expectation
and belief of all America.

But in France itself one American had grave misgivings as to the outcome. "The materials for a revolution in this country are very indifferent. Everybody agrees that there is an utter prostration of
morals; but this general position can never convey
to an American mind the degree of depravity. . . . A
hundred thousand examples are required to show the
extreme rottenness. . . . The virtuous . . . stand forward from a background deeply and darkly shaded.
. . . From such crumbling matter . . . the great edi-
fice of freedom is to be erected here [in France]. . . .
[There is] a perfect indifference to the violation of
engagements. . . . Inconstancy is mingled in the
blood, marrow, and very essence of this people. . . .
Consistency is a phenomenon. . . . The great mass
of the common people have . . . no morals but their
interest. These are the creatures who, led by drunken
curates, are now in the high road *à la liberté.*" [1]
Such was the report sent to Washington by Gouverneur Morris, the first American Minister to
France under the Constitution.

Three months later Morris, writing officially, declares that "this country is . . . as near to anarchy
as society can approach without dissolution." [2] And
yet, a year earlier, Lafayette had lamented the

---

[1] Gouverneur Morris to Washington, Paris, April 29, 1789; *Cor.
Rev.*: Sparks, iv, 256. Even Jefferson had doubted French capacity
for self-government because of what he described as French light-
mindedness. (Jefferson to Mrs. Adams, Feb. 22, 1787; *Works:* Ford,
v, 263; also see vol. I, chap. VIII, of this work.)

[2] Morris to Washington, July 31, 1789; *Cor. Rev.*: Sparks, iv,
270.

French public's indifference to much needed reforms; "The people . . . have been so dull that it has made me sick" was Lafayette's doleful account of popular enthusiasm for liberty in the France of 1788.[1]

Gouverneur Morris wrote Robert Morris that a French owner of a quarry demanded damages because so many bodies had been dumped into the quarry that they "choked it up so that he could not get men to work at it." These victims, declared the American Minister, had been "the best people," killed "without form of trial, and their bodies thrown like dead dogs into the first hole that offered."[2] Gouverneur Morris's diary abounds in such entries as "[Sept. 2, 1792] the murder of the priests, . . . murder of prisoners, . . . [Sept. 3] The murdering continues all day. . . . [Sept. 4th] . . . And still the murders continue."[3]

John Marshall was now the attorney of Robert

---

[1] Lafayette to Washington, May 25, 1788; *Cor. Rev.*: Sparks, iv, 216. Lafayette's letters to Washington, from the beginning of the French Revolution down to his humiliating expulsion from France, constitute a thermometer of French temperature, all the more trustworthy because his letters are so naïve. For example, in March, 1790: "Our revolution is getting on as well as it can, with a nation that has swallowed liberty at once, and is still liable to mistake licentiousness for freedom." Or, in August of the same year: "I have lately lost some of my favor with the mob, and displeased the frantic lovers of licentiousness, as I am bent on establishing a legal subordination." Or, six months later: "I still am tossed about in the ocean of factions and commotions of every kind." Or, two months afterwards: "There appears a kind of phenomenon in my situation; all parties against me, and a national popularity which, in spite of every effort, has been unshakable." (Lafayette to Washington, March 17, 1790; *ib.*, 321; Aug. 28, *ib.*, 345; March 7, 1791, *ib.*, 361; May 3, 1791, *ib.*, 372.)

[2] G. Morris to R. Morris, Dec. 24, 1792; Morris, ii, 15.

[3] *Ib.*, i, 582–84.

Morris; was closely connected with him in business transactions; and, as will appear, was soon to become his relative by the marriage of Marshall's brother to the daughter of the Philadelphia financier. Gouverneur Morris, while not related to Robert Morris, was "entirely devoted" to and closely associated with him in business; and both were in perfect agreement of opinions.[1] Thus the reports of the scarlet and revolting phases of the French Revolution that came to the Virginia lawyer were carried through channels peculiarly personal and intimate.

They came, too, from an observer who was thoroughly aristocratic in temperament and conviction.[2] Little of appreciation or understanding of the basic causes and high purposes of the French Revolution appears in Gouverneur Morris's accounts and comments, while he portrays the horrible in unrelieved ghastliness.[3]

Such, then, were the direct and first-hand accounts that Marshall received; and the impression made upon him was correspondingly dark, and as lasting as it was somber. Of this, Marshall himself leaves us in no doubt. Writing more than a decade later he gives his estimate of Gouverneur Morris and of his accounts of the French Revolution.

[1] Louis Otto to De Montmorin, March 10, 1792; *Writings:* Conway, iii, 153.

[2] *Ib.*, 154–56.

[3] Morris associated with the nobility in France and accepted the aristocratic view. (*Ib.*; and see A. Esmein, Membre de l'Institut: *Gouverneur Morris, un témoin américain de la révolution française.* Paris, 1906.)

"The private correspondence of Mr. Morris with the president [and, of course, much more so with Robert Morris] exhibits a faithful picture, drawn by the hand of a master, of the shifting revolutionary scenes which with unparalleled rapidity succeeded each other in Paris. With the eye of an intelligent, and of an unimpassioned observer, he marked all passing events, and communicated them with fidelity. He did not mistake despotism for freedom, because it was sanguinary, because it was exercised by those who denominated themselves the people, or because it assumed the name of liberty. Sincerely wishing happiness and a really free government to France, he could not be blind to the obvious truth that the road to those blessings had been mistaken." [1]

Everybody in America echoed the shouts of the Parisian populace when the Bastille fell. Was it not the prison where kings thrust their subjects to perish of starvation and torture? [2] Lafayette, "as a missionary of liberty to its patriarch," hastened to present Washington with "the main key of the

---

[1] Marshall, ii, note xvi, p. 17.

[2] Recent investigation establishes the fact that the inmates of the Bastille generally found themselves very well off indeed. The records of this celebrated prison show that even prisoners of mean station, when incarcerated for so grave a crime as conspiracy against the King's life, had, in addition to remarkably abundant meals, an astonishing amount of extra viands and refreshments including comfortable quantities of wine, brandy, and beer. Prisoners of higher station fared still more generously, of course. (Funck-Brentano: *Legends of the Bastille*, 85–113; see also *ib.*, introduction.) It should be said, however, that the *lettres de cachet* were a chief cause of complaint, although the stories, generally exaggerated, concerning the cruel treatment of prisoners came to be the principal count of the public indictment of the Bastille.

fortress of despotism." [1] Washington responded that he accepted the key of the Bastille as "a token of the victory gained by liberty." [2] Thomas Paine wrote of his delight at having been chosen by Lafayette to "convey . . . the first ripe fruits of American principles, transplanted into Europe, to his master and patron." [3] Mutual congratulations were carried back and forth by every ship.

Soon the mob in Paris took more sanguinary action and blood flowed more freely, but not in sufficient quantity to quench American enthusiasm for the cause of liberty in France. We had had plenty of mobs ourselves and much crimson experience. Had not mobs been the precursors of our own Revolution?

The next developments of the French uprising and the appearance of the Jacobin Clubs, however, alarmed some and gave pause to all of the cautious friends of freedom in America and other countries.

Edmund Burke hysterically sounded the alarm. On account of his championship of the cause of American Independence, Burke had enjoyed much credit with all Americans who had heard of him. "In the last age," exclaimed Burke in Parliament, February 9, 1790, "we were in danger of being entangled by the example of France in the net of a relentless despotism. . . . Our present danger from

[1] Lafayette to Washington, March 17, 1790; *Cor. Rev.*: Sparks, iv, 322.

[2] Washington to Lafayette, August 11, 1790; *Writings:* Ford, xi, 493.

[3] Paine to Washington, May 1, 1790; *Cor. Rev.*: Sparks, iv, 328. Paine did not, personally, bring the key, but forwarded it from London.

the example of a people whose character knows no medium, is, with regard to government, a danger from anarchy; a danger of being led, through an admiration of successful fraud and violence, to an imitation of the excesses of an irrational, unprincipled, proscribing, confiscating, plundering, ferocious, bloody, and tyrannical democracy." [1]

Of the French declaration of human rights Burke declared: "They made and recorded a sort of *institute* and *digest* of anarchy, called the rights of man, in such a pedantic abuse of elementary principles as would have disgraced boys at school. . . . They systematically destroyed every hold of authority by opinion, religious or civil, on the minds of the people.[2] . . . On the scheme of this barbarous philosophy, which is the offspring of cold hearts and muddy understandings," exclaimed the great English liberal, "laws are to be supported only by their own terrours. . . . In the groves of *their* academy, at the end of every vista, you see nothing but the gallows." [3]

Burke's extravagant rhetoric, although reprinted in America, was little heeded. It would have been better if his pen had remained idle. For Burke's wild language, not yet justified by the orgy of blood

[1] Burke in the House of Commons; *Works:* Burke, i, 451–53.
[2] *Ib.*
[3] *Reflections on the Revolution in France; ib.*, i, 489. Jefferson well stated the American radical opinion of Burke: "The Revolution of France does not astonish me so much as the Revolution of Mr. Burke. . . . How mortifying that this evidence of the rottenness of his mind must oblige us now to ascribe to wicked motives those actions of his life which were the mark of virtue & patriotism." (Jefferson to Vaughan, May 11, 1791; *Works :* Ford, vi, 260.)

in which French liberty was, later, to be baptized,
caused a voice to speak to which America did listen,
a page to be written that America did read. Thomas
Paine, whose "Common Sense" had made his name
better known to all people in the United States than
that of any other man of his time except Washington, Franklin, Jefferson, and Henry, was then in
France. This stormy petrel of revolution seems always to have been drawn by instinct to every part of
the human ocean where hurricanes were brooding.[1]

Paine answered Burke with that ferocious indictment of monarchy entitled "The Rights of Man,"
in which he went as far to one extreme as the English political philosopher had gone to the other; for
while Paine annihilated Burke's Brahminic laudation of rank, title, and custom, he also penned a
doctrine of paralysis to all government. As was the
case with his "Common Sense," Paine's "Rights
of Man" abounded in attractive epigrams and striking sentences which quickly caught the popular ear
and were easily retained by the shallowest memory.

"The cause of the French people is that of . . . the
whole world," declared Paine in the preface of his
flaming essay;[2] and then, the sparks beginning to
fly from his pen, he wrote: "Great part of that order
which reigns among mankind is not the effect of
government. . . . It existed prior to government,
and would exist if the formality of government was

---

[1] Paine had not yet lost his immense popularity in the United
States. While, later, he came to be looked upon with horror by great
numbers of people, he enjoyed the regard and admiration of nearly
everybody in America at the time his *Rights of Man* appeared.

[2] *Writings*: Conway, ii, 272.

abolished. . . . The instant formal government is abolished," said he, "society begins to act; . . . and common interest produces common security." And again: "The more perfect civilization is, the less occasion has it for government. . . . It is but few general laws that civilised life requires."

Holding up our own struggle for liberty as an illustration, Paine declared: "The American Revolution . . . laid open the imposition of governments"; and, using our newly formed and untried National Government as an example, he asserted with grotesque inaccuracy: "In America . . . all the parts are brought into cordial unison. There the poor are not oppressed, the rich are not privileged. . . . Their taxes are few, because their government is just." [1]

Proceeding thence to his assault upon all other established governments, especially that of England, the great iconoclast exclaimed: "It is impossible that such governments as have hitherto [1790] existed in the world, could have commenced by any other means than a violation of every principle sacred and moral."

Striking at the foundations of all permanent authority, Paine declared that "Every age and generation must be . . . free to act for itself *in all cases.* . . . The vanity and presumption of governing beyond the grave is the most ridiculous and insolent of all tyrannies." The people of yesterday have "no right . . . to bind or to control . . . the people of the present day . . . *in any shape whatever.* . . .

---

[1] *Writings:* Conway, ii, 406. At this very moment the sympathizers with the French Revolution in America were saying exactly the reverse.

Every generation is, and must be, competent to all the purposes which its occasions require." [1] So wrote the incomparable pamphleteer of radicalism.

Paine's essay, issued in two parts, was a torch successively applied to the inflammable emotions of the American masses. Most newspapers printed in each issue short and appealing excerpts from it. For example, the following sentence from Paine's "Rights of Man" was reproduced in the "Columbian Centinel" of Boston on June 6, 1792: "Can we possibly suppose that if government had originated in right principles and had not an interest in pursuing a wrong one, that the world could have been in the wretched and quarrelsome condition it is?" Such quotations from Paine appeared in all radical and in some conservative American publications; and they were repeated from mouth to mouth until even the backwoodsmen knew of them — and believed them.

"Our people . . . love what you write and read it with delight" ran the message which Jefferson sent across the ocean to Paine. "The printers," continued Jefferson, "season every newspaper with extracts from your last, as they did before from your first part of the *Rights of Man*. They have both served here to separate the wheat from the chaff. . . . Would you believe it possible that in this country there should be high & important characters [2] who need your lessons in republicanism & who do not heed them. It is but too true that we have a sect preaching up & pouting after an English constitu-

[1] *Writings:* Conway, ii, 278–79, 407, 408, 413, 910.
[2] Compare with Jefferson's celebrated letter to Mazzei (*infra*, chap. vii). Jefferson was now, however, in Washington's Cabinet.

tion of king, lords, & commons, & whose heads are
itching for crowns, coronets & mitres. . . .

"Go on then," Jefferson urged Paine, "in doing
with your pen what in other times was done with
the sword, . . . and be assured that it has not a
more sincere votary nor you a more ardent well-
wisher than . . . Thos Jefferson." [1]

And the wheat was being separated from the
chaff, as Jefferson declared. Shocked not more by
the increasing violence in France than by the principles which Paine announced, men of moderate
mind and conservative temperament in America
came to have misgivings about the French Revolution, and began to speak out against its doings and
its doctrines.

A series of closely reasoned and well-written articles were printed in the "Columbian Centinel" of
Boston in the summer of 1791, over the *nom de
guerre* "Publicola"; and these were widely copied.
They were ascribed to the pen of John Adams, but
were the work of his brilliant son.[2]

---

[1] Jefferson to Paine, June 19, 1792; *Works:* Ford, vii, 121–22;
and see Hazen, 157–60. Jefferson had, two years before, expressed
precisely the views set forth in Paine's *Rights of Man.* Indeed, he
stated them in even more startling terms. (See Jefferson to Madison,
Sept. 6, 1789; *ib.,* vi, 1–11.)

[2] *Writings, J. Q. A.:* Ford, i, 65–110. John Quincy Adams wrote
these admirable essays when he was twenty-four years old. Their
logic, wit, and style suggest the writer's incomparable mother.
Madison, who remarked their quality, wrote to Jefferson: "There is
more of method . . . in the arguments, and much less of clumsiness
& heaviness in the style, than characterizes his [John Adams's] writings." (Madison to Jefferson, July 13, 1791; *Writings:* Hunt, vi, 56.)

The sagacious industry of Mr. Worthington C. Ford has made
these and all the other invaluable papers of the younger Adams accessible, in his *Writings of John Quincy Adams* now issuing.

⌡ The American edition of Paine's "Rights of Man" was headed by a letter from Secretary of State Jefferson to the printer, stating his pleasure that the essay was to be printed in this country and "that something is at length to be publickly said against the political heresies which have sprung up among us." [1] Publicola called attention to this and thus, more conspicuously, displayed Jefferson as an advocate of Paine's doctrines. [2]

All Americans had "seen with pleasure the temples of despotism levelled with the ground," wrote the keen young Boston law student. [3] There was "but one sentiment . . . — that of exultation." But what did Jefferson mean by "heresies"? asked Publicola. Was Paine's pamphlet "the canonical book of scripture?" If so, what were its doctrines? "That

---

[1] Jefferson to Adams, July 17, 1791; *Works:* Ford, vi, 283, and footnote; also see Jefferson to Washington, May 8, 1791; *ib.*, 255–56.

Jefferson wrote Washington and the elder Adams, trying to evade his patronage of Paine's pamphlet; but, as Mr. Ford moderately remarks, "the explanation was somewhat lame." (*Writings, J. Q. A.:* Ford, i, 65; and see Hazen, 156–57.) Later Jefferson avowed that "Mr. Paine's principles . . . were the principles of the citizens of the U. S." (Jefferson to Adams, Aug. 30, 1791; *Works:* Ford, vi, 314.) To his intimate friend, Monroe, Jefferson wrote that "Publicola, in attacking all Paine's principles, is very desirous of involving me in the same censure with the author. I certainly merit the same, for I profess the same principles." (Jefferson to Monroe, July 10, 1791; *ib.*, 280.)

Jefferson at this time was just on the threshold of his discovery of and campaign against the "deep-laid plans" of Hamilton and the Nationalists to transform the newborn Republic into a monarchy and to deliver the hard-won "liberties" of the people into the rapacious hands of "monocrats," "stockjobbers," and other "plunderers" of the public. (See next chapter.)

[2] *Writings, J. Q. A.:* Ford, i, 65–66.

[3] Although John Quincy Adams had just been admitted to the bar, he was still a student in the law office of Theophilus Parsons at the time he wrote the Publicola papers.

which a whole nation chooses to do, it has a right
to do" was one of them.

Was that "principle" sound? No! avowed Publicola, for "the eternal and immutable laws of justice
and of morality are paramount to all human legislation." A nation might have the power but never
the right to violate these. Even majorities have no
right to do as they please; if so, what security has
the individual citizen? Under the unrestrained rule
of the majority "the principles of liberty must still
be the sport of arbitrary power, and the hideous
form of despotism must lay aside the diadem and the
scepter, only to assume the party-colored garments
of democracy."

"The only genuine liberty consists in a mean
equally distant from the despotism of an individual
and of a million," asserted Publicola. "Mr. Paine
seems to think it as easy for a nation to change its
government as for a man to change his coat." But
"the extreme difficulty which impeded the progress
of its [the American Constitution's] adoption . . .
exhibits the fullest evidence of what a more than
Herculean task it is to unite the opinions of a free
people on any system of government whatever."

The "mob" which Paine exalted as the common
people, but which Publicola thought was really only
the rabble of the cities, "can be brought to act in
concert" only by "a frantic enthusiasm and ungov-
ernable fury; their profound ignorance and deplor-
able credulity make them proper tools for any man
who can inflame their passions; . . . and," warned
Publicola, "as they have nothing to lose by the total

dissolution of civil society, their rage may be easily
directed against any victim which may be pointed
out to them. . . . To set in motion this inert mass,
the eccentric vivacity of a madman is infinitely better calculated than the sober coolness of phlegmatic
reason."

"Where," asked Publicola, "is the power that
should control them [Congress]?" if they violate the
letter of the Constitution. Replying to his own
question, he asserted that the real check on Congress "is the spirit of the people." [1] John Marshall
had said the same thing in the Virginia Constitutional Convention; but even at that early period
the Richmond attorney went further and flatly
declared that the temporary "spirit of the people"
was not infallible and that the Supreme Court could
and would declare void an unconstitutional act of
Congress — a truth which he was, unguessed at
that time by himself or anybody else, to announce
with conclusive power within a few years and at
an hour when dissolution confronted the forming
Nation.

Such is a rapid *précis* of the conservative essays
written by the younger Adams. Taken together,
they were a rallying cry to those who dared to
brave the rising hurricane of American sympathy
with the French Revolution; but they also strengthened the force of that growing storm. Multitudes
of writers attacked Publicola as the advocate of
"aristocracy" and "monarchy." "The papers under the signature of PUBLICOLA have called forth

[1] *Writings, J. Q. A.*: Ford, i, 65–110.

a torrent of abuse," declared the final essay of the series.

Brown's "Federal Gazette" of Philadelphia branded Publicola's doctrines as "abominable heresies"; and hoped that they would "not procure many proselytes either to *monarchy* or *aristocracy*." [1] The "Independent Chronicle" of Boston asserted that Publicola was trying to build up a "system of MONARCHY AND ARISTOCRACY . . . on the ruins both of the REPUTATION and LIBERTIES of the PEOPLE." [2] Madison reported to Jefferson that because of John Adams's reputed authorship of these unpopular letters, the supporters of the Massachusetts statesman had become "perfectly insignificant in . . . number" and that "in Boston he is . . . distinguished for his unpopularity." [3]

In such fashion the controversy began in America over the French Revolution.

But whatever the misgivings of the conservative, whatever the alarm of the timid, the overwhelming majority of Americans were for the French Revolution and its doctrines; [4] and men of the highest ability and station gave dignity to the voice of the people.

[1] *Writings, J. Q. A.*: Ford, i, footnote to 107.
"As soon as Publicola attacked Paine, swarms appeared in his defense. . . . Instantly a host of writers attacked Publicola in support of those [Paine's] principles." (Jefferson to Adams, Aug. 30, 1791; *Works:* Ford, vi, 314; and see Jefferson to Madison, July 10, 1791; *ib.*, 279.)
[2] *Writings, J. Q. A.*: Ford, i, 110.
[3] Madison to Jefferson, July 13, 1791; *Writings;* Hunt, vi, 56; and see Monroe to Jefferson, July 25, 1791; Monroe's *Writings:* Hamilton, i, 225–26.
[4] A verse of a song by French Revolutionary enthusiasts at a Boston "CIVIC FESTIVAL in commemoration of the SUCCESSES of their French

In most parts of the country politicians who sought election to public office conformed, as usual, to the popular view. It would appear that the prevailing sentiment was influential even with so strong a conservative and extreme a Nationalist as Madison, in bringing about his amazing reversal of views which occurred soon after the Constitution was adopted.[1] But those who, like Marshall, were not shaken, were made firmer in their opinions by the very strength of the ideas thus making headway among the masses.

An incident of the French Revolution almost within sight of the American coast gave to the dogma of equality a new and intimate meaning in the eyes of those who had begun to look with disfavor upon the results of Gallic radical thought. Marshall and Jefferson best set forth the opposite impressions made by this dramatic event.

"Early and bitter fruits of that malignant philosophy," writes Marshall, "which . . . can coolly

brethren in their glorious enterprise for the ESTABLISHMENT of EQUAL LIBERTY," as a newspaper describes the meeting, expresses in reserved and moderate fashion the popular feeling: —

> "See the bright flame arise,
> In yonder Eastern skies
> Spreading in veins;
> 'T is pure Democracy
> Setting all Nations free
> Melting their chains."

At this celebration an ox with gilded horns, one bearing the French flag and the other the American; carts of bread and two or three hogsheads of rum; and other devices of fancy and provisions for good cheer were the material evidence of the radical spirit. (See *Columbian Centinel*, Jan. 26, 1793.)

[1] It is certain that Madison could not possibly have continued in public life if he had remained a conservative and a Nationalist. (See next chapter.)

and deliberately pursue, through oceans of blood, abstract systems for the attainment of some fancied untried good, were gathered in the French West Indies. . . . The revolutionists of France formed the mad and wicked project of spreading their doctrines of equality among persons [negroes and white people] between whom distinctions and prejudices exist to be subdued only by the grave. The rage excited by the pursuit of this visionary and baneful theory, after many threatening symptoms, burst forth on the 23d day of August 1791, with a fury alike destructive and general.

"In one night, a preconcerted insurrection of the blacks took place throughout the colony of St. Domingo; and the white inhabitants of the country, while sleeping in their beds, were involved in one indiscriminate massacre, from which neither age nor sex could afford an exemption. Only a few females, reserved for a fate more cruel than death, were intentionally spared; and not many were fortunate enough to escape into the fortified cities. The insurgents then assembled in vast numbers, and a bloody war commenced between them and the whites inhabiting the towns." [1]

After the African disciples of French liberty had overthrown white supremacy in St. Domingo, Jefferson wrote his daughter that he had been informed "that the Patriotic party [St. Domingo revolutionists] had taken possession of 600 aristocrats & monocrats, had sent 200 of them to France, & were sending 400 here. . . . I wish," avowed Jef-

[1] Marshall, ii, 239.

ferson, in this intimate family letter, "we could distribute our 400 [white French exiles] among the Indians, who would teach them lessons of liberty & equality." [1]

Events in France marched swiftly from one bloody climax to another still more scarlet. All were faithfully reflected in the views of the people of the United States. John Marshall records for us "the fervour of democracy" as it then appeared in our infant Republic. He repeats that, at first, every American wished success to the French reformers. But the later steps of the movement "impaired this . . . unanimity of opinion. . . . A few who had thought deeply on the science of government . . . believed that . . . the influence of the galleries over the legislature, and of mobs over the executive; . . . the tumultuous assemblages of the people and their licentious excesses . . . did not appear to be the symptoms of a healthy constitution, or of genuine freedom. . . . They doubted, and they feared for the future."

Of the body of American public opinion, however, Marshall chronicles that: "In total opposition to this sentiment was that of the public. There seems to be something infectious in the example of a powerful and enlightened nation verging towards democracy, which imposes on the human mind, and leads human reason in fetters. . . . Long settled opinions yield to the overwhelming weight of such dazzling authority. It wears the semblance of be-

[1] Jefferson to Martha Jefferson Randolph, May 26, 1793; *Works:* Ford, vii, 345.

ing the sense of mankind, breaking loose from the shackles which had been imposed by artifice, and asserting the freedom, and the dignity, of his nature."

American conservative writers, says Marshall, "were branded as the advocates of royalty, and of aristocracy. To question the duration of the present order of things [in France] was thought to evidence an attachment to unlimited monarchy, or a blind prejudice in favour of British institutions. . . . The war in which the several potentates of Europe were engaged against France, although in almost every instance declared by that power, was pronounced to be a war for the extirpation of human liberty, and for the banishment of free government from the face of the earth. The preservation of the constitution of the United States was supposed to depend on its issue; and the coalition against France was treated as a coalition against America also." [1]

Marshall states, more clearly, perhaps, than any one else, American conservative opinion of the time: "The circumstances under which the abolition of royalty was declared, the massacres which preceded it, the scenes of turbulence and violence which were acted in every part of the nation, appeared to them [American conservatives] to present an awful and doubtful state of things. . . . The idea that a republic was to be introduced and supported by force, was, to them, a paradox in politics."

Thus it was, he declares, that "the French revolution will be found to have had great influence

[1] Marshall, ii, 249-51.

on the strength of parties, and on the subsequent political transactions of the United States." [1]

As the French storm increased, its winds blew ever stronger over the responsive waters of American opinion. Jefferson, that accurate barometer of public weather, thus registers the popular feeling: "The sensations it [the French Revolution] has produced here, and the indications of them in the public papers, have shown that the form our own government was to take depended much more on the events of France than anybody had before imagined." [2] Thus both Marshall and Jefferson bear testimony as to the determining effect produced in America by the violent change of systems in France.

William Short, whom Jefferson had taken to France as his secretary, when he was the American Minister to France, and who, when Jefferson returned to the United States, remained as *chargé d'affaires*,[3] had written both officially and privately of what was going on in France and of the increasing dominance of the Jacobin Clubs.[4] Perhaps no

[1] Marshall, ii, 251–52.

[2] Jefferson to T. M. Randolph, Jan. 7, 1793; *Works:* Ford, vii, 207.

[3] Mass. Hist. Collections (7th Series), i, 138.

[4] Typical excerpts from Short's reports to Jefferson are: July 20, 1792: "Those mad & corrupted people in France who under the name of liberty have destroyed their own government [French Constitution of 1791] & disgusted all . . . men of honesty & property. . . . All the rights of humanity . . . are daily violated with impunity . . . universal anarchy prevails. . . . There is no succour . . . against mobs & factions which have assumed despotic power."

July 31: "The factions which have lately determined the system . . . for violating all the bonds of civil society . . . have disgusted all, except the *sans culottes* . . . with the present order of things . . . the most perfect & universal disorder that ever reigned in any country.

more trustworthy statement exists of the prevailing
American view of the French cataclysm than that
given in Jefferson's fatherly letter to his protégé: —
"The tone of your letters had for some time given
me pain," wrote Jefferson, "on account of the extreme warmth with which they censured the proceedings of the Jacobins of France.[1] . . . Many
guilty persons [aristocrats] fell without the forms
of trial, and with them some innocent: . . . It was
necessary to use the arm of the people, a machine

Those who from the beginning took part in the revolution . . . have
been disgusted, by the follies, injustice, & atrocities of the Jacobins.
. . . All power [is] in the hands of the most mad, wicked & atrocious
assembly that ever was collected in any country."

August 15: "The Swiss guards have been massacred by the people
& . . . streets literally are red with blood."

October 12: "Their [French] successes abroad are unquestionably
evils for humanity. The spirit which they will propagate is so destructive of all order . . . so subversive of all ideas of justice — the system
they aim at so absolutely visionary & impracticable — that their
efforts can end in nothing but despotism after having bewildered the
unfortunate people, whom they render free in their way, in violence
& crimes, & wearied them with sacrifices of blood, which alone they
consider worthy of the furies whom they worship under the names
of *Liberté* & *Egalité!*"

August 24: "I sh^d not be at all surprized to hear of the present
leaders being hung by the people. Such has been the moral of this
revolution from the beginning. The people have gone farther than
their leaders. . . . We may expect . . . to hear of such proceedings, under the cloak of liberty, *égalité* & patriotism as would disgrace any
chambre ardente that has ever created in humanity shudders at the
idea." (Short MSS., Lib. Cong.)

These are examples of the statements to which Jefferson's letter,
quoted in the text following, was the reply. Short's most valuable letters are from The Hague, to which he had been transferred. They are
all the more important, as coming from a young radical whom events
in France had changed into a conservative. And Jefferson's letter
is conclusive of American popular sentiment, which he seldom opposed.

[1] Almost at the same time Thomas Paine was writing to Jefferson
from Paris of "the Jacobins who act without either prudence or morality." (Paine to Jefferson, April 20, 1793; *Writings;* Conway, iii, 132.)

not quite so blind as balls and bombs, but blind to a certain degree. . . .

"The liberty of the whole earth," continued Jefferson, "was depending on the issue of the contest, and was ever such a prize won with so little innocent blood? My own affections have been deeply wounded by some of the martyrs to this cause, but rather than it should have failed, I would have seen half the earth desolated.

"Were there but an Adam & an Eve left in every country, & left free, it would be better than as it now is," declared Jefferson; and "my sentiments . . . are really those of 99 in an hundred of our citizens," was that careful political observer's estimate of American public opinion. "Your temper of mind," Jefferson cautions Short, "would be extremely disrelished if known to your countrymen.

"There are in the U.S. some characters of opposite principles. . . . Excepting them, this country is entirely republican, friends to the constitution. . . . The little party above mentioned have espoused it only as a stepping stone to monarchy. . . . The successes of republicanism in France have given the coup de grace to their prospects, and I hope to their projects.

"I have developed to you faithfully the sentiments of your country," Jefferson admonishes Short, "that you may govern yourself accordingly." [1]

[1] Jefferson to Short, Jan. 3, 1793; *Works:* Ford, vii, 202–05. Short had written Jefferson that Morris, then in Paris, would inform him of French conditions. Morris had done so. For instance, he wrote officially to Jefferson, nearly four months before the latter's letter to Short quoted in the text, that: "We have had one

Jefferson's count of the public pulse was accurate. "The people of this country [Virginia] . . . are unanimous & explicit in their sympathy with the Revolution" was the weather-wise Madison's report.[1] And the fever was almost as high in other States.

When, after many executions of persons who had been "denounced" on mere suspicion of unfriendliness to the new order of things, the neck of Louis XVI was finally laid beneath the knife of the guillotine and the royal head rolled into the executioner's basket, even Thomas Paine was shocked. In a judicious letter to Danton he said: —

"I now despair of seeing the great object of European liberty accomplished" because of "the tumultuous misconduct" of "the present revolution" which "injure[s its] character . . . and discourage[s] the progress of liberty all over the world. . . . There ought to be some regulation with respect to the spirit of denunciation that now prevails."[2]

So it was that Thomas Paine, in France, came to speak privately the language which, in America, at that very hour, was considered by his disciples to be the speech of "aristocracy," "monarchy," and

week of unchecked murders, in which some thousands have perished in this city [Paris]. It began with between two and three hundred of the clergy, who would not take the oath prescribed by law. Thence these *executors of speedy justice* went to the Abbaye, where the prisoners were confined who were at Court on the 10th. Madame de Lamballe . . . was beheaded and disembowelled; the head and entrails paraded on pikes through the street, and the body dragged after them," etc., etc. (Morris to Jefferson, Sept. 10, 1792; Morris, i, 583–84.)

[1] Madison to Jefferson, June 17, 1793; *Writings:* Hunt, vi, 133.
[2] Paine to Danton, May 6, 1793; *Writings:* Conway, iii, 135–38.

"despotism"; for the red fountains which drenched the fires of even Thomas Paine's enthusiasm did not extinguish the flames his burning words had lighted among the people of the United States. Indeed Paine, himself, was attacked for regretting the execution of the King.[1]

Three months after the execution of the French King, the new Minister of the French Republic, "Citizen" Genêt, arrived upon our shores. He landed, not at Philadelphia, then our seat of government, but at Charleston, South Carolina. The youthful [2] representative of Revolutionary France was received by public officials with obsequious flattery and by the populace with a frenzy of enthusiasm almost indescribable in its intensity.

He acted on the welcome. He fitted out privateers, engaged seamen, issued letters of marque and reprisal, administered to American citizens oaths of "allegiance" to the authority then reigning in Paris. All this was done long before he presented his credentials to the American Government. His progress to our Capital was an unbroken festival of triumph. Washington's dignified restraint was interpreted as hostility, not only to Genêt, but also to "liberty." But if Washington's heart was ice, the people's heart was fire.

"We expect Mr. Genest here within a few days,"

---

[1] "Truth," in the *General Advertiser* (Philadelphia), May 8, 1793. "Truth" denied that Louis XVI had aided us in our Revolution and insisted that it was the French Nation that had come to our assistance. Such was the disregard of the times for even the greatest of historic facts, and facts within the personal knowledge of nine tenths of the people then living.

[2] See *Writings, J. Q. A.*: Ford, i, 151.

wrote Jefferson, just previous to the appearance of
the French Minister in Philadelphia and before our
ignored and offended President had even an opportunity to receive him. "It seems," Jefferson continued, "as if his arrival would furnish occasion for
the *people* to testify their affections without respect
to the cold caution of their government."[1]

Again Jefferson measured popular sentiment accurately. Genêt was made an idol by the people.
Banquets were given in his honor and extravagant
toasts were drunk to the Republic and the guillotine.
Showers of fiery "poems" filled the literary air.[2]
"What hugging and tugging! What addressing
and caressing! What mountebanking and chanting!
with liberty caps and other wretched trumpery of
sans culotte foolery!" exclaimed a disgusted conservative.[3]

While all this was going on in America, Robespierre, as the incarnation of liberty, equality, and
fraternity in France, achieved the summit of power
and "The Terror" reached high tide. Marie Antoinette met the fate of her royal husband, and the
executioners, overworked, could not satisfy the lust
of the Parisian populace for human life. All this,
however, did not extinguish American enthusiasm
for French liberty.

Responding to the wishes of their subscribers, who
at that period were the only support of the press, the
Republican newspapers suppressed such atrocities
as they could, but when concealment was impossible,

---

[1] Jefferson to Madison, April 28, 1793; *Works:* Ford, vii, 301.
[2] For examples of these, see Hazen, 220–45.   [3] Graydon, 363.

they defended the deeds they chronicled.[1] It was a
losing game to do otherwise, as one of the few
journalistic supporters of the American Government
discovered to his sorrow. Fenno, the editor of the
"Gazette of the United States," found opposition to
French revolutionary ideas, in addition to his support of Hamilton's popularly detested financial
measures,[2] too much for him. The latter was load
enough; but the former was the straw that broke the
conservative editor's back.

"I am . . . incapacitate[d] . . . from printing another paper without the aid of a considerable loan,"
wrote the bankrupt newspaper opponent of French
doctrines and advocate of Washington's Administration. "Since the 18th September, [1793] I have rec'd
only $35\frac{1}{4}$ dollars," Fenno lamented. "Four years &
an half of my life is gone for nothing; & worse (for I
have a Debt of 2500 Dollars on my Shoulders), if
at this crisis the hand of benevolence & *patriotism*
is not extended." [3]

---

[1] Freneau's *National Gazette* defended the execution of the King
and the excesses of the Terror. (Hazen, 256; and see Cobbett, iii, 4.)
While Cobbett, an Englishman, was a fanatic against the whole democratic movement, and while his opinions are violently prejudiced,
his statements of fact are generally trustworthy. "I have seen a
bundle of Gazettes published all by the same man, wherein Mirabeau,
Fayette, Brissot, Danton, Robespierre, and Barras, are all pane-
gyrized and execrated in due succession." (*Ib.*, i, 116.) Cobbett did
his best to turn the radical tide, but to no purpose. "Alas!" he exclaimed, "what can a straggling pamphlet . . . do against a hundred
thousand volumes of miscellaneous falsehood in folio?" (*Ib.*, iii, 5.)

[2] See next chapter.

[3] Fenno to Hamilton, Nov. 9, 1793; King, i, 501–02. "The hand
of benevolence & *patriotism*" was extended, it appears: "If you
can . . . raise 1000 Dollars in New York, I will endeavor to raise
another Thousand at Philadelphia. If this cannot be done, we
must lose his [Fenno's and the *Gazette of the United States*] services

Forgotten by the majority of Americans was the
assistance which the demolished French Monarchy
and the decapitated French King had given the
American army when, but for that assistance, our
cause had been lost. The effigy of Louis XVI was
guillotined by the people, many times every day in
Philadelphia, on the same spot where, ten years before, as a monument of their gratitude, these same
patriots had erected a triumphal arch, decorated
with the royal lilies of France bearing the motto,
"They exceed in glory," surmounted by a bust of
Louis inscribed, "His merit makes us remember
him." [1]

At a dinner in Philadelphia upon the anniversary
of the French King's execution, the dead monarch
was represented by a roasted pig. Its head was cut
off at the table, and each guest, donning the liberty
cap, shouted "tyrant" as with his knife he chopped
the sundered head of the dead swine.[2] The news of
the beheading of Louis's royal consort met with a
like reception. "I have heard more than one young
woman under the age of twenty declare," testifies
Cobbett, "that they would willingly have dipped
their hands in the blood of the queen of France." [3]

& he will be the Victim of his honest public spirit." (Hamilton to
King, Nov. 11, 1793; King, i, 502.)

[1] Cobbett, i, footnote to 114. Curiously enough Louis XVI had
believed that he was leading the French people in the reform movement. Thomas Paine, who was then in Paris, records that "The
King . . . prides himself on being the head of the revolution." (Paine
to Washington, May 1, 1790; *Cor. Rev.*: Sparks, iv, 328.)

[2] Cobbett, i, 113–14; and see Hazen, 258. For other accounts of
the "feasts" in honor of *liberté, égalité, et fraternité*, in America, see
ib., 165–73.

[3] Cobbett, i, 113.

But if the host of American radicals whom Jefferson led and whose spirit he so truly interpreted were forgetful of the practical friendship of French Royalty in our hour of need, American conservatives, among whom Marshall was developing leadership, were also unmindful of the dark crimes against the people which, at an earlier period, had stained the Monarchy of France and gradually cast up the account that brought on the inevitable settlement of the Revolution. The streams of blood that flowed were waters of Lethe to both sides.

Yet to both they were draughts which produced in one an obsession of reckless unrestraint and in the other a terror of popular rule no less exaggerated. [1] Of the latter class, Marshall was, by far, the most moderate and balanced, although the tragic aspect of the convulsion in which French liberty was born, came to him in an especially direct fashion, as we have seen from the Morris correspondence already cited.

Another similar influence on Marshall was the case of Lafayette. The American partisans of the French Revolution accused this man, who had fought for

[1] For instance, the younger Adams wrote that the French Revolution had "contributed more to . . . Vandalic ignorance than whole centuries can retrieve. . . . The myrmidons of Robespierre were as ready to burn libraries as the followers of Omar; and if the principle is finally to prevail which puts the sceptre of Sovereignty in the hands of European Sans Culottes, they will soon reduce everything to the level of their own ignorance." (John Quincy Adams to his father, July 27, 1795; *Writings, J. Q. A.*: Ford, i, 389.)

And James A. Bayard wrote that: "The Barbarians who inundated the Roman Empire and broke to pieces the institutions of the civilized world, in my opinion innovated the state of things not more than the French revolution." (Bayard to Bassett, Dec. 30, 1797; *Bayard Papers:* Donnan, 47.)

us in our War for Independence, of deserting the
cause of liberty because he had striven to hold the
Gallic uprising within orderly bounds. When, for
this, he had been driven from his native land and
thrown into a foreign dungeon, Freneau thus sang
the conviction of the American majority:—

> "Here, bold in arms, and firm in heart,
> He help'd to gain our cause,
> Yet could not from a tyrant part,
> But, turn'd to embrace his laws!" [1]

Lafayette's expulsion by his fellow Republicans
and his imprisonment by the allied monarchs, was
brought home to John Marshall in a very direct and
human fashion. His brother, James M. Marshall,
was sent by Washington [2] as his personal representative, to plead unofficially for Lafayette's release.
Marshall tells us of the strong and tender personal
friendship between Washington and Lafayette
and of the former's anxiety for the latter. But,
writes Marshall: "The extreme jealousy with which
the persons who administered the government of
France, as well as a large party in America, watched
his [Washington's] deportment towards all those
whom the ferocious despotism of the jacobins had
exiled from their country" rendered "a formal
interposition in favour of the virtuous and unfortunate victim [Lafayette] of their furious passions . . .
unavailing."

Washington instructed our ministers to do all they
could "unofficially" to help Lafayette, says Marshall; and "a confidential person [Marshall's brother

---

[1] Freneau, iii, 86.   [2] Marshall, ii, 387.

James] had been sent to Berlin to solicit his discharge: but before this messenger had reached his destination, the King of Prussia had delivered over his illustrious prisoner to the Emperor of Germany."[1] Washington tried "to obtain the powerful mediation of Britain" and hoped "that the cabinet of St. James would take an interest in the case; but this hope was soon dissipated." Great Britain would do nothing to secure from her allies Lafayette's release.[2]

Thus Marshall, in an uncommonly personal way, was brought face to face with what appeared to him to be the injustice of the French revolutionists. Lafayette, under whom John Marshall had served at Brandywine and Monmouth; Lafayette, leader of the movement in France for a free government like our own; Lafayette, hated by kings and aristocrats because he loved genuine liberty, and yet exiled from his own country by his own countrymen for the same reason [3] — this picture, which was the one Marshall saw, influenced him profoundly and permanently.

Humor as well as horror contributed to the repugnance which Marshall and men of his type felt ever more strongly for what they considered to be mere popular caprice. The American passion for equality had its comic side. The public hatred of all

---

[1] Austria.   [2] Marshall, ii, 387.

[3] "They have long considered the Mis de lafayette as really the firmest supporter of the principles of liberty in France — & as they are for the most part no friends to these principles anywhere, they cannot conceal the pleasure they [the aristocracy at The Hague] feel at their [principles of liberty] supporters' being thus expelled from the country where he laboured to establish them." (Short to Jefferson, Aug. 24, 1792; Short MSS., Lib. Cong.)

rank did not stop with French royalty and nobility. Because of his impassioned plea in Parliament for the American cause, a statue of Lord Chatham had been erected at Charleston, South Carolina; the people now suspended it by the neck in the air until the sculptured head was severed from the body. But Chatham was dead and knew only from the spirit world of this recognition of his bold words in behalf of the American people in their hour of trial and of need. In Virginia the statue of Lord Botetourt was beheaded.[1] This nobleman was also long since deceased, guilty of no fault but an effort to help the colonists, more earnest than some other royal governors had displayed. Still, in life, he had been called a "lord"; so off with the head of his statue!

In the cities, streets were renamed. "Royal Exchange Alley" in Boston became "Equality Lane"; and "Liberty Stump" was the name now given to the base of a tree that formerly had been called "Royal." In New York, "*Queen Street* became *Pearl Street;* and *King Street*, Liberty Street."[2] The liberty cap was the popular headgear and everybody wore the French cockade. Even the children, thus decorated, marched in processions,[3] singing, in a mixture of French and English words, the meaning

---

[1] Cobbett, i, 112.

[2] *Ib.* When the corporation of New York City thus took all monarchy out of its streets, Noah Webster suggested that, logically, the city ought to get rid of "this vile aristocratical name New York"; and, why not, inquired he, change the name of Kings County, Queens County, and Orange County? "Nay," exclaimed the sarcastic savant, "what will become of the people named King? Alas for the liberties of such people!" (Hazen, 216.)

[3] Hazen, 218.

of which they did not in the least understand, the
glories of "liberté, égalité, fraternité."

At a town meeting in Boston resolutions asking
that a city charter be granted were denounced as an
effort to "destroy the liberties of the people; . . . a
link in the chain of aristocratic influence." [1] Titles
were the especial aversion of the masses. Even before the formation of our government, the people had
shown their distaste for all formalities, and especially for terms denoting official rank; and, after the
Constitution was adopted, one of the first things
Congress did was to decide against any form of address to the President. Adams and Lee had favored
some kind of respectful designation of public officials. This all-important subject had attracted the
serious thought of the people more than had the
form of government, foreign policy, or even taxes.

Scarcely had Washington taken his oath of office
when David Stuart warned him that "nothing could
equal the ferment and disquietude occasioned by the
proposition respecting titles. As it is believed to have
originated from Mr. Adams and Mr. Lee, they are
not only unpopular to an extreme, but highly odious.
. . . It has given me much pleasure to hear every
part of your conduct spoken of with high approbation, and particularly your dispensing with cere-
mony, occasionally walking the streets; while Adams
is never seen but in his carriage and six. As trivial
as this may appear," writes Stuart, "it appears to
be more captivating to the generality, than matters

[1] J. Q. Adams, to T. B. Adams, Feb. 1, 1792; *Writings, J. Q. A.*:
Ford, i, 111–13.

of more importance. Indeed, I believe the great herd of mankind form their judgments of characters, more from such slight occurrences, than those of greater magnitude." [1]

This early hostility to ostentation and rank now broke forth in rabid virulence. In the opinion of the people, as influenced by the French Revolution, a Governor or President ought not to be referred to as "His Excellency"; nor a minister of the gospel as "Reverend." Even "sir" or "esquire" were, plainly, "monarchical." The title "Honorable" or "His Honor," when applied to any official, even a judge, was base pandering to aristocracy. "Mr." and "Mrs." were heretical to the new religion of equality. Nothing but "citizen" [2] would do — citizen judge, citizen governor, citizen clergyman, citizen colonel, major, or general, citizen baker, shoemaker, banker, merchant, and farmer, — citizen everybody.

To address the master of ceremonies at a dinner or banquet or other public gathering as "Mr. Chairman" or "Mr. Toastmaster" was aristocratic: only "citizen chairman" or "citizen toastmaster" was the true speech of genuine liberty. [3] And the name of the *Greek* letter college fraternity, Phi Beta Kappa, was the trick of kings to ensnare our unsuspecting youth. Even "Φ.Β.Κ." was declared to be "an infringement of the natural rights of society." A college fraternity was destructive of the spirit of equality in American

[1] Stuart to Washington, July 14, 1789; *Cor. Rev.*: Sparks, iv, 265–66; and see Randolph to Madison, May 19, 1789; Conway, 124.

[2] See Hazen, 209–15.   [3] *Ib.*, 213.

colleges.[1] "*Lèse-républicanisme*" was the term applied to good manners and politeness.[2]

Such were the surface and harmless evidences of the effect of the French Revolution on the great mass of American opinion. But a serious and practical result developed. Starting with the mother organization at Philadelphia, secret societies sprang up all over the Union in imitation of the Jacobin Clubs of France. Each society had its corresponding committee; and thus these organizations were welded into an unbroken chain. Their avowed purpose was to cherish the principles of human freedom and to spread the doctrine of true republicanism. But they soon became practical political agencies; and then, like their French prototype, the sowers of disorder and the instigators of insurrection.[3]

The practical activities of these organizations aroused, at last, the open wrath of Washington. They "are spreading mischief far and wide," he wrote; [4] and he declared to Randolph that "if these self-created societies cannot be discountenanced, they will destroy the government of this country." [5]

Conservative apprehensions were thus voiced by George Cabot: "We have seen . . . the . . . representatives of the people butchered, and a band of

---

[1] See Hazen, 215.   [2] Cobbett, i, 111.

[3] For an impartial and comprehensive account of these clubs see Hazen, 188–208; also, Marshall, ii, 269 *et seq.* At first many excellent and prominent men were members; but these withdrew when the clubs fell under the control of less unselfish and high-minded persons.

[4] Washington to Thruston, Aug. 10, 1794; *Writings:* Ford, xii, 451.

[5] Washington to Randolph, Oct. 16, 1794; *ib.*, 475; and see Washington to Lee, Aug. 26, 1794; *ib.*, 455.

relentless murderers ruling in their stead with rods
of iron. Will not this, or something like it, be the
wretched fate of our country? ... Is not this hostility and distrust [to just opinions and right senti-
ments] chiefly produced by the slanders and falsehoods which the anarchists incessantly inculcate?" [1]

Young men like John Quincy Adams of Massachusetts and John Marshall of Virginia thought that
"the rabble that followed on the heels of Jack Cade
could not have devised greater absurdities than"
the French Revolution had inspired in America; [2]
but they were greatly outnumbered by those for
whom Jefferson spoke when he said that "I feel that
the permanence of our own [Government] leans" on
the success of the French Revolution. [3]

The American democratic societies, like their
French originals, declared that theirs was the voice
of "the people," and popular clamor justified the
claim. [4] Everybody who dissented from the edicts
of the clubs was denounced as a public robber or
monarchist. "What a continual yelping and barking
are our Swindlers, Aristocrats, Refugees, and British Agents making at the Constitutional Societies"
which were "like a noble mastiff ... with ... im-
potent and noisy puppies at his heels," cried the
indignant editor of the "Independent Chronicle"
of Boston, [5] to whom the democratic societies were
"guardians of liberty."

[1] Cabot to Parsons, Aug. 12, 1794; Lodge: *Cabot*, 79.
[2] J. Q. Adams to John Adams, Oct. 19, 1790; *Writings, J. Q. A.:*
Ford, i, 64.
[3] Jefferson to Rutledge, Aug. 29, 1791; *Works:* Ford, vi, 309.
[4] See Hazen, 203–07.   [5] September 18, 1794.

While these organizations strengthened radical opinion and fashioned American sympathizers of the French Revolution into disciplined ranks, they also solidified the conservative elements of the United States. Most viciously did the latter hate these "Jacobin Clubs," the principles they advocated, and their interference with public affairs. "They were born in sin, the impure offspring of Genêt," wrote Fisher Ames.

"They are the few against the many; the sons of darkness (for their meetings are secret) against those of the light; and above all, it is a *town* cabal, attempting to rule the *country*." [1] This testy New Englander thus expressed the extreme conservative feeling against the "insanity which is epidemic": [2] "This French mania," said Ames, "is the bane of our politics, the mortal poison that makes our peace so sickly." [3] "They have, like toads, sucked poison from the earth. They thirst for vengeance." [4] "The spirit of mischief is as active as the element of fire and as destructive." [5] Ames describes the activities of the Boston Society and the aversion of the "better classes" for it: "The club is despised here by men of right heads," he writes. "But . . . they [the members of the Club] poison every spring; they whisper lies to every gale; they are everywhere, always acting like Old Nick and his imps. . . . They will be as busy as Macbeth's witches at the election." [6]

[1] Ames to Dwight, Sept. 11, 1794; *Works:* Ames, i, 150.
[2] Cabot to King, July 25, 1795; Lodge: *Cabot*, 80.
[3] Ames to Gore, March 26, 1794; *Works:* Ames, i, 139.
[4] Ames to Minot, Feb. 20, 1793; *ib.*, 128.
[5] Ames to Gore, Jan. 28, 1794; *ib.*, 134.
[6] Ames to Dwight, Sept. 3, 1794; *ib.*, 148.

In Virginia the French Revolution and the American "Jacobins" helped to effect that change in Patrick Henry's political sentiments which his increasing wealth had begun. "If my Country," wrote Henry to Washington, "is destined in my day to encounter the horrors of anarchy, every power of mind or body which I possess will be exerted in support of the government under which I live." [1] As to France itself, Henry predicted that "anarchy will be succeeded by despotism" and Bonaparte, "Caesar-like, subvert the liberties of his country." [2]

Marshall was as much opposed to the democratic societies as was Washington, or Cabot, or Ames, but he was calmer in his opposition, although vitriolic enough. When writing even ten years later, after time had restored perspective and cooled feeling, Marshall says that these "pernicious societies" [3] were "the resolute champions of all the encroachments attempted by the agents of the French republic on the government of the United States, and the steady defamers of the views and measures of the American executive." [4] He thus describes their decline: —

"The colossean power of the [French] clubs, which had been abused to an excess that gives to faithful history the appearance of fiction, fell with that of their favourite member, and they sunk into long merited disgrace. The means by which their political influence had been maintained were wrested

---

[1] Henry to Washington, Oct. 16, 1795; Henry, ii, 559.
[2] *Ib.*, 576.   [3] Marshall, ii, 353.   [4] *Ib.*, 269.

from them; and, in a short time, their meetings were prohibited. Not more certain is it that the boldest streams must disappear, if the fountains which fed them be emptied, than was the dissolution of the democratic societies of America, when the Jacobin clubs were denounced by France. As if their destinies depended on the same thread, the political death of the former was the unerring signal for that of the latter." [1]

Such was the effect of the French Revolution on American thought at the critical period of our new Government's first trials. To measure justly the speech and conduct of men during the years we are now to review, this influence must always be borne in mind. It was woven into every great issue that arose in the United States. Generally speaking, the debtor classes and the poorer people were partisans of French revolutionary principles; and the creditor classes, the mercantile and financial interests, were the enemies of what they called "Jacobin philosophy." In a broad sense, those who opposed taxes, levied to support a strong National Government, sympathized with the French Revolution and believed in its ideas; those who advocated taxes for that purpose, abhorred that convulsion and feared its doctrines.

Those who had disliked government before the Constitution was established and who now hated National control, heard in the preachings of the French revolutionary theorists the voice of their hearts; while those who believed that government is essen-

[1] Marshall, ii, 353–54.

tial to society and absolutely indispensable to the building of the American Nation, heard in the language and saw in the deeds of the French Revolution the forces that would wreck the foundations of the state even while they were but being laid and, in the end, dissolve society itself. Thus were the ideas of Nationality and localism in America brought into sharper conflict by the mob and guillotine in France.

All the passion for irresponsible liberty which the French Revolution increased in America, as well as all the resentment aroused by the financial measures and foreign policy of the "Federal Administrations," were combined in the opposition to and attacks upon a strong National Government. Thus provincialism in the form of States' Rights was given a fresh impulse and a new vitality. Through nearly all the important legislation and diplomacy of those stirring and interpretative years ran, with ever increasing clearness, the dividing line of Nationalism as against localism.

Such are the curious turns of human history. Those whom Jefferson led profoundly believed that they were fighting for human rights; and in their view and as a practical matter at that particular time this sacred cause meant State Rights. For everything which they felt to be oppressive, unjust, and antagonistic to liberty, came from the National Government. By natural contrast in their own minds, as well as by assertions of their leaders, the State Governments were the sources of justice and the protectors of the genuine rights of man.

In the development of John Marshall as well as of his great ultimate antagonist, Thomas Jefferson, during the formative decade which we are now to consider, the influence of the French Revolution must never be forgotten. Not a circumstance of the public lives of these two men and scarcely an incident of their private experience but was shaped and colored by this vast series of human events. Bearing in mind the influence of the French Revolution on American opinion, and hence, on Marshall and Jefferson, let us examine the succeeding years in the light of this determining fact.

CHAPTER II

A VIRGINIA NATIONALIST

Lace Congress up straitly within the enumerated powers. (Jefferson.)

Construe the constitution liberally in advancement of the common good. (Hamilton.)

To organize government, to retrieve the national character, to establish a system of revenue, to create public credit, were among the duties imposed upon them. (Marshall.)

I trust in that Providence which has saved us in six troubles, yea, in seven, to rescue us again. (Washington.)

THE Constitution's narrow escape from defeat in the State Conventions did not end the struggle against the National principle that pervaded it.[1] The Anti-Nationalists put forth all their strength to send to the State Legislatures and to the National House and Senate as many antagonists of the National idea as possible.[2] "Exertions will be made to engage two thirds of the legislatures in the task of regularly undermining the government" was Madison's "hint" to Hamilton.[3]

Madison cautioned Washington to the same effect, suggesting that a still more ominous part of the plan was "to get a Congress appointed in the

[1] Marshall, ii, 150–51. "The agitation had been too great to be suddenly calmed; and for the active opponents of the system [Constitution] to become suddenly its friends, or even indifferent to its fate, would have been a victory of reason over passion." (*Ib.*; and see Beard: *Econ. O. J. D.*, 85, 101, 102–07.)

[2] "The effort was made to fill the legislature with the declared enemies of the government, and thus to commit it, in its infancy, to the custody of its foes." (Marshall, ii, 151.)

[3] Madison to Hamilton, June 27, 1788; Hamilton MSS., Lib. Cong. Madison adds this cryptic sentence: "This hint may not be unworthy of your attention."

first instance that will commit suicide on their own
Authority." [1] Not yet had the timorous Madison
personally felt the burly hand of the sovereign people so soon to fall upon him. Not yet had he undergone that familiar reversal of principles wrought
in those politicians who keep an ear to the ground.
But that change was swiftly approaching. Even
then the *vox populi* was filling the political heavens
with a clamor not to be denied by the ambitious.
The sentiment of the people required only an organ-
izer to become formidable and finally omnipotent.

Such an artisan of public opinion was soon to appear. Indeed, the master political potter was even
then about to start for America where the clay for
an Anti-Nationalist Party was almost kneaded for
the moulder's hands. Jefferson was preparing to leave
France; and not many months later the great politician landed on his native soil and among his fellow citizens, who, however, welcomed him none too
ardently. [2]

[1] Madison to Washington, June 27, 1788; *Writings:* Hunt, v, 234.
Madison here refers to the project of calling a new Federal Convention for the purpose of amending the Constitution or making a new one.

Randolph was still more apprehensive. "Something is surely
meditated against the new Constitution more animated, forcible, and
violent than a simple application for calling a Convention." (Randolph to Madison, Oct. 23, 1788; Conway, 118.)

[2] When Jefferson left Virginia for France, his political fortunes
were broken. (Eckenrode: *R. V.*, chap. viii; and Dodd, 63–64; and
Ambler, 35–36.) The mission to France at the close of the American
Revolution, while "an honor," was avoided rather than sought by
those who were keen for career. (Dodd, 36–39.)

Seldom has any man achieved such a recovery as that of Jefferson
in the period now under review. Perhaps Talleyrand's rehabilitation
most nearly approaches Jefferson's achievement. From the depths
of disfavor this genius of party management climbed to the heights
of popularity and fame.

No one knew just where Jefferson stood on the fundamental question of the hour when, with his two daughters, he arrived in Virginia in 1789. The brilliant Virginian had uttered both Nationalist and Anti-Nationalist sentiments. "I am not of the party of the Federalists," he protested, "but I am much farther from that of the Antifederalists." Indeed, declared Jefferson, "If I could not go to heaven but with a party, I would not go there at all." [1]

His first opinions of the Constitution were, as we have seen, unfavorable. But after he had learned that the new Government was to be a fact, Jefferson wrote Washington: "I have seen with infinite pleasure our new constitution accepted." Careful study had taught him, he said, "that circumstances may arise, and probably will arise, wherein all the resources of taxation will be necessary for the safety of the state." He saw probability of war which "requires every resource of taxation & credit." He thought that "the power of making war often prevents it." [2]

Thus Jefferson could be quoted on both sides and claimed by neither or by both. But, because of his absence in France and of the reports he had received from the then extreme Nationalist, Madison, he had not yet apprehended the people's animosity to National rule. Upon his arrival in Virginia, however, he discovered that "Antifederalism is not yet dead

---

[1] Jefferson to Hopkinson, March 13, 1789; *Works:* Ford, v, 456.

[2] Jefferson to Washington, Paris, Dec. 4, 1788; *Works:* Ford, v, 437–38. Compare with Jefferson's statements when the fight was on against ratifying the Constitution. (See vol. I, chap. VIII; also Jefferson to Humphreys, Paris, March 18, 1789; *Works:* Ford, v, 470.)

in this country." [1] That much, indeed, was clear at
first sight. The Legislature of Virginia, which met
three months after her Convention had ratified the
Constitution, was determined to undo that work, as
Madison had foreseen. [2]

That body was militantly against the new Government as it stood. "The conflict between the powers
of the general and state governments was coeval
with those governments," declares Marshall. "The
old line of division was still as strongly marked as
ever." The enemies of National power thought that
"liberty could be endangered only by encroachments
upon the states; and that it was the great duty of
patriotism to restrain the powers of the general government within the narrowest possible limits." On
the other hand, the Nationalists, says Marshall,
"sincerely believed that the real danger which
threatened the republic was to be looked for in the
undue ascendency of the states." [3]

Patrick Henry was supreme in the House of Delegates. Washington was vastly concerned at the
prospect. He feared that the enemies of Nationalism would control the State Legislature and that

[1] Jefferson to Short, Dec. 14, 1789; *Works:* Ford, vi, 24.

[2] The Legislature which met on the heels of the Virginia Constitutional Convention hastened to adjourn in order that its members
might attend to their harvesting. (Monroe to Jefferson, July 12,
1788; Monroe's *Writings;* Hamilton, i, 188.) But at its autumn session, it made up for lost time in its practical display of antagonism
to the Nationalist movement.

[3] Marshall, ii, 205–26. Throughout this chapter the terms "Nationalist" and "Anti-Nationalist" are used instead of the customary terms "Federalist" and "Anti-Federalist," the latter not clearly
expressing the fundamental difference between the contending political forces at that particular time.

it would respond to New York's appeal for a new
Federal Constitutional Convention. He was "particularly alarmed" that the General Assembly
would elect Senators "entirely anti-Federal."[1] His
apprehension was justified. Hardly a week passed
after the House convened until it passed resolutions, drawn by Henry,[2] to answer Clinton's letter,
to ask Congress to call a new Federal Convention, and to coöperate with other States in that
business.

In vain did the Nationalist members strive to
soften this resolution. An amendment which went
so far as to request Congress to recommend to the
several States "the ratification of a bill of rights"
and of the twenty amendments proposed by the Virginia Convention, was defeated by a majority of
46 out of a total vote of 124.[3] Swiftly and without
mercy the triumphant opposition struck its next
blow. Washington had urged Madison to stand for
the Senate,[4] and the Nationalists exerted themselves
to elect him. Madison wrote cleverly in his own
behalf.[5] But he had no hope of success because it
was "certain that a clear majority of the assembly
are enemies to the Gov.ᵗ."[6] Madison was still the
ultra-Nationalist, who, five years earlier, had wanted

[1] Carrington to Madison, Oct. 19, 1788; quoted in Henry, ii, 415.
[2] Ib., 416–18.
[3] Journal, H.D. (Oct. 30, 1788), 16–17; see Grigsby, ii, 319; also
see the vivid description of the debate under these resolutions in
Henry, ii, 418–23.
[4] Carrington to Madison, Oct. 19, 1788; quoted in Henry, ii, 415.
[5] Madison to Randolph Oct. 17, 1788; to Pendleton, Oct. 20, 1788;
Writings: Hunt, v, 269–79.
[6] Madison to Randolph, Nov. 2, 1788; Writings: Hunt, v, 296.

the National Government to have an absolute veto on *every* State law.[1]

Henry delivered "a tremendous philippic" against Madison as soon as his name was placed before the General Assembly.[2] Madison was badly beaten, and Richard Henry Lee and William Grayson were chosen as the first Senators from Virginia under the new National Government.[3] The defeated champion of the Constitution attributed Henry's attack and his own misfortune to his Nationalist principles: Henry's "enmity was levelled . . . agst the *whole system;* and the destruction of the whole system, I take to be the secret wish of his heart."[4]

In such fashion did Madison receive his first chastisement for his Nationalist views and labors. He required no further discipline of a kind so rough and humiliating; and he sought and secured election to the National House of Representatives,[5] with opinions much subdued and his whole being made pliant for the wizard who so soon was to invoke his spell over that master mind.

Though Marshall was not in the Virginia Legislature at that session, it is certain that he worked with its members for Madison's election as Senator.

[1] See vol. i of this work.

[2] Henry, ii, 427; see also Scott, 172.

[3] Journal, H.D. (Nov. 8, 1788), 32; see also Conway, 120; and Henry, ii, 427–28.

[4] Madison to Randolph, Nov. 2, 1788; *Writings:* Hunt, v, 295.

[5] Monroe became a candidate against Madison and it was "thought that he [would] . . . carry his election." (Mason to John Mason, Dec. 18, 1788; Rowland, ii, 304.) But so ardent were Madison's assurances of his modified Nationalist views that he was elected. His majority, however, was only three hundred. (Monroe to Jefferson, Feb. 15, 1789; Monroe's *Writings:* Hamilton, i, 199.)

But even Marshall's persuasiveness was unavailing. "Nothing," wrote Randolph to Madison, "is left undone which can tend to the subversion of the new government."[1]

Hard upon its defeat of Madison the Legislature adopted an ominous address to Congress. "The sooner . . . the [National] government is possessed of the confidence of the people . . . *the longer its duration*" — such was the language and spirit of Virginia's message to the lawmakers of the Nation, even before they had assembled.[2] The desperate Nationalists sought to break the force of this blow. They proposed a substitute which even suggested that the widely demanded new Federal Convention should be called by Congress if that body thought best. But all to no purpose. Their solemn [3] amendment was beaten by a majority of 22 out of a total vote of 122.[4]

Thus again was displayed that hostility to Nationalism which was to focus upon the newborn National Government every burning ray of discontent from the flames that sprang up all over the country during the constructive but riotous years that followed. Were the people taxed to pay obligations incurred in our War for Independence? — the Na-

[1] Randolph to Madison, Nov. 10, 1788; Conway, 121.

[2] Journal, H.D. (Nov. 14, 1788), 42–44. Also see *Annals*, 1st Cong., 1st Sess., 259.

[3] The Nationalist substitute is pathetic in its apprehensive tone. It closes with a prayer "that Almighty God in his goodness and wisdom will direct your councils to such measures as will establish our lasting peace and welfare and secure to our latest posterity the blessings of freedom; and that he will always have you in his holy keeping." (Journal, H.D. (Nov. 14, 1788), 43.)

[4] *Ib.*, 44.

tional Government was to blame. Was an excise laid on whiskey, "the common drink of the nation" [1] — it was the National Government which thus wrung tribute from the universal thirst. Were those who owed debts compelled, at last, to pay them? — it was the National Government which armed the creditor with power to recover his own.

Why did we not aid French Republicans against the hordes of "despotism"? Because the National Government, with its accursed Neutrality, would not let us! And who but the National Government would dare make a treaty with British Monarchy, sacrificing American rights? Speculation and corruption, parade and ostentation, — everything that could, reasonably or unreasonably, be complained of, — were, avowed the Anti-Nationalists, the wretched but legitimate offspring of Nationalism. The remedy, of course, was to weaken the power of the Nation and strengthen that of the States. Such was the course pursued by the foes of Nationalism, that we shall trace during the first three administrations of the Government of the United States.

Thus, the events that took place between 1790 and 1800, supplemented and heated by the French Revolution, developed to their full stature those antagonistic theories of which John Marshall and Thomas Jefferson were to become the chief expounders. Those events also finished the preparation of these two men for the commanding stations they were to

[1] Pennsylvania Resolutions: Gallatin's *Writings:* Adams, i, 3. This was unjust to New England, where rum was "the common drink of the nation" and played an interesting part in our tariff laws and New England trade.

occupy. The radical politician and States' Rights leader on the one hand, and the conservative politician and Nationalist jurist on the other hand, were finally settled in their opinions during these developing years, at the end of which one of them was to occupy the highest executive office and the other the highest judicial office in the Government.

It was under such circumstances that the National Government, with Washington at its head, began its uncertain career. If the Legislature of Virginia had gone so far before the infant National establishment was under way, how far might not succeeding Legislatures go? No one knew. But it was plain to all that every act of the new Administration, even with Washington at the helm, would be watched with keen and jealous eyes; and that each Nationalist turn of the wheel would meet with prompt and stern resistance in the General Assembly of the greatest of American Commonwealths. Mutiny was already aboard.

John Marshall, therefore, determined again to seek election to the House of Delegates.

Immediately upon the organization of the National Government, Washington appointed Marshall to be United States Attorney for the District of Virginia. The young lawyer's friends had suggested his name to the President, intimating that he wished the place.[1] Marshall, high in the esteem of every one, had been consulted as to appointments on the National bench,[2] and Washington gladly named

[1] Washington to Marshall, Nov. 23, 1789; MS., Lib. Cong.
[2] Randolph to Madison, July 19, 1789; Conway, 127.

him for District Attorney. But when notified of his appointment, Marshall declined the honor.

A seat in the Virginia Legislature, was, however, quite another matter. Although his work as a legislator would interfere with his profession much more than would his duties as United States Attorney, he could be of practical service to the National Government in the General Assembly of the State where, it was plain, the first battle for Nationalism must be fought.

The Virginia Nationalists, much alarmed, urged him to make the race. The most popular man in Richmond, he was the only Nationalist who could be elected by that constituency; and, if chosen, would be the ablest supporter of the Administration in the Legislature. Although the people of Henrico County were more strongly against a powerful National Government than they had been when they sent Marshall to the Constitutional Convention the previous year, they nevertheless elected him; and in 1789 Marshall once more took his seat as a member of Virginia's law-making and law-marring body.

He was at once given his old place on the two principal standing committees; [1] and on special committees to bring in various bills, [2] among them one concerning descents, a difficult subject and of particular concern to Virginians at that time. [3] As a member of the Committee of Privileges and Elections, he passed on a hotly contested election case. [4] He was made a

---

[1] Journal, H.D. (Oct. 20, 1789), 4.   [2] Ib., 7–16.

[3] Ib., 16. Marshall probably drew the bill that finally passed. He carried it from the House to the Senate. (Ib., 136.)

[4] Ib. (Oct. 28, 1790), 19-22. Whether or not a voter owned land was weighed in delicate scales. Even "treating" was examined.

member of the important special committee to
report upon the whole body of laws in force in Virginia, and helped to draw the committee's report,
which is comprehensive and able.[1] The following
year he was appointed a member of the committee
to revise the tangled laws of the Commonwealth.[2]

The irrepressible subject of paying taxes in something else than money soon came up. Marshall voted
against a proposition to pay the taxes in hemp and
tobacco, which was defeated by a majority of 37
out of a total vote of 139; and he voted for the resolution "that the taxes of the present year ought to
be paid in specie only or in warrants equivalent
thereto," which carried.[3] He was added to the committee on a notable divorce case.[4]

Marshall was, of course, appointed on the special
committee to bring in a bill giving statehood to the
District of Kentucky.[5] Thus he had to do with the
creation of the second State to be admitted after
the Constitution was adopted. A bill was passed
authorizing a lottery to raise money to establish an

[1] Journal, H.D. (Oct. 28, 1790), 24–29.
[2] Ib., 1st Sess. (1790), 41; and 2d Sess. (Dec. 8), 121–22. For
extent of this revision see Conway, 130.
[3] Journal, H.D. (1789), 57–58.
[4] Ib., 78. See report of the committee in this interesting case.
(Ib., 103.) The bill was passed. (Ib., 141.) At that time divorces
in Virginia could be had only by an act of the Legislature. Contrast
the above case, where the divorce was granted for cruelty, abandonment, waste of property, etc., with that of the Mattauer case (ib.
(1793), 112, 126), where the divorce was refused for admitted infidelity on the part of the wife who bore a child by the brother of her
husband while the latter was abroad.
[5] Ib. (1789), 96. Kentucky was then a part of Virginia and legislation by the latter State was necessary. It is more than probable
that Marshall drew this important statute, which passed. (Ib., 115,
131, 141.)

academy in Marshall's home county, Fauquier.[1] He
voted with the majority against the perennial Bap-
tist petition to democratize religion;[2] and for the
bill to sell lands for taxes.[3]

Marshall was appointed on the committee to
bring in bills for proceeding against absent debtors;[4]
on another to amend the penal code;[5] and he was
made chairman of the special committee to examine
the James River Company,[6] of which he was a stock-

[1] Journal, H.D. (1789), 112. At this period, lotteries were the
common and favorite methods of raising money for schools, and other
public institutions and enterprises. Even the maintenance of ceme-
teries was provided for in this way. The Journals of the House of
Delegates are full of resolutions and Hening's Statutes contain many
acts concerning these enterprises. (See, for example, Journal, H.D.
(1787), 16–20; (1797), 39.)

[2] An uncommonly able state paper was laid before the House of
Delegates at this session. It was an arraignment of the Virginia Constitution of 1776, and mercilessly exposed, without the use of direct
terms, the dangerous political machine which that Constitution made
inevitable; it suggested "that as harmony with the Federal Government . . . is to be desired our own Constitution ought to be compared
with that of the United States and retrenched where it is repugnant";
and it finally recommended that the people instruct their representatives in the Legislature to take the steps for reform. The
author of this admirable petition is unknown. (Journal, H.D. (1789),
113.)

From this previous vote for a new Constitution, it is probable that
Marshall warmly supported this resolution. But the friends of the
old and vicious system instantly proposed an amendment "that the
foregoing statement contains principles repugnant to Republican
Government and dangerous to the freedom of this country, and, therefore, ought not to meet with the approbation of this House or be
recommended to the consideration of the people"; and so strong were
they that the whole subject was dropped by postponement, without
further contest. (Journal, H.D. (1789), 108–09.)

[3] Ib. (Nov. 17, 1789), 20.   [4] Ib. (Nov. 13, 1789), 12.

[5] Ib. (Nov. 16, 1789), 14.

[6] Ib. (Nov. 27, 1789), 49. The James River Company was formed in
1784. Washington was its first president. (Randolph to Washington,
Aug. 8, 1784; Conway, 58.) Marshall's Account Book shows many
payments on stock in this company.

holder. Such are examples of his routine activities in the Legislature of 1789.

The Legislature instructed the Virginia Senators in Congress "to use their utmost endeavors to procure the admission of the citizens of the United States to hear the debates of their House, whenever they are sitting in their legislative capacity." [1] An address glowing with love, confidence, and veneration was sent to Washington.[2] Then Jefferson came to Richmond; and the Legislature appointed a committee to greet him with polite but coldly formal congratulations.[3] No one then foresaw that a few short years would turn the reverence and affection for Washington into disrespect and hostility; and the indifference toward Jefferson into fiery enthusiasm.

The first skirmish in the engagement between the friends and foes of a stronger National Government soon came on. On November 30, 1789, the House ratified the first twelve amendments to the Constitution,[4] which the new Congress had submitted to the States; but three days later it was proposed

[1] Journal, H.D. (1789), 117, 135. For many years after the Constitution was adopted the United States Senate sat behind closed doors. The Virginia Legislature continued to demand public debate in the National Senate until that reform was accomplished. (See Journal, H.D. (Oct. 25, 1791), 14; (Nov. 8, 1793), 57, etc.)

In 1789 the Nationalists were much stronger in the Legislatures of the other States than they had been in the preceding year. Only three States had answered Virginia's belated letter proposing a new Federal Convention to amend the Constitution. Disgusted and despondent, Henry quitted his seat in the House of Delegates in the latter part of November and went home in a sulk. (Henry, ii, 448–49; Conway, 131.)

[2] Journal, H.D. (1789), 17, 19, 98.   [3] Ib., 107–12.

[4] Ib., 90–91.

that the Legislature urge Congress to reconsider the amendments recommended by Virginia which Congress had not adopted.[1] An attempt to make this resolution stronger was defeated by the deciding vote of the Speaker, Marshall voting against it.[2]

The Anti-Nationalist State Senate refused to concur in the House's ratification of the amendments proposed by Congress;[3] and Marshall was one of the committee to hold a conference with the Senate committee on the subject.

After Congress had passed the laws necessary to set the National Government in motion, Madison had reluctantly offered his summary of the volume of amendments to the Constitution recommended by the States "in order," as he said, "to quiet that anxiety which prevails in the public mind."[4] The debate is illuminating. The amendments, as agreed to, fell far short of the radical and extensive alterations which the States had asked and were understood to be palliatives to popular discontent.[5]

---

[1] Journal, H.D. (1789), 96.   [2] Ib., 102.

[3] Ib., 119. The objections were that the liberty of the press, trial by jury, freedom of speech, the right of the people to assemble, consult, and "to instruct their representatives," were not guaranteed; and in general, that the amendments submitted "fall short of affording security to personal rights." (Senate Journal, December 12, 1789; MS., Va. St. Lib.)

[4] Annals, 1st Cong., 1st Sess., 444; and see entire debate. The amendments were offered as a measure of prudence to mollify the disaffected. (Rives, iii, 38–39.)

[5] The House agreed to seventeen amendments. But the Senate reduced these to twelve, which were submitted to the States. The first of these provided for an increase of the representation in the House; the second provided that no law "varying" the salaries of Senators or Representatives "shall take effect until an election of Representatives shall have intervened." (Annals, 1st Cong., 1st Sess., Appendix to ii, 2033.) The States ratified only the last ten.

Randolph in Richmond wrote that the amendments were "much approved by the *strong* federalists . . . being considered as an anodyne to the discontented. Some others . . . expect to hear, . . . that a real amelioration of the Constitution was not so much intended, as a soporific draught to the restless. I believe, indeed," declared Randolph, "that nothing — nay, not even the abolishment of direct taxation — would satisfy those who are most clamorous." [1]

The amendments were used by many, who changed from advocates to opponents of broad National powers, as a pretext for reversed views and conduct; but such as were actually adopted were not a sufficient justification for their action.[2]

The great question, however, with which the First Congress had to deal, was the vexed and vital problem of finance. It was the heart of the whole constitutional movement.[3] Without a solution of it the National Government was, at best, a doubtful experiment. The public debt was a chaos of variegated obligations, including the foreign and domestic debts contracted by the Confederation, the debts of the various States, the heavy accumulation of interest on all.[4] Public and private credit, which had risen when

(For good condensed treatment of the subject see Hildreth, iv, 112–24.) Thus the Tenth Amendment, as ratified, was the twelfth as submitted and is sometimes referred to by the latter number in the documents and correspondence of 1790–91, as in Jefferson's "Opinion on the Constitutionality of the Bank of the United States." (See *infra*.) New York, Virginia, Maryland, South Carolina, North Carolina, and Rhode Island accepted the twelve amendments as proposed. The other States rejected one or both of the first two amendments.

[1] Randolph to Madison, June 30, 1789; Conway, 126.
[2] See Beard: *Econ. O. J. D.*, 76.   [3] *Ib.*, 86.   [4] *Ib.*, 132-33.

the Constitution finally became an accomplished
fact, was now declining with capital's frail timidity
of the uncertain.

In his "First Report on the Public Credit," Hamilton showed the way out of this maddening jungle.
Pay the foreign debt, said Hamilton, assume as a
National obligation the debts of the States and
fund them, together with those of the Confederation.
All had been contracted for a common purpose in a
common cause; all were "the price of liberty." Let
the owners of certificates, both State and Continental, be paid in full with arrears of interest, without discrimination between original holders and
those who had purchased from them. And let this
be done by exchanging for the old certificates those
of the new National Government bearing interest
and transferable. These latter then would pass as
specie;[1] the country would be supplied with a great
volume of sound money, so badly needed,[2] and the
debt be in the process of extinguishment.[3]

Hamilton's entire financial system was assailed
with fury both in Congress and among the people.
The funding plan, said its opponents, was a stock-
jobbing scheme, the bank a speculator's contrivance,
the National Assumption of State debts a dishonest

---

[1] Marshall, ii, 192.

[2] Money was exceedingly scarce. Even Washington had to borrow
to travel to New York for his inauguration, and Patrick Henry could
not attend the Federal Constitutional Convention for want of cash.
(Conway, 132.)

[3] "First Report on the Public Credit"; *Works;* Lodge, ii, 227 *et
seq.* The above analysis, while not technically precise, is sufficiently
accurate to give a rough idea of Hamilton's plan. (See Marshall's
analysis; Marshall, ii, 178–80.)

trick. The whole was a plot designed to array the moneyed interests in support of the National Government.[1] Assumption of State debts was a device to increase the National power and influence and to lessen still more the strength and importance of the States.[2] The speculators, who had bought the depreciated certificates of the needy, would be enriched from the substance of the whole people.

Without avail had Hamilton answered every objection in advance; the careful explanations in Congress of his financial measures went for naught; the materials for popular agitation against the National Government were too precious to be neglected by its foes.[3] "The first regular and systematic opposition

[1] This, indeed, was a portion of Hamilton's plan and he succeeded in it as he did in other parts of his broad purpose to combine as much strength as possible in support of the National Government. "The northern states and the commercial and monied people are zealously attached to . . . the new government." (Wolcott to his father, Feb. 12, 1791; Gibbs, i, 62.)

[2] This was emphatically true. From the National point of view it was the best feature of Hamilton's plan.

[3] In his old age, John Adams, Hamilton's most venomous and unforgiving enemy, while unsparing in his personal abuse, paid high tribute to the wisdom and necessity of Hamilton's financial statesmanship. "I know not," writes Adams, "how Hamilton could have done otherwise." (Adams to Rush, Aug. 23, 1805; *Old Family Letters*, 75.) "The sudden rise of public securities, after the establishment of the funding system was no misfortune to the Public but an advantage. The necessity of that system arose from the inconsistency of the People in contracting debts and then refusing to pay them." (Same to same, Jan. 25, 1806; *ib.*, 93.)

Fisher Ames thus states the different interests of the sections: "The funding system, they [Southern members of Congress] say, is in favor of the moneyed interest — oppressive to the land; that is, favorable to us [Northern people], hard on them. They pay tribute, they say, and the middle and eastern people . . . receive it. And here is the burden of the song, almost all the little [certificates of State or Continental debts] that they had and which cost them twenty shillings, for sup-to the principles on which the affairs of the union were administered," writes Marshall, "originated in the measures which were founded on it [the "First Report on the Public Credit"]."[1]

The Assumption of State debts was the strategic point of attack, especially for the Virginia politicians; and upon Assumption, therefore, they wisely concentrated their forces. Nor were they without plausible ground of opposition; for Virginia, having given as much to the common cause as any State and more than most of her sisters, and having suffered greatly, had by the sale of her public lands paid off more of her debt than had any of the rest of them.

It seemed, therefore, unjust to Virginians to put their State on a parity with those Commonwealths who had been less prompt. On the other hand, the certificates of debt, State and Continental, had accumulated in the North and East;[2] and these sections were determined that the debt should be assumed by the Nation.[3] So the debate in Congress was heated and prolonged, the decision doubtful. On various

plies or services, has been bought up, at a low rate, and now they pay more tax towards the interest than they received for the paper. This *tribute*, they say, is aggravating." (Ames to Minot, Nov. 30, 1791; *Works;* Ames, i, 104.)

[1] Marshall, ii, 181. The attack on Hamilton's financial plan and especially on Assumption was the beginning of the definite organization of the Republican Party. (Washington's *Diary:* Lossing, 166.)

[2] Gore to King, July 25, 1790; King, i, 392; and see McMaster, ii, 22.

[3] At one time, when it appeared that Assumption was defeated, Sedgwick of Massachusetts intimated that his section might secede. (*Annals,* 1st Cong., April 12, 1790, pp. 1577–78; and see Rives, iii, 90 *et seq.*)

amendments, sometimes one side and sometimes the other prevailed, often by a single vote.[1]

At the same time the question of the permanent location of the National Capital arose.[2] On these two subjects Congress was deadlocked. Both were disposed of finally by the famous deal between Jefferson and Hamilton, by which the latter agreed to get enough votes to establish the Capital on the Potomac and the former enough votes to pass the Assumption Bill.

Washington had made Jefferson his Secretary of State purely on merit. For similar reasons of efficiency Hamilton had been appointed Secretary of the Treasury, after Robert Morris, Washington's first choice, had declined that office.

At Jefferson's dinner table, the two Secretaries discussed the predicament and made the bargain. Thereupon, Jefferson, with all the zeal of his ardent temperament, threw himself into the contest to pass Hamilton's financial measure; and not only secured the necessary votes to make Assumption a law, but wrote letters broadcast in support of it.

"Congress has been long embarrassed," he advised Monroe, "by two of the most irritating questions that ever can be raised, . . . the funding the public debt and . . . the fixing on a more central residence. . . . Unless they can be reconciled by

[1] Marshall's statement of the debate is the best and fairest brief account of this historic conflict. (See Marshall, ii, 181–90. See entire debate in *Annals*, 1st Cong., i, ii, under caption "Public Debt.")

[2] "This despicable grog-shop contest, whether the taverns of New York or Philadelphia shall get the custom of Congress, keeps us in discord and covers us all with disgrace." (Ames to Dwight, June 11, 1790; *Works:* Ames, i, 80.)

some plan of compromise, there will be no funding
bill agreed to, our credit . . . will burst and vanish
and the states separate to take care every one of
itself." Jefferson outlines the bargain for fixing the
Capital and assuming the debts, and concludes:
"If this plan of compromise does not take place,
I fear one infinitely worse." [1] To John Harvie he
writes: "With respect to Virginia the measure is
. . . divested of . . . injustice." [2]

Jefferson delivered three Southern votes to pass
the bill for Assumption of the State debts, and
Hamilton got enough Northern votes to locate the
National Capital permanently where it now stands.[3]
Thus this vital part of Hamilton's comprehensive
financial plan was squeezed through Congress by
only two votes.[4] But Virginia was not appeased and
remained the center of the opposition.[5]

Business at once improved. "The sudden increase
of monied capital," writes Marshall, "invigorated
commerce, and gave a new stimulus to agriculture." [6]

[1] Jefferson to Monroe, June 20, 1790; *Works:* Ford, vi, 78–80; and
see *ib.*, 76; to Gilmer, June 27, *ib.*, 83; to Rutledge, July 4, *ib.*, 87–88;
to Harvie, July 25, *ib.*, 108.

[2] *Ib.*; and see also Jefferson to Eppes, July 25, *ib.*, 106; to Randolph,
March 28, *ib.*, 37; to same, April 18, *ib.*, 47; to Lee, April 26, *ib.*, 53;
to Mason, June 13, *ib.*, 75; to Randolph, June 20, *ib.*, 76–77; to
Monroe, June 20, *ib.*, 79; to Dumas, June 23, *ib.*, 82; to Rutledge,
July 4, *ib.*, 87–88; to Dumas, July 13, *ib.*, 96. Compare these letters
with Jefferson's statement, February, 1793; *ib.*, vii, 224–26; and with
the "Anas," *ib.*, i, 171–78. Jefferson then declared that "I was really
a stranger to the whole subject." (*Ib.*, 176.)

[3] Jefferson's statement; *Works:* Ford, vii, 224–26, and i, 175–77.

[4] Gibbs, i, 32; and see Marshall, ii, 190–91.

[5] Henry, ii, 453. But Marshall says that more votes would have
changed had that been necessary to consummate the bargain. (See
Marshall, ii, footnote to 191.)

[6] *Ib.*, 192.

But the "immense wealth which individuals acquired" by the instantaneous rise in the value of the certificates of debt caused popular jealousy and discontent. The debt was looked upon, not as the funding of obligations incurred in our War for Independence, but as a scheme newly hatched to strengthen the National Government by "the creation of a monied interest . . . subservient to its will." [1]

The Virginia Legislature, of which Marshall was now the foremost Nationalist member, convened soon after Assumption had become a National law. A smashing resolution, drawn by Henry,[2] was proposed, asserting that Assumption "is repugnant to the constitution of the United States, as it goes to the exercise of a power not expressly granted to the general government." [3] Marshall was active among and, indeed, led those who resisted to the uttermost the attack upon this thoroughly National measure of the National Government.

Knowing that they were outnumbered in the Legislature and that the people were against Assumption, Marshall and his fellow Nationalists in the House of Delegates employed the expedient of compromise. They proposed to amend Henry's resolution by stating that Assumption would place on Virginia a "heavy debt . . . which never can be extinguished" so long as the debt of any other State remained unpaid; that it was "inconsistent with justice"; that it would "alienate the affections of good citizens of this Commonwealth from the gov-

---

[1] Marshall, ii, 191–92. [2] Henry, ii, 453–55.
[3] Journal, H.D. (1790), 35.

ernment of the United States . . . and finally tend
to produce measures extremely unfavorable to the
interests of the Union." [1]

Savage enough for any one, it would seem, was this
amendment of the Nationalists in the Virginia
Legislature; but its fangs were not sufficiently poi-
sonous to suit the opposition. It lacked, particularly,
the supreme virtue of asserting the law's unconstitutionality. So the Virginia Anti-Nationalists rejected
it by a majority of 41 votes out of a total of 135.

Marshall and his determined band of Nationalists labored hard to retrieve this crushing defeat.
On Henry's original resolution, they slightly increased their strength, but were again beaten by a
majority of 23 out of 127 voting.[2]

Finally, the triumphant opposition reported a
protest and remonstrance to Congress. This brilliant
Anti-Nationalist State paper — the Magna Charta
of States' Rights — sounded the first formal call to
arms for the doctrine that all powers not expressly
given in the Constitution were reserved to the States.
It also impeached the Assumption Act as an effort
"to erect and concentrate and perpetuate a large
monied interest in opposition to the landed interests," which would prostrate "agriculture at the
feet of commerce" or result in a "change in the
present form of Federal Government, fatal to the
existence of American liberty." [3]

But the unconstitutionality of Assumption was
the main objection. The memorial declared that
"during the whole discussion of the federal consti-

[1] Journal, H.D. (1790), 35.   [2] Ib.   [3] Ib., 80–81.

tution by the convention of Virginia, your memorialists were taught to believe 'that every power not expressly granted was retained' . . . and upon this positive condition" the Constitution had been adopted. But where could anything be found in the Constitution "authorizing Congress to express terms or to assume the debts of the states?" Nowhere! Therefore, Congress had no such power.

"As the guardians, then, of the rights and interests of their constituents; as sentinels placed by them over the ministers of the Federal Government, to shield it from their encroachments," the Anti-Nationalists in the Virginia Legislature sounded the alarm.[1] It was of this jealous temper of the States that Ames so accurately wrote a year later: "The [National] government is too far off to gain the affections of the people. . . . Instead of feeling as a Nation, a State is our country. We look with indifference, often with hatred, fear, and aversion, to the other states."[2]

Marshall and his fellow Nationalists strove earnestly to extract from the memorial as much venom as possible, but were able to get only three or four lines left out;[3] and the report was adopted practically as originally drafted.[4] Thus Marshall was in

[1] Journal, H.D. (1790), 80–81; and see *Am. St. Prs., Finance*, i, 90–91. The economic distinction is here clearly drawn. Jefferson, who later made this a chief part of his attack, had not yet raised the point.

[2] Ames to Minot, Feb. 16, 1792; *Works; Ames*, i, 113.

[3] This was the sentence which declared that Hamilton's reasoning would result in "fictitious wealth through a paper medium," referring to his plan for making the transferable certificates of the National debt serve as currency.

[4] Journal, H.D. (1790), 141.

the first skirmish, after the National Government had been established, of that constitutional engagement in which, ultimately, Nationalism was to be challenged on the field of battle. Sumter and Appomattox were just below the horizon.

The remainder of Hamilton's financial plan was speedily placed upon the statute books of the Republic, though not without determined resistance which, more and more, took on a grim and ugly aspect both in Congress and throughout the country.

When Henry's resolution, on which the Virginia remonstrance was based, reached Hamilton, he instantly saw its logical result. It was, he thought, the major premise of the syllogism of National disintegration. "This," exclaimed Hamilton, of the Virginia resolution, "is the first symptom of a spirit which must either be killed or it will kill the Constitution of the United States." [1]

[1] Hamilton to Jay, Nov. 13, 1790; *Works:* Lodge, ix, 473–74. Virginia was becoming very hostile to the new Government. First, there was a report that Congress was about to emancipate the slaves. Then came the news of the Assumption of the State debts, with the presence in Virginia of speculators from other States buying up State securities; and this added gall to the bitter cup which Virginians felt the National Government was forcing them to drink. Finally the tidings that the Senate had defeated the motion for public sessions inflamed the public mind still more. (Stuart to Washington, June 2, 1790; *Writings:* Ford, xi, footnote to 482.)

Even close friends of Washington deeply deplored a "spirit so subversive of the true principles of the constitution. . . . If Mr. Henry has sufficient boldness to aim the blow at its [Constitution's] existence, which he has threatened, I think he can never meet with a more favorable opportunity if the assumption should take place." (*Ib.*)

Washington replied that Stuart's letter pained him. "The public mind in Virginia . . . seems to be more irritable, sour, and discontented than . . . it is in any other State in the Union except Massachusetts." (Washington to Stuart, June 15, 1790; *ib.*, 481–82.)

Marshall's father most inaccurately reported to Washington that

The Anti-Nationalist memorial of the Legislature of Virginia accurately expressed the sentiment of the State. John Taylor of Caroline two years later, in pamphlets of marked ability, attacked the Administration's entire financial system and its management. While he exhaustively analyzed its economic features, yet he traced all its supposed evils to the Nationalist idea. The purpose and result of Hamilton's whole plan and of the manner of its execution was, declared Taylor, to "Swallow up . . . the once sovereign . . . states. . . . Hence all assumptions and . . . the enormous loans." Thus "the state governments will become only speculative commonwealths to be read for amusement, like Harrington's *Oceana* or Moore's *Utopia*." [1]

The fight apparently over, Marshall declined to become a candidate for the Legislature in the following year. The Administration's financial plan was now enacted into law and the vital part of the National machinery thus set up and in motion. The country was responding with a degree of prosperity hitherto unknown, and, for the time, all seemed secure. [2] So Marshall did not again consent to serve

Kentucky favored the measures of the Administration; and the President, thanking him for the welcome news, asked the elder Marshall for "any information of a public or private nature . . . from your district." (Washington to Thomas Marshall, Feb., 1791; Washington's Letter Book, MS., Lib. Cong.) Kentucky was at that time in strong opposition and this continued to grow.

[1] Taylor's "An Enquiry, etc.," as quoted in Beard: *Econ. O. J. D.*, 209. (*Ib.*, chap. vii.) Taylor's pamphlet was revised by Pendleton and then sent to Madison before publication. (Monroe to Madison, May 18, 1793; Monroe's *Writings*: Hamilton, i, 254.) Taylor wanted "banks . . . demolished" and bankers "excluded from public councils." (Beard: *Econ. O. J. D.*, 209.)

[2] Marshall, ii, 192.

in the House of Delegates until 1795. But the years between these periods of his public life brought forth events which were determinative of the Nation's future. Upon the questions growing out of them, John Marshall was one of the ever-decreasing Virginia minority which stanchly upheld the policies of the National Government.

Virginia's declaration of the unconstitutionality of the Assumption Act had now thundered in Jefferson's ears. He himself was instrumental in the enactment of this law and its unconstitutionality never occurred to him [1] until Virginia spoke. But, faithful to the people's voice,[2] Jefferson was already publicly opposing, through the timid but resourceful Madison [3] and the fearless and aggressive [4] Giles, the Nationalist statesmanship of Hamilton.[5]

---

[1] In Jefferson's letters, already cited, not the faintest suggestion appears that he thought the law unconstitutional. Not until Patrick Henry's resolution, and the address of the Virginia Legislature to Congress based thereon, made the point that Assumption was in violation of this instrument, because the power to pass such a law was not expressly given in the Constitution, did Jefferson take his stand against implied powers.

[2] "Whether . . . right or wrong, abstractedly, more attention should be paid to the general opinion." (Jefferson to Mason, Feb. 4, 1791; *Works: Ford*, vi, 186.)

[3] Monroe had advised Madison of the hostility of Virginia to Assumption and incidentally asked for an office for his own brother-in-law. (Monroe to Madison, July 2, 1790; Monroe's *Writings:* Hamilton, i, 208; and see Monroe to Jefferson, July 3, 1790; *ib.,* 209.)

[4] Anderson, 21.

[5] Jefferson himself, a year after he helped pass the Assumption Act, had in a Cabinet paper fiercely attacked Hamilton's plan; and the latter answered in a formal statement to the President. These two documents are the ablest summaries of the opposing sides of this great controversy. (See Jefferson to President, May 23, 1792; *Works: Ford*, vi, 487–95; and Hamilton to Washington, Aug. 18, 1792; *Works: Lodge*, ii, 426–72.)

Thus it came about that when Washington asked his Cabinet's opinion upon the bill to incorporate the Bank of the United States, Jefferson promptly expressed with all his power the constitutional theory of the Virginia Legislature. The opposition had reached the point when, if no other objection could be found to any measure of the National Government, its "unconstitutionality" was urged against it. "We hear, incessantly, from the old foes of the Constitution 'this is unconstitutional and that is,' and, indeed, what is not? I scarce know a point which has not produced this cry, not excepting a motion for adjourning."[1] Jefferson now proceeded "to produce this cry" against the Bank Bill.

Hamilton's plan, said Jefferson, violated the Constitution. "To take a single step beyond the boundaries thus specially drawn around the powers of Congress [the Twelfth Amendment][2] is to take possession of a boundless field of power, no longer susceptible of any definition." Even if the bank were "convenient" to carry out any power specifically granted in the Constitution, yet it was not "*necessary*," argued Jefferson; all powers expressly given could be exercised without the bank. It was only indispensable powers that the Constitution permitted to be implied from those definitely bestowed on Congress — "convenience is not necessity."[3]

[1] Ames to Minot, March 8, 1792; *Works:* Ames, i, 114.
[2] Tenth Amendment, as ratified.
[3] "Opinion on the Constitutionality of a National Bank of the United States"; *Works:* Ford, vi, 198; and see Madison's argument against the constitutionality of the Bank Act in *Annals*, 1st Cong., Feb. 2, 1791, pp. 1944–52; Feb. 8, 2008–12; also, *Writings:* Hunt,

Hamilton answered with his argument for the doctrine of implied powers.[1] Banks, said he, are products of civilized life — all enlightened commercial nations have them. He showed the benefits and utility of banks; answered all the objections to these financial agencies; and then examined the disputed constitutionality of the bill for the incorporation of the Bank of the United States.

All the powers of the National Government were not set down in words in the Constitution and could not be. For instance, there are the "resulting powers," as over conquered territory. Nobody could deny the existence of such powers — yet they were not granted by the language of the fundamental law. As to Jefferson's argument based on the word "necessary," his contention meant, said Hamilton, that "no means are to be considered *necessary* without which the power would be *nugatory*" — which was absurd. Jefferson's reasoning would require that an implied power should be "*absolutely* or *indispensably* necessary."

But this was not the ordinary meaning of the word and it was by this usual and customary understanding of terms that the Constitution must be interpreted. If Jefferson was right, Congress could act only in "a case of extreme necessity." Such a construction of the Constitution would prevent

vi, 19–42. This argument best shows Madison's sudden and radical change from an extreme Nationalist to an advocate of the most restricted National powers.

[1] Hamilton's "Opinion as to the Constitutionality of the Bank of the United States"; *Works:* Lodge, iii, 445–93. Adams took the same view. (See Adams to Rush, Dec. 27, 1810; *Old Family Letters,* 272.)

the National Government even from erecting light-
houses, piers, and other conveniences of commerce
which *could* be carried on without them. These
illustrations revealed the paralysis of government
concealed in Jefferson's philosophy.

The true test of implied powers, Hamilton showed,
was the "natural relation [of means] to the . . . lawful ends of the government." Collection of taxes,
foreign and interstate trade, were, admittedly, such
ends. The National power to "*regulate*" these is
"*sovereign*"; and therefore "to employ all the means
which will relate to their regulation to the best and
greatest advantage" is permissible.

"This *general principle* is *inherent* in the very
definition of government," declared he, "and *essential* to every step of the progress to be made by that
of the United States, namely: That every power
vested in a government is in its nature *sovereign* and
included by *force* of the *term*, a right to employ all
the *means* requisite and fairly applicable to the
attainment of the *ends* of such power, and which are
not precluded by restrictions and exceptions specified in the Constitution or not immoral, or not contrary to the *essential* ends of political society. . . .

"The powers of the Federal Government, as to
its objects are sovereign"; the National Constitution, National laws, and treaties are expressly
declared to be "the supreme law of the land."
And he added, sarcastically: "The power which
can create *the supreme law of the land* in *any case*
is doubtless *sovereign* as to such case." But, said
Hamilton, "it is unquestionably incident to *sove-*

reign power to erect corporations, and consequently
to *that* of the United States, in *relation* to the *objects* intrusted to the management of the government."

And, finally: "The powers contained in a constitution of government . . . ought to be construed
liberally in advancement of the public good. . . . The
means by which natural exigencies are to be provided
for, national inconveniences obviated, national prosperity promoted are of such infinite variety, extent,
and complexity, that there must of necessity be
great latitude of discretion in the selection and application of those means." [1]

So were stated the opposing principles of liberal
and narrow interpretation of the Constitution, about
which were gathering those political parties that,
says Marshall, "in their long and dubious conflict
. . . have shaken the United States to their centre." [2]
The latter of these parties, under the name "Republican," was then being shaped into a compact
organization. Its strength was increasing. The object of Republican attack was the National Government; that of Republican praise and affection
was the sovereignty of the States.

"The hatred of the Jacobites towards the house
of Hanover was never more deadly than that . . .
borne by many of the partisans of State power towards the government of the United States," testi-

---

[1] "Opinion as to the Constitutionality of the Bank of the United
States"; *Works:* Lodge, iii, 445–93. Washington was sorely perplexed
by the controversy and was on the point of vetoing the Bank Bill.
(See Rives, iii, 170–71.)
[2] Marshall, ii, 206–07.

fies Ames.[1] In the Republican view the basis of the two parties was faith as against disbelief in the ability of the people to govern themselves; the former favored the moneyed interests, the latter appealed to the masses.[2] Such was the popular doctrine preached by the opponents of the National Government; but all economic objections centered in a common assault on Nationalism.

Thus a clear dividing line was drawn separating the people into two great political divisions; and political parties, in the present-day sense of definite organizations upon fundamental and popularly recognized principles, began to emerge. Henceforth the terms "Federalist" and "Republican" mean opposing party groups, the one standing for the National and the other for the provincial idea. The various issues that arose were referred to the one or the other of these hostile conceptions of government.

In this rise of political parties the philosophy of the Constitution was negatived; for our fundamental law, unlike those of other modern democracies, was built on the non-party theory and did not contemplate party government. Its architects did not foresee parties. Indeed, for several years after the Constitution was adopted, the term "party" was used as an expression of reproach. The correspondence of the period teems with illustrations of this important fact.

For a considerable time most of the leading men

[1] Ames to Dwight, Jan. 23, 1792; *Works: Ames*, i, 110–11.
[2] "A Candid State of Parties" — *National Gazette*, Sept. 26, 1792.

of the period looked with dread upon the growing idea of political parties; and the favorite rebuke to opponents was to accuse them of being a "party" or a "faction," those designations being used interchangeably. The "Farewell Address" is a solemn warning against political parties [1] almost as much as against foreign alliances.

[1] "I was no party man myself and the first wish of my heart was, if parties did exist, to reconcile them." (Washington to Jefferson, July 6, 1796; *Writings:* Ford, xiii, 230.)

CHAPTER III .

LEADING THE VIRGINIA FEDERALISTS

I think nothing better could be done than to make him [Marshall] a judge. (Jefferson to Madison, June 29, 1792.)

To doubt the holiness of the French cause was the certain road to odium and proscription. (Alexander Graydon.)

The trouble and perplexities have worn away my mind. (Washington.)

In Richmond, Marshall was growing ever stronger in his belief in Nationalism. Hamilton's immortal plea for a vital interpretation of the fundamental law of the Nation and his demonstration of the constitutionality of extensive implied powers was a clear, compact statement of what Marshall himself had been thinking. The time was coming when he would announce it in language still more lucid, expressive of a reasoning even more convincing. Upon Hamilton's constitutional doctrine John Marshall was to place the seal of finality.[1]

But Marshall did not delay until that great hour to declare his Nationalist opinions. Not only did he fight for them in the House of Delegates; but in his club at Farmicola's Tavern, on the street corners, riding the circuit, he argued for the constitutionality and wisdom of those measures of Washington's

[1] Compare Hamilton's "Opinion as to the Constitutionality of the Bank of the United States" with Marshall's opinion in McCulloch vs. Maryland. The student of Marshall cannot devote too much attention to Hamilton's great state papers, from the "First Report on the Public Credit" to "Camillus." It is interesting that Hamilton produced all these within five years, notwithstanding the fact that this was the busiest and most crowded period of his life.

Administration which strengthened and broadened
the powers of the National Government.[1]

Although he spoke his mind, in and out of season,
for a cause increasingly unpopular, Marshall, as yet,
lost little favor with the people. At a time when
political controversy severed friendship and interrupted social relations,[2] his personality still held
sway over his associates regardless of their political
convictions. Even Mason, the ultra-radical foe of
broad National powers, wrote, at this heated juncture, that Marshall "is an intimate friend of mine." [3]

His winning frankness, easy manner, and warm-
heartedness saved him from that dislike which his
bold views otherwise would have created. "Independent principles, talents, and integrity are denounced [in Virginia] as badges of aristocracy; but
if you add to these good manners and a decent
appearance, his political death is decreed without
the benefit of a hearing," testifies Francis Corbin.[4]

"Independent principles, talents, and integrity"
Marshall possessed in fullest measure, as all admitted; but his manners were far from those which
men like the modish Corbin called "good," and his
appearance would not have passed muster under the
critical eye of that fastidious and disgruntled young
Federalist. We shall soon hear Jefferson denouncing
Marshall's deportment as the artifice of a cunning

[1] Binney, in Dillon, iii, 301-02.

[2] La Rochefoucauld, iii, 73. For a man even "to be passive . . .
is a satisfactory proof that he is on the wrong side." (Monroe to
Jefferson, July 17, 1792; Monroe's *Writings:* Hamilton, i, 238.)

[3] George Mason to John Mason, July 12, 1791; Rowland, ii, 338.

[4] Corbin to Hamilton March 17, 1793; as quoted in Beard: *Econ.
O. J. D.*, 226.

and hypocritical craft. As yet, however, Jefferson
saw in Marshall only an extremely popular young
man who was fast becoming the most effective supporter in Virginia of the National Government.

In the year of the Bank Act, Jefferson and Madison went on their eventful "vacation," swinging up
the Hudson and through New England. During this
journey Jefferson drew around Madison "the magic
circle" of his compelling charm and won entirely to
the extreme Republican cause [1] the invaluable aid
of that superb intellect. In agreement as to common
warfare upon the Nationalist measures of the Administration,[2] the two undoubtedly talked over the
Virginia Federalists.[3]

Marshall's repeated successes at the polls with a
constituency hostile to the young lawyer's views particularly impressed them. Might not Marshall become a candidate for Congress? If elected, here would
be a skillful, dauntless, and captivating supporter of
all Nationalist measures in the House of Representatives. What should be done to avert this misfortune?

[1] "Patrick Henry once said 'that he could forgive anything else
in Mr. Jefferson, but his corrupting Mr. Madison.'" (Pickering to
Marshall, Dec. 26, 1828; Pickering MSS., Mass. Hist. Soc.) "His
[Madison's] placing himself under the pupilage of Mr. Jefferson and
supporting his public deceptions, are sufficient to put him out of my
book." (Pickering to Rose, March 22, 1808; ib.)

[2] Madison's course was irreconcilable with his earlier Nationalist
stand. (See Beard: Econ. O. J. D., 77; and see especially the remarkable and highly important letter of Hamilton to Carrington, May 26,
1792; Works: Lodge, ix, 513–35, on Madison's change, Jefferson's conduct, and the politics of the time.) Carrington was now the brother-
in-law of Marshall and his most intimate friend. Their houses in
Richmond almost adjoined. (See infra, chap. v.)

[3] See brief but excellent account of this famous journey in Gay:
Madison (American Statesmen Series), 184–85; and contra, Rives, iii,
191.

Jefferson's dexterous intellect devised the idea of getting rid of Marshall, politically, by depositing him on the innocuous heights of the State bench. Better, far better, to make Marshall a Virginia judge than to permit him to become a Virginia Representative in Congress. So, upon his return, Jefferson wrote to Madison: —

"I learn that he [Hamilton] has expressed the strongest desire that Marshall should come into Congress from Richmond, declaring that there is no man in Virginia whom he wishes so much to see there; and I am told that Marshall has expressed half a mind to come. Hence I conclude that Hamilton has plyed him well with flattery & sollicitation and I think nothing better could be done than to make him a judge." [1]

Hamilton's "plying" Marshall with "flattery & solicitation" occurred only in Jefferson's teeming, but abnormally suspicious, mind. Marshall was in Virginia all this time, as his Account Book proves, while Hamilton was in New York, and no letters seem to have passed between them.[2] But Jefferson's information that his fellow Secretary wished the Nationalist Richmond attorney in Congress was probably correct. Accounts of Marshall's striking ability and of his fearless zeal in support of the Administration's measures had undoubtedly reached Hamilton, perhaps through Washington himself; and so sturdy and capable a Federalist in Congress

[1] Jefferson to Madison, June 29, 1792; *Works:* Ford, vii, 129–30.

[2] No letters have been discovered from Hamilton to Marshall or from Marshall to Hamilton dated earlier than three years after Jefferson's letter to Madison.

from Virginia would have been of great strategic value.

But Jefferson might have spared his pains to dispose of Marshall by cloistering him on the State bench. Nothing could have induced the busy lawyer to go to Congress at this period. It would have been fatal to his law practice [1] which he had built up until it was the largest in Richmond and upon the returns from which his increasing family depended for support. Six years later, Washington himself labored with Marshall for four days before he could persuade him to stand for the National House, and Marshall then yielded to his adored leader only as a matter of duty, at one of the Nation's most critical hours, when war was on the horizon.[2]

The break-up of Washington's Cabinet was now approaching. Jefferson was keeping pace with the Anti-Nationalist sentiment of the masses — drilling his followers into a sternly ordered political force. "The discipline of the [Republican] party," wrote Ames, "is as severe as the Prussian."[3] Jefferson and Madison had secured an organ in the "National Gazette," [4] edited by Freneau, whom Jefferson employed as translator in the State Department. Through this paper Jefferson attacked Hamilton without mercy. The spirited Secretary of the Treas-

[1] "The length of the last session has done me irreparable injury in my profession, as it has made an impression on the general opinion that two occupations are incompatible." (Monroe to Jefferson, June 17, 1792; Monroe's *Writings:* Hamilton, i, 230.)

[2] See *infra*, chap. x.

[3] Ames to Dwight, Jan., 1793; *Works:* Ames, i, 126–27.

[4] Rives, iii, 192–94; and see McMaster, ii, 52–53; also Hamilton to Carrington, May 26, 1792; *Works:* Lodge, ix, 513–35.

ury keenly resented the opposition of his Cabinet
associate which was at once covert and open.

In vain the President pathetically begged Jefferson for harmony and peace.[1] Jefferson responded
with a bitter attack on Hamilton. "I was duped,"
said he, "by the Secretary of the Treasury and made
a tool for forwarding his schemes, not then sufficiently understood by me."[2] To somewhat, but not
much, better purpose did Washington ask Hamilton
for "mutual forbearances."[3] Hamilton replied with
spirit, yet pledged his honor that he would "not,
directly or indirectly, say or do a thing that shall
endanger a feud."[4]

The immense speculation, which had unavoidably
grown out of the Assumption and Funding Acts, inflamed popular resentment against the whole financial statesmanship of the Federalists.[5] More material, this, for the hands of the artificer who was
fashioning the Republican Party into a capacious
vessel into which the people might pour all their
discontent, all their fears, all their woes and all their

---

[1] Washington to Jefferson, Aug. 23, 1792; *Writings:* Ford, xii,
174–75. This letter is almost tearful in its pleading.

[2] Jefferson to Washington, Sept. 9, 1792; *Works:* Ford, vii, 137
et seq. The quotation in the text refers to Jefferson's part in the deal
fixing the site of the Capital and passing the Assumption Act. Compare with Jefferson's letters written at the time. (*Supra,* 64.) It is
impossible that Jefferson was not fully advised; the whole country
was aroused over Assumption, Congress debated it for weeks, it was
the one subject of interest and conversation at the seat of government,
and Jefferson himself so testifies in his correspondence.

[3] Washington to Hamilton, Aug. 26, 1792; *Writings:* Ford, xii,
177–78.

[4] Hamilton to Washington, Sept. 9, 1792; *Works:* Lodge, vii,
306.

[5] See Marshall, ii, 191–92.

hopes. And Jefferson, with practical skill, used for that purpose whatever material he could find.

Still more potter's earth was brought to Jefferson. The National Courts were at work. Creditors were securing judgments for debts long due them. In Virginia the debtors of British merchants, who for many years had been rendered immune from payment, were brought to the bar of this "alien" tribunal. Popular feeling ran high. A resolution was introduced into the House of Delegates requesting the Virginia Senators and Representatives in Congress to "adopt such measures as will tend, not only to suspend all executions and the proceedings thereon, but prevent any future judgments to be given by the Federal Courts in favor of British creditors until" Great Britain surrendered the posts and runaway negroes.[1] Thus was the practical overthrow of the National Judiciary proposed.[2]

Nor was this all. A State had been haled before a National Court.[3] The Republicans saw in this the monster "consolidation." The Virginia Legislature passed a resolution instructing her Senators and Representatives to "unite their utmost and earliest exertions" to secure a constitutional amendment preventing a State from being sued "in any court of

[1] Journal, H.D. (Nov. 28, 1793), 101.

[2] Ib. The Legislature instructed Virginia's Senators and Representatives to endeavor to secure measures to "suspend the operation and completion" of the articles of the treaty of peace looking to the payment of British debts until the posts and negroes should be given up. (Ib., 124–25; also see Virginia Statutes at Large, New Series, i, 285.) Referring to this Ames wrote: "Thus, murder, at last, is out." (Ames to Dwight, May 6, 1794; Works: Ames, i, 143–44.)

[3] Chisholm vs. Georgia, 2 Dallas, 419.

the United States." [1] The hostility to the National
Bank took the form of a resolution against a director
or stockholder of the Bank of the United States being
a Senator or Representative in Congress. [2] But apparently this trod upon the toes of too many ambitious Virginians, for the word "stockholders" was
stricken out. [3]

The slander that the Treasury Department had
misused the public funds had been thoroughly answered; [4] but the Legislature of Virginia by a majority of 111 out of a total vote of 124, applauded her
Senators and Representatives who had urged the
inquiry. [5] Such was the developing temper of Republicanism as revealed by the emotionless pages
of the public records; but these furnish scarcely a
hint of the violence of public opinion.

Jefferson was now becoming tigerish in his assaults on the measures of the Administration. Many

[1] Journal, H.D. (1793), 92–99; also see Virginia Statutes at Large,
New Series, i, 284. This was the origin of the Eleventh Amendment to
the Constitution. The Legislature "Resolved, That a State cannot,
under the Constitution of the United States, be made a defendant at the
suit of any individual or individuals, and that the decision of the
Supreme Federal Court, that a State may be placed in that situation,
is incompatible with, and dangerous to the sovereignty and independence of the individual States, as the same tends to a general consolidation of these confederated republics." Virginia Senators were
"instructed" to make "their utmost exertions" to secure an amendment to the Constitution regarding suits against States. The Governor was directed to send the Virginia resolution to all the other States.
(Journal, H.D. (1793), 99.)

[2] Ib., 125.

[3] Ib.; also Statutes at Large, supra, 284.

[4] See Annals, 2d Cong., 900–63.

[5] Journal, H.D. (1793), 56–57. Of Giles's methods in this attack on
Hamilton the elder Wolcott wrote that it was "such a piece of baseness as would have disgraced the council of Pandemonium." (Wolcott to his son, March 25, 1793; Gibbs, i, 91.)

members of Congress had been holders of certificates which Assumption and Funding had made valuable. Most but not all of them had voted for every feature of Hamilton's financial plan.[1] Three or four were directors of the Bank, but no dishonesty existed.[2] Heavy speculation went on in Philadelphia.[3] This, said Republicans, was the fruit which Hamilton's Nationalist financial scheme gathered from the people's industry to feed to "monocrats."

"Here [Philadelphia]," wrote Jefferson, "*the unmonied farmer* . . . his cattle & corps [*sic*] are no more thought of than if they did not feed us. Script & stock are food & raiment here. . . . The credit & fate of the nation seem to hang on the desperate throws & plunges of gambling scoundrels."[4] But Jefferson comforted himself with the prophecy that

[1] Beard: *Econ. O. J. D.*, chap. vi.

[2] Professor Beard, after a careful treatment of this subject, concludes that "The charge of mere corruption must fall to the ground." (*Ib.*, 195.)

[3] "To the northward of Baltimore everybody . . . speculates, trades, and jobs in the stocks. The judge, the advocate, the physician and the minister of divine worship, are all, or almost all, more or less interested in the sale of land, in the purchase of goods, in that of bills of exchange, and in lending money at two or three per cent." (La Rochefoucauld, iv, 474.) The French traveler was also impressed with the display of riches in the Capital. "The profusion of luxury of Philadelphia, on great days, at the tables of the wealthy, in their equipages and the dresses of their wives and daughters, are . . . extreme. I have seen balls on the President's birthday where the splendor of the rooms, and the variety and richness of the dresses did not suffer, in comparison with Europe." The extravagance extended to working-men who, on Sundays, spent money with amazing lavishness. Even negro servants had balls; and negresses with wages of one dollar per week wore dresses costing sixty dollars. (*Ib.*, 107–09.)

[4] Jefferson to T. M. Randolph, March 16, 1792; *Works: Ford*, vi, 408.

"this nefarious business" would finally "tumble its authors headlong from their heights." [1]

The National law taxing whiskey particularly aroused the wrath of the multitude. Here it was at last! — a direct tax laid upon the universal drink of the people, as the razor-edged Pennsylvania resolutions declared. [2] Here it was, just as the patriotic foes of the abominable National Constitution had predicted when fighting the ratification of that "oppressive" instrument. Here was the exciseman at every man's door, just as Henry and Mason and Grayson had foretold — and few were the doors in the back counties of the States behind which the owner's private still was not simmering. [3] And why was this tribute exacted? To provide funds required by the corrupt Assumption and Funding laws, asserted the agitators.

[1] Jefferson to Short, May 18, 1792; *Works:* Ford, vi, 413; and see "A Citizen" in the *National Gazette,* May 3, 1792, for a typical Republican indictment of Funding and Assumption.

[2] Gallatin's *Writings:* Adams, i, 3.

[3] Pennsylvania alone had five thousand distilleries. (Beard: *Econ. O. J. D.,* 250.) Whiskey was used as a circulating medium. (McMaster, ii, 29.) Every contemporary traveler tells of the numerous private stills in Pennyslvania and the South. Practically all farmers, especially in the back country, had their own apparatus for making whiskey or brandy. (See chap. vii, vol. i, of this work.)

Nor was this industry confined to the lowly and the frontiersmen. Washington had a large distillery. (Washington to William Augustine Washington, Feb. 27, 1798; *Writings:* Ford, xiii, 444.)

New England's rum, on the other hand, was supplied by big distilleries; and these could include the tax in the price charged the consumer. Thus the people of Pennsylvania and the South felt the tax personally, while New Englanders were unconscious of it. Otherwise there doubtless would have been a New England "rum rebellion," as Shays's uprising and as New England's implied threat in the Assumption fight would seem to prove. (See Beard: *Econ. O. J. D.,* 250–51.)

Again it was the National Government that was to blame; in laying the whiskey tax it had invaded the rights of the States, hotly declared the Republicans. "All that powerful party," Marshall bears witness, "which attached itself to the local [State] rather than to the general [National] government ... considered ... a tax by Congress on any domestic manufacture as the intrusion of a foreign power into their particular concerns which excited serious apprehensions for state importance and for liberty." [1] The tariff did not affect most people, especially those in the back country, because they used few or no imported articles; but the whiskey tax did reach them, directly and personally. [2]

Should such a despotic law be obeyed? Never! It was oppressive! It was wicked! Above all, it was "unconstitutional"! But what to do! The agencies of the detested and detestable National Government were at work! To arms, then! That was the only thing left to outraged freemen about to be ravaged of their liberty! [3] Thus came the physical defiance of the law in Pennsylvania; Washington's third proclamation [4] demanding obedience to the National statutes after his earnest pleas [5] to the disaffected to observe the laws; the march of the troops accompanied by Hamilton [6] against the insurgents; the

[1] Marshall, ii, 200.   [2] Ib., 238.   [3] Graydon, 372.

[4] Sept. 25, 1794; *Writings: Ford*, xii, 467.

[5] Sept. 15, 1792; Richardson, i, 124; Aug. 7, 1794; *Writings: Ford*, xii, 445.

[6] Hamilton remained with the troops until the insurrection was suppressed and order fully established. (See Hamilton's letters to Washington, written from various points, during the expedition, from Oct. 25 to Nov. 19, 1794; *Works: Lodge*, vi, 451–60.)

forcible suppression of this first armed assault on
the laws of the United States in which men had been
killed, houses burned, mails pillaged — all in the
name of the Constitution,[1] which the Republicans
now claimed as their peculiar property.[2]

Foremost in the fight for the whiskey insurgents
were the democratic societies, which, as has been
seen, were the offspring of the French Jacobin
Clubs. Washington finally became certain that these
organizations had inspired this uprising against
National law and authority. While the Whiskey
Rebellion was economic in its origin, yet it was sustained by the spirit which the French Revolution
had kindled in the popular heart. Indeed, when the
troops sent to put down the insurrection reached
Harrisburg, they found the French flag flying over
the courthouse.[3]

Marshall's old comrade in the Revolution, close
personal friend, and business partner,[4] Henry Lee,
was now Governor of Virginia. He stood militantly
with Washington and it was due to Lee's efforts that

[1] Marshall, ii, 200, 235–38, 340–48; Gibbs, i, 144–55; and see Hamilton's Report to the President, Aug. 5, 1794; *Works*: Lodge, vi, 358–
88. But see Gallatin's *Writings:* Adams, i, 2–12; Beard: *Econ. O. J. D.*,
250–60. For extended account of the Whiskey Rebellion from the
point of view of the insurgents, see Findley: *History of the Insurrection*,
etc., and Breckenridge: *History of the Western Insurrection*.

[2] The claim now made by the Republicans that they were the only
friends of the Constitution was a clever political turn. Also it is an
amusing incident of our history. The Federalists were the creators of
the Constitution; while the Republicans, generally speaking and
with exceptions, had been ardent foes of its adoption. (See Beard:
Econ. O. J. D.)

[3] Graydon, 374. Jefferson's party was called Republican because
of its championship of the French Republic. (Ambler, 63.)

[4] In the Fairfax purchase. (See *infra*, chap. v.)

the Virginia militia responded to help suppress the Whiskey Rebellion. He was made Commander-in-Chief of all the forces that actually took the field.[1] To Lee, therefore, Washington wrote with unrestrained pen.

"I consider," said the President, "this insurrection as the first *formidable* fruit of the Democratic Societies . . . instituted by . . . *artful and designing* members [of Congress] . . . to sow the seeds of jealousy and distrust among the people of the government. . . . I see, under a display of popular and fascinating guises, the most diabolical attempts to destroy . . . the government."[2] He declared: "That they have been the fomenters of the western disturbances admits of no doubt."[3]

Never was that emphatic man more decided than now; he was sure, he said, that, unless lawlessness were overcome, republican government was at an end, "and nothing but anarchy and confusion is to be expected hereafter."[4] If "the daring and factious spirit" is not crushed, "adieu to all government in this country, except mob and club government."[5]

Such were Washington's positive and settled opinions, and they were adopted and maintained by Marshall, his faithful supporter.

And not only by argument and speech did Marshall uphold the measures of Washington's Adminis-

[1] See Hamilton's orders to General Lee; *Works:* Lodge, vi, 445–51; and see Washington to Lee, Oct. 20, 1794; *Writings:* Ford, xii, 478–80.

[2] Washington to Lee, Aug. 26, 1794; *Writings:* Ford, xii, 454–56.

[3] Washington to Jay, Nov. 1, 1794; *ib.*, 486.

[4] Washington to Thruston, Aug. 10, 1794; *ib.*, 452.

[5] Washington to Morgan, Oct. 8, 1794; *ib.*, 470. The Virginia militia were under the Command of Major-General Daniel Morgan.

tration. In 1793 he had been commissioned as Brigadier-General of Militia, and when the President's
requisition came for Virginia troops to enforce the
National revenue law against those who were violently resisting the execution of it, he was placed in
command of one of the detachments to be raised for
that purpose.[1] Although it is not established that
his brigade was ordered to Pennsylvania, the proba-
bilities are that it was and that Marshall, in command of it, was on the scene of the first armed opposition to the National Government. And it is certain
that Marshall was busy and effective in the work of
raising and properly equipping the troops for duty.
He suggested practical plans for expediting the muster and for economizing the expenditure of the public
money, and his judgment was highly valued.[2]

All the ability, experience, and zeal at the disposal
of the State were necessary, for the whiskey tax was
only less disliked in Virginia than in Pennsylvania,
and a portion of the Commonwealth was inclined
to assist rather than to suppress the insurrection.[3]
Whether or not he was one of the military force that,
on the ground, overawed the whiskey insurgents,
it is positively established that Marshall was ready,
in person, to help put down with arms all forcible
opposition to the National laws and authority.

Jefferson, now the recognized commander-in-chief
of the new party, was, however, heartily with the
popular outbreak. He had approved Washington's

---

[1] General Order, June 30, 1794; *Cal. Va. St. Prs.*, vii, 202.

[2] Carrington to Lieutenant-Governor Wood, Sept. 1, 1794; *ib.*, 287.

[3] Major-General Daniel Morgan to the Governor of Virginia, Sept.
7, 1794; *ib.*, 297.

first proclamations against the whiskey producers; [1] but, nevertheless, as the anger of the people grew, it found Jefferson responsive. "The excise law is an infernal one," he cried; the rebellion against it, nothing more than "riotous" at the worst. [2]

And Jefferson wielded his verbal cat-o'-nine-tails on Washington's order to put the rebellion down by armed forces. [3] It was all "for the favorite purpose of strengthening government and increasing public debt." [4] Washington thought the Whiskey Rebellion treasonable; and Jefferson admitted that "there was . . . a meeting to consult about a separation" from the Union; but talking was not acting. [5] Thus the very point was raised which Marshall enforced in the Burr trial twelve years later, when Jefferson took exactly opposite grounds. But to take the popular view now made for Republican solidarity and strength. Criticism is ever more profitable politics than building.

All this had different effects on different public men. The Republican Party was ever growing stronger, and under Jefferson's skillful guidance, was fast becoming a seasoned political army. The sentiment of the multitude against the National Government continued to rise. But instead of weakening John Marshall's Nationalist principles, this turbulent opposition strengthened and hardened them. So did other and larger events of that period which tumultuously crowded fast upon one another's heels.

[1] Jefferson to Washington, Sept. 18, 1792; *Works:* Ford, vii, 153.
[2] Jefferson to Madison, Dec. 28, 1794; *ib.*, viii, 157.   [3] *Ib.*
[4] Jefferson to Monroe, May 26, 1795; *ib.*, 177.
[5] Jefferson to Madison, Dec. 28, 1794; *ib.*, 157.

As we have seen, the horrors of the Reign of Terror in Paris did not chill the frenzied enthusiasm of the masses of Americans for France. "By a strange kind of reasoning," wrote Oliver Wolcott to his brother, "some suppose the liberties of America depend on the right of cutting throats in France." [1]

In the spring of 1793 France declared war against England. The popular heart in America was hot for France, the popular voice loud against England. The idea that the United States was an independent nation standing aloof from foreign quarrels did not enter the minds of the people. But it was Washington's one great conception. It was not to make the American people the tool of any foreign government that he had drawn his sword for their independence. It was to found a separate nation with dignity and rights equal to those of any other nation; a nation friendly to all, and allied with none [2] — this was the supreme purpose for which he had fought, toiled, and suffered. And Washington believed that only on this broad highway could the American people travel to ultimate happiness and power. [3] He determined upon a policy of absolute impartiality.

On the same day that the Minister of the new French Republic landed on American shores, Wash-

[1] Wolcott to Wolcott, Dec. 15, 1792; Gibbs, i, 85.

[2] Marshall, ii, 256; see Washington's "Farewell Address."

[3] John Adams claimed this as his particular idea. "Washington learned it from me . . . and practiced upon it." (Adams to Rush, July 7, 1805; *Old Family Letters*, 71.)

"I trust that we shall have too just a sense of our own interest to originate any cause, that may involve us in it [the European war]." (Washington to Humphreys, March 23, 1793; *Writings:* Ford, xii, 276.)

ington proclaimed Neutrality.[1] This action, which to-day all admit to have been wise and far-seeing statesmanship, then caused an outburst of popular resentment against Neutrality and the Administration that had dared to take this impartial stand. For the first time Washington was openly abused by Americans.[2]

"A great majority of the American people deemed it criminal to remain unconcerned spectators of a conflict between their ancient enemy [Great Britain] and republican France," declares Marshall. The people, he writes, thought Great Britain was waging war "with the sole purpose of imposing a monarchical government on the French people. The few who did not embrace these opinions, and they were certainly very few, were held up as objects of public detestation; and were calumniated as the tools of Britain and the satellites of despotism." [3]

The National Government was ungrateful, cried the popular voice; it was aiding the tyrants of Europe against a people struggling for freedom; it was cowardly, infamous, base. "Could any friend of his kind be neutral?" was the question on the popular tongue; of course not! unless, indeed, the miscreant who dared to be exclusively American was a monarchist at heart. "To doubt the holiness of their [the French] cause was the certain road to odium

[1] Marshall, ii, 259; and see Rules of Neutrality, *ib.*, note 13, p. 15. Washington's proclamation was drawn by Attorney-General Randolph. (Conway, 202.)

[2] Marshall, ii, 259-60. "The publications in Freneau's and Bache's papers are outrages on common decency." (Washington to Lee, July 21, 1793; *Writings:* Ford, xii, 310.)

[3] Marshall, ii, 256.

and proscription," testifies an observer.[1] The Republican press, following Paine's theory, attacked "all governments, including that of the United States, as naturally hostile to the liberty of the people," asserts Marshall.[2] Few were the friends of Neutrality outside of the trading and shipping interests.[3]

Jefferson, although still in Washington's Cabinet, spoke of "the pusillanimity of the proclamation"[4] and of "the sneaking neutrality" it set up.[5] "In every effort made by the executive to maintain the neutrality of the United States," writes Marshall,

[1] Graydon, 382.

[2] Marshall, ii, 260. "A Freeman" in the *General Advertiser* of Philadelphia stated the most moderate opinion of those who opposed Neutrality. "France," said he, "is not only warring against the despotism of monarchy but the despotism of aristocracy and it would appear rather uncommon to see men [Washington and those who agreed with him] welcoming the Ambassador of republicanism who are warring [against] their darling aristocracy. But ... shall the officers of our government prescribe rules of conduct to freemen? Fellow citizens, view this conduct [Neutrality] well and you will discover principles lurking at bottom at variance with your liberty. Who is the superior of the people? Are we already so degenerate as to acknowledge a superior in the United States?" (*General Advertiser*, April 25, 1793.)

[3] "Our commercial and maritime people feel themselves deeply interested to prevent every act that may put our peace at hazard." (Cabot to King, Aug. 2, 1793; Lodge: *Cabot*, 74.)

The merchants and traders of Baltimore, "as participants in the general prosperity resulting from peace, and the excellent laws and constitution of the United States ... beg leave to express the high sense they entertain of the provident wisdom and watchfulness over the concerns and peace of a happy people which you have displayed in your late proclamation declaring neutrality ... well convinced that the true interests of America consist in a conduct, impartial, friendly, and unoffending to all the belligerent powers." (Address of the Merchants and Traders of Baltimore to George Washington, President of the United States; *General Advertiser*, Philadelphia, June 5, 1793.)

[4] Jefferson to Madison, May 19, 1793; *Works:* Ford, vii, 336.

[5] Jefferson to Monroe, May 5, 1793; *ib.*, 309.

"that great party [Republican] which denominated itself 'THE PEOPLE' could perceive only a settled hostility to France and to liberty."[1]

And, of course, Washington's proclamation of Neutrality was "unconstitutional," shouted the Republican politicians. Hamilton quickly answered. The power to deal with foreign affairs was, he said, lodged somewhere in the National Government. Where, then? Plainly not in the Legislative or Judicial branches, but in the Executive Department, which is "the *organ* of intercourse between the nation and foreign nations" and "the *interpreter* of . . . treaties in those cases in which the judiciary is not competent — that is between government and government. . . . The *executive power* of the United States is completely lodged in the President," with only those exceptions made by the Constitution, as that of declaring war. But if it is the right of Congress to declare war, "it is the duty of the Executive to preserve peace till the declaration is made."[2]

Washington's refusal to take sides in the European war was still more fuel for the Republican furnace. The bill to maintain Neutrality escaped defeat in Congress by a dangerously narrow margin: on amendments and motions in the Senate it was rescued time and again only by the deciding vote of the Vice-President.[3] In the House, resolutions were introduced which, in the perspective of history, were stupid. Public speakers searched for expressions strong enough for the popular taste; the newspapers

[1] Marshall, ii, 273.
[2] Pacificus No. 1; *Works:* Lodge, iv, 432–44.
[3] Marshall, ii, 327.

blazed with denunciation. "The artillery of the press," declares Marshall, "was played with unceasing fury on" the supporters of Neutrality; "and the democratic societies brought their whole force into operation. Language will scarcely afford terms of greater outrage, than were employed against those who sought to stem the torrent of public opinion and to moderate the rage of the moment." [1]

At the most effective hour, politically, Jefferson resigned [2] from the Cabinet, as he had declared, two years before, he intended to do. [3] He had prepared well for popular leadership. His stinging criticism of the Nationalist financial measures, his warm championship of France, his bitter hostility to Great Britain, and most of all, his advocacy of the popular view of the Constitution, secured him the favor of the people. Had he remained Secretary of State, he would have found himself in a hazardous political situation. But now, freed from restraint, he could openly lead the Republican forces which so eagerly awaited his formal command. [4]

As in the struggle for the Constitution, so now Neutrality was saved by the combined efforts of the mercantile and financial interests who dreaded the effect of the war on business and credit; [5] and by

[1] Marshall, ii, 322.
[2] Jefferson to Washington, Dec. 31, 1793; *Works:* Ford, viii, 136.
[3] Jefferson to Short, Jan. 28, 1792; *ib.*, vi, 382.
[4] Marshall, ii, 233.
[5] Generally speaking, the same classes that secured the Constitution supported all the measures of Washington's Administration. (See Beard: *Econ. O. J. D.*, 122–24.)

While the Republicans charged that Washington's Neutrality was inspired by favoritism to Great Britain, as it was certainly championed by trading and moneyed interests which dealt chiefly with British

the disinterested support of those who wished the United States to become a nation, distinct from, unconnected with, and unsubservient to any other government.

Among these latter was John Marshall, although he also held the view of the commercial classes from which most of his best clients came; and his personal loyalty to Washington strengthened his opinions. Hot as Virginia was against the Administration, Marshall was equally hot in its favor. Although he was the most prudent of men, and in Virginia silence was the part of discretion for those who approved Washington's course, Marshall would not be still. He made speeches in support of Washington's stand, wrote pamphlets, and appealed in every possible way to the solid reason and genuine Americanism of his neighbors. He had, of course, read Hamilton's great defense of Neutrality; and he asserted that sound National policy required Neutrality and that it was the duty of the President to proclaim and enforce it. Over and over again, by tongue and pen,

houses, the Federalists made the counter-charge, with equal accuracy, that the opponents of Neutrality were French partisans and encouraged by those financially interested.

The younger Adams, who was in Europe during most of this period and who carefully informed himself, writing from The Hague, declared that many Americans, some of them very important men, were "debtors to British merchants, creditors to the French government, and speculators in the French revolutionary funds, all to an immense amount," and that other Americans were heavily indebted in England. All these interests were against Neutrality and in favor of war with Great Britain — those owing British debts, because "war . . . would serve as a sponge for their debts," or at least postpone payment, and the creditors of the French securities, because French success would insure payment. (J. Q. Adams to his father, June 24, 1796; *Writings, J. Q. A.*: Ford, i, 506.)

he demonstrated the constitutional right of the
Executive to institute and maintain the Nation's
attitude of aloofness from foreign belligerents.[1]

Marshall rallied the friends of the Administration,
not only in Richmond, but elsewhere in Virginia.
"The [Administration] party in Richmond was soon
set in motion," Monroe reported to Jefferson; " from
what I have understood here [I] have reason to
believe they mean to produce the most extensive
effect they are capable of. M⁹ Marshall has written
G. Jones [2] on the subject and the first appearances
threatened the most furious attack on the French
Minister [Genêt]." [3]

At last Marshall's personal popularity could no
longer save him from open and public attack. The
enraged Republicans assailed him in pamphlets;
he was criticized in the newspapers; his character
was impugned.[4] He was branded with what, in
Virginia, was at that time the ultimate reproach:
Marshall, said the Republicans, was the friend and
follower of Alexander Hamilton, the monarchist,
the financial manipulator, the father of Assumption, the inventor of the rotten Funding system, the
designer of the stock-jobbing Bank of the United
States, and, worst of all, the champion of a power-

[1] Story, in Dillon, iii, 350.

[2] Gabriel Jones, the ablest lawyer in the Valley, and, of course, a
stanch Federalist.

[3] Monroe to Jefferson, Sept. 3, 1793; Monroe's *Writings:* Hamilton,
i, 274–75. Considering the intimate personal friendship existing between Monroe and Marshall, the significance and importance of this
letter cannot be overestimated.

[4] It was at this point, undoubtedly, that the slander concerning
Marshall's habits was started. (See *infra*, 101–03.)

ful Nationalism and the implacable foe of the sovereignty of the States.

Spiritedly Marshall made reply. He was, indeed, a disciple of Washington's great Secretary of the Treasury, he said, and proud of it; and he gloried in his fealty to Washington, for which also he had been blamed. In short, Marshall was aggressively for the Administration and all its measures. These were right, he said, and wise and necessary. Above all, since that was the chief ground of attack, all of them, from Assumption to Neutrality, were plainly constitutional. At a public meeting at Richmond, Marshall offered resolutions which he had drawn up in support of the Administration's foreign policy, spoke in their favor, and carried the meeting for them by a heavy majority.[1]

Marshall's bold course cost him the proffer of an honor. Our strained relations with the Spaniards required an alert, able, and cool-headed representative to go to New Orleans. Jefferson[2] confided to Madison the task of finding such a man in Virginia. "My imagination has hunted thro' this whole state," Madison advised the Secretary of State in reply, "without being able to find a single character fitted for the mission to N. O. Young Marshall seems to possess some of the qualifications, but there would be objections of several sorts to

---

[1] The above paragraphs are based on Justice Story's account of Marshall's activities at this period, supplemented by Madison and Monroe's letters; by the well-known political history of that time; and by the untrustworthy but not negligible testimony of tradition. While difficult to reconstruct a situation from such fragments, the account given in the text is believed to be substantially accurate.

[2] See *Works:* Ford, xii, footnote to 451.

him." [1] Three months later Madison revealed one
of these "several objections" to Marshall; but the
principal one was his sturdy, fighting Nationalism.
This "objection" was so intense that anybody who
was even a close friend of Marshall was suspected
and proscribed by the Republicans. The Jacobin
Clubs of Paris were scarcely more intolerant than
their disciples in America.

So irritated, indeed, were the Republican leaders by Marshall's political efforts in support of
Neutrality and other policies of the Administration,
that they began to hint at improper motives. With
his brother, brother-in-law, and General Henry Lee
(then Governor of Virginia) Marshall had purchased
the Fairfax estate.[2] This was evidence, said the Republicans, that he was the tool of the wicked financial
interests. Madison hastened to inform Jefferson.

"The circumstances which derogate from full confidence in W[ilson] N[icholas]," cautioned Madison,
"are . . . his connection & intimacy with Marshall,
of whose *disinterestedness* as well as understanding he has the highest opinion. It is said that
Marshall, who is at the head of the great purchase
from Fairfax, has lately obtained pecuniary aids
from the bank [of the United States] or people connected with it. I think it certain that he must have
felt, in the moment of purchase, an absolute confidence in the monied interests which will explain
him to everyone that reflects in the active character
he is assuming." [3]

---

[1] Madison to Jefferson, June 17, 1793; *Writings:* Hunt, vi, 134.
[2] See *infra*, chap. v.
[3] Madison to Jefferson, Sept. 2, 1793; *Writings:* Hunt, vi, 196.

In such fashion do the exigencies of politics gener-
ate suspicion and false witness. Marshall received
no money from the Bank for the Fairfax purchase
and it tied him to "the monied interests" in no way
except through business sympathy. He relied for
help on his brother's father-in-law, Robert Morris,
who expected to raise the funds for the Fairfax purchase from loans negotiated in Europe on the security
of Morris's immense real-estate holdings in America.[1]
But even the once poised, charitable, and unsuspicious Madison had now acquired that state of mind
which beholds in any business transaction, no matter
how innocent, something furtive and sinister. His
letter proves, however, that the fearless Richmond
lawyer was making himself effectively felt as a practical power for Washington's Administration, to the
serious discomfort of the Republican chieftains.

While Marshall was beloved by most of those
who knew him and was astonishingly popular with
the masses, jealousy of his ability and success had
made remorseless enemies for him. It appears, indeed, that a peculiarly malicious envy had pursued
him almost from the time he had gone to William and Mary College. His sister-in-law, with hot
resentment, emphasizes this feature of Marshall's
career. "Notwithstanding his amiable and correct
conduct," writes Mrs. Carrington, "there were
those who would catch at the most trifling circumstance to throw a shade over his fair fame." He had
little education, said his detractors; "his talents

---

[1] See *infra,* chap. v. Robert Morris secured in this way all the
money he was able to give his son-in-law for the Fairfax purchase.

were greatly overrated"; his habits were bad. "Tho' no man living ever had more ardent friends, yet there does not exist one who had at one time more slanderous enemies." [1]

These now assailed Marshall with all their pent-up hatred. They stopped at no charge, hesitated at no insinuation. For instance, his conviviality was magnified into reports of excesses and the tale was carried to the President. "It was cruelly insinuated to G[eorge] W[ashington]," writes Marshall's sister-in-law, "by an after great S[olo?]n that to Mr. M[arsha]lls fondness for play was added an increasing fondness for liquor." Mrs. Carrington loyally defends Marshall, testifying, from her personal knowledge, that "this S——n knew better than most others how Mr. M——ll always played for amusement and never, never for gain, and that he was, of all men, the most temperate." [2]

Considering the custom of the time [3] and the habits of the foremost men of that period,[4] Marshall's

---

[1] Mrs. Carrington to her sister Nancy; undated; MS.   [2] *Ib.*

[3] See *supra*, vol. I, chap. VII.

[4] See, for instance, Jefferson to Short (Sept 6, 1790; *Works:* Ford, VI, 146), describing a single order of wine for Washington and one for himself; and see Chastellux's account of an evening with Jefferson: "We were conversing one evening over a bowl of punch after Mrs. Jefferson had retired. Our conversation turned on the poems of Ossian. . . . The book was sent for and placed near the bowl, where by their mutual aid the night far advanced imperceptibly upon us." (Chastellux, 229.)

Marshall's Account Book does not show any purchases of wine at all comparable with those of other contemporaries. In March, 1791, Marshall enters, "wine £60"; August, ditto, "£14–5–8"; September, 1792, "Wine £70"; in July, 1793, "Whisky 6.3.9" (pounds, shillings, and pence); in May, 1794, "Rum and brandy 6–4"; August, 1794, ditto, five shillings, sixpence; May, 1795, "Whisky £6.16"; Sept., "wine £3"; Oct., ditto, "£17.6."

sister-in-law is entirely accurate. Certainly this political slander did not impress Washington, for his confidence in Marshall grew steadily; and, as we shall presently see, he continued to tender Marshall high honors and confide to him political tasks requiring delicate judgment.

Such petty falsehoods did not disturb Marshall's composure. But he warmly resented the assault made upon him because of his friendship for Hamilton; and his anger was hot against what he felt was the sheer dishonesty of the attacks on the measures of the National Government. "I wish very much to see you," writes Marshall to Archibald Stuart at this time: "I want to observe [illegible] how much honest men you and I are [illegible] half our acquaintance. Seriously there appears to me every day to be more folly, envy, malice, and damn rascality in the world than there was the day before and I do verily begin to think that plain downright honesty and unintriguing integrity will be kicked out of doors." [1]

A picturesque incident gave to the Virginia opponents of Washington's Administration more substantial cause to hate Marshall than his pamphlets, speeches, and resolutions had afforded. At Smithfield, not far from Norfolk, the ship Unicorn was fitting out as a French privateer. The people of Isle of Wight County were almost unanimous in their sympathy with the project, and only seven or eight men could be procured to assist the United States Marshal in seizing and holding the vessel. [2] Twenty-

---

[1] Marshall to Stuart, March 27, 1794; MS., Va. Hist. Soc.

[2] Major George Keith Taylor to Brigadier-General Mathews, July 19, 1794; *Cal. Va. St. Prs.*, vii, 223.

five soldiers and three officers were sent from Norfolk in a revenue cutter; [1] but the Governor, considering this force insufficient to outface resistance and take the ship, dispatched Marshall, with a considerable body of militia, to Smithfield.

Evidently the affair was believed to be serious; "the Particular Orders . . . to Brigadier General Marshall" placed under his command forces of cavalry, infantry, and artillery from Richmond and another body of troops from Petersburg. The Governor assures Marshall that "the executive know that in your hands the dignity and rights of the Commonwealth will ever be safe and they are also sure that prudence, affection to our deluded fellow citizens, and marked obedience to law in the means you will be compelled to adopt, will equally characterize every step of your procedure." He is directed to "collect every information respecting this daring violation of order," and particularly "the conduct of the Lieutenant Colonel Commandant of Isle of Wight," who had disregarded his instructions.[2]

Clad in the uniform of a brigadier-general of the Virginia Militia,[3] Marshall set out for Smithfield riding at the head of the cavalry, the light infantry and

---

[1] Mathews to Taylor, July 20, 1794; *ib.*, 224.

[2] Governor Henry Lee "Commander-in-chief," to Marshall, July 21, 1794; MS., "War 10," Archives, Va. St. Lib.

[3] "Dark blue coat, skirts lined with buff, capes, lapels and cuffs buff, buttons yellow. Epaulets gold one on each shoulder, black cocked hat, with black cockade, black stock, boots and side arms." (Division Orders, July 4, 1794; *Cal. Va. St. Prs.*, vii, 204. But see Schoepf (ii, 43), where a uniform worn by one brigadier-general of Virginia Militia is described as consisting of "a large white hat, a blue coat, a brown waistcoat, and green breeches.")

artillery following by boat.[1] He found all thought of resistance abandoned upon his arrival. A "peaceable search" of Captain Sinclair's house revealed thirteen cannon with ball, grape-shot, and powder. Three more pieces of ordnance were stationed on the shore. Before General Marshall and his cavalry arrived, the United States Marshal had been insulted, and threatened with violence. Men had been heard loading muskets in Sinclair's house, and fifteen of these weapons, fully charged, were discovered. The house so "completely commanded the Deck of the" Unicorn "that . . . one hundred men placed in the vessel could not have protected her ten minutes from fifteen placed in the house."[2]

The State and Federal officers had previously been able to get little aid of any kind, but "since the arrival of distant militia," reports Marshall, "those of the County are as prompt as could be wished in rendering any service required of them," and he suggests that the commandant of the county, rather than the men, was responsible for the failure to act earlier. He at once sent messengers to the infantry and artillery detachment which had not yet arrived, with orders that they return to Richmond and Petersburg.[3]

Marshall "had . . . frequent conversations with individuals of the Isle of Wight" and found them much distressed at the necessity for calling distant militia "to protect from violence the laws of our

---

[1] Particular Orders, *supra*.
[2] Marshall to Governor of Virginia, July 23, 1794; *Cal. Va. St. Prs.*, vii, 228; and same to same, July 28, 1794; *ib.*, 234.
[3] *Ib.*

common country. . . . The commanding officers [of
the county] . . . seem not to have become sufficiently
impressed with the importance of maintaining the
Sovereignty of the law" says Marshall, but with unwarranted optimism he believes "that a more proper
mode of thinking is beginning to prevail." [1]

Thus was the Smithfield defiance of Neutrality
and the National laws quelled by strong measures,
taken before it had gathered dangerous headway.
"I am very much indebted to Brig.-Gen'l Marshall
and Major Taylor [2] for their exertions in the execution of my orders," writes Governor Lee to the
Secretary of War.[3]

But the efforts of the National Government and
the action of Governor Lee in Virginia to enforce
obedience to National laws and observance of Neutrality, while they succeeded locally in their immediate purpose, did not modify the public temper toward the Administration. Neutrality, in particular,
grew in disfavor among the people. When the congressional elections of 1794 came on, all complaints
against the National Government were vivified by
that burning question. As if, said the Republicans,
there could be such a status as neutrality between
"right and wrong," between "liberty" and "tyranny." [4]

Thus, in the campaign, the Republicans made the
French cause their own. Everything that Washing-

---

[1] Marshall to Governor of Virginia, July 28, 1794; *Cal. Va. St. Prs.*
vii, 235.

[2] George Keith Taylor; see *infra*, chaps. x and xii.

[3] Lee to the Secretary of War, July 28, 1794; *Cal. Va. St. Prs.*, vii, 234.

[4] See, for instance, Thompson's speech, *infra*, chap. vi.

ton's Administration had accomplished was wrong, said the Republicans, but Neutrality was the work of the Evil One. The same National power which had dared to issue this "edict" against American support of French "liberty" had foisted on the people Assumption, National Courts, and taxes on whiskey. This identical Nationalist crew had, said the Republicans, by Funding and National Banks, fostered, nay, created, stock-jobbing and speculation by which the few "monocrats" were made rich, while the many remained poor. Thus every Republican candidate for Congress became a knight of the flaming sword, warring upon all evil, but especially and for the moment against the dragon of Neutrality that the National Government had uncaged to help the monarchs of Europe destroy free government in France.[1] Chiefly on that question the Republicans won the National House of Representatives.

But if Neutrality lit the flames of public wrath, Washington's next act in foreign affairs was powder and oil cast upon fires already fiercely burning. Great Britain, by her war measures against France, did not spare America. She seized hundreds of American vessels trading with her enemy and even with neutrals; in order to starve France [2] she lifted cargoes from American bottoms; to man her warships she forcibly took sailors from American ships, "often leaving scarcely hands enough to navigate the vessel into port";[3] she conducted herself as if she were not only mistress of the seas, but their sole pro-

[1] Marshall, ii, 293. [2] *Ib.*, 285. [3] *Ib.*, 285.

prietor. And the British depredations were committed in a manner harsh, brutal, and insulting.

Even Marshall was aroused and wrote to his friend Stuart: "We fear, not without reason, a war. The man does not live who wishes for peace more than I do; but the outrages committed upon us are beyond human bearing. Farewell — pray Heaven we may weather the storm." [1] If the self-contained and cautious Marshall felt a just resentment of British outrage, we may, by that measure, accurately judge of the inflamed and dangerous condition of the general sentiment.

Thus it came about that the deeply rooted hatred of the people for their former master [2] was heated to the point of reckless defiance. This was the same Monarchy, they truly said, that still kept the military and trading posts on American soil which, more than a decade before, it had, by the Treaty of Peace, solemnly promised to surrender. [3] The Government that was committing these savage outrages was the same faithless Power, declared the general voice, that had pledged compensation for the slaves its armies had carried away, but not one shilling of which had been paid.

If ever a country had good cause for war, Great Britain then furnished it to America; and, had we been prepared, it is impossible to believe that we

---

[1] Marshall to Stuart, March 27, 1794; MS., Va. Hist. Soc.

[2] "The idea that Great Britain was the natural enemy of America had become habitual" long before this time. (Marshall, ii, 154.)

[3] One reason for Great Britain's unlawful retention of these posts was her purpose to maintain her monopoly of the fur trade. (*Ib.*, 194. And see Beard: *Econ. O. J. D.*, 279.)

should not have taken up arms to defend our ravaged interests and vindicate our insulted honor. In Congress various methods of justifiable retaliation were urged with intense earnestness, marred by loud and extravagant declamation.[1] "The noise of debate was more deafening than a mill. . . . We sleep upon our arms," wrote a member of the National House.[2] But these bellicose measures were rejected because any one of them would have meant immediate hostilities.

For we were not prepared. War was the one thing America could not then afford. Our Government was still tottering on the unstable legs of infancy. Orderly society was only beginning and the spirit of unrest and upheaval was strong and active. In case of war, wrote Ames, expressing the conservative fears, "I dread anarchy more than great guns."[3] Our resources had been bled white by the Revolution and the desolating years that followed. We had no real army, no adequate arsenals,[4] no efficient ships of war; and the French Republic, surrounded by hostile bayonets and guns and battling for very existence, could not send us armies, fleets, munitions, and money as the French Monarchy had done.

Spain was on our south eager for more territory on the Mississippi, the mouth of which she con-

[1] Marshall, ii, 320–21; and see *Annals*, 3d Cong., 1st Sess., 1793, 274–90; also Anderson, 29; and see prior war-inviting resolves and speeches in *Annals*, 3d Cong., *supra*, 21, 30, 544 *et seq.*; also Marshall, ii, 324 *et seq.*

[2] Ames to Dwight, Dec. 12, 1794; *Works: Ames*, i, 154.

[3] Ames to Gore, March 26, 1794; *Works: Ames*, i, 140. And see Marshall, ii, 324 *et seq.*

[4] See Washington to Ball, Aug. 10, 1794; *Writings: Ford*, xii, 449.

trolled; and ready to attack us in case we came to blows with Great Britain. The latter Power was on our north, the expelled Loyalists in Canada burning with that natural resentment [1] which has never cooled; British soldiers held strategic posts within our territory; hordes of Indians, controlled and their leaders paid by Great Britain,[2] and hostile to the United States, were upon our borders anxious to avenge themselves for the defeats we had inflicted on them and their kinsmen in the savage wars incited by their British employers.[3] Worst of all, British warships covered the oceans and patrolled every mile of our shores just beyond American waters. Our coast defenses, few, poor, and feeble in their best estate, had been utterly neglected for more than ten years and every American port was at the mercy of British guns.[4]

Evidence was not wanting that Great Britain courted war.[5] She had been cold and unresponsive to every approach for a better understanding with us. She had not even sent a Minister to our Government until eight years after the Treaty of Peace had been signed.[6] She not only held our posts, but established

---

[1] See Van Tyne, chap. xi.   [2] Marshall, ii, 286, 287.   [3] *Ib.*

[4] John Quincy Adams, who was in London and who was intensely irritated by British conduct, concluded that: "A war at present with Great Britain must be total destruction to the commerce of our country; for there is no maritime power on earth that can contend with the existing naval British force." (J. Q. Adams to Sargent, The Hague, Oct. 12, 1795; *Writings, J. Q. A.*: Ford, i, 419.)

[5] "I believe the intention is to draw the United States into it [war] merely to make tools of them. . . . The conduct of the British government is so well adapted to increasing our danger of war, that I cannot but suppose they are secretly inclined to produce it." (J. Q. Adams to his father, The Hague, Sept. 12, 1795; *ib.*, 409.)

[6] Marshall, ii, 194.

a new one fifty miles south of Detroit; and her entire conduct indicated, and Washington believed, that she meant to draw a new boundary line which would give her exclusive possession of the Great Lakes.[1] She had the monopoly of the fur trade[2] and plainly meant to keep it.

Lord Dorchester, supreme representative of the British Crown in Canada, had made an ominous speech to the Indians predicting hostilities against the United States within a year and declaring that a new boundary line would then be drawn "by the warriors." [3] Rumors flew and gained volume and color in their flight. Even the poised and steady Marshall was disturbed.

"We have some letters from Philadelphia that wear a very ugly aspect," he writes Archibald Stuart. "It is said that Simcoe, the Governor of Upper Canada, has entered the territory of the United States at the head of about 500 men and has possessed himself of Presque Isle." But Marshall cannot restrain his humor, notwithstanding the gravity of the report: "As this is in Pennsylvania," he observes, "I hope the democratic society of Philadelphia will at once demolish him and if they should fail I still trust that some of our upper brothers [Virginia Republicans] will at one stride place themselves by him and prostrate his post. But seriously," continues Marshall,

---

[1] Marshall, ii, 337.

[2] *Ib.*, 195; and see Beard: *Econ. O. J. D.*, 279.

[3] See this speech in Rives, iii, footnote to 418-19. It is curious that Marshall, in his *Life of Washington*, makes the error of asserting that the account of Dorchester's speech was "not authentic." It is one of the very few mistakes in Marshall's careful book. (Marshall, ii, 320.)

"if this be true we must bid adieu to all hope of peace and prepare for serious war. My only hope is that it is a mere speculating story."[1]

Powerless to obtain our rights by force or to prevent their violation by being prepared to assert them with arms, Washington had no recourse but to diplomacy. At all hazards and at any cost, war must be avoided for the time being. It was one of Great Britain's critical mistakes that she consented to treat instead of forcing a conflict with us; for had she taken the latter course it is not improbable that, at the end of the war, the southern boundary of British dominion in America would have been the Ohio River, and it is not impossible that New York and New England would have fallen into her hands. At the very least, there can be little doubt that the Great Lakes and the St. Lawrence would have become exclusively British waters.[2]

Amid a confusion of counsels, Washington determined to try for a treaty of amity, commerce, and

[1] Marshall to Stuart, May 28, 1794; MS., Va. Hist. Soc.

[2] It must not be forgotten that we were not so well prepared for war in 1794 as the colonies had been in 1776, or as we were a few years after Jay was sent on his mission. And on the traditional policy of Great Britain when intending to make war on any country, see J. Q. Adams to his father, June 24, 1796; *Writings, J. Q. A.*: Ford, i, 499–500.

Also, see same to same, The Hague, June 9, 1796; *ib.*, 493, predicting dissolution of the Union in case of war with Great Britain. "I confess it made me doubly desirous to quit a country where the malevolence that is so common against America was exulting in triumph." (*Ib.*)

"The truth is that the American *Government* . . . have not upon earth more rancorous enemies, than the springs which move the machine of this Country [England] . . . Between Great Britain and the United States no *cordiality* can exist." (Same to same, London, Feb. 10, 1796; *ib.*, 477; also, March 24, 1794; *ib.*, 18, 183, 187.)

navigation with Great Britain, a decision, the outcome of which was to bring Marshall even more conspicuously into politics than he ever had been before.
Indeed, the result of the President's policy, and
Marshall's activity in support of it, was to become
one of the important stepping-stones in the latter's
career.

Chief Justice Jay was selected for the infinitely
delicate task of negotiation. Even the news of
such a plan was received with stinging criticism.
What! Kiss the hand that smote us! It was "a
degrading insult to the American people; a pusil-
lanimous surrender of their honor; and an insidious
injury to France." [1] And our envoy to carry out this
shameful programme! — was it not that same Jay
who once tried to barter away the Mississippi? [2]

It was bad enough to turn our backs on France;
but to treat with the British Government was infamous. So spoke the voice of the people. The
democratic societies were especially virulent; "Let
us unite with France and stand or fall together" [3]
was their heroic sentiment. But abhorrence of the
mission did not blind the Republicans to the advantages of political craft. While the negotiations
were in progress they said that, after all, everything
would be gained that America desired, knowing that
they could say afterward, as they did and with just
cause, that everything had been lost. [4]

At last Jay secured from Great Britain the famous

[1] Marshall, ii, 363.   [2] *American Remembrancer*, i, 9.
[3] Resolution of Wythe County (Va.) Democratic Society, quoted
in Anderson, 32.
[4] Ames to Dwight, Feb. 3, 1795; *Works:* Ames, i, 166.

treaty that bears his name. It is perhaps the most humiliating compact into which America ever entered. He was expected to secure the restriction of contraband — it was enlarged; payment for the slaves — it was refused; recognition of the principle that "free ships make free goods" — it was denied; equality with France as to belligerent rights — it was not granted; opening of the West Indian trade — it was conceded upon hard and unjust conditions; payment for British spoliation of American commerce — it was promised at some future time, but even then only on the award of a commission; immediate surrender of the posts — their evacuation was agreed to, but not until a year and a half after the treaty was signed.

On the other hand, the British secured from us free navigation and trading rights on the Mississippi —never contemplated; agreement that the United States would pay all debts due from American citizens to British creditors — a claim never admitted hitherto; prohibition of any future sequestration of British debts; freedom of all American ports to British vessels, with a pledge to lay no further restrictions on British commerce — never before proposed; liberty of Indians and British subjects to pass our frontiers, trade on our soil, retain lands occupied without becoming American citizens, but privileged to become such at pleasure — an odious provision, which, formerly, had never occurred to anybody.

Thus, by the Treaty of 1794, we yielded everything and gained little not already ours. But we secured peace; we were saved from war. That supreme

end was worth the sacrifice and that, alone, justified
it. It more than demonstrated the wisdom of the
Jay Treaty.

While the Senate was considering the bitter terms
which Great Britain, with unsheathed sword, had
forced upon us, Senator Stephen H. Mason of Virginia, in violation of the Senate rules, gave a copy
of the treaty to the press.[1] Instantly the whole land
shook with a tornado of passionate protest.[2] From
one end of the country to the other, public meetings
were held. Boston led off.[3] Washington was smothered with violent petitions that poured in upon him
from every quarter praying, demanding, that he withhold his assent.[4] As in the struggle for the Constitution and in the violent attacks on Neutrality, so now
the strongest advocates of the Jay Treaty were the

[1] Marshall, ii, 362–64.   [2] *Ib.*, 366.

[3] The Boston men, it appears, had not even read the treaty, as
was the case with other meetings which adopted resolutions of protest. (Marshall, ii, 365 *et seq.*) Thereupon the Boston satirists lam-
pooned the hasty denunciators of the treaty as follows: —

"I've never read it, but I say 't is bad.
If it goes down, I'll bet my ears and eyes,
It will the people all unpopularize;
Boobies may hear it read ere they decide,
I move it quickly be unratified."

On Dr. Jarvis's speech at Faneuil Hall against the Jay Treaty; Loring:
Hundred Boston Orators, 232. The Republicans were equally sarcastic:
"I say the treaty is a good one . . . for I do not think about it. . . .
What did we choose the Senate for . . . but to think for us. . . . Let
the people remember that it is their sacred right to submit and obey;
and that all those who would persuade them that they have a right to
think and speak on the sublime, mysterious, and to them incompre-
hensible affairs of government are factious Democrats and outrageous
Jacobins." (Essay on Jacobinical Thinkers: *American Remembrancer*,
i, 141.)

[4] See Marshall's vivid description of the popular reception of the
treaty; Marshall, ii, 365–66.

commercial interests. "The common opinion among
men of business of all descriptions is," declares Hamilton, "that a disagreement would greatly shock
and stagnate pecuniary plans and operations in
general." [1]

The printing presses belched pamphlets and
lampoons, scurrilous, inflammatory, even indecent.
An example of these was a Boston screed. This
classic of vituperation, connecting the treaty with
the financial measures of Washington's Administration, represented the Federalist leaders as servants
of the Devil; Independence, after the death of his
first wife, Virtue, married a foul creature, Vice, and
finally himself expired in convulsions, leaving Speculation, Bribery, and Corruption as the base offspring of his second marriage. [2]

Everywhere Jay was burned in effigy. Hamilton
was stoned in New York when he tried to speak to
the mob; and with the blood pouring down his face
went, with the few who were willing to listen to
him, to the safety of a hall. [3] Even Washington's
granite resolution was shaken. Only once in our
history have the American people so scourged a
great public servant. [4] He was no statesman, raged
the Republicans; everybody knew that he had been
a failure as a soldier, they said; and now, having

[1] Hamilton to King, June 20, 1795; *Works:* Lodge, x, 103.

[2] "An Emetic for Aristocrats. . . . Also a History of the Life and
Death of Independence; Boston, 1795." Copies of such attacks were
scattered broadcast — "Emissaries flew through the country spreading alarm and discontent." (Camillus, no. 1; *Works:* Lodge, v, 189–99.)

[3] McMaster, ii, 213–20; Gibbs, i, 207; and Hildreth, iv, 548.

[4] Present-day detraction of our public men is gentle reproof contrasted with the savagery with which Washington was, thenceforth,
assailed.

trampled on the Constitution and betrayed America, let him be impeached, screamed the infuriated opposition.[1] Seldom has any measure of our Government awakened such convulsions of popular feeling as did the Jay Treaty, which, surrendering our righteous and immediate demands, yet saved our future. Marshall, watching it all, prepared to defend the popularly abhorred compact; and thus he was to become its leading defender in the South.

When, finally, Washington reluctantly approved its ratification by the Senate,[2] many of his friends deserted him.[3] "The trouble and perplexities . . . have worn away my mind," wrote the abused and distracted President.[4] Mercer County, Kentucky,

[1] Marshall, ii, 370. Of the innumerable accounts of the abuse of Washington, Weld may be cited as the most moderate. After testifying to Washington's unpopularity this acute traveler says: "It is the spirit of dissatisfaction which forms a leading trait in the character of the Americans as a people, which produces this malevolence [against Washington]; if their public affairs were regulated by a person sent from heaven, I firmly believe his acts, instead of meeting with universal approbation, would by many be considered as deceitful and flagitious." (Weld, i, 108–09.)

[2] Washington almost determined to withhold ratification. (Marshall, ii, 362.) The treaty was signed November 19, 1794; received by the President, March 7, 1795; submitted to the Senate June 8, 1795; ratified by the Senate June 24; and signed by Washington August 12, 1795. (*Ib.*, 360, 361, 368.)

[3] "Washington now defies the whole Sovereign that made him what he is —— and can unmake him again. Better his hand had been cut off when his glory was at its height before he blasted all his Laurels!" (Dr. Nathaniel Ames's Diary, Aug. 14, 1795; *Dedham (Mass.) Historical Register*, vii, 33.) Of Washington's reply to the address of the merchants and traders of Philadelphia "An Old Soldier of '76," wrote: "Has adulation . . . so bewildered his senses, that relinquishing even common decency, he tells 408 merchants and traders of Philadelphia that they are more immediately concerned than any other class of his fellow citizens?" (*American Remembrancer*, ii, 280–81.)

[4] Washington to Jay, May 8, 1796; *Writings:* Ford, xiii, 189.

denounced Senator Humphrey Marshall for voting
for ratification and demanded a constitutional
amendment empowering State Legislatures to recall Senators at will.[1] The Legislature of Virginia
actually passed a resolution for an amendment of
the National Constitution to make the House
of Representatives a part of the treaty-making
power.[2] The Lexington, Kentucky, resolutions
branded the treaty as "shameful to the American
name."[3] It was reported that at a dinner in Virginia this toast was drunk: "A speedy death to
General Washington."[4] Orators exhausted invec-
tive; poets wrote in the ink of gall.[5]

Jefferson, in harmony, of course, with the public
temper, was against the treaty. "So general a burst
of dissatisfaction," he declared, "never before appeared against any transaction. . . . The whole body
of the people . . . have taken a greater interest in
this transaction than they were ever known to do
in any other."[6] The Republican chieftain carefully
observed the effect of the popular commotion on his
own and the opposite party. "It has in my opinion
completely demolished the monarchical party here[7]

---

[1] *American Remembrancer*, ii, 265.
[2] Journal, H.D. (1795), 54–55; and see Anderson, 43.
[3] *American Remembrancer*, ii, 269.
[4] Ames to Gore, Jan. 10, 1795; *Works: Ames*, i, 161.
[5]   "This treaty in one page confines,
                The sad result of base designs;
                The wretched purchase here behold
                Of Traitors — who their country sold.
                Here, in their proper shape and mien,
                Fraud, perjury, and guilt are seen."

                                              (Freneau, iii, 133.)
[6] Jefferson to Monroe, Sept. 6, 1795; *Works: Ford*, viii, 187–88.
[7] *Ib.*

[Virginia]." Jefferson thought the treaty itself so bad that it nearly turned him against all treaties. "I am not satisfied," said he, "we should not be better without treaties with any nation. But I am satisfied we should be better without such as this."[1]

The deadliest charge against the treaty was the now familiar one of "unconstitutionality." Many urged that the President had no power to begin negotiations without the assent of the Senate;[2] and all opponents agreed that it flagrantly violated the Constitution in several respects, especially in regulating trade, to do which was the exclusive province of Congress.[3] Once more, avowed the Jeffersonians, it was the National Government which had brought upon America this disgrace. "Not one in a thousand would have resisted Great Britain . . . in the be-

[1] Jefferson to Tazewell, Sept. 13, 1795; *Works:* Ford, viii, 191. The Jay Treaty and Neutrality must be considered together, if the temper of the times is to be understood. "If our neutrality be still preserved, it will be due to the President alone," writes the younger Adams from Europe. "Nothing but his weight of character and reputation, combined with his firmness and political intrepidity could have stood against the torrent that is still tumbling with a fury that resounds even across the Atlantic. . . . If his system of administration now prevails, ten years more will place the United States among the most powerful and opulent nations on earth. . . . Now, when a powerful party at home and a mighty influence from abroad, are joining all their forces to assail his reputation, and his character I think it my duty as an American to avow my sentiments." (J. Q. Adams to Bourne, Dec. 24, 1795; *Writings, J. Q. A.:* Ford, i, 467.)

[2] Charles Pinckney's Speech; *American Remembrancer,* i, 7.

[3] Marshall, ii, 378. The Republicans insisted that the assent of the House of Representatives is necessary to the ratification of any treaty that affects commerce, requires appropriation of money, or where any act of Congress whatever may be necessary to carry a treaty into effect. (*Ib.;* and see Livingston's resolutions and debate; *Annals,* 4th Cong., 1st Sess., 1795, 426; 628.)

ginning of the Revolution" if the vile conduct of
Washington had been foreseen; and it was plain, at
this late day, that "either the Federal or State
governments must fall" — so wrote Republican
pamphleteers, so spoke Republican orators.[1]

Again Hamilton brought into action the artillery
of his astounding intellect. In a series of public letters under the signature of "Camillus," he vindi-
cated every feature of the treaty, evading nothing,
conceding nothing. These papers were his last great
constructive work. In numbers three, six, thirty-
seven, and thirty-eight of "Camillus," he expounded
the Constitution on the treaty-making power; demonstrated the exclusive right of the President to
negotiate, and, with the Senate, to conclude, treaties; and proved, not only that the House should
not be consulted, but that it is bound by the Constitution itself to pass all laws necessary to carry
treaties into effect.[2]

Fearless, indeed, and void of political ambition
were those who dared to face the tempest. "The
cry against the Treaty is like that against a mad-
dog," wrote Washington from Mount Vernon.[3] Particularly was this true of Virginia, where it raged un-

[1] "Priestly's Emigration," printed in Cobbett, i, 196, quoting
"Agricola."

[2] "Camillus"; *Works:* Lodge, v and vi. It is impossible to give a
satisfactory condensation of these monumental papers. Struck off
in haste and under greatest pressure, they equal if not surpass Hamilton's "First Report on the Public Credit," his "Opinion as to
the Constitutionality of the Bank of the United States," or his
"Report on Manufactures." As an intellectual performance, the
"Letters of Camillus" come near being Hamilton's masterpiece.

[3] Washington to Hamilton, July 29, 1795; *Writings:* Ford, xiii,
76.

governably.[1] A meeting of Richmond citizens "have outdone all that has gone before them" in the resolutions passed,[2] bitterly complained Washington. Virginians, testified Jefferson, "were never more unanimous. 4. or 5. individuals of Richmond, distinguished however, by their talents as by their devotion to all the sacred acts of the government, & the town of Alexandria constitute the whole support of that instrument [Jay Treaty] here."[3] These four or five devoted ones, said Jefferson, were "Marshall, Carrington, Harvey, Bushrod Washington, Doctor Stewart."[4] But, as we are now to see, Marshall made up in boldness and ability what the Virginia friends of the Administration lacked in numbers.

[1] The whole country was against the treaty on general grounds; but Virginia was especially hostile because of the sore question of runaway slaves and the British debts.

[2] Washington to Randolph, Aug. 4, 1795; *Writings: Ford,* xiii, footnote to 86. See Resolutions, which were comparatively mild; *American Remembrancer,* i, 133–34; and see *Richmond and Manchester Advertiser,* of July 30, and Aug. 6, 1795.

[3] Jefferson to Coxe, Sept. 10, 1795; *Works: Ford,* viii, 190.

[4] Jefferson to Monroe, Sept. 6, 1795; *ib.,* 188.

CHAPTER IV.

WASHINGTON'S DEFENDER

His [Marshall's] lax, lounging manners have made him popular. (Jefferson.)

Having a high opinion of General Marshall's honor, prudence, and judgment, consult him. (Washington.)

The man [Washington] who is the source of all the misfortunes of our country is no longer possessed of the power to multiply evils on the United States. (The *Aurora* on Washington's retirement from the Presidency.)

JEFFERSON properly named Marshall as the first of Washington's friends in Virginia. For, by now, he had become the leader of the Virginia Federalists. His lucid common sense, his level poise, his steady courage, his rock-like reliability — these qualities, together with his almost uncanny influence over his constituents, had made him chief in the Virginia Federalist councils.

So high had Marshall risen in Washington's esteem and confidence that the President urged him to become a member of the Cabinet.

"The office of Attorney Gen! of the United States has become vacant by the death of Will Bradford, Esq.[1] I take the earliest opportunity of asking if you will accept the appointment? The salary annexed thereto, and the prospects of lucrative practice in this city [Philadelphia] — the present seat of the Gen! Government, must be as well known to you, perhaps better, than they are to me, and therefore I shall say nothing concerning them.

[1] When Jefferson resigned, Randolph succeeded him as Secretary of State, and continued in that office until driven out of public life by the famous Fauchet disclosure. William Bradford of Pennsylvania succeeded Randolph as Attorney-General.

"If your answer is in the affirmative, it will readily occur to you that no unnecessary time should be lost in repairing to this place. If, on the contrary, it should be the negative (which would give me concern) it might be as well to say nothing of this offer. But in either case, I pray you to give me an answer as promptly as you can." [1]

Marshall decided instantly; he could not possibly afford to accept a place yielding only fifteen hundred dollars annually, the salary of the Attorney-General at that period,[2] and the duties of which permitted little time for private practice which was then allowable.[3] So Marshall, in a "few minutes" declined Washington's offer in a letter which is a model of good taste.

"I had the honor of receiving a few minutes past your letter of the 26th inst.

"While the business I have undertaken to complete in Richmond,[4] forbids me to change my situation tho for one infinitely more eligible, permit me Sir to express my sincere acknowledgments for the offer your letter contains & the real pride & gratification I feel at the favorable opinion it indicates.

"I respect too highly the offices of the present government of the United States to permit it to be suspected that I have declined one of them." [5]

[1] Washington to Marshall, Aug. 26, 1795; Washington MSS., Lib. Cong.

[2] Act of 1789, *Annals*, 1st Cong., 1st Sess., Appendix, 2238.

[3] For Randolph's pathetic account of his struggles to subsist as Attorney-General, see Conway, chap. xv.

[4] The Fairfax purchase. See *infra*, chap. v.

[5] Marshall to Washington, Aug. 31, 1795; Washington MSS., Lib. Cong.

When he refused the office of Attorney-General,
Washington, sorely perplexed, wrote Marshall's
brother-in-law,[1] Edward Carrington, United States
Marshal and Collector of Internal Revenue for the
District of Virginia,[2] a letter, "the *whole*" of which
"is perfectly confidential, written, perhaps, with more
candor than prudence," concerning Innes or Henry
for the place; but, says the President, "having a
high opinion of General [3] Marshall's honor, prudence,
and judgment," Carrington must consult him.[4]

The harassed President had now come to lean
heavily on Marshall in Virginia affairs; indeed, it
may be said that he was Washington's political agent
at the State Capital. Carrington's answer is typical
of his reports to the President: "The inquiry [con-
cerning the selection of an Attorney-General] which
you have been pleased to submit to Gen! Marshall
and myself demands & receives our most serious attention — On his [Marshall's] aid I rely for giving
you accurate information." [5]

Later Carrington advises Washington that Mar-
shall "wishes an opportunity of conversing with
Col. Innes before he decides." [6] Innes was absent at
Williamsburg; and although the matter was urgent,
Marshall and Carrington did not write Innes, be-

[1] See *infra*, chap. v.

[2] Executive Journal, U.S. Senate, i, 81, 82. And see Washington's
Diary: Lossing, 166. Carrington held both of these offices at the same
time.

[3] Referring to Marshall's title as General of Virginia Militia. He
was called "General" from that time until he became Chief Justice
of the United States.

[4] Washington to Carrington, Oct. 9, 1795; *Writings:* Ford, xiii, 116.

[5] Carrington to Washington, Oct. 2, 1795; MS., Lib. Cong.   [6] *Ib.*

cause, to do so, would involve a decisive offer from Washington which "Gen! Marshall does not think advisable." [1]

When Washington's second letter, suggesting Patrick Henry, was received by Carrington, he "immediately consulted Gen. Marshall thereon"; and was guided by his opinion. Marshall thought that Washington's letter should be forwarded to Henry because "his nonacceptance, from domestic considerations, may be calculated on"; the offer "must tend to soften" Henry "if he has any asperities"; and the whole affair would make Henry "active on the side of Government & order." [2]

Marshall argued that, if Henry should accept, his friendship for the Administration could be counted on. But Marshall's strongest reason for trying to induce Henry to become a member of the Cabinet was, says Carrington, that "we are fully persuaded that a more deadly blow could not be given to the Faction [Republican party] in Virginia, & perhaps elsewhere, than that Gentleman's acceptance of the" Attorney-Generalship. "So much have the opposers of the Government held him [Henry] up as their oracle, even since he has ceased to respond to them, that any event demonstrating his active support to Government, could not but give the [Republican] party a severe shock." [3]

[1] Carrington to Washington, Oct. 8, 1795; MS., Lib. Cong.

[2] *Ib.*, Oct. 13, 1795; MS., Lib. Cong.

[3] *Ib.* A passage in this letter clearly shows the Federalist opinion of the young Republican Party and suggests the economic line dividing it from the Federalists. "In the present crisis Mr. H.[enry] may reasonably be calculated on as taking the side of Government, even though he may retain his old prejudices against the Constitution. He has

A week later Carrington reports that Henry's "conduct & sentiments generally both as to government & yourself [Washington] are such as we [Marshall and Carrington] calculated on . . . which assure us of his discountenancing calumny of every description & disorder,"[1] meaning that Henry was hostile to the Republicans.

In the rancorous assaults upon the Jay Treaty in Virginia, Marshall, of course, promptly took his position by Washington's side, and stoutly defended the President and even the hated compact itself. Little cared Marshall for the effect of his stand upon his popularity. Not at all did he fear or hesitate to take that stand. And high courage was required to resist the almost universal denunciation of the treaty in Virginia. Nor was this confined to the masses of the people; it was expressed also by most of the leading men in the various communities. At every meeting of protest, well-drawn and apparently convincing resolutions were adopted, and able, albeit extravagant, speeches were made against the treaty and the Administration.

Typical of these was the address of John Thompson at Petersburg, August 1, 1795.[2] With whom,

indubitably an abhorrence of Anarchy. . . . We know too that he is improving his fortune fast, which must additionally attach him to the existing Government & order, the only Guarantees of property. Add to all this, that he has no affection for the present leaders of the opposition in Virg.ª " (Carrington to Washington, Oct. 13, 1795; MS., Lib. Cong.)

[1] Carrington to Washington, Oct. 20, 1795; MS., Lib. Cong. Carrington's correspondence shows that everything was done on Marshall's judgment and that Marshall himself personally handled most of the negotiations. (See *ib.*, Oct. 28; Oct. 30, 1795.)

[2] *American Remembrancer*, i, 21 *et seq.* John Thompson was nineteen years old when he delivered this address. His extravagant

asked Thompson, was the treaty made? With the British King "who had sworn eternal enmity to republics"; that hateful monarch who was trying "to stifle the liberty of France" and "to starve thirty millions of men" by "intercepting the correspondence and plundering the commerce of neutral nations," especially that of the United States. The British, declared Thompson, sought "the destruction of our rising commerce; the annihilation of our growing navigation," and were pursuing that object "with all the . . . oppression which rapacity can practice."

Sequestration of British debts and other justifiable measures of retaliation would, said he, have stopped Great Britain's lawless practices. But the Administration preferred to treat with that malign Power; and our envoy, Jay, instead of "preserving the attitude of dignity and speaking the language of truth . . . basely apostatizing from republican principles, stooped to offer the incense of flattery to a tyrant, the scourge of his country, the foe of mankind. . . . Yes!" exclaimed the radical orator, "we hesitated to offend a proud King, who had captured our vessels, enslaved our fellow-citizens, ruined our merchants, invaded our territory and trampled on our sovereignty." In spite of these wrongs and insults, "we prostrated ourselves before him, smiled in his face, flattered, and obtained this treaty."

The treaty thus negotiated was, declared Thompson, the climax of the Funding system which had

rhetoric rather than his solid argument is quoted in the text as better illustrating the public temper and prevailing style of oratory. (See sketch of this remarkable young Virginian, *infra*, chap. x.)

"organized a great aristocracy . . . usurped the dominion of the senate . . . often preponderated in the house of representatives and which proclaims itself in servile addresses to our supreme executive, in dangerous appointments, in monstrous accumulations of debt, in violation of the constitution, in proscriptions of democrats, and, to complete the climax of political infamy, in this treaty."

Concerning the refusal to observe the principle that "free bottoms make free goods," our yielding the point rendered us, avowed Thompson, "a cowardly confederate . . . of . . . ruthless despots, who march to desolate France, to restore the altars of barbarous superstition and to extinguish the celestial light which has burst upon the human mind. O my countrymen, when you are capable of such monstrous baseness, even the patriot will invoke upon you the contempt of ages." This humiliation had been thrust upon us as a natural result of Washington's Neutrality proclamation — "a sullen neutrality between freemen and despots."

Thompson's searching, if boyish, rhetoric truly expressed the feeling in the hearts of the people; it was a frenzied sentiment with which Marshall had to contend. Notwithstanding his blazing language, Thompson analyzed the treaty with ability. In common with opponents of the treaty everywhere, he laid strongest emphasis on its unconstitutionality

---

[1] A favorite Republican charge was that the treaty would separate us from France and tie us to Great Britain: "A treaty which children cannot read without discovering that it tends to disunite us from our present ally, and unite us to a government which we abhor, detest and despise." ("An Old Soldier of '76"; *American Remembrancer*, ii, 281.)

and the "usurpation" by the President and Senate of the rights and powers of the House of Representatives.

But Thompson also mentioned one point that touched Marshall closely. "The ninth article," said he, "invades the rights of this commonwealth, by contemplating the case of Denny Fairfax." [1] Marshall and his brother were now the owners of this estate; [2] and the Jay Treaty confirmed all transfers of British property and authorized British subjects to grant, sell, or devise lands held in America in the same manner as if they were citizens of the United States. In Congress a few months later, Giles, who, declared Ames, "has no scruples and certainly less sense," [3] touched lightly on this same chord.[4] So did Heath, who was from that part of Virginia lying within the Fairfax grant.[5]

Such was the public temper in Virginia, as accurately if bombastically expressed by the youthful Thompson, when the elections for the Legislature of 1795 were held. It was certain that the General Assembly would take drastic and hostile action against the treaty; and, perhaps, against Washington himself, in case the Republicans secured a majority in that body. The Federalists were in terror and justly so; for the Republicans, their strength much increased by the treaty, were aggressive and confident.

---

[1] *American Remembrancer*, i, 27.   [2] See *infra*, chap. v.

[3] Ames to Gore, March 11, 1796; *Works:* Ames, i, 189.

[4] *Annals*, 4th Cong., 1st Sess., 1033–34.

[5] *Ib.*, 1063. See Anderson, 41–43. As one of the purchasers of the Fairfax estate, Marshall had a personal interest in the Jay Treaty, though it does not appear that this influenced him in his support of it.

The Federalist candidate in Richmond was the
member of the Legislature whom the Federalists had
succeeded in electing after Marshall's retirement
three years before. He was Marshall's intimate friend
and a stanch supporter of Washington's Administration. But it appears that in the present crisis
his popularity was not sufficient to secure his election, nor his courage robust enough for the stern
fight that was certain to develop in the General
Assembly.

The polls were open and the voting in progress.
Marshall was among the first to arrive; and he
announced his choice.[1] Upon his appearance "a
gentleman demanded that a poll be opened for
Mr. Marshall." [2] Marshall, of course, indignantly
refused; he had promised to support his friend, he
avowed, and now to become a candidate was against
"his wishes and feeling and honor." But Marshall
promised that he would stand for the Legislature
the following year.

Thereupon Marshall left the polls and went to the
court-house to make an argument in a case then
pending. No sooner had he departed than a poll
was opened for him in spite of his objections;[3] he
was elected; and in the evening was told of the
undesired honor with which the freeholders of
Richmond had crowned him.

[1] The voting was *viva voce*. See *infra*, chap. X.

[2] Undoubtedly this gentleman was one of the perturbed Federalist
managers.

[3] *North American Review*, xxvi, 22. While this story seems improbable, no evidence has appeared which throws doubt upon it. At any
rate, it serves to illustrate Marshall's astonishing popularity.

Washington was apprehensive of the newly elected Legislature. He anxiously questioned Carrington "as to the temper of our Assembly." The latter reported that he did not "expect an extravagant conduct during the session." [1] He thought that "the spirit of dissatisfaction is considerably abated abroad" (throughout Virginia and away from Richmond), because recent attempts to hold county and district meetings "for the avowed purpose of condemning the Administration & the Treaty" had been "abortive." It seemed to him, however, that "there is a very general impression unfavorable to the Treaty, owing to the greater industry of those who revile, over the supporters of it." [2]

Still, Carrington was not sure about the Legislature itself; for, as he said, "it has every year for several past been observable, that, at meeting [of the Legislature] but few hot heads were to be seen, while the great body were rational; but in the course of the session it has seldom happened otherwise than

[1] Carrington's reports to Washington were often absurd in their optimistic inaccuracy. They are typical of those which faithful office-holding politicians habitually make to the appointing power. For instance, Carrington told Washington in 1791 that, after traveling all over Virginia as United States Marshal and Collector of Internal Revenue, he was sure the people were content with Assumption and the whiskey tax (Washington's *Diary:* Lossing, footnote to 166), when, as a matter of fact, the State was boiling with opposition to those very measures.

[2] The mingling, in the Republican mind, of the Jay Treaty, Neutrality, unfriendliness to France, and the Federalist Party is illustrated in a toast at a dinner in Lexington, Virginia, to Senator Brown, who had voted against the treaty: "The French Republic — May every power or party who would attempt to throw any obstacle in the way of its independence or happiness receive the reward due to corruption." (*Richmond and Manchester Advertiser,* Oct. 15, 1795.)

that the spirit of party has been communicated so
as to infect a majority. In the present instance I
verily believe a question put on this day [the first
day of the session] for making the Treaty a subject
of consideration would be negatived — yet sundry
members are here who will attempt every injury
to both the Administration & the Treaty. The
party will want ability in their leaders. . . . General
Lee, C. Lee, Gen! Marshall & Mr. Andrews will act
with ability on the defensive." [1]

Three days later the buoyant official advised the
President that the Republicans doubted their own
strength and, at worst, would delay their attack
"in order that, as usual, a heat may be generated."
Marshall was still busy searching for a properly qualified person to appoint to the unfilled vacancy in
the office of Attorney-General; and Carrington tells
Washington that "Gen! Marshall and myself have
had a private consultation" on that subject and had
decided to recommend Judge Blain. But, he adds,
"The suggestion rests entirely with Gen! M[arshall]
& myself & will there expire, should you, for any
consideration, forbear to adopt it." His real message
of joy, however, was the happy frame of mind of
the Legislature. [2]

Alas for this prophecy of optimism! The Legislature had not been in session a week before the
anti-Administration Banquo's ghost showed its grim
visage. The Republicans offered a resolution approving the vote of Virginia Senators against the

[1] Carrington to Washington, Nov. 10, 1795; MS., Lib. Cong.
[2] *Ib.*, Nov. 13, 1795; MS.; Lib. Cong.

Jay Treaty. For three days the debate raged. Marshall led the Federalist forces. "The support of the Treaty has fallen altogether on Gen! Marshall and Mr. Chas. Lee," Carrington reports to Washington.[2]

Among the many objections to the treaty the principal one, as we have seen, was that it violated the Constitution. The treaty regulated commerce; the Constitution gave that power to Congress, which included the House of Representatives; yet the House had not been consulted. The treaty involved naturalization, the punishment of piracies, the laying of imposts and the expenditure of money — all of these subjects were expressly placed under the control of Congress and one of them[3] (the raising and expending of public money) must originate in the House; yet that popular branch of the Government had been ignored. The treaty provided for a quasi-judicial commission to settle the question of the British debts; yet "all the power of the Federal government with respect to debts is given [Congress] by a concise article of the Constitution. ... What article of the Constitution authorizes President and Senate to establish a judiciary colossus which is to stand with one foot on America and the other on Britain, and drag the reluctant governments of those countries to the altar of justice?"[4]

[1] The resolution "was warmly agitated three whole days." (Randolph to Jefferson, Nov. 22, 1795; *Works:* Ford, viii, footnote to 197.)

[2] Carrington to Washington, Nov. 20, 1795; MS., Lib. Cong.

[3] See debates; *Annals*, 4th Cong., 1st Sess., 423–1291; also see Petersburg Resolutions; *American Remembrancer*, i, 102–07.

[4] Thompson's address, Aug. 1, 1795, at Petersburg; *ib.*, 21 *et seq.*

Thus the question was raised whether a commercial treaty, or an international compact requiring an appropriation of money, or, indeed, any treaty whatever in the execution of which any action of any kind on the part of the House of Representatives was necessary, could be made without the concurrence of the House as well as the Senate. On this, the only vital and enduring question involved, Marshall's views were clear and unshakable.

The defense of the constitutional power of the President and Senate to make treaties was placed solely on Marshall's shoulders. The Federalists considered his argument a conclusive demonstration. Carrington wrote Washington that "on the point of constitutionality many conversions were acknowledged." [1] He was mistaken; the Republicans were not impressed. On the contrary, they thought that the treaty "was much less ably defended than opposed." [2]

The Republicans had been very much alarmed over Marshall and especially feared the effect of one clever move. "John Marshall," wrote Jefferson's son-in-law from Richmond to the Republican commander in Monticello, "it was once apprehended would make a great number of converts by an argument which cannot be considered in any other light than an uncandid artifice. To prevent what would be a virtual censure of the President's conduct he maintained *that the treaty in all its commercial parts*

[1] Carrington to Washington, Nov. 20, 1795; MS., Lib. Cong.

[2] Randolph to Jefferson, Nov. 22, 1795; *Works:* Ford, viii, footnote to 197.

was still under the power of the H.[ouse] of R.[epre-sentatives]." [1]

Marshall, indeed, did make the most of this point. It was better, said he, and "more in the spirit of the constitution" for the National House to refuse support after ratification than to have a treaty "stifled in embryo" by the House passing upon it before ratification. "He compared the relation of the Executive and the Legislative department to that between the states and the Congress under the old confederation. The old Congress might have given up the right of laying discriminating duties in favor of any nation by treaty; it would never have thought of taking beforehand the assent of each state thereto. Yet, no one would have pretended to deny the power of the states to lay such [discriminating duties]." [2]

Such is an unfriendly report of this part of Marshall's effort which, wrote Jefferson's informant, "is all that is original in his argument. The sophisms of Camillus, & the nice distinctions of the Examiner made up the rest." [3] Marshall's position was that a "treaty is as completely a valid and obligatory contract when negotiated by the President and ratified by him, with the assent and advice of the Senate, as if sanctioned by the House of Representatives also, under a constitution requiring such sanction"; and he admitted only that the powers of the House in

[1] Randolph to Jefferson, Nov. 22, 1795; *Works:* Ford, viii, footnote to 197.
[2] *Ib.*
[3] *Ib.* See Hamilton's dissertation on the treaty-making power in numbers 36, 37, 38, of his "Camillus"; *Works:* Lodge, vi, 160-97.

reference to a treaty were limited to granting or refusing appropriations to carry it into effect.[1]

But as a matter of practical tactics to get votes,
Marshall appears to have put this in the form of an
assertion — no matter what treaty the President and
Senate made, the House held the whip hand, he argued, and in the end, could do what it liked; why
then unnecessarily affront and humiliate Washington
by applauding the Virginia Senators for their vote
against the treaty? This turn of Marshall's, thought
the Republicans, "was brought forward for the
purpose of gaining over the unwary & wavering. It
has never been admitted by the writers in favor of
the treaty to the northward."[2]

But neither Marshall's unanswerable argument
on the treaty-making power, nor his cleverness in
holding up the National House of Representatives as
the final arbiter, availed anything. The Federalists
offered an amendment affirming that the President
and Senate "have a right to make" a treaty; that
discussion of a treaty in a State Legislature, "except
as to its constitutionality," was unnecessary; and
that the Legislature could not give "any mature
opinion upon the conduct of the Senators from
Virginia . . . without a full investigation of the
treaty." They were defeated by a majority of 46
out of a total of 150 members present and voting;
John Marshall voting for the amendment.[3] On the
main resolution proposed by the Republicans the

[1] Marshall to Hamilton, April 25, 1796; *Works:* Hamilton, vi,
109.

[2] Randolph to Jefferson, Nov. 22, 1795; *Works:* Ford, viii, 198.

[3] Journal, H.D. (Nov. 20, 1795), 27–28.

Federalists lost two votes and were crushed by a majority of two to one; Marshall, of course, voting with the minority.[1]

Carrington hastily reported to Washington that though "the discussion has been an able one on the side of the Treaty," yet, "such was the apprehension that a vote in its favor would be unpopular, that argument was lost"; and that, notwithstanding many members were convinced by Marshall's constitutional argument, "obligations of expediency" held them in line against the Administration. The sanguine Carrington assured the President, however, that "during the discussion there has been preserved a decided respect for & confidence in you."[2]

But alas again for the expectations of sanguinity! The Republican resolution was, as Jefferson's son-in-law had reported to the Republican headquarters at Monticello, "a virtual censure of the President's conduct." This was the situation at the close of the day's debate. Realizing it, as the night wore on, Washington's friends determined to relieve the President of this implied rebuke by the Legislature of his own State. The Republicans had carried their point; and surely, thought Washington's supporters, the Legislature of Virginia would not openly affront the greatest of all Americans, the pride of the State, and the President of the Nation.

Infatuated imagination! The next morning the friends of the Administration offered a resolution

[1] Journal, H.D. (Nov. 20, 1795), 28.
[2] Carrington to Washington, Nov. 20, 1795; MS., Lib. Cong.

that Washington's "motives" in approving the treaty met "the entire approbation of this House"; and that Washington, "for his great abilities, *wisdom* and integrity merits and possesses the undiminished confidence of his country." The resolution came near passing. But some lynx-eyed Republican discovered in the nick of time the word "*wisdom*." [1] That would never do. The Republicans, therefore, offered an amendment "that this House do entertain the highest sense of the integrity and patriotism of the President of the United States; and that while they approve of the vote of the Senators of this State" on the treaty, "they in no wise censure the motives which influenced him in his [Washington's] conduct thereupon." [2]

The word "wisdom" was carefully left out. Marshall, Lee, and the other Federalists struggled hard to defeat this obnoxious amendment; but the Republicans overwhelmed them by a majority of 33 out of a total of 145 voting, Marshall, of course, casting his vote against it. [3]

In worse plight than ever, Washington's friends moved to amend the Republican amendment by resolving: "That the President of the United States, for his great abilities, *wisdom*, and integrity, merits

---

[1] The italics are mine. "The word 'wisdom' in expressing the confidence of the House in the P.[resident] was so artfully introduced that if the fraudulent design had not been detected in time the vote of the House, as to its effect upon the P. would have been entirely done away. ... A resolution so worded as to acquit the P. of all evil intention, but at the same time silently censuring his error, was passed by a majority of 33." (Letter of Jefferson's son-in-law, enclosed by Jefferson to Madison; *Works:* Ford, viii, footnote to 198.)

[2] Journal, H.D. (Nov. 21, 1795), 29.   [3] *Ib.*

and possesses the undiminished confidence of this House." But even this, which omitted all reference to the treaty and merely expressed confidence in Washington's "abilities, wisdom, and integrity," was beaten by a majority of 20 out of a total of 138 voting.[1]

As soon as Jefferson got word of Marshall's support of Washington's Administration in the Legislature, he poured out his dislike which had long been distilling: —

"Though Marshall will be able to embarras [sic] the republican party in the assembly a good deal," wrote Jefferson to Madison, "yet upon the whole his having gone into it will be of service. He has been, hitherto, able to do more mischief acting under the mask of Republicanism than he will be able to do after throwing it plainly off. His lax lounging manners have made him popular with the bulk of the people of Richmond; & a profound hypocrisy, with many thinking men of our country. But having come forth in the plenitude of his English principles the latter will see that it is high time to make him known." [2]

Such was Jefferson's inability to brook any opposition, and his readiness to ascribe improper motives to any one having views different from his own. So far from Marshall's having cloaked his opinions, he had been and was imprudently outspoken in avowing them. Frankness was as much a part of Marshall's mental make-up as his "lax, lounging manners"

[1] Journal, H.D. (Nov. 21, 1795), 29.
[2] Jefferson to Madison, Nov. 26, 1795; *Works:* Ford, viii, 197–98.

were a part of his physical characteristics. Of all
the men of the period, not one was cleaner of hypocrisy than he. From Patrick Henry in his early life
onward to his associates on the bench at the end
of his days the testimony as to Marshall's open-
mindedness is uniform and unbroken.

With the possible exception of Giles and Roane,
Jefferson appears to have been the only man who
even so much as hinted at hypocrisy in Marshall.
Although strongly opposing his views and suggesting the influence of supposed business connections,
Madison had supreme confidence in Marshall's integrity of mind and character. So had Monroe.
Even Jefferson's most panegyrical biographer declares Marshall to have been "an earnest and sincere
man." [1]

The House of Delegates having refused to approve
Washington, even indirectly, the matter went to
the State Senate. There for a week Washington's
friends fought hard and made a slight gain. The
Senate struck out the House resolution and inserted
instead: "The General Assembly entertain the highest sense of the integrity, patriotism and wisdom of
the President of the United States, and in approving
the vote of the Senators of the State in the Congress
of the United States, relative to the treaty with
Great Britain, they in no wise mean to censure the
motives which influenced him in his conduct thereupon." To this the House agreed, although by a
slender majority, Marshall, of course, voting for
the Senate amendment. [2]

[1] Randall, ii, 36.　　　　[2] Journal, H.D. (1795), 72.

During this session Marshall was, as usual, on the principal standing committees and did his accustomed share of general legislative work. He was made chairman of a special committee to bring in a bill "authorizing one or more branches of the bank of the United States in this commonwealth"; [1] and later presented the bill, [2] which finally passed, December 8, 1795, though not without resistance, 38 votes being cast against it. [3]

But the Republicans had not yet finished with the Jay Treaty or with its author. On December 12, 1795, they offered a resolution instructing Virginia's Senators and Representatives in Congress to attempt to secure amendments to the Constitution providing that: "Treaties containing stipulations upon the subject of powers vested in Congress shall be approved by the House of Representatives"; that "a tribunal other than the Senate be instituted for trying impeachments"; that "Senators shall be chosen for three years"; and that "U.S. Judges shall hold no other appointments." [4]

The Federalists moved to postpone this resolution until the following year "and print and distribute proposed amendments for the consideration of the people"; but they were beaten by a majority of 11 out of a total vote of 129, Marshall voting for the resolution. The instruction to secure these radical constitutional changes then passed the House by a majority of 56 out of a total vote of 120, Marshall voting against it. [5]

<hr />

[1] Journal, H.D. (1795), 50.   [2] Ib., 53.
[3] Ib., 79.   [4] Ib., 90.   [5] Ib., 91–92.

Marshall's brother-in-law, United States Marshal
Carrington, had a hard time explaining to Washington his previous enthusiasm. He writes: "The active
powers of the [Republican] party . . . unveiled themselves, & carried in the House some points very extraordinary indeed, manifesting disrespect towards
you." But, he continues, when the Virginia Senate
reversed the House, "the zealots of Anarchy were
backward to act . . . while the friends of Order were
satisfied to let it [the Virginia Senate amendment]
remain for farther effects of reflection"; and later
succeeded in carrying it.

"The fever has raged, come to its crisis, and is
abating." Proof of this, argued Carrington, was
the failure of the Republicans to get signatures to
"some seditious petitions [against the Jay Treaty]
which was sent in vast numbers from Philadelphia"
and which "were at first patronized with great zeal
by many of our distinguished anarchists; but . . .
very few copies will be sent to Congress fully
signed." [1]

Never was appointive officer so oblivious of facts
in his reports to his superior, as was Carrington.
Before adjournment on December 12, 1795, the Legislature adopted part of the resolution which had
been offered in the morning: "No treaty containing
any stipulation upon the subject of powers vested
in Congress by the eighth section of the first article
[of the Constitution] shall become the Supreme law
of the land until it shall have been approved in
those particulars by a majority in the House of

[1] Carrington to Washington, Dec. 6, 1795; MS., Lib. Cong.

Representatives; and that the President, before he shall ratify *any* treaty, shall submit the same to the House of Representatives." [1]

Carrington ignored or failed to understand this amazing resolution of the Legislature of Virginia; for nearly three months later he again sought to solace Washington by encouraging reports. "The public mind in Virginia was never more tranquil than at present. The fever of the late session of our assembly, had not been communicated to the Country. . . . The people do not approve of the violent and petulant measures of the Assembly, because, in several instances, public meetings have declared a decided disapprobation." In fact, wrote Carrington, Virginia's "hostility to the treaty has been exaggerated." Proof "of the mass of the people being less violent than was asserted" would be discovered "in the failure of our Zealots in getting their signatures to certain printed papers, sent through the Country almost by Horse loads, as copies of a petition to Congress on the subject of the Treaty." [2] But a few short months would show how rose-colored were the spectacles which Mr. Carrington wore when he wrote this reassuring letter.

The ratification of the British treaty; the rage against England; and the devotion to France which already had made the Republican a French party; the resentment of the tri-color Republic toward the American Government — all forged a new and desperate menace. It was, indeed, Scylla or Charybdis,

[1] Journal, H.D. (Dec. 12, 1795), 91–92.
[2] Carrington to Washington, Feb. 24, 1796; MS., Lib. Cong.

as Washington had foreseen, and bluntly stated, that confronted the National Government. War with France now seemed the rock on which events were driving the hard-pressed Administration — war for France or war from France.

The partisan and simple-minded Monroe had been recalled from his diplomatic post at Paris. The French mission, which at the close of our Revolution was not a place of serious moment,[1] now became critically — vitally — important. Level must be the head and stout the heart of him who should be sent to deal with that sensitive, proud, and now violent country. Lee thus advises the President: "No person would be better fitted than John Marshall to go to France for supplying the place of our minister; but it is scarcely short of absolute certainty that he would not accept any such office."[2]

But Washington's letter was already on the way, asking Marshall to undertake this delicate task: —

"In confidence I inform you," wrote Washington to Marshall, "that it has become indispensably necessary to recall our minister at Paris & to send one in his place, who will explain faithfully the views of this government & ascertain those of France.

"Nothing would be more pleasing to me than that you should be this organ, if it were only for a temporary absence of a few months; but it being feared that even this could not be made to comport with your present pursuits, I have in order that as little delay as possible may be incurred put the enclosed

[1] Dodd, 39.
[2] Lee to Washington, July 7, 1796; *Writings: Sparks*, xi, 487.

letter [to Charles Cotesworth Pinckney] under cover
to be forwarded to its address, if you decline the
present offer or to be returned to me if you accept
it. Your own correct knowledge of circumstances
renders details unnecessary." [1]

Marshall at once declined this now high distinction and weighty service, as he had already refused
the United States district attorneyship and a place
in Washington's Cabinet. Without a moment's delay, he wrote the President: —

"I will not attempt to express those sensations
which your letter of the 8th instant has increased.
Was it possible for me in the present crisis of my affairs to leave the United States, such is my conviction of the importance of that duty which you would
confide to me, &, pardon me if I add, of the fidelity with which I shoud attempt to perform it, that
I woud certainly forego any consideration not decisive with respect to my future fortunes, & woud
surmount that just diffidence I have entertain^d of
myself, to make one effort to convey truly & faithfully to the government of France those sentiments
which I have ever believed to be entertained by that
of the United States.

"I have forwarded your letter to Mr. Pinckney.
The recall of our minister at Paris has been conjectured while its probable necessity has been regretted
by those who love more than all others, our own
country. I will certainly do myself the honor of
waiting on you at Mt. Vernon." [2]

[1] Washington to Marshall, July 8, 1796; Washington MSS., Lib.
Cong.

[2] Marshall to Washington, July 11, 1796; *ib.*

Washington, although anticipating Marshall's refusal of the French mission, promptly answered: "I . . . regret that present circumstances should deprive our Country of the services, which, I am confident, your going to France would have rendered it"; and Washington asks Marshall's opinion on the proper person to appoint to the office of Surveyor-General.[1]

The President's letter, offering the French post to Pinckney, was lost in the mails; and the President wrote Marshall about it, because it also enclosed a note "containing three bank bills for one hundred dollars each for the sufferers by fire in Charlestown."[2] In answer, Marshall indulged in a flash of humor, even at Washington's expense. "Your letter to General Pinckney was delivered by myself to the post master on the night on which I received it and was, as he says, immediately forwarded by him. Its loss is the more remarkable, as it could not have been opened from a hope that it contained bank notes." He also expressed his gratification "that a gentleman of General Pinckney's character will represent our government at the court of France."[3]

The office of Secretary of State now became vacant, under circumstances apparently forbidding. The interception of Fauchet's[4] famous dispatch number 10[5] had been fatal to Randolph. The French

---

[1] Washington to Marshall, July 15, 1796; Washington's Private Letter Book; MS., Lib. Cong.

[2] Washington to Marshall, Oct. 10, 1796; *ib.*

[3] Marshall to Washington, Oct. 12, 1796; Washington MSS., Lib. Cong.

[4] Genêt's successor as French Minister to the United States.

[5] *Interesting State Papers*, 48 *et seq.*

Minister, in this communication to his Government, portrays a frightful state of corrupt public thinking in America; ascribes this to the measures of Washington's Administration; avows that a revolution is imminent; declares that powerful men, "all having without doubt" Randolph at their head, are balancing to decide on their party; asserts that Randolph approached him with suggestions for money; and concludes: —

"Thus with some thousands of dollars the [French] republic could have decided on civil war or on peace [in America]! Thus the consciences of the pretended patriots of America have already their prices! . . . What will be the old age of this [American] government, if it is thus early decrepid!" [1]

The discovery of this dispatch of the French Minister destroyed Randolph politically. Washington immediately forced his resignation. [2]

The President had great difficulty in finding a suitable successor to the deposed Secretary of State. He tendered the office to five men, all of whom declined. [3] "What am I to do for a Secretary of State?" he asks Hamilton; and after recounting his fruitless efforts to fill that office the President adds that "Mr. Marshall, of Virginia, has declined the office of Attorney General, and I am pretty certain, would accept of

---

[1] *Interesting State Papers*, 55.

[2] For able defense of Randolph see Conway, chap. xxiii; but *contra*, see Gibbs, i, chap. ix.

[3] Patterson of New Jersey, Johnson of Maryland, C. C. Pinckney of South Carolina, Patrick Henry of Virginia, and Rufus King of New York. (Washington to Hamilton, Oct. 29, 1795; *Writings:* Ford, xiii, 129–30.) King declined because of the abuse heaped upon public officers. (Hamilton to Washington, Nov. 5, 1795; *ib.*, footnote to 130.)

no other." [1] It is thus made clear that Washington would have made Marshall the head of his Cabinet in 1795 but for the certainty that his Virginia champion would refuse the place, as he had declined other posts of honor and power.

Hardly had the Virginia Legislature adjourned when the conflict over the treaty was renewed in Congress. The Republicans had captured the House of Representatives and were full of fight. They worked the mechanism of public meetings and petitions to its utmost. On March 7 the House plunged into a swirl of debate over the British treaty; time and again it seemed as though the House would strangle the compact by withholding appropriations to make it effective. [2] If the treaty was to be saved, all possible pressure must be brought to bear on Congress. So the Federalists took a leaf out of the book of Republican tactics, and got up meetings wherever they could to petition Congress to grant the necessary money.

In Virginia, as elsewhere, the merchants were the principal force in arranging these meetings. [3] As we have seen, the business and financial interests had from the first been the stanchest supporters of Washington's Administration. "The commercial and monied people are zealously attached to" and support the Government, wrote Wolcott in 1791. [4] And now Hamilton advised King that "men of busi-

---

[1] Washington to Hamilton, Oct. 29, 1795; *Writings:* Ford, xiii, 131.

[2] For debate see *Annals*, 4th Cong., 1st Sess., 423–1291.

[3] Carrington to Washington, May 9, 1796; MS., Lib. Cong.

[4] Oliver Wolcott to his father, Feb. 12, 1791; Gibbs, i, 62.

ness of all descriptions" thought the defeat of the treaty "would greatly shock and stagnate pecuniary plans and operations in general." [1] Indeed, the one virtue of the treaty, aside from its greatest purpose, that of avoiding war, was that it prevented the collapse of credit and the wreck of Hamilton's financial system.

Washington, with the deceptive hopefulness of responsibility, had, even when it seemed that the people were as one man against the treaty, "doubted much whether the great body of the yeomanry have formed any opinions on the subject." [2] The Federalist meetings were designed to show that the "yeomanry," having been "educated," had at last made up its mind in favor of Washington's policy.

Marshall and Carrington arranged for the Richmond gathering. "The disorganizing machinations of a faction [Republicans]," reported the busy United States Marshal, "are no longer left to be nourished and inculcated on the minds of the credulous by clamorous demagogues, while the great mass of citizens, viewing these, as evils at a distance, remain inactive. . . . All who are attached to peace and order, . . . will now come forward and speak for themselves. . . . A meeting of the people of this city will take place on Monday next" to petition the National House of Representatives to support the treaty. So Carrington advised the President; and the same thing, said he, was to be done "exten-

---

[1] Hamilton to King, June 20, 1795; *Works:* Lodge, x, 103.
[2] Washington to Knox, Sept. 20, 1795; *Writings:* Ford, xiii, 105–06.

sively" by "public meetings and Petitions throughout Virginia." [1]

Washington was expecting great results from the
Richmond demonstration. "It would give me and
. . . every friend to order and good government
throughout the United States very great satisfaction," he wrote to encourage the Virginia Federalists; "more so than similar sentiments from any
other State in the Union; for people living at a distance from it [Virginia] know not how to believe
it possible" that the Virginia Legislature and her
Senators and Representatives in Congress should
speak and act as they had done.[2] "It is," phil-
osophized Washington, "on *great* occasions *only* and
after time has been given for cool and deliberate
reflection that the *real* voice of the people can be
known. The present . . . is one of those great
occasions, than which none more important has
occurred, or probably may occur again to call forth
their decision." [3]

By such inspiration and management the historic
Federalist gathering was brought about at Richmond on April 25, 1796, where the "Marshall eloquence" was to do its utmost to convert a riotously
hostile sentiment into approval of this famous
treaty and of the Administration which was responsible for it. All day the meeting lasted. Marshall
put forth his whole strength. At last a "decided
majority" adopted a favorable resolution drawn by

[1] Carrington to the President, April 22, 1796; *Writings:* Ford, xiii,
footnote to 185.
[2] Washington to Carrington, May 1, 1796; *ib.*, 185.
[3] *Ib.*, 186.

an "original opponent" of the treaty. Thus were
sweetened the bitter resolutions adopted by these
same freeholders of Richmond some months before,
which had so angered Washington.

The accounts of this all-day public discussion
are as opposite as were the prejudices and interests
of the narrators. Justice Story tells us that Marshall's speech was "masterly," the majority for the
resolution "flattering," and the assemblage itself
made up of the "same citizens" who formerly had
"denounced" the treaty.[1] But there was present at
the meeting an onlooker who gives a different version. Randolph, who, in disgrace, was then sweating
venom from every pore, thus reports to Madison
at the end of the hard-fought day: —

"Between 3 & 400 persons were present; a large
proportion of whom were British merchants, some
of whom pay for the British purchases of horses —
their clerks — officers, who have held posts under
the President at his will, — stockholders — expec-
tants of office — and many without the shadow of
a freehold.[2] Notwithstanding this, the numbers on
the republican side, tho' inferior, were inferior in a
small degree only; and it is believed on good grounds
that the majority of free-holders were on the side
of the house of representatives [against the treaty].

"Campbell[3] and Marshall the principal combat-
ants [word illegible] as you know without being

[1] Story, in Dillon, iii, 352.
[2] Senator Stephen Thompson Mason wrote privately to Tazewell
that the Fairfax purchasers and British merchants were the only
friends of the treaty in Virginia. (Anderson, 42.)
[3] Alexander Campbell. (See *infra*, chap. v.)

told. Marshall's argument was inconsistent, and
shifting; concluding every third sentence with the
horrors of war. Campbell spoke elegantly and
forcibly; and threw ridicule and absurdity upon his
antagonist with success. Mr. Clofton [Clopton, member of Congress from Richmond] will receive two
papers; one signed by the treaty men, many of
whom he will know to have neither interest nor feeling in common with the citizens of Virginia, and
to have been transplanted hither from England or
Caledonia since the war, interspersed pretty considerably with fugitive tories who have returned under
the amnesty of peace.

"The notice, which I sent you the other day,"
he goes on to say, "spoke of instructions and a
petition; but Marshall, suspecting that he would be
outnumbered by freeholders, and conscious that
none should instruct those who elect, quitted the
idea of instruction, and betook himself to a petition,
in which he said all the inhabitants of Richmond,
though not freeholders, might join. Upon which
Campbell gave notice, that it would be published
that he (Marshall) declined hazarding the question on the true sense of the country. Very few of
the people [freeholders] of the county were present;
but three-fourths of those who were present voted
with Campbell. Dr. Foushee was extremely active
and influential." [1]

Marshall, on the contrary, painted in rich colors
his picture of this town-hall contest. He thus reports

[1] Randolph to Madison, Richmond, April 25, 1796; Conway, 362.
Only freeholders could vote.

to Hamilton: "I had been informed of the temper of the House of Representatives and we [Richmond Federalists] had promptly taken such measures as appeared to us fitted to the occasion. We could not venture an expression of the public mind under the violent prejudices with which it has been impressed, so long as a hope remained, that the House of Representatives might ultimately consult the interest or honor of the nation. . . . But now, when all hope of this has vanished, it was deemed advisable to make the experiment, however hazardous it might be.

"A meeting was called," continues Marshall, "which was more numerous than I have ever seen at this place; and after a very ardent and zealous discussion which consumed the day, a decided majority declared in favor of a resolution that the wellfare and honor of the nation required us to give full effect to the treaty negotiated with Britain. This resolution, with a petition drawn by an original opponent of the treaty, will be forwarded by the next post to Congress." [1]

The resolution which Marshall's speech caused an "original opponent" [2] of the treaty to draw was "that the Peace, Happiness, & Wellfare, not less than the National Honor of the United States, depend in a great degree upon giving, with good faith, Full effect to the Treaty lately negotiated with Great Britain." The same newspaper that printed this resolution, in another account of the meeting

[1] Marshall to Hamilton, April 25, 1796; *Works: Hamilton,* vi, 109.
[2] Author unknown.

"which was held at the instance of some friends of the British Treaty," says that "in opposition to that resolution a vast number of the meeting" subscribed to counter-declarations which "are now circulated throughout this City and the county of Henrico for the subscription of all those who" are opposed to the treaty.[1] Even the exultant Carrington reported "that the enemies of the Treaty or rather of the Government, are putting in practice every part and effort to obtain subscriptions to a counteracting paper."

Carrington denounced the unfavorable newspaper account as "a most absolute falsehood." He tells Washington that the opposition resolution "was not even listened [to] in the meeting." But still he is very apprehensive — he beholds the politician's customary "crisis" and strives to make the people see it: "There never was a crisis at which the activity of the Friends of Government was more urgently called for — some of us here have endeavored to make this impression in different parts of the Country."[2] The newspaper reported that the Federalists had induced "school boys & apprentices" to sign the petition in favor of the treaty; Carrington adds a postscript stating that this was, "I believe, a little incorrect."

Marshall foresaw that the Republicans would make this accusation and hastened to anticipate it by advancing the same charge against his opponents. The Republicans, says Marshall, secured the signa-

---

[1] *Richmond and Manchester Advertiser*, April 27, 1796.
[2] Carrington to the President, April 27, 1796; MS., Lib. Cong.

tures to their petition not only "of many respectable persons but of still a greater number of mere boys. . . . Altho' some caution has been used by us in excluding those who might not be considered as authorized to vote," yet, Marshall advises King, "they [Republicans] will not fail to charge us with having collected a number of names belonging to foreigners and to persons having no property in the place. The charge is as far untrue," asserts Marshall, "as has perhaps ever happened on any occasion of the sort. We could, by resorting to that measure, have doubled our list of petitioners." And he adds that "the ruling party [Republican] of Virginia are extremely irritated at the vote of to-day, and will spare no exertion to obtain a majority in other counties. Even here they will affect to have the greater number of freeholders." [1]

It was in this wise that petitions favorable to the Jay Treaty and to Washington were procured in the President's own State. It was thus that the remainder of the country was assured that the Administration was not without support among the people of Virginia. Unsuspected and wholly unforeseen was the influence on Marshall's future which his ardent championship of this despised treaty was to exercise.

The Federalists were wise to follow the Republican practice of petition to Congress; for, "nothing . . . but the torrent of petitions and remonstrances . . . would have produced a division (fifty-one to forty-

[1] Marshall to King, April 25, 1796; King, ii, 45–46.

eight) in favor of the appropriation." [1] So great was
the joy of the commercial classes that in Philadelphia, the financial heart of the country, a holiday
was celebrated when the House voted the money.[2]

Marshall's activity, skill, courage, ability, and
determination in the Legislature and before the
people at this critical hour lifted him higher than
ever, not only in the regard of Washington, but in
the opinion of the Federalist leaders throughout
the country.[3] They were casting about for a
successor to Washington who could be most easily
elected. The Hamiltonian Federalists were already
distrustful of Adams as his successor, and, even then,
were casting about for some other candidate. Why
not Patrick Henry? Great changes had occurred
in the old patriot's mind and manner of thinking.
He was now a man of wealth and had come to lean
strongly toward the Government. His friendship
for Washington, Marshall, and other Virginia Federalists had grown; while for Jefferson and other
Virginia Republicans it had turned to dislike. Still,
with Henry's lifelong record, the Federalists could
not be sure of him.

To Marshall's cautious hands the Federalist leaders committed the delicate business of sounding
Henry. King of New York had written Marshall on
the subject. "Having never been in habits of correspondence with Mr. H.[enry]," replies Marshall,

[1] Washington to Thomas Pinckney, May 22, 1796; *Writings:* Ford,
xiii, 208.
[2] Robert Morris to James M. Marshall, May 1, 1796; Morris's
Private Letter Book; MS., Lib. Cong.
[3] Story, in Dillon, iii, 350.

"I cou'd not by letter ask from him a decision on the proposition I was requested to make him without giving him at the same time a full statement of the whole conversation & of the persons with whom that conversation was held." Marshall did not think this wise, for "I am not positively certain what course that Gentleman might take. The proposition might not only have been rejected but mentioned publickly to others in such manner as to have become an unpleasant circumstance."

A prudent man was Marshall. He thought that Lee, who "corresponds familiarly with Mr. H. & is in the habit of proposing offices to him," was the man to do the work; and he asked Lee "to sound Mr. H. as from himself or in such manner as might in any event be perfectly safe." Lee did so, but got no answer. However, writes Marshall, "Mr. H.[enry] will be in Richmond on the 22ᵈ of May. I can then sound him myself & if I find him (as I suspect I shall) totally unwilling to engage in the contest, I can stop where prudence may direct. I trust it will not then be too late to bring forward to public view Mr. H. or any other gentleman who may be thought of in his stead. Shou'd anything occur to render it improper to have any communication with Mᴿ H. on this subject, or shou'd you wish the communication to take any particular shape you will be so obliging as to drop me a line concerning it."[1]

[1] Marshall to King, April 19, 1796; Hamilton MSS., Lib. Cong. Hamilton, it seems, had also asked Marshall to make overtures to Patrick Henry for the Presidency. (King, ii, footnote to 46.) But no correspondence between Hamilton and Marshall upon this subject has been discovered. Marshall's correspondence about Henry was with King.

Marshall finally saw Henry and at once wrote the New York lieutenant of Hamilton the result of the interview. "Mr. Henry has at length been sounded on the subject you communicated to my charge," Marshall advises King. "Gen! Lee and myself have each conversed with him on it, tho' without informing him particularly of the persons who authorized the communication. He is unwilling to embark in the business. His unwillingness, I think, proceeds from an apprehension of the difficulties to be encountered by those who shall fill high Executive offices." [1]

The autumn of 1796 was at hand. Washington's second term was closing in Republican cloudbursts and downpours of abuse of him. He was, said the Republicans, an aristocrat, a "monocrat," a miser, an oppressor of the many for the enrichment of the few. Nay, more! Washington was a thief, even a murderer, charged the Republicans. His personal habits were low and base, said these champions of purity.[2] Washington had not even been true to the cause of the Revolution, they declared; and to prove this, an ancient slander, supported by forged letters alleged to have been written by Washington during the war, was revived.[3]

Marshall, outraged and insulted by these assaults on the great American, the friend of his father and himself and the commander of the patriots who had,

[1] Marshall to King, May 24, 1796; King, ii, 48.
[2] For an accurate description of the unparalleled abuse of Washington, see McMaster, ii, 249–50, 289–91, 302–06.
[3] Marshall, ii, 391–92. Also see Washington to Pickering, March 3, 1797; *Writings:* Ford, xiii, 378–80; and to Gordon, Oct. 15; *ib.*, 427.

by arms, won liberty and independence for the very men who were now befouling Washington's name, earnestly defended the President. Although his law practice and private business called for all his strength and time, Marshall, in order to serve the President more effectively, again stood for the Legislature, and again he was elected.

In the Virginia House of Delegates, Marshall and the other friends of Washington took the initiative. On November 17, 1796, they carried a motion for an address to the President, declaratory of Virginia's "gratitude for the services of their most excellent fellow citizen"; who "has so wisely and prosperously administrated the national concerns." [1] But how should the address be worded? The Republicans controlled the committee to which the resolution was referred. Two days later that body reported a cold and formal collection of sentences as Virginia's address to Washington upon his leaving, apparently forever, the service of America. Even Lee, who headed the committee, could not secure a declaration that Washington was or had been wise.

This stiff "address" to Washington, reported by the committee, left out the word "wisdom." Commendation of Washington's conduct of the Government was carefully omitted. Should his friends submit to this? No! Better to be beaten in a manly contest. Marshall and the other supporters of the President resolved to try for a warmer expression. On December 10, they introduced a substitute declaring that, if Washington had not declined, the

[1] Journal, H.D. (1796), 46–47; MS. Archives, Va. St. Lib.

people would have reëlected him; that his whole life had been "strongly marked by wisdom, valor, and patriotism"; that "posterity to the most remote generations and the friends of true and genuine liberty and of the rights of man throughout the world, and in all succeeding ages, will unite" in acclaiming "that you have never ceased to deserve well of your country"; that Washington's "valor and wisdom . . . had essentially contributed to establish and maintain the happiness and prosperity of the nation." [1]

But the Republicans would have none of it. After an acrid debate and in spite of personal appeals made to the members of the House, the substitute was defeated by a majority of three votes. John Marshall was the busiest and most persistent of Washington's friends, and of course voted for the substitute,[2] which, almost certainly, he drew. Cold as was the original address which the Federalists had failed to amend, the Republicans now made it still more frigid. They would not admit that Washington deserved well of the whole country. They moved to strike out the word "country" and in lieu thereof insert "native state." [3]

Many years afterward Marshall told Justice Story his recollection of this bitter fight: "In the session of 1796 . . . which," said Marshall, "called forth all

[1] Journal, H.D. (1796), 153; MS. Archives, Va. St. Lib.   [2] *Ib.*

[3] *Ib.* This amendment is historically important for another reason. It is the first time that the Virginia Legislature refers to that Commonwealth as a "State" in contra-distinction to the country. Although the Journal shows that this important motion was passed, the manuscript draft of the resolution signed by the presiding officer of both Houses does not show the change. (MS. Archives, Va. St. Lib.)

the strength and violence of party, some Federalist moved a resolution expressing the high confidence of the House in the virtue, patriotism, and wisdom of the President of the United States. A motion was made to strike out the word *wisdom*. In the debate the whole course of the Administration was reviewed, and the whole talent of each party was brought into action. Will it be believed that the word was retained by a very small majority? A very small majority in the legislature of Virginia acknowledged the wisdom of General Washington!" [1]

Dazed for a moment, the Federalists did not resist. But, their courage quickly returning, they moved a brief amendment of twenty words declaring that Washington's life had been "strongly marked by wisdom, in the cabinet, by valor, in the field, and by the purest patriotism in both." Futile effort! The Republicans would not yield. By a majority of nine votes [2] they flatly declined to declare that Washington had been wise in council, brave in battle, or patriotic in either; and the original address, which, by these repeated refusals to endorse either Washington's sagacity, patriotism, or even courage, had now been made a dagger of ice, was sent to Washington as the final comment of his native

[1] Story, in Dillon, iii, 355. Marshall's account was inaccurate, as we have seen. His memory was confused as to the vote in the two contests (*supra*), a very natural thing after the lapse of twenty years. In the first contest the House of Delegates voted overwhelmingly against including the word "wisdom" in the resolutions; and on the Senate amendment restored it by a dangerously small majority. On the second contest in 1796, when Marshall declares that Washington's friends won "by a very small majority," they were actually defeated.

[2] Journal, H.D., 153–90.

State upon his lifetime of unbearable suffering and incalculable service to the Nation.

Arctic as was this sentiment of the Virginia Republicans for Washington, it was tropical compared with the feeling of the Republican Party toward the old hero as he retired from the Presidency. On Monday, March 5, 1797, the day after Washington's second term expired, the principal Republican newspaper of America thus expressed the popular sentiment: —

"'Lord, now lettest thou thy servant depart in peace, for mine eyes have seen thy salvation,' was the pious ejaculation of a man who beheld a flood of happiness rushing in upon mankind. . . .

"If ever there was a time that would license the reiteration of the exclamation, that time is now arrived, for the man [Washington] who is the source of all the misfortunes of our country, is this day reduced to a level with his fellow citizens, and is no longer possessed of power to multiply evils upon the United States.

"If ever there was a period for rejoicing this is the moment — every heart, in unison with the freedom and happiness of the people ought to beat high with exultation, that the name of Washington from this day ceases to give a currency to political iniquity, and to legalize corruption. . . .

"A new æra is now opening upon us, an æra which promises much to the people; for public measures must now stand upon their own merits, and nefarious projects can no longer be supported by a name.

"When a retrospect is taken of the Washingtonian

administration for eight years, it is a subject of
the greatest astonishment, that a single individual
should have cankered the principles of republicanism
in an enlightened people, just emerged from the
gulph of despotism, and should have carried his designs against the public liberty so far as to have put
in jeopardy its very existence.

"Such however are the facts, and with these star-
ing us in the face, this day ought to be a JUBILEE
in the United States." [1]

Such was Washington's greeting from a great body
of his fellow citizens when he resumed his private
station among them after almost twenty years of
labor for them in both war and peace. Here rational
imagination must supply what record does not reveal. What must Marshall have thought? Was this
the fruit of such sacrifice for the people's welfare as no
other man in America and few in any land throughout all history had ever made — this rebuke of
Washington — Washington, who had been the soul
as well as the sword of the Revolution; Washington,
who alone had saved the land from anarchy; Washington, whose level sense, far-seeing vision, and
mighty character had so guided the newborn Government that the American people had taken their

---

[1] *Aurora*, Monday, March 5, 1797. This paper, expressing Republican hatred of Washington, had long been assailing him. For
instance, on October 24, 1795, a correspondent, in the course of a
scandalous attack upon the President, said: "The consecrated ermine
of Presidential chastity seems too foul for time itself to bleach."
(See Cobbett, i, 411; and *ib.*, 444, where the *Aurora* is represented
as having said that "Washington has the ostentation of an eastern
bashaw.") From August to September the *Aurora* had accused Washington of peculation. (See "Calm Observer" in *Aurora*, Oct. 23 to
Nov. 5, 1795.)

place as a separate and independent Nation? Could any but this question have been asked by Marshall?

He was not the only man to whom such reflections came. Patrick Henry thus expressed his feelings: "I see with concern our old commander-in-chief most abusively treated — nor are his long and great services remembered. . . . If he, whose character as our leader during the whole war, was above all praise, is so roughly handled in his old age, what may be expected by men of the common standard of character?" [1]

And Jefferson! Had he not become the voice of the majority?

Great as he was, restrained as he had arduously schooled himself to be, Washington personally resented the brutal assaults upon his character with something of the fury of his unbridled youth: "I had no conception that parties would or even could go to the length I have been witness to; nor did I believe, until lately, that it was within the bounds of probability — hardly within those of possibility — that . . . every act of my administration would be tortured and the grossest and most insidious misrepresentations of them be made . . . and that too in such exaggerated and indecent terms as could scarcely be applied to a Nero — a notorious defaulter — or even to a common pickpocket." [2]

[1] Henry to his daughter, Aug. 20, 1796; Henry, ii, 569-70. Henry was now an enemy of Jefferson and his dislike was heartily reciprocated.

[2] Washington to Jefferson, July 6, 1796; *Writings:* Ford, xiii, 230-31. This letter is in answer to a letter from Jefferson denying responsibility for the publication of a Cabinet paper in the *Aurora.* (Jefferson to Washington, June 19, 1796; *Works:* Ford, viii, 245; and

Here, then, once more, we clearly trace the development of that antipathy between Marshall and Jefferson, the seeds of which were sown in those desolating years from 1776 to 1780, and in the not less trying period from the close of the Revolution to the end of Washington's Administration. Thus does circumstance mould opinion and career far more than abstract thinking; and emotion quite as much as reason shape systems of government. The personal feud between Marshall and Jefferson, growing through the years and nourished by events, gave force and speed to their progress along highways which, starting at the same point, gradually diverged and finally ran in opposite directions.

see Marshall, ii, 390–91.) Even in Congress Washington did not escape. In the debate over the last address of the National Legislature to the President, Giles of Virginia declared that Washington had been "neither wise nor firm." He did not think "so much of the President." He "wished him to retire . . . the government of the United States could go on very well without him." (*Annals*, 4th Cong., 2d Sess. (Dec. 14, 1796), 1614–18.) On the three roll-calls and passage of the address Giles voted against Washington. (*Ib.*, 1666–68.) So did Andrew Jackson, a new member from Tennessee. (*Ib.*)

The unpopularity of Washington's Administration led to the hostile policy of Bache's paper, largely as a matter of business. This provident editor became fiercely "Republican" because, as he explained to his relative, Temple Franklin, in England, he "could not [otherwise] maintain his family," and "he had determined to adopt a bold experiment and to come out openly against the Administration. He thought the public temper would bear it." (Marshall to Pickering, Feb. 28, 1811, relating the statement of Temple Franklin to James M. Marshall while in England in 1793.)

CHAPTER V.

THE MAN AND THE LAWYER

Tall, meagre, emaciated, his muscles relaxed, his joints loosely connected, his head small, his complexion swarthy, his countenance expressing great good humor and hilarity. (William Wirt.)

Mr. Marshall can hardly be regarded as a learned lawyer. (Gustavus Schmidt.)

His head is one of the best organized of any I have known. (Rufus King.)

ON a pleasant summer morning when the cherries were ripe, a tall, ungainly man in early middle life sauntered along a Richmond street. His long legs were encased in knee breeches, stockings, and shoes of the period; and about his gaunt, bony frame hung a roundabout or short linen jacket. Plainly, he had paid little attention to his attire. He was bareheaded and his unkempt hair was tied behind in a queue. He carried his hat under his arm, and it was full of cherries which the owner was eating as he sauntered idly along.[1] Mr. Epps's hotel (The Eagle) faced the street along which this negligently appareled person was making his leisurely way. He greeted the landlord as he approached, cracked a joke in passing, and rambled on in his unhurried walk.

At the inn was an old gentleman from the country who had come to Richmond where a lawsuit, to which he was a party, was to be tried. The venerable litigant had a hundred dollars to pay to the lawyer who should conduct the case, a very large fee for those

[1] *Southern Literary Messenger*, 1836, ii, 181-91; also see Howe, 266.

days. Who was the best lawyer in Richmond, asked
he of his host? "The man who just passed us, John
Marshall by name," said the tavern-keeper. But
the countryman would have none of Marshall. His
appearance did not fill the old man's idea of a practi-
tioner before the courts. He wanted, for his hundred
dollars, a lawyer who looked like a lawyer. He
would go to the court-room itself and there ask for
further recommendation. But again he was told by
the clerk of the court to retain Marshall, who, meanwhile, had ambled into the court-room.

But no! This searcher for a legal champion would
use his own judgment. Soon a venerable, dignified
person, solemn of face, with black coat and powdered
wig, entered the room. At once the planter retained
him. The client remained in the court-room, it appears, to listen to the lawyers in the other cases that
were ahead of his own. Thus he heard the pompous
advocate whom he had chosen; and then, in astonishment, listened to Marshall.

The attorney of impressive appearance turned out
to be so inferior to the eccentric-looking advocate
that the planter went to Marshall, frankly told him
the circumstances, and apologized. Explaining that
he had but five dollars left, the troubled old farmer
asked Marshall whether he would conduct his case
for that amount. With a kindly jest about the power
of a black coat and a powdered wig, Marshall good-
naturedly accepted.[1]

[1] *Southern Literary Messenger*, ii, 181–91; also Howe, 266. Apparently the older lawyer had been paid the one hundred dollars, for
prepayment was customary in Virginia at the time. (See La Rochefoucauld, iii, 76.) This tale, fairly well authenticated, is so charac-
ter-

This not too highly colored story is justified by all reports of Marshall that have come down to us. It is some such picture that we must keep before us as we follow this astonishing man in the henceforth easy and giant, albeit accidental, strides of his great career. John Marshall, after he had become the leading lawyer of Virginia, and, indeed, throughout his life, was the simple, unaffected man whom the tale describes. Perhaps consciousness of his own strength contributed to his disregard of personal appearance and contempt for studied manners. For Marshall knew that he carried heavier guns than other men. "No one," says Story, who knew him long and intimately, "ever possessed a more entire sense of his own extraordinary talents . . . than he." [1]

Marshall's most careful contemporary observer, William Wirt, tells us that Marshall was "in his person, tall, meagre, emaciated; his muscles relaxed and his joints so loosely connected, as not only to disqualify him, apparently, for any vigorous exertion of body, but to destroy everything like elegance and harmony in his air and movements.

"Indeed, in his whole appearance, and demeanour; dress, attitudes, gesture; sitting, standing, or walking; he is as far removed from the idolized graces of lord Chesterfield, as any other gentleman on earth.

"To continue the portrait; his head and face are small in proportion to his height; his complexion swarthy; the muscles of his face being relaxed; . . .

istic of Marshall that it is important. It visualizes the man as he really was. (See Jefferson's reference, in his letter to Madison, to Marshall's "lax, lounging manners," *supra*, 139.)

[1] Story, in Dillon, iii, 363.

his countenance has a faithful expression of great
good humour and hilarity; while his black eyes —
that unerring index — possess an irradiating spirit
which proclaims the imperial powers of the mind that
sits enthroned within. . . .

"His voice is dry, and hard; his attitude, in his
most effective orations, often extremely awkward;
as it was not unusual for him to stand with his left
foot in advance, while all his gesture proceeded from
his right arm, and consisted merely in a vehement,
perpendicular swing of it from about the elevation
of his head to the bar, behind which he was accustomed to stand." [1]

During all the years of clamorous happenings, from
the great Virginia Convention of 1788 down to the
beginning of Adams's Administration and in the
midst of his own active part in the strenuous politics
of the time, Marshall practiced his profession, although intermittently. However, during the critical
three weeks of plot and plan, debate and oratory in
the famous month of June, 1788, he managed to do
some "law business": while Virginia's Constitutional Convention was in session, he received twenty
fees, most of them of one and two pounds and the
largest from "Col? W. Miles Cary 6.4." He drew
a deed for his fellow member of the Convention,
James Madison, while the Convention was in session, for which he charged his colleague one pound
and four shillings.

But there was no time for card-playing during this
notable month and no whist or backgammon en-

---

[1] Wirt: *The British Spy*, 110–12.

tries appear in Marshall's Account Book. Earlier in the year we find such social expenses as "Card table 5.10 Cards 8/ paper 2/–6" and "expenses and loss at billiards at dif^t times 3" (pounds). In September, 1788, occurs the first entry for professional literature, "Law books 20/–1"; but a more important book purchase was that of "Mazai's book sur les etats unis [1] 18" (shillings), an entry which shows that some of Marshall's family could read French.[2]

Marshall's law practice during this pivotal year was fairly profitable. He thus sums up his earnings and outlay, "Rec^d in the year 1788 1169.05; and expended in year 1788, 515–13–7" which left Marshall more than 653 pounds or about $1960 Virginia currency clear profit for the year.[3]

The following year (1789) he did a little better, his net profit being a trifle over seven hundred pounds, or about $2130 Virginia currency. In 1790 he earned a few shillings more than 1427 pounds and had about $2400 Virginia currency remaining, after paying all expenses. In 1791 he did not do so well, yet he cleared over $2200 Virginia currency. In 1792 his earnings fell off a good deal, yet he earned more than he expended, over 402 pounds (a little more than $1200 Virginia currency).

In 1793 Marshall was slightly more successful, but

[1] Mazzei's *Recherches sur les États-Unis*, published in this year (1788) in four volumes.

[2] Marshall himself could not read French at this time. (See *infra*, chap. VI.)

[3] In this chapter of Marshall's receipts and expenditures all items are from his Account Book, described in vol. I, chap. V, of this work.

his expenses also increased, and he ended this year with a trifle less than 400 pounds clear profit. He makes no summary in 1794, but his Account Book shows that he no more than held his own. This business barometer does not register beyond the end of 1795,[1] and there is no further evidence than the general understanding current in Richmond as to the amount of his earnings after this date. La Rochefoucauld reported in 1797 that "Mr. Marshall does not, from his practice, derive above four or five thousand dollars per annum and not even that sum every year." [2] We may take this as a trustworthy estimate of Marshall's income; for the noble French traveler and student was thorough in his inquiries and took great pains to verify his statements.

In 1789 Marshall bought the tract of land amounting to an entire city "square" of two acres,[3] on which, four years later, he built the comfortable brick residence where he lived, while in Richmond, during the remainder of his life. This house still stands (1916) and is in excellent repair. It contains nine rooms, most of them commodious, and one of them of generous dimensions where Marshall gave the "lawyer dinners" which, later, became so celebrated. This structure was one of a number of the important houses of Richmond.[4] Near by were the residences of Colonel Edward Carrington, Daniel Call, an ex-

---

[1] Marshall's third child, Mary, was born Sept. 17, of this year.

[2] La Rochefoucauld, iii, 75–76.

[3] Records, Henrico County, Virginia, Deed Book, iii, 74.

[4] In 1911 the City Council of Richmond presented this house to the Association for the Preservation of Virginia Antiquities, which now owns and occupies it.

cellent lawyer, and George Fisher, a wealthy merchant; these men had married the three sisters of
Marshall's wife. The house of Jacquelin Ambler was
also one of this cluster of dwellings. So that Marshall
was in daily association with four men to whom he
was related by marriage, a not negligible circumstance; for every one of them was a strong and successful man, and all of them were, like Marshall,
pronounced Federalists. Their views and tastes were
the same, they mutually aided and supported one
another; and Marshall was, of course, the favorite
of this unusual family group.

In the same locality lived the Leighs, Wickhams,
Ronalds, and others, who, with those just mentioned,
formed the intellectual and social aristocracy of the
little city.[1] Richmond grew rapidly during the first
two decades that Marshall lived there. From the vil-
lage of a few hundred people abiding in small wooden
houses, in 1783, the Capital became, in 1795, a vigorous town of six thousand inhabitants, dwelling mostly
in attractive brick residences.[2] This architectural
transformation was occasioned by a fire which, in
1787, destroyed most of the buildings in Richmond.[3]
Business kept pace with the growth of the city,
wealth gradually and healthfully accumulated, and
the comforts of life appeared. Marshall steadily
wove his activities into those of the developing Virginia metropolis and his prosperity increased in
moderate and normal fashion.

[1] Mordecai, 63–70; and *ib.*, chap. vii.

[2] La Rochefoucauld, iii, 63. Negroes made up one third of the
population.

[3] *Ib.*, 64; also Christian, 30.

JOHN MARSHALL'S HOUSE, RICHMOND

THE LARGE ROOM WHERE THE FAMOUS "LAWYERS' DINNERS"
WERE GIVEN

In his personal business affairs Marshall showed a childlike faith in human nature which sometimes worked to his disadvantage. For instance, in 1790 he bought a considerable tract of land in Buckingham County, which was heavily encumbered by a deed of trust to secure "a debt of a former owner" of the land to Caron de Beaumarchais.[1] Marshall knew of this mortgage "at the time of the purchase, but he felt no concern . . . because" the seller verbally "promised to pay the debt and relieve the land from the incumbrance."

So he made the payments through a series of years, in spite of the fact that Beaumarchais's mortgage remained unsatisfied, that Marshall urged its discharge, and, finally, that disputes concerning it arose. Perhaps the fact that he was the attorney of the Frenchman in important litigation quieted apprehension. Beaumarchais having died, his agent, unable to collect the debt, was about to sell the land under the trust deed, unless Marshall would pay the obligation it secured. Thus, thirteen years after this improvident transaction, Marshall was forced to take the absurd tangle into a court of equity.[2]

But he was as careful of matters entrusted to him by others as this land transaction would suggest

[1] This celebrated French playwright and adventurer is soon to appear again at a dramatic moment of Marshall's life. (See *infra*, chaps. VI to VIII.)

[2] Marshall's bill in equity in the "High Court of Chancery sitting in Richmond," January 1, 1803; Chamberlin MSS., Boston Public Library. Marshall, then Chief Justice, personally drew this bill. After the Fairfax transaction, he seems to have left to his brother and partner, James M. Marshall, the practical handling of his business affairs.

that he was negligent of his own affairs. Especially was he in demand, it would seem, when an enterprise was to be launched which required public confidence for its success. For instance, the subscribers to a fire insurance company appointed him on the committee to examine the proposed plan of business and to petition the Legislature for a charter,[1] which was granted under the name of the "Mutual Assurance Society of Virginia." [2] Thus Marshall was a founder of one of the oldest American fire insurance companies.[3] Again, when in 1792 the "Bank of Virginia," a State institution, was organized,[4] Marshall was named as one of the committee to receive and approve subscriptions for stock.[5]

No man could have been more watchful than was Marshall of the welfare of members of his family. At one of the most troubled moments of his life, when greatly distressed by combined business and political complications,[6] he notes a love affair of his sister and, unasked, carefully reviews the eligibility of her suitor. Writing to his brother James on business and politics, he says: —

"I understand that my sister Jane, while here [Richmond], was addressed by Major Taylor and that his addresses were encouraged by her. I am not by any means certain of the fact nor did I suspect

[1] Memorial of William F. Ast and others; MS. Archives, Va. St. Lib.

[2] Christian, 46.

[3] This company is still doing business in Richmond.

[4] Christian, 46.

[5] The enterprise appears not to have filled the public with investing enthusiasm and no subscriptions to it were received.

[6] See *infra*, chap. x.

it until we had separated the night preceding her departure and consequently I could have no conversation with her concerning it.

"I believe that tho' Major Taylor was attach'd to her, it would probably have had no serious result if Jane had not manifested some partiality for him. This affair embarrasses me a good deal. Major Taylor is a young gentleman of talents and integrity for whom I profess and feel a real friendship. There is no person with whom I should be better pleased if there were not other considerations which ought not to be overlook'd. Mr. Taylor possesses but little if any fortune, he is encumbered with a family, and does not like his profession. Of course he will be as eminent in his profession as his talents entitle him to be. These are facts unknown to my sister but which ought to be known to her.

"Had I conjectured that Mr. Taylor was contemplated in the character of a lover I shou'd certainly have made to her all proper communications. I regret that it was concealed from me. I have a sincere and real affection and esteem for Major Taylor but I think it right in affairs of this sort that the real situation of the parties should be mutually understood. Present me affectionately to my sister." [1]

[1] Marshall to James M. Marshall, April 3, 1799; MS. This was the only one of Marshall's sisters then unmarried. She was twenty years of age at this time and married Major George Keith Taylor within a few months. He was a man of unusual ability and high character and became very successful in his profession. In 1801 he was appointed by President Adams, United States Judge for a Virginia district. (See *infra*, chap. XII.) The union of Mr. Taylor and Jane Marshall turned out to be very happy indeed. (Paxton, 77.)

Compare this letter of Marshall with that of Washington to his niece,

From the beginning of his residence in Richmond, Marshall had been an active member of the Masonic Order. He probably had become a Free Mason while in the Revolutionary army, which abounded in camp lodges. It was due to his efforts as City Recorder of Richmond that a lottery was successfully conducted to raise funds for the building of a Masonic hall in the State Capital in 1785.[1] The following year Marshall was appointed Deputy Grand Master. In 1792 he presided over the Grand Lodge as Grand Master *pro tempore;* and the next year he was chosen as the head of the order in Virginia. He was reëlected as Grand Master in 1794; and presided over the meetings of the Grand Lodge held during 1793 until 1795 inclusive. During the latter year the Masonic hall in Manchester was begun and he assisted in the ceremonies attending the laying of the corner-stone, which bore this inscription: "This stone was laid by the Worshipful Archibald Campbell, Master of the Manchester Lodge of free & accepted Masons Assisted by & in the presence of the Most Worshipful John Marshall Grand Master of Masons to Virginia." [2]

Upon the expiration of his second term in this office, the Grand Lodge "Resolved, that the Grand Lodge are truly sensible of the great attention of our late Grand Master, John Marshall, to the duties of Masonry, and that they entertain an high sense

in which he gives extensive advice on the subject of love and marriage. (Washington to Eleanor Parke Custis, Jan. 16, 1795; *Writings:* Ford, xiii, 29–32.)

[1] Christian, 28.

[2] *Richmond and Manchester Advertiser*, Sept. 24, 1795.

of the wisdom displayed by him in the discharge of the duties of his office; and as a token of their entire approbation of his conduct do direct the Grand Treasurer to procure and present him with an elegant Past Master's jewel." [1]

From 1790 until his election to Congress, nine years later,[2] Marshall argued one hundred and thirteen cases decided by the Court of Appeals of Virginia. Notwithstanding his almost continuous political activity, he appeared, during this time, in practically every important cause heard and determined by the supreme tribunal of the State. Whenever there was more than one attorney for the client who retained Marshall, the latter almost invariably was reserved to make the closing argument. His absorbing mind took in everything said or suggested by counsel who preceded him; and his logic easily marshaled the strongest arguments to support his position and crushed or threw aside as unimportant those advanced against him.

Marshall preferred to close rather than open an argument. He wished to hear all that other counsel might have to say before he spoke himself; for, as has appeared, he was but slightly equipped with legal learning[3] and he informed himself from the knowledge displayed by his adversaries. Even after he had become Chief Justice of the Supreme Court of the United States and throughout his long and epochal occupancy of that high place, Marshall

---

[1] *Proceedings* of the M. W. Grand Lodge of Ancient York Masons of the State of Virginia, from 1778 to 1822, by John Dove, i, 144; see also 121, 139.

[2] See *infra*, chap. x.   [3] See vol. i, chap. v, of this work.

showed this same peculiarity which was so prominent in his practice at the bar.

Every contemporary student of Marshall's method
and equipment notes the meagerness of his learning
in the law. "Everyone has heard of the gigantick
abilities of John Marshall; as a most able and profound reasoner he deserves all the praise which has
been lavished upon him," writes Francis Walker
Gilmer, in his keen and brilliant contemporary
analysis of Marshall. "His mind is not very richly
stored with knowledge," he continues, "but it is so
creative, so well organized by nature, or disciplined
by early education, and constant habits of syste-
matick thinking, that he embraces every subject
with the clearness and facility of one prepared by
previous study to comprehend and explain it." [1]

Gustavus Schmidt, who was a competent critic
of legal attainments and whose study of Marshall
as a lawyer was painstaking and thorough, bears
witness to Marshall's scanty acquirements. "Mr.
Marshall," says Schmidt, "can hardly be regarded
as a learned lawyer. . . . His acquaintance with the
Roman jurisprudence as well as with the laws of
foreign countries was not very extensive. He was
what is called a common law lawyer in the best &
noblest acceptation of that term."

Mr. Schmidt attempts to excuse Marshall's want
of those legal weapons which knowledge of the books
supply.

"He was educated for the bar," writes Schmidt,
"at a period when digests, abridgments & all the

[1] Gilmer, 23-24.

numerous facilities, which now smooth the path of
the law student were almost unknown & when you
often sought in vain in the Reporters which usually
wore the imposing form of folios, even for an index
of the decisions & when marginal notes of the points
determined in a case was a luxury not to be either
looked for or expected.

"At this period when the principles of the Common Law had to be studied in the black-letter pages
of Coke upon Littleton, a work equally remarkable
for quaintness of expression, profundity of research
and the absence of all method in the arrangements of
its very valuable materials; when the rules of pleading had to be looked for in Chief Justice Saunders's
Reports, while the doctrinal parts of the jurisprudence, based almost exclusively on the precedents
had to be sought after in the reports of Dyer, Plow-
den, Coke, Popham. . . . it was . . . no easy task to
become an able lawyer & it required no common
share of industry and perseverance to amass sufficient knowledge of the law to make even a decent
appearance in the forum." [1]

It would not be strange, therefore, if Marshall did
cite very few authorities in the scores of cases argued
by him. But it seems certain that he would not have
relied upon the "learning of the law" in any event;
for at a later period, when precedents were more
abundant and accessible, he still ignored them.
Even in these early years other counsel exhibited
the results of much research; but not so Marshall.
In most of his arguments, as reported in volumes one,

[1] Gustavus Schmidt, in *Louisiana Law Journal* (1841), 81–82.

two, and four of Call's Virginia Reports and in volumes one and two of Washington's Virginia Reports,[1] he depended on no authority whatever. Frequently when the arguments of his associates and of opposing counsel show that they had explored the whole field of legal learning on the subject in hand, Marshall referred to no precedent.[2] The strongest feature of his argument was his statement of the case.

The multitude of cases which Marshall argued before the General Court of Appeals and before the High Court of Chancery at Richmond covered every possible subject of litigation at that time. He lost almost as frequently as he won. Out of one hundred and twenty-one cases reported, Marshall was on the winning side sixty-two times and on the losing side fifty times. In two cases he was partly successful and partly unsuccessful, and in seven it is impossible to tell from the reports what the outcome was.

Once Marshall appeared for clients whose cause was so weak that the court decided against him on his own argument, refusing to hear opposing counsel.[3] He was extremely frank and honest with the

---

[1] For a list of cases argued by Marshall and reported in Call and Washington, with title of case, date, volume, and page, see Appendix I.

[2] A good illustration of a brilliant display of legal learning by associate and opposing counsel, and Marshall's distaste for authorities when he could do without them, is the curious and interesting case of Coleman *vs.* Dick and Pat, decided in 1793, and reported in 1 Washington, 233. Wickham for appellant and Campbell for appellee cited ancient laws and treaties as far back as 1662. Marshall cited no authority whatever.

[3] See Stevens *vs.* Taliaferro, Adm'r, 1 Washington, 155, Spring Term, 1793.

court, and on one occasion went so far as to say that the opposing counsel was in the right and himself in the wrong.[1] "My own opinion," he admitted to the court in this case, "is that the law is correctly stated by Mr. Ronald [the opposing counsel], but the point has been otherwise determined in the General Court." Marshall, of course, lost.[2]

Nearly all the cases in which Marshall was engaged concerned property rights. Only three or four of the controversies in which he took part involved criminal law. A considerable part of the litigation in which he was employed was intricate and involved; and in this class of cases his lucid and orderly mind made him the intellectual master of the contending lawyers. Marshall's ability to extract from the confusion of the most involved question its vital elements and to state those elements in simple terms was helpful to the court, and frankly appreciated by the judges.

Few letters of Marshall to his fellow lawyers written during this period are extant. Most of these are very brief and confined strictly to the particular cases which he had been retained by his associate attorneys throughout Virginia to conduct before the Court of Appeals. Occasionally, however, his humor breaks forth.

"I cannot appear for Donaghoe," writes Marshall to a country member of the bar who lived in the Valley over the mountains. "I do not decline his business from any objection to his *bank*. To that I should like very well to have free access & wou'd certainly

---

[1] Johnson *vs.* Bourn, 1 Washington, 187, Spring Term, 1793. [2] *Ib.*

discount *from* it as largely as he wou'd permit, but I am already fixed by Rankin & as those who are once in the bank do not I am told readily get out again I despair of being ever able to touch the guineas of Donaghoe.

"Shall we never see you again in Richmond? I was very much rejoiced when I heard that you were happily married but if that amounts to a ne exeat which is to confine you entirely to your side of the mountain, I shall be selfish enough to regret your good fortune & almost wish you had found some little crooked rib among the fish and oysters which would once a year drag you into this part of our terraqueous globe.

"You have forgotten I believe the solemn compact we made to take a journey to Philadelphia together this winter and superintend for a while the proceedings of Congress."[1]

Again, writing to Stuart concerning a libel suit, Marshall says: "Whether the truth of the libel may be justified or not is a perfectly unsettled question. If in that respect the law here varies from the law of England it must be because such is the will of their Honors for I know of no legislative act to vary it. It will however be right to appeal was it only to secure a compromise."[2]

Marshall's sociableness and love of play made him the leader of the Barbecue Club, consisting of thirty of the most agreeable of the prominent men in Richmond. Membership in this club was eagerly

[1] Marshall to Archibald Stuart, March 27, 1794; MS., Va. Hist. Soc.
[2] *Ib.*, May 28, 1794.

sought and difficult to secure, two negatives being sufficient to reject a candidate. Meetings were held each Saturday, in pleasant weather, at "the springs" on the farm of Mr. Buchanan, the Episcopal clergyman. There a generous meal was served and games played, quoits being the favorite sport. One such occasion of which there is a trustworthy account shows the humor, the wit, and the good-fellowship of Marshall.

He welcomed the invited guests, Messrs. Blair and Buchanan, the famous "Two Parsons" of Richmond, and then announced that a fine of a basket of champagne, imposed on two members for talking politics at a previous meeting of the club, had been paid and that the wine was at hand. It was drunk from tumblers and the Presbyterian minister joked about the danger of those who "drank from tumblers *on* the table becoming tumblers *under* the table." Marshall challenged "Parson" Blair to a game of quoits, each selecting four partners. His quoits were big, rough, heavy iron affairs that nobody else could throw, those of the other players being smaller and of polished brass. Marshall rang the meg and Blair threw his quoit directly over that of his opponent. Loud were the cries of applause and a great controversy arose as to which player had won. The decision was left to the club with the understanding that when the question was determined they should "crack another bottle of champagne."

Marshall argued his own case with great solemnity and elaboration. The one first ringing the meg must be deemed the winner, unless his adversary knocked

off the first quoit and put his own in its place. This
required perfection, which Blair did not possess.
Blair claimed to have won by being on top of Marshall; but suppose he tried to reach heaven "by riding on my back," asked Marshall. "I fear that from
my many backslidings and deficiencies, he may be
badly disappointed." Blair's method was like playing leap frog, said he. And did anybody play backgammon in that way? Also there was the ancient
legal maxim, "*Cujus est solum, ejus est usque ad
cœlum*": being "the first occupant his right extended
from the ground up to the vault of heaven and no one
had a right to become a squatter on his back." If
Blair had any claim "he must obtain a writ of eject-
ment or drive him [Marshall] from his position *vi et
armis*." Marshall then cited the boys' game of
marbles and, by analogy, proved that he had won
and should be given the verdict of the club.

Wickham argued at length that the judgment of
the club should be that "where two adversary quoits
are on the same meg, neither is victorious." Marshall's quoit was so big and heavy that no ordinary
quoit could move it and "no rule requires an impos-
sibility." As to Marshall's insinuation that Blair
was trying to reach "Elysium by mounting on his
back," it was plain to the club that such was not the
parson's intention, but that he meant only to get a
more elevated view of earthly things. Also Blair, by
"riding on that pinnacle," will be apt to arrive in
time at the upper round of the ladder of fame. The
legal maxim cited by Marshall was really against his
claim, since the ground belonged to Mr. Buchanan

and Marshall was as much of a "squatter" as Blair was. "The first squatter was no better than the second." And why did Marshall talk of ejecting him by force of arms? Everybody knew that "parsons are men of peace and do not vanquish their antagonists *vi et armis*. We do not deserve to prolong this riding on Mr. Marshall's back; he is too much of a *Rosinante* to make the ride agreeable." The club declined to consider seriously Marshall's comparison of the manly game of quoits with the boys' game of marbles, for had not one of the clergymen present preached a sermon on "marvel not"? There was no analogy to quoits in Marshall's citation of leap frog nor of backgammon; and Wickham closed, amid the cheers of the club, by pointing out the difference between quoits and leap frog.

The club voted with impressive gravity, taking care to make the vote as even as possible and finally determined that the disputed throw was a draw. The game was resumed and Marshall won.[1]

Such were Marshall's diversions when an attorney at Richmond. His "lawyer dinners" at his house,[2] his card playing at Farmicola's tavern, his quoit-throwing and pleasant foolery at the Barbecue Club, and other similar amusements which served to take his mind from the grave problems on which, at other times, it was constantly working, were continued, as we shall see, and with increasing zest, after he became the world's leading jurist-statesman of his time. But neither as lawyer nor judge did these wholesome frivolities interfere with his serious work.

[1] Munford, 326-38.   [2] See vol. III of this work.

Marshall's first case of nation-wide interest, in which his argument gave him fame among lawyers throughout the country, was the historic controversy over the British debts. When Congress enacted the Judiciary Law of 1789 and the National Courts were established, British creditors at once began action to recover their long overdue debts. During the Revolution, other States as well as Virginia had passed laws confiscating the debts which their citizens owed British subjects and sequestering British property.

Under these laws, debtors could cancel their obligations in several ways. The Treaty of Peace between the United States and Great Britain provided, among other things, that "It is agreed that creditors on either side shall meet with no legal impediments to the recovery of the full value in sterling money of all bona fide debts heretofore contracted." The Constitution provided that "All treaties made, or which shall be made, under the authority of the United States, shall be the supreme law of the land; and the judges in every State shall be bound thereby, anything in the Constitution or laws of any State to the contrary notwithstanding," [1] and that "The judicial power shall extend to all cases in law and equity arising under this Constitution, the laws of the United States, and treaties made, or which shall be made, under their authority; to all cases . . . between a State, or the citizens thereof, and foreign States citizens, or subjects." [2]

Thus the case of Ware, Administrator, *vs.* Hylton

---

[1] Constitution of the United States, article vi.
[2] *Ib.*, article iii, section 2.

et al., which involved the validity of a State law in conflict with a treaty, attracted the attention of the whole country when finally it reached the Supreme Court. The question in that celebrated controversy was whether a State law, suspending the collection of a debt due to a subject of Great Britain, was valid as against the treaty which provided that no "legal impediment" should prevent the recovery of the obligation.

Ware *vs.* Hylton was a test case; and its decision involved immense sums of money. Large numbers of creditors who had sought to cancel their debts under the confiscation laws were vitally interested. Marshall, in this case, made the notable argument that carried his reputation as a lawyer beyond Virginia and won for him the admiration of the ablest men at the bar, regardless of their opinion of the merits of the controversy.

It is an example of "the irony of fate" that in this historic legal contest Marshall supported the theory which he had opposed throughout his public career thus far, and to demolish which his entire after life was given. More remarkable still, his efforts for his clients were opposed to his own interests; for, had he succeeded for those who employed him, he would have wrecked the only considerable business transaction in which he ever engaged.[1] He was employed by the debtors to uphold those laws of Virginia which sequestered British property and prevented the collection of the British debts; and he put forth all his power in this behalf.

[1] The Fairfax deal; see *infra,* 203 *et seq.*

Three such cases were pending in Virginia; and these were heard twice by the National Court in Richmond as a consolidated cause, the real issue being the same in all. The second hearing was during the May Term of 1793 before Chief Justice Jay, Justice Iredell of the Supreme Court, and Judge Griffin of the United States District Court. The attorneys for the British creditors were William Ronald, John Baker, John Stark, and John Wickham. For the defendants were Alexander Campbell, James Innes, Patrick Henry, and John Marshall. Thus we see Marshall, when thirty-six years of age, after ten years of practice at the Richmond bar, interrupted as those years were by politics and legislative activities, one of the group of lawyers who, for power, brilliancy, and learning, were unsurpassed in America.

The argument at the Richmond hearing was a brilliant display of eloquence, reasoning, and erudition, and, among lawyers, its repute has reached even to the present day. Counsel on both sides exerted every ounce of their strength. When Patrick Henry had finished his appeal, Justice Iredell was so overcome that he cried, "Gracious God! He is an orator indeed!" [1] The Countess of Huntingdon, who was then in Richmond and heard the arguments of all the attorneys, declared: "If every one had spoken in Westminster Hall, they would have been honored with a peerage." [2]

In his formal opinion, Justice Iredell thus expressed his admiration: "The cause has been spoken to, at the bar, with a degree of ability equal to any

---

[1] Henry, ii, 475.   [2] Howe, 221-22.

occasion. . . . I shall as long as I live, remember with pleasure and respect the arguments which I have heard on this case: they have discovered an ingenuity, a depth of investigation, and a power of reasoning fully equal to anything I have ever witnessed. . . . Fatigue has given way under its influence; the heart has been warmed, while the understanding has been instructed." [1]

Marshall's argument before the District Court of Richmond must have impressed his debtor clients more than that of any other of their distinguished counsel, with the single exception of Alexander Campbell; for when, on appeal to the Supreme Court of the United States, the case came on for hearing in 1796, we find that only Marshall and Campbell appeared for the debtors.

It is unfortunate that Marshall's argument before the Supreme Court at Philadelphia is very poorly reported. But inadequate as the report is, it still reveals the peculiar clearness and the compact and simple reasoning which made up the whole of Marshall's method, whether in legal arguments, political speeches, diplomatic letters, or judicial opinions.

Marshall argued that the Virginia law barred the recovery of the debts regardless of the treaty. "It has been conceded," said he, "that independent

[1] 3 Dallas, 256–57, and footnote. In his opinion Justice Iredell decided for the debtors. When the Supreme Court of the United States, of which he was a member, reversed him in Philadelphia, the following year, Justice Iredell, pursuant to a practice then existing, and on the advice of his brother justices, placed his original opinion on record along with those of Justices Chase, Patterson, Wilson, and Cushing, each of whom delivered separate opinions in favor of the British creditors.

nations have, in general, the right to confiscation; and that Virginia, at the time of passing her law, was an independent nation." A State engaged in war has the powers of war, "and confiscation is one of those powers, weakening the party against whom it is employed and strengthening the party that employs it." Nations have equal powers; and, from July 4, 1776, America was as independent a nation as Great Britain. What would have happened if Great Britain had been victorious? "Sequestration, confiscation, and proscription would have followed in the train of that event," asserted Marshall.

Why, then, he asked, "should the confiscation of British property be deemed less just in the event of an American triumph?" Property and its disposition is not a natural right, but the "creature of civil society, and subject in all respects to the disposition and control of civil institutions." Even if "an individual has not the power of extinguishing his debts," still "the community to which he belongs . . . may . . . upon principles of public policy, prevent his creditors from recovering them." The ownership and control of property "is the offspring of the social state; not the incident of a state of nature. But the Revolution did not reduce the inhabitants of America to a state of nature; and if it did, the plaintiff's claim would be at an end." Virginia was within her rights when she confiscated these debts.

As an independent nation Virginia could do as she liked, declared Marshall. Legally, then, at the time of the Treaty of Peace in 1783, "the defendant owed nothing to the plaintiff." Did the treaty revive the debt thus extinguished? No: For the treaty provides "that creditors on either side shall meet with no lawful impediment to the recovery" of their debts. Who are the creditors? "There cannot be a creditor where there is not a debt; and the British debts were extinguished by the act of confiscation," which was entirely legal.

Plainly, then, argued Marshall, the treaty "must be construed with reference to those creditors" whose debts had not been extinguished by the sequestration laws. There were cases of such debts and it was to these only that the treaty applied. The Virginia law must have been known to the commissioners who made the treaty; and it was unthinkable that they should attempt to repeal those laws in the treaty without using plain words to that effect.

Such is an outline of Marshall's argument, as inaccurately and defectively reported.[1]

Cold and dry as it appears in the reporter's notes, Marshall's address to the Supreme Court made a tremendous impression on all who heard it. When he left the court-room, he was followed by admiring crowds. The ablest public men at the Capital were watching Marshall narrowly and these particularly were captivated by his argument. "His head is one of the best organized of any one that I have known," writes the keenly observant King, a year later, in giving to Pinckney his estimate of Marshall. "This I say from general Reputation, and more satisfactorily from an Argument that I heard him de-

[1] For Marshall's argument in the British Debts case before the Supreme Court, see 3 Dallas, 199–285.

liver before the fed'l Court at Philadelphia." [1] King's judgment of Marshall's intellectual strength was that generally held.

Marshall's speech had a more enduring effect on those who listened to it than any other address he ever made, excepting that on the Jonathan Robins case. [2] Twenty-four years afterwards William Wirt, then at the summit of his brilliant career, advising Francis Gilmer upon the art of oratory, recalled Marshall's argument in the British Debts case as an example for Gilmer to follow. Wirt thus contrasts Marshall's method with that of Campbell on the same occasion: —

"Campbell played off all his Apollonian airs; but they were lost. Marshall spoke, as he always does, to the judgment merely and for the simple purpose of convincing. Marshall was justly pronounced one of the greatest men of the country; he was followed by crowds, looked upon, and courted with every evidence of admiration and respect for the great powers of his mind. Campbell was neglected and slighted, and came home in disgust.

"Marshall's maxim seems always to have been, 'aim exclusively *at Strength:*' and from his eminent success, I say, if I had my life to go over again, I would practice on his maxim with the most rigorous severity, until the character of my mind was established." [3]

[1] King to Pinckney, Oct. 17, 1797; King, ii, 234–35. King refers to the British Debts case, the only one in which Marshall had made an argument before the Supreme Court up to this time.

[2] See *infra*, chap. XI.

[3] Kennedy, ii, 76. Mr. Wirt remembered the argument well; but twenty-four years having elapsed, he had forgotten the case in which

In another letter to Gilmer, Wirt again urges his son-in-law to imitate Marshall's style. In his early career Wirt had suffered in his own arguments from too much adornment which detracted from the real solidity and careful learning of his efforts at the bar. And when, finally, in his old age he had, through his own mistakes, learned the value of simplicity in statement and clear logic in argument, he counseled young Gilmer accordingly.

"In your arguments at the bar," he writes, "*let argument strongly predominate*. Sacrifice your flowers. . . . Avoid as you would the gates of death, the reputation for floridity. . . . Imitate . . . Marshall's simple process of reasoning." [1]

Following the advice of his distinguished father-in-law, Gilmer studied Marshall with the hungry zeal of ambitious youth. Thus it is that to Francis Gilmer we owe what is perhaps the truest analysis, made by a personal observer, of Marshall's method as advocate and orator.

"So perfect is his analysis," records Gilmer, "that he extracts the whole matter, the kernel of the inquiry, unbroken, undivided, clean and entire. In this process, such is the instinctive neatness and precision of his mind that no superfluous thought, or even word, ever presents itself and still

it was made. He says that it was the Carriage Tax case and that Hamilton was one of the attorneys. But it was the British Debts case and Hamilton's name does not appear in the records.

[1] Kennedy, ii, 66. Francis W. Gilmer was then the most brilliant young lawyer in Virginia. His health became too frail for the hard work of the law; and his early death was universally mourned as the going out of the brightest light among the young men of the Old Dominion.

he says everything that seems appropriate to the subject.

"This perfect exemption from any unnecessary encumbrance of matter or ornament, is in some degree the effect of an aversion for the labour of thinking. So great a mind, perhaps, like large bodies in the physical world, is with difficulty set in motion. That this is the case with Mr. Marshall's is manifest, from his mode of entering on an argument both in conversation and in publick debate.

"It is difficult to rouse his faculties; he begins with reluctance, hesitation, and vacancy of eye; presently his articulation becomes less broken, his eye more fixed, until finally, his voice is full, clear, and rapid, his manner bold, and his whole face lighted up, with the mingled fires of genius and passion; and he pours forth the unbroken stream of eloquence, in a current deep, majestick, smooth, and strong.

"He reminds one of some great bird, which flounders and flounces on the earth for a while before it acquires the impetus to sustain its soaring flight.

"The characteristick of his eloquence is an irresistible cogency, and a luminous simplicity in the order of his reasoning. His arguments are remarkable for their separate and independent strength, and for the solid, compact, impenetrable order in which they are arrayed.

"He certainly possesses in an eminent degree the power which had been ascribed to him, of mastering the most complicated subjects with facility, and when moving with his full momentum, even without the appearance of resistance."

Comparing Marshall and Randolph, Gilmer says:—

"The powers of these two gentlemen are strikingly contrasted by nature. In Mr. Marshall's speeches, all is reasoning; in Mr. Randolph's everything is declamation. The former scarcely uses a figure; the latter hardly an abstraction. One is awkward; the other graceful.

"One is indifferent as to his words, and slovenly in his pronunciation; the other adapts his phrases to the sense with poetick felicity; his voice to the sound with musical exactness.

"There is no breach in the train of Mr. Marshall's thoughts; little connection between Mr. Randolph's. Each has his separate excellence, but either is far from being a finished orator." [1]

Another invaluable first-hand analysis of Marshall's style and manner of argument is that of William Wirt, himself, in the vivacious descriptions of "The British Spy": —

"He possesses one original, and, almost supernatural faculty, the faculty of developing a subject by a single glance of his mind, and detecting at once, the very point on which every controversy depends. No matter what the question; though ten times more knotty than 'the gnarled oak,' the lightning of heaven is not more rapid nor more resistless, than his astonishing penetration.

"Nor does the exercise of it seem to cost him an effort. On the contrary, it is as easy as vision. I am persuaded that his eye does not fly over a landscape and take in its various objects with more prompti-

---

[1] Gilmer, 23–24.

tude and facility, than his mind embraces and analyses the most complex subject.

"Possessing while at the bar this intellectual elevation, which enabled him to look down and comprehend the whole ground at once, he determined immediately and without difficulty, on which side the question might be most advantageously approached and assailed.

"In a bad cause his art consisted in laying his premises so remotely from the point directly in debate, or else in terms so general and so spacious, that the hearer, seeing no consequence which could be drawn from them, was just as willing to admit them as not; but his premises once admitted, the demonstration, however distant, followed as certainly, as cogently, as inevitably, as any demonstration in Euclid." [1]

Marshall's supremacy, now unchallenged, at the Virginia bar was noted by foreign observers. La Rochefoucauld testifies to this in his exhaustive volumes of travel: —

"Mr. J. Marshall, conspicuously eminent as a professor of the law, is beyond all doubt one of those who rank highest in the public opinion at Richmond. He is what is termed a federalist, and perhaps somewhat warm in support of his opinions, but never exceeding the bounds of propriety, which a man of his goodness and prudence and knowledge is incapable of transgressing.

"He may be considered as a distinguished character in the United States. His political enemies

[1] Wirt: *The British Spy*, 112-13.

allow him to possess great talents but accuse him of ambition. I know not whether the charge be well or ill grounded, or whether that ambition might ever be able to impel him to a dereliction of his principles — a conduct of which I am inclined to disbelieve the possibility on his part.

"He has already refused several employments under the general government, preferring the income derived from his professional labours (which is more than sufficient for his moderate system of economy), together with a life of tranquil ease in the midst of his family and in his native town.

"Even by his friends he is taxed with some little propensity to indolence; but even if this reproach were well founded, he nevertheless displays great superiority in his profession when he applies his mind to business." [1]

When Jefferson foresaw Marshall's permanent transfer to public life he advised James Monroe to practice law in Richmond because "the business is very profitable; [2] . . . and an opening of great importance must be made by the retirement of Marshall." [3]

[1] La Rochefoucauld, iii, 120. Doubtless La Rochefoucauld would have arrived at the above conclusion in any event, since his estimate of Marshall is borne out by every contemporary observer; but it is worthy of note that the Frenchman while in Richmond spent much of his time in Marshall's company. (*Ib.*, 119.)

[2] *Ib.*, 75. "The profession of a lawyer is . . . one of the most profitable. . . . In Virginia the lawyers usually take care to insist on payment before they proceed in a suit; and this custom is justified by the general disposition of the inhabitants to pay as little and as seldom as possible."

[3] Jefferson to Monroe, Feb. 8, 1798; *Works:* Ford, viii, 365. Marshall was in France at the time. (See *infra*, chaps. VI to VIII inclusive.)

Marshall's solid and brilliant performance in the British Debts case before the Supreme Court at Philadelphia did much more than advance him in his profession. It also focused upon him the keen scrutiny of the politicians and statesmen who at that time were in attendance upon Congress in the Quaker City. Particularly did the strength and personality of the Virginia advocate impress the Federalist leaders.

These vigilant men had learned of Marshall's daring championship of the Jay Treaty in hostile Virginia. And although in the case of Ware *vs.* Hylton, Marshall was doing his utmost as a lawyer before the Supreme Court to defeat the collection of the British debts, yet his courageous advocacy of the Jay Treaty outweighed, in their judgment, his professional labors in behalf of the clients who had employed him.

The Federalist leaders were in sore need of Southern support; and when Marshall was in Philadelphia on the British Debts case, they were prompt and unsparing in their efforts to bind this strong and able man to them by personal ties. Marshall himself unwittingly testifies to this. "I then [during this professional visit to Philadelphia] became acquainted," he relates, "with Mr. Cabot, Mr. Ames, Mr. Dexter, and Mr. Sedgwick of Massachusetts, Mr. Wadsworth of Connecticut, and Mr. King of New York. I was delighted with these gentlemen. The particular subject (the British Treaty) which introduced me to their notice was at that time so interesting, and a Virginian who supported, with any sort of repu-

tation, the measures of the government, was such a
rara avis, that I was received by them all with a
degree of kindness which I had not anticipated. I
was particularly intimate with Mr. Ames, and could
scarcely gain credit with him when I assured him
that the appropriations [to effectuate the treaty]
would be seriously opposed in Congress." [1]

As we shall presently see, Marshall became associated with Robert Morris in the one great business
undertaking of the former's life. Early in this transaction when, for Marshall, the skies were still clear
of financial clouds, he appears to have made a small
purchase of bank stock and ventured modestly into
the commercial field. "I have received your letter
of 18 ulto," Morris writes Marshall, "& am negotiating for Bank Stock to answer your demand." [2]

And again: "I did not succeed in the purchase of
the Bank Stock mentioned in my letter of the 3ᵈ Ulto
to you and as Mʳ Richard tells me in his letter of the
4 Inst that you want the money for the Stock, you
may if you please draw upon me for $7000 giving
me as much time in the sight as you can, and I will
most certainly pay your drafts as they become due.
The Brokers shall fix the price of the Stock at the
market price at the time I pay the money & I will
then state the Amᵗ including Dividends & remit
you the Balance but if you prefer having the Stock

[1] Story, in Dillon, iii, 354. Ware *vs.* Hylton was argued Feb. 6, 8, 9,
10, 11, and 12. The fight against the bill to carry out the Jay Treaty
did not begin in the National House of Representatives until March
7, 1796.

[2] Morris to Marshall, May 3, 1796; Morris's Private Letter Book;
MS., Lib. Cong. The stock referred to in this correspondence is
probably that of the Bank of the United States.

I will buy it on receiving your Answer to this, cost what it may." [1]

Soon afterward, Morris sent Marshall the promised shares of stock, apparently to enable him to return shares to some person in Richmond from whom he had borrowed them.

"You will receive herewith enclosed the Certificates for four shares of Bank Stock of the United States placed in your name to enable you to return the four shares to the Gentlemen of whom you borrowed them, this I thought better than remitting the money lest some difficulty should arise about price of shares. Two other shares in the name of Mr Geo Pickett is also enclosed herewith and I will go on buying and remitting others untill the number of Ten are completed for him which shall be done before the time limited in your letter of the 12^h Ins^t The dividends shall also be remitted speedily." [2]

Again Washington desired Marshall to fill an important public office, this time a place on the joint commission, provided for in the Jay Treaty, to settle the British claims. These, as we have seen, had been for many years a source of grave trouble between the two countries. Their satisfactory adjustment would mean, not only the final settlement of this serious controversy, but the removal of an ever-present cause of war. [3] But since Marshall had re-

[1] Morris to Marshall, June 16, 1796; Morris's Private Letter Book; MS., Lib. Cong.

[2] Morris to Marshall, Aug. 24, 1796; *ib.*

[3] The commission failed and war was narrowly averted by the payment of a lump sum to Great Britain. It is one of the curious turns of

fused appointment to three offices tendered him by
Washington, the President did not now communicate with him directly, but inquired of Charles Lee,
Attorney-General of Virginia, whether Marshall
might be prevailed upon to accept this weighty and
delicate business.

"I have very little doubt," replied Lee, "that
Mr. John Marshall would not act as a Commissioner
under the Treaty with Great Britain, for deciding
on the claims of creditors. I have been long acquainted with his private affairs, and I think it almost impossible for him to undertake that office. If
he would, I know not any objection that subsists
against him.

"First, he is not a debtor.[1] Secondly, he cannot
be benefitted or injured by any decision of the Commissioners. Thirdly, his being employed as counsel,
in suits of that kind, furnishes no reasonable objection; nor do I know of any opinions that he has
published, or professes, that might, with a view of
impartiality, make him liable to be objected to.

"Mr. Marshall is at the head of his profession in
Virginia, enjoying every convenience and comfort;
in the midst of his friends and the relations of his
wife at Richmond; in a practice of his profession
that annually produces about five thousand dollars
on an average; with a young and increasing family;
and under a degree of necessity to continue his pro-

history that Marshall, as Secretary of State, made the proposition that
finally concluded the matter and that Jefferson consummated the
transaction. (See *infra*, chap. XII.)

[1] Lee means a debtor under the commission. Marshall was a debtor
to Fairfax. (See *infra*.)

fession, for the purpose of complying with contracts not yet performed." [1]

The "contracts" which Marshall had to fulfill concerned the one important financial adventure of his life. It was this, and not, as some suppose, the condition of his invalid wife, to which Marshall vaguely referred in his letter to Washington declining appointment as Attorney-General and as Minister to France.

The two decades following the establishment of the National Government under the Constitution were years of enormous land speculation. Hardly a prominent man of the period failed to secure large tracts of real estate, which could be had at absurdly low prices, and to hold the lands for the natural advance which increasing population would bring. The greatest of these investors was Robert Morris, the financier of the Revolution, the second richest man of the time,[2] and the leading business man of the country.

[1] Lee to Washington, March 20, 1796; *Cor. Rev.*: Sparks, iv, 481–82.

[2] William Bingham of Philadelphia was reputed to be "the richest man of his time." (Watson: *Annals of Philadelphia* i. 414.) Chastellux estimates Morris's wealth at the close of the Revolution at 8,000,000 francs. (Chastellux, 107.) He increased his fortune many fold from the close of the war to 1796.

The operations of Robert Morris in land were almost without limit. For instance, one of the smaller items of his purchases was 199,480 acres in Burke County, North Carolina. (Robert Morris to James M. Marshall, Sept. 24, 1795; Morris's Private Letter Book; MS., Lib. Cong.)

Another example of Morris's scattered and detached deals was his purchase of a million acres "lying on the western counties of Virginia . . . purchased of William Cary Nicholas. . . . I do not consider one shilling sterling as one fourth the real value of the lands. . . . If, therefore," writes Morris to James M. Marshall, "a little over £5000 Stg. could be made on this security it would be better than selling especially at 12$^\text{d}$ per acre." (Robert Morris to James M. Marshall, Oct. 10, 1795; *ib.*)

Morris owned at one time or another nearly all of the western half

John Marshall had long been the attorney in Virginia for Robert Morris, who frequently visited that State, sometimes taking his family with him. In all probability, it was upon some such journey that James M. Marshall, the brother of John Marshall, met and became engaged to Hester Morris, daughter of the great speculator, whom he married on April 19, 1795.[1] James M. Marshall — nine years younger than his brother — possessed ability almost equal to John Marshall and wider and more varied accomplishments.[2]

It is likely that the Pennsylvania financier, before the marriage, suggested to the Marshall brothers the purchase of what remained of the Fairfax estate in the Northern Neck, embracing over one hundred and sixty thousand acres of the best land in Virginia.[3] At any rate, sometime during 1793 or 1794 John

of New York State. (See Oberholtzer, 301 *et seq.*) "You knew of Mr. Robert Morris's purchase ... of one million, three hundred thousand acres of land of the State of Massachusetts, at five pence per acre. It is said he has sold one million two hundred thousand acres of these in Europe." (Jefferson to Washington, March 27, 1791; *Cor. Rev.*: Sparks, iv, 365.)

Patrick Henry acquired considerable holdings which helped to make him, toward the end of his life, a wealthy man. Washington, who had a keen eye for land values, became the owner of immense quantities of real estate. In 1788 he already possessed two hundred thousand acres. (De Warville, 243.)

[1] Oberholtzer, 266 *et seq.* Hester Morris, at the time of her marriage to John Marshall's brother, was the second greatest heiress in America.

[2] Grigsby, i, footnote to 150.

[3] Deed of Lieutenant-General Phillip Martin (the Fairfax heir who made the final conveyance) to Rawleigh Colston, John Marshall, and James M. Marshall; Records at Large, Fauquier County (Virginia) Circuit Court, 200 *et seq.* At the time of the contract of purchase, however, the Fairfax estate was supposed to be very much larger than the quantity of land conveyed in this deed. It was considerably reduced before the Marshalls finally secured the title.

Marshall, his brother, James M. Marshall, his
brother-in-law, Rawleigh Colston, and General
Henry Lee contracted for the purchase of this valuable holding.[1] In January of that year James
M. Marshall sailed for England to close the bargain.[2]
The money to buy the Fairfax lands was to be
advanced by Robert Morris, who, partly for this
purpose, sent James M. Marshall to Europe to
negotiate[3] loans, immediately after his marriage
to Hester Morris.

At Amsterdam "some Capitalists proposed to
supply on very hard terms a Sum more than Sufficient to pay Mr. Fairfax," writes Morris, and
James M. Marshall "has my authority to apply the
first Monies he receives on my acco^t to that Payment."[4] By the end of 1796 Morris's over-specula-
tions had gravely impaired his fortune. The old
financier writes pathetically to James M. Marshall:
"I am struggling hard, very hard, indeed to re-
gain my Position." He tells his son-in-law that if a
loan cannot be obtained on his other real estate he
"expects these Washington Lotts will be the most

[1] Lee is mentioned in all contemporary references to this transaction as one of the Marshall syndicate, but his name does not appear
in the Morris correspondence nor in the deed of the Fairfax heir to
the Marshall brothers and Colston.

[2] J^s Marshall to——[Edmund Randolph] Jan. 21, 1794; MS.
Archives Department of State. Marshall speaks of dispatches which
he is carrying to Pinckney, then American Minister to Great Britain.
This letter is incorrectly indexed in the Archives as from John Marshall.
It is signed "J^s Marshall" and is in the handwriting of James M.
Marshall. John Marshall was in Richmond all this year, as his Ac-
count Book shows.

[3] Morris to John Marshall, Nov. 21, 1795; and Aug. 24, 1796;
Morris's Private Letter Book; MS., Lib. Cong.

[4] Morris to Colston, Nov. 11, 1796; ib.

certain of any Property to raise Money on"; and
that "[I] will have a number of them Placed under
your Controul." [1]

The loan failed, for the time being, but, writes
Morris to John Marshall, "Mr. Hottenguer [2] who
first put the thing in motion says it will come on
again" and succeed; "if so, your brother will, of
course, be ready for Mr. Fairfax." Morris is trying,
he says, to raise money from other sources lest that
should fail. "I am here distressed exceedingly in
money matters," continues the harried and aging
speculator "as indeed every body here are but I will
immediately make such exertions as are in my power
to place funds with your brother and I cannot but
hope that his and my exertions will produce the
needful in proper time to prevent mischief." [3]

A month later Morris again writes John Marshall
that he is "extremely anxious & fearing that it [the

---

[1] Robert Morris to James M. Marshall, Dec. 3, 1796; Morris's
Private Letter Book; MS., Lib. Cong. By the expression "Washington Lotts" Morris refers to his immense real estate speculations on the
site of the proposed National Capital. Morris bought more lots in the
newly laid out ' Federal City" than all other purchasers put together.
Seven thousand two hundred and thirty-four lots stood in his name
when the site of Washington was still a primeval forest. (Oberholtzer,
308–12.) Some of these he afterwards transferred to the Marshall
brothers, undoubtedly to make good his engagement to furnish the
money for the Fairfax deal, which his failure prevented him from advancing entirely in cash. (For account of Morris's real estate transactions in Washington see La Rochefoucauld, iii, 622–26.)

[2] This Hottenguer soon appears again in John Marshall's life as
one of Talleyrand's agents who made the corrupt proposals to Marshall, Pinckney, and Gerry, the American Commissioners to France
in the famous X.Y.Z. transaction of 1797–98. (See *infra*, chaps. VI
to VIII.)

[3] Robert Morris to John Marshall, Dec. 30, 1796; Morris's Private
Letter Book; MS., Lib. Cong.

Amsterdam loan] may fall through I am trying to obtain a loan here for the purposes of your Brother in London. This," says the now desperate financier, "is extremely difficult, for those who have money or credit in Europe seem to dread every thing that is American." He assures John Marshall that he will do his utmost. "My anxiety . . . [to make good the Fairfax purchase] is beyond what I can express." Alexander Baring "could supply the money . . . but he parries me. He intends soon for the Southward I will introduce him to you." [1]

The title to the Fairfax estate had been the subject of controversy for many years. Conflicting grants, overlapping boundaries, sequestration laws, the two treaties with Great Britain, were some of the elements that produced confusion and uncertainty in the public mind and especially in the minds of those holding lands within the grant. The only real and threatening clouds upon the title to the lands purchased by the Marshall syndicate, however, were the confiscatory laws passed during the Revolution [2] which the Treaty of Peace and the Jay Treaty nullified. [3] There were also questions growing out of grants made by the colonial authorities between 1730 and 1736, but these were not weighty.

The case of Hunter *vs.* Fairfax, Devisee, involving these questions, was pending in the Supreme Court of the United States. John Marshall went to Phila-

---

[1] Morris to John Marshall, Jan. 23, 1797; Morris's Private Letter Book; MS., Lib. Cong.

[2] Hening, ix, chap. ix, 377 *et seq.*; also *ib.*, x, chap. xiv, 66 *et seq.*; xi, chap. xliv, 75–76; xi, chap. xlv, 176 *et seq.*; xi, chap. xlvii, 81 *et seq.*; xi, chap. xxx, 349 *et seq.*

[3] Such effect of these treaties was not yet conceded, however.

delphia and tried to get the cause advanced and decided. He was sadly disappointed at his failure and so wrote his brother. "Your Brother has been here," writes Morris to his son-in-law, " as you will see by a letter from him forwarded by this conveyance. He could not get your case brought forward in the Supreme Court of the U. S. at which he was much dissatisfied & I am much concerned thereat, fearing that real disadvantage will result to your concern thereby." [1]

The case came on for hearing in regular course during the fall term. Hunter, on the death of his attorney, Alexander Campbell, prayed the Court, by letter, for a continuance, which was granted over the protest of the Fairfax attorneys of record, Lee and Ingersoll of Philadelphia, who argued that "from the nature of the cause, delay would be worse for the defendant in error [the Fairfax heir] than a decision adverse to his claim." The Attorney-General stated that the issue before the Court was "whether . . . the defendant in error being an alien can take and hold the lands by devise. And it will be contended that his title is completely protected by the treaty of peace." Mr. Justice Chase remarked: "I recollect that . . . a decision in favor of such a devisee's title was given by a court in Maryland. It is a matter, however, of great moment and ought to be deliberately and finally settled." [2] The Marshalls, of course, stood in the shoes of the Fairfax devisee; had the Supreme Court decided against the Fairfax title,

---

[1] Morris to James M. Marshall, March 4, 1796; Morris's Private Letter Book; MS., Lib. Cong.

[2] Hunter *vs.* Fairfax, Devisee, 3 Dallas, 303, and footnote.

their contract of purchase would have been nullified and, while they would not have secured the estate, they would have been relieved of the Fairfax indebtedness. It was, then, a very grave matter to the Marshalls, in common with all others deriving their titles from Fairfax, that the question be settled quickly and permanently.

A year or two before this purchase by the Marshalls of what remained of the Fairfax estate, more than two hundred settlers, occupying other parts of it, petitioned the Legislature of Virginia to quiet their titles.[1] Acting on these petitions and influenced, perhaps, by the controversy over the sequestration laws which the Marshall purchase renewed, the Legislature in 1796 passed a resolution proposing to compromise the dispute by the State's relinquishing "all claim to any lands specifically appropriated by . . . Lord Fairfax to his own use either by deed or actual survey . . . if the devises of Lord Fairfax, or those claiming under them, will relinquish all claims to lands . . . which were waste and unappropriated at the time of the death of Lord Fairfax." [2]

Acting for the purchasing syndicate, John Marshall, in a letter to the Speaker of the House, accepted this legislative offer of settlement upon the condition that "an act passes during this session confirming . . . the title of those claiming under Mr. Fairfax the lands specifically appropriated and

[1] Originals in Archives of Virginia State Library. Most of the petitions were by Germans, many of their signatures being in German script. They set forth their sufferings and hardships, their good faith, loss of papers, death of witnesses, etc.

[2] Laws of Virginia, Revised Code (1819), i, 352.

reserved by the late Thomas Lord Fairfax or his ancestors for his or their use." [1]

When advised of what everybody then supposed to be the definitive settlement of this vexed controversy, Robert Morris wrote John Marshall that "altho' you were obliged to give up a part of your claim yet it was probably better to do that than to hold a contest with such an opponent [State of Virginia]. I will give notice to M: Ja: Marshall of this compromise." [2] John Marshall, now sure of the title, and more anxious than ever to consummate the deal by paying the Fairfax heir, hastened to Philadelphia to see Morris about the money.

"Your Brother John Marshall Esq: is now in this City," writes Robert Morris to his son-in-law, "and his principal business I believe is to see how you are provided with Money to pay Lord Fairfax.

---

[1] Laws of Virginia, Revised Code (1819), i, 352. Marshall's letter accepting the proposal of compromise is as follows: —

"RICHMOND, November 24th, 1796.

"SIR, being one of the purchasers of the lands of Mr. Fairfax, and authorized to act for them all, I have considered the resolution of the General Assembly on the petitions of sundry inhabitants of the counties of Hampshire, Hardy, and Shenandoah, and have determined to accede to the proposition it contains.

"So soon as the conveyance shall be transmitted to me from Mr. Fairfax, deeds extinguishing his title to the waste and unappropriated lands in the Northern Neck shall be executed, provided an act passes during this session, confirming, on the execution of such deeds, the title of those claiming under Mr. Fairfax the lands specifically appropriated and reserved by the late Thomas Lord Fairfax, or his ancestors, for his or their use.

"I remain Sir, with much respect and esteem,
              "Your obedient servant,   JOHN MARSHALL.
"The Honorable, the Speaker of the House of Delegates."
(Laws of Virginia.)

[2] Morris to John Marshall, Dec. 30, 1796; Morris's Private Letter Book; MS., Lib. Cong.

. . . I am so sensible of the necessity there is for your being prepared for Lord Fairfax's payment that there is nothing within my power that I would not do to enable you to meet it." [1]

The members of the Marshall syndicate pressed their Philadelphia backer unremittingly, it appears, for a few days later he answers what seems to have been a petulant letter from Colston assuring that partner in the Fairfax transaction that he is doing his utmost to "raise the money to enable Mr. James Marshall to meet the Payments for your Purchase at least so far as it is incumbent on me to supply the means. . . . From the time named by John Marshall Esq[re] when here, I feel perfect Confidence, because I will furnish him before that period with such Resources & aid as I think cannot fail." [2]

Finally Marshall's brother negotiated the loan, an achievement which Morris found "very pleasing, as it enables you to take the first steps with Lord Fairfax for securing your bargain." [3] Nearly forty thousand dollars of this loan was thus applied. In his book of accounts with Morris, James M. Marshall enters: "Jany 25 '97 To £7700 paid the Rev[d] Denny Fairfax and credited in your [Morris's] account with me 7700" (English pounds sterling).[4]

---

[1] Morris to James M. Marshall, Feb. 10, 1797; Morris's Private Letter Book; MS., Lib. Cong. Morris adds that "I mortgaged to Col? Hamilton 100,000 acres of Genesee Lands to secure payment of $75,000 to Mr. Church in five years. This land is worth at this moment in Cash two Dollars pr Acre."

[2] Morris to Colston, Feb. 25, 1797; *ib.*

[3] Morris to James M. Marshall, April 27, 1797; *ib.*

[4] MS. The entry was made in Amsterdam and Morris learned of the loan three months afterwards.

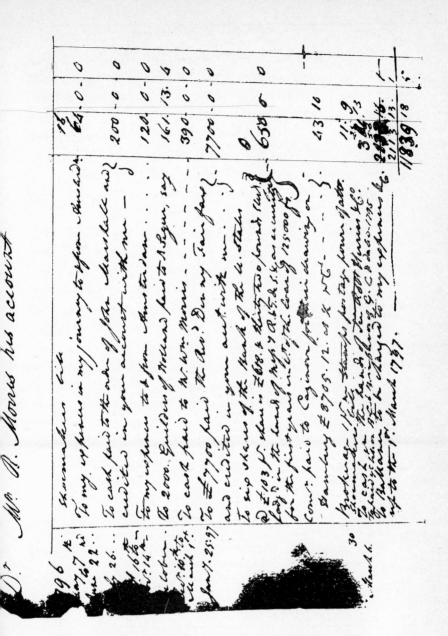

PAGE OF JAMES MARSHALL'S ACCOUNT WITH ROBERT MORRIS
SHOWING PAYMENT OF £7700 TO FAIRFAX
(*Facsimile*)

The total amount which the Marshalls had agreed to pay for the remnant of the Fairfax estate was "fourteen thousand pounds British money." [1] When Robert Morris became bankrupt, payment of the remainder of the Fairfax indebtedness fell on the shoulders of Marshall and his brother.

This financial burden caused Marshall to break his rule of declining office and to accept appointment as one of our envoys to France at the time of Robert Morris's failure and imprisonment for debt; for from that public employment of less than one year, Marshall, as we shall see, received in the sorely needed cash, over and above his expenses, three times the amount of his annual earnings at the bar. [2] "Mr. John Marshall has said here," relates Jefferson after Marshall's return, "that had he not been appointed minister [envoy] to France, he was desperate in his affairs and must have sold his estate [the Fairfax purchase] & that immediately. That that appointment was the greatest God-send that could ever have befallen a man." [3] Jefferson adds: "I have this from J. Brown and S. T. Mason [Senator Mason]." [4]

[1] Records at Large in Clerk's Office of Circuit Court of Fauquier County, Virginia, 200 *et seq.* The deed was not filed until 1806, at which time, undoubtedly, the Marshalls made their last payment.

[2] See *infra*, chap. VIII. It was probably this obligation too, that induced Marshall, a few years later, to undertake the heavy task of writing the *Life of Washington*, quite as much as his passionate devotion to that greatest of Americans. (See vol. III of this work.)

[3] "Anas," March 21, 1800; *Works:* Ford, i, 355.

[4] *Ib.* Misleading as Jefferson's "Anas" is, his information in this matter was indisputably accurate.

So it was that Marshall accepted a place on the mission to France[1] when it was offered to him by

---

[1] See *infra*, chap. vi. A short time before the place on the French mission was tendered Marshall, his father in Kentucky resigned the office of Supervisor of Revenue for the District of Ohio. In his letter of resignation Thomas Marshall gives a résumé of his experiences as an official under Washington's Administrations. Since this is one of the only two existing letters of Marshall's father on political subjects, and because it may have turned Adams's mind to John Marshall, it is worthy of reproduction: —

Sir,

Having determined to resign my Commission as Supervisor of the Revenue for the district of Ohio, on the 30th day of June next, which terminates the present fiscal year, I have thought it right to give this timely notice to you as President of the United States, in whom the nomination and appointment of my successor is vested; in order that you may in the meantime select some fit person to fill the office. You will therefore be pleased to consider me as out of office on the first day of July ensuing.

It may possibly be a subject of enquiry, why, after holding the office during the most critical & troublesome times, I should now resign it, when I am no longer insulted, and abused, for endeavoring to execute the Laws of my Country — when those Laws appear to be, more than formerly, respected — and when the probability is, that in future they may be carried into effect with but little difficulty?

In truth this very change, among other considerations, furnishes a reason for the decision I have made. For having once engaged in the business of revenue I presently found myself of sufficient importance with the enemies of the Government here to be made an object of their particular malevolence — and while this was the case, I was determined not to be driven from my post.

At this time, advanced in years and declining in health, I find myself unfit for the cares, and active duties of the office; and therefore cheerfully resign a situation, which I at first accepted and afterwards held, more from an attachment to the Government, than from any pecuniary consideration, to be filled by some more active officer, as still more conducive to the public service.

To the late President I had the honor of being known, and combined, with respect and veneration for his public character, the more social and ardent affections of the man, and of the friend.

You Sir I have not the honor to know personally, but you have filled too many important stations in the service of your country; & fame has been too busy with your name to permit me to remain ignorant of

Adams, who "by a miracle," as Hamilton said, had been elected President.[1]

your character; for which in all its public relations permit me to say, I feel the most entire respect and esteem: Nor is it to me among the smallest motives for my rejoicing that you are the President; and of my attachment to your administration to know that you have ever been on terms of friendship with the late President — that you have approved his administration, — and that you propose to yourself his conduct as an example for your imitation.

On this occasion I may say without vanity that I have formerly and not infrequently, given ample testimony of my attachment to Republican Government, to the peace, liberty and happiness of my country and that it is not now to be supposed that I have changed my principles — or can esteem those who possess different ones.

And altho' I am too old [Thomas Marshall was nearly sixty-five years of age when he wrote this letter] and infirm for active services, (for which I pray our country may not feel a call) yet my voice shall ever be excited in opposition to foreign influence, (from whence the greatest danger seems to threaten, as well as against internal foes) and in support of a manly, firm, and independent, exercise of those constitutional rights, which belong to the President, and Government of the United States. And, *even opinions*, have their effect.

I am Sir with the most

JOHN ADAMS, ESQ.   entire respect and esteem
President of the   Your very humble Servt,
United States.   T. MARSHALL.

(Thomas Marshall to Adams, April 28, 1797; MS., Dept. of State.)

[1] See *infra*, chaps. XI and XII.

CHAPTER VI

ENVOY TO FRANCE

My dearest life, continue to write to me, as my heart clings with delight only to what comes from you. (Marshall to his wife.)

He is a plain man, very sensible and cautious. (Adams.)

Our poor insulted country has not before it the most flattering prospects. (Marshall at Antwerp.)

"PHILADELPHIA July 2nd 1797.

"MY DEAREST POLLY

"I am here after a passage up the bay from Baltimore . . . I dined on saturday in private with the President whom I found a sensible plain candid good tempered man & was consequently much pleased with him. I am not certain when I shall sail. . . . So you . . . my dearest life continue to write to me as your letters will follow me should I be gone before their arrival & as my heart clings with real pleasure & delight only to what comes from you. I was on friday evening at the faux hall of Philadelphia. . . . The amusements were walking, sitting, punch ice cream etc Music & conversation. . . . Thus my dearest Polly do I when not engaged in the very serious business which employs a large portion of my time endeavor by a-[muse]ments to preserve a mind at ease & [keep] it from brooding too much over my much loved & absent wife. By all that is dear on earth, I entreat you to do the same, for separation will not I trust be long & letters do everything to draw its sting I am my dearest life your affectionate

"J MARSHALL." [1]

[1] Marshall to his wife, July 2, 1797; MS.

My dearest Polly   Philadelphia July 2d 97

I am here after a passage up the bay
from Baltimore which would have been very
unpleasant but for the company of a very
agreable family which greatly alleviated the
vexatious calamity of a dead calm under an
excessive hot suns. I dined on saturday in private
with the President whom I found a sensible
plain candid good tempered man & was con
sequently much pleased with him I am not certain
when I shall sail nor have I yet taken a vessel
but I conjecture it will be early in the next
week. Do you however my dearest life
continue to write to me as your letters will
follow me should I be gone before their arrival
& as my heart clings with real pleasure &
delight only to what comes from you.

FIRST PAGE OF A LETTER FROM JOHN MARSHALL TO HIS WIFE
(*Facsimile*)

So wrote John Marshall at the first stage of his journey upon that critical diplomatic mission which was to prove the most dramatic in our history and which was to be the turning-point in Marshall's life. From the time when Mary Ambler became his bride in 1783, Marshall had never been farther away from his Richmond home than Philadelphia, to which city he had made three flying visits in 1796, one to argue the British Debts case, the other two to see Robert Morris on the Fairfax deal and to hasten the decision of the Supreme Court in that controversy.

But now Marshall was to cross the ocean as one of the American envoys to "the terrible Republic" whose "power and vengeance" everybody dreaded.[1] He was to go to that now arrogant Paris whose streets were resounding with the shouts of French victories. It was the first and the last trans-Atlantic voyage Marshall ever undertook; and although he was to sail into a murky horizon to grapple with vast difficulties and unknown dangers, yet the mind of the home-loving Virginian dwelt more on his Richmond fireside than on the duties and hazards before him.

Three days after his arrival at Philadelphia, impressionable as a boy, he again writes to his wife: "My dearest Polly I have been extremely chagrined at not having yet received a letter from you. I hope you are well as I hear nothing indicating the contrary but you know not how solicitous how anxiously solicitous I am to hear it from yourself. Write me that

[1] Sedgwick to King, June 24, 1797; King, ii, 192.

you are well & in good spirits & I shall set out on my
voyage with a lightened heart . . . you will hear
from me more than once before my departure."

The Virginia envoy was much courted a[...]
delphia before he sailed. "I dined yesterd[...]
shall tells his wife, "in a very large co[...]any of
Senators & members of the house of repr[...]entatives
who met to celebrate the 4th of July. T[...] company
was really a most respectable one & I [...]xperienced
from them the most flattering attent[...]n. I have
much reason to be satisfied & pleas[...]d with the
manner in which I am received here." But flattery
did not soothe Marshall — "Somethi[...]g is wanting
to make me happy," he tells his "[...]arest Polly."
"Had I my dearest wife with me I should be delighted indeed." [1]

Washington had sent letters in Marshall's care
to acquaintances in France com[...]ending him to
their attention and good offices[...] and the retired
President wrote Marshall himsel[...] a letter of hearty
good wishes. "Receive sir," rep[...]es Marshall, "my
warm & grateful acknowledgme[...]ts for the polite &,
allow me to add, friendly wish[...] which you express
concerning myself as well as f[...] the honor of being
mentioned in your letters." [2]

A less composed man, total[...]y unpracticed as Marshall was in diplomatic usag[...]s, when embarking on
an adventure involving wa[...] or peace, would have
occupied himself constantly in preparing for the vast
business before him. Not so Marshall. While waiting

[1] Marshall to his wife, July 5, 1797; MS.
[2] Marshall to Washington, July 7, 1797; MS., Lib. Cong.

for his ship, he indulged his love of the theater. Again he tells his wife how much he misses her. "I cannot avoid writing to you because while doing so I seem to myself to be in some distant degree enjoying your company. I was last night at the play & saw the celebrated Mrs. Mary in the character of Juliet. She performs that part to admiration indeed but I really do not think Mrs. Westig is far her inferior in it. I saw," gossips Marshall, "Mrs. Heyward there. I have paid that lady one visit to one of the most delightful & romantic spots on the river Schuylkil. . . . She expressed much pleasure to see me & has pressed me very much to repeat my visit. I hope I shall not have time to do so."

Marshall is already bored with the social life of Philadelphia. "I am beyond expression impatient to set out on the embassy," he informs his wife. "The life I lead here does not suit me I am weary of it I dine out every day & am now engaged longer I hope than I shall stay. This disipated life does not long suit my temper. I like it very well for a day or two but I begin to require a frugal repast with good cold water" — There was too much wine, it would seem, at Philadelphia to suit Marshall.

"I would give a great deal to dine with you to day on a piece of cold meat with our boys beside us to see Little Mary running backwards & forwards over the floor playing the sweet little tricks she [is] full of. . . . I wish to Heaven the time which must intervene before I can repass these delightful scenes was now terminated & that we were looking back on our separation instead of seeing it before us. Farewell my dearest Polly. Make yourself happy & you will bless your ever affectionate

"J. MARSHALL." [1]

If Marshall was pleased with Adams, the President was equally impressed with his Virginia envoy to France. "He [Marshall] is a plain man very sensible, cautious, guarded, and learned in the law of nations.[2] I think you will be pleased with him," [3] Adams writes Gerry, who was to be Marshall's associate and whose capacity for the task even his intimate personal friend, the President, already distrusted. Hamilton was also in Philadelphia at the time [4] — a circumstance which may or may not have been significant. It was, however, the first time, so far as definite evidence attests, that these men had met since they had been comrades and fellow officers in the Revolution.

The "Aurora," the leading Republican newspaper, was mildly sarcastic over Marshall's ignorance of the French language and general lack of equipment for his diplomatic task. "Mr. Marshall, one of our extra envoys to France, will be eminently qualified for the mission by the time he reaches that country," says the "Aurora." Some official of great legal learning was coaching Marshall, it seems, and advised him to read certain monarchical books on the old France and on the fate of the ancient republics.

[1] Marshall to his wife, July 11, 1797; MS.

[2] This, of course, was untrue, at that time. Marshall probably listened with polite interest to Adams, who was a master of the subject, and agreed with him. Thus Adams was impressed, as is the way of human nature.

[3] Adams to Gerry, July 17, 1797; *Works:* Adams, viii, 549.

[4] *Aurora*, July 17, 1797.

The "Aurora" asks "whether some history of France since the overthrow of the Monarchy would not have been more instructive to Mr. Marshall. The Envoy, however," continues the "Aurora," "approved the choice of his sagacious friend, but very shrewdly observed 'that he must first purchase Chambaud's grammar, English and French.' We understand that he is a very apt scholar, and no doubt, during the passage, he will be able to acquire enough of the French jargon for all the purposes of the embassy." [1]

Having received thirty-five hundred dollars for his expenses,[2] Marshall set sail on the brig Grace for Amsterdam where Charles Cotesworth Pinckney, the expelled American Minister to France and head of the mission, awaited him. As the land faded, Marshall wrote, like any love-sick youth, another letter to his wife which he sent back by the pilot.

"The land is just escaping from my view," writes Marshall to his "dearest Polly"; "the pilot is about to leave us & I hasten from the deck into the cabin once more to give myself the sweet indulgence of writing to you. . . . There has been so little wind that we are not yet entirely out of the bay. It is so wide however that the land has the appearance of a light blue cloud on the surface of the water & we shall very soon lose it entirely."

Marshall assures his wife that his "cabin is neat & clean. My berth a commodious one in which I

---

[1] *Aurora*, July 19, 1797. For documents given envoys by the Government, see *Am. St. Prs., For. Rel.,* Class I, ii, 153.

[2] Marshall to Secretary of State, July 10, 1797; Memorandum by Pickering; Pickering MSS., in *Proc.,* Mass. Hist. Soc., xxi, 177.

have my own bed & sheets of which I have a plenty so that I lodge as conveniently as I could do in any place whatever & I find I sleep very soundly altho on water." He is careful to say that he has plenty of creature comforts. "We have for the voyage, the greatest plenty of salt provisions live stock & poultry & as we lay in our own liquors I have taken care to provide myself with a plenty of excellent porter wine & brandy. The Captain is one of the most obliging men in the world & the vessel is said by every body to be a very fine one."

There were passengers, too, who suited Marshall's sociable disposition and who were "well disposed to make the voyage agreeable. . . . I have then my dearest Polly every prospect before me of a passage such as I could wish in every respect but one . . . fear of a lengthy passage. We have met in the bay several vessels. One from Liverpool had been at sea nine weeks, & the others from other places had been proportionately long. . . . I shall be extremely impatient to hear from you & our dear children."

Marshall tells his wife how to direct her letters to him, "some . . . by the way of London to the care of Rufus King esquire our Minister there, some by the way of Amsterdam or the Hague to the care of William Vanns [sic] Murr[a]y esquire our Minister at the Hague & perhaps some directed to me as Envoy extraordinary of the United States to the French Republic at Paris.

"Do not I entreat you omit to write. Some of your letters may miscarry but some will reach me & my heart can feel till my return no pleasure comparable to what will be given it by a line from you telling me that all remains well. Farewell my dearest wife. Your happiness will ever be the first prayer of your unceasingly affectionate

"J MARSHALL." [1]

So fared forth John Marshall upon the adventure which was to open the door to that historic career that lay just beyond it; and force him, against his will and his life's plans, to pass through it. But for this French mission, it is certain that Marshall's life would have been devoted to his law practice and his private affairs. He now was sailing to meet the ablest and most cunning diplomatic mind in the contemporary world whose talents, however, were as yet known to but few; and to face the most venal and ruthless governing body of any which then directed the affairs of the nations of Europe. Unguessed and unexpected by the kindly, naïve, and inexperienced Richmond lawyer were the scenes about to unroll before him; and the manner of his meeting the emergencies so soon to confront him was the passing of the great divide in his destiny.

Even had the French rulers been perfectly honest and simple men, the American envoys would have had no easy task. For American-French affairs were sadly tangled and involved. Gouverneur Morris, our first Minister to France under the Constitution, had made himself unwelcome to the French Revolutionists; and to placate the authorities then reigning in Paris, Washington had recalled Morris and appointed

[1] Marshall to his wife, "The Bay of Delaware," July 20, 1797; MS.

Monroe in his place "after several attempts had failed to obtain a more eligible character." [1]

Monroe, a partisan of the Revolutionists, had begun his mission with theatrical blunders; and these he continued until his recall, [2] when he climaxed his imprudent conduct by his attack on Washington. [3] During most of his mission Monroe was under the influence of Thomas Paine, [4] who had then become the venomous enemy of Washington.

Monroe had refused to receive from his fellow Minister to England, John Jay, "confidential informal statements" as to the British treaty which Jay prudently had sent him by word of mouth only. When the Jay Treaty itself arrived, Monroe

[1] Washington's remarks on Monroe's "View"; *Writings:* Ford, xiii, 452.

[2] See McMaster, ii, 257–59, 319, 370. But Monroe, although shallow, was well meaning; and he had good excuse for over-enthusiasm; for his instructions were: "Let it be seen that in case of a war with any nation on earth, we shall consider France as our first and natural ally." (*Am. St. Prs., For. Rel.,* Class I, ii, 669.)

[3] "View of the Conduct of the Executive of the United States, etc.," by James Monroe (Philadelphia, Bache, Publisher, 1797). This pamphlet is printed in full in Monroe's *Writings:* Hamilton, iii, as an Appendix.

Washington did not deign to notice Monroe's attack publicly; but on the margin of Monroe's book answered every point. Extracts from Monroe's "View" and Washington's comments thereon are given in Washington's *Writings:* Ford, xiii, 452–90.

Jefferson not only approved but commended Monroe's attack on Washington. (See Jefferson to Monroe, Oct. 25, 1797; *Works:* Ford, viii, 344–46.) It is more than probable that he helped circulate it. (Jefferson to Eppes, Dec. 21, 1797; *ib.,* 347; and to Madison, Feb. 8, 1798; *ib.,* 362; see also Jefferson to Monroe, Dec. 27; *ib.,* 350. "Your book was later coming than was to have been wished: however it works irresistibly. It would have been very gratifying to you to hear the unqualified eulogies . . . by all who are not hostile to it from principle.")

[4] Ticknor, ii, 113.

publicly denounced the treaty as "shameful," [1] a grave indiscretion in the diplomatic representative of the Government that had negotiated the offending compact.

Finally Monroe was recalled and Washington, after having offered the French mission to John Marshall, appointed Charles Cotesworth Pinckney of South Carolina as his successor. The French Revolutionary authorities had bitterly resented the Jay compact, accused the American Government of violating its treaty with France, denounced the United States for ingratitude, and abused it for undue friendship to Great Britain.

In all this the French Directory had been and still was backed up by the Republicans in the United States, who, long before this, had become a distinctly French party. Thomas Paine understated the case when he described "the Republican party in the United States" as "that party which is the sincere ally of France." [2]

The French Republic was showing its resentment by encouraging a piratical warfare by French privateers upon American commerce. Indeed, vessels of the French Government joined in these depredations. In this way, it thought to frighten the United States into taking the armed side of France against Great Britain. The French Republic was emulating the recent outrages of that Power; and, except that

[1] For a condensed but accurate and impartial statement of Monroe's conduct while Minister, see Gilman: *James Monroe* (American Statesmen Series), 36–73.

[2] Paine to editors of the *Bien-Informé*, Sept. 27, 1797; *Writings: Conway*, iii, 368–69.

the French did not impress Americans into their service, as the British had done, their Government was furnishing to America the same cause for war that Great Britain had so brutally afforded.

In less than a year and a half before Marshall sailed from Philadelphia, more than three hundred and forty American vessels had been taken by French privateers.[1] Over fifty-five million dollars' worth of American property had been destroyed or confiscated under the decrees of the Directory.[2] American seamen, captured on the high seas, had been beaten and imprisoned. The officers and crew of a French armed brig tortured Captain Walker, of the American ship Cincinnatus, four hours by thumbscrews.[3]

When Monroe learned that Pinckney had been appointed to succeed him, he began a course of insinuations to his French friends against his successor; branded Pinckney as an "aristocrat"; and thus sowed the seeds for the insulting treatment the latter received upon his appearance at the French Capital.[4] Upon Pinckney's arrival, the French Directory refused to receive him, threatened him with arrest by the Paris police, and finally ordered the new American Minister out of the territory of the Republic.[5]

To emphasize this affront, the Directory made a great ado over the departure of Monroe, who re-

[1] *Am. St. Prs., For. Rel.*, ii, 55–63.

[2] See condensed summary of the American case in instructions to Pinckney, Marshall, and Gerry; *ib.*, 153–57.

[3] *Ib.*, 64; and for numerous other examples see *ib.*, 28–64.

[4] Ticknor, ii, 113.

[5] Pinckney to Secretary of State, Amsterdam, Feb. 18, 1797; *Am. St. Prs., For. Rel.*, vii, 10.

sponded with a characteristic address. To this speech Barras, then President of the Directory, replied in a harangue insulting to the American Government; it was, indeed, an open appeal to the American people to repudiate their own Administration,[1] of the same character as, and no less offensive than, the verbal performances of Genêt.

And still the outrages of French privateers on American ships continued with increasing fury.[2] The news of Pinckney's treatment and the speech of Barras reached America after Adams's inauguration. The President promptly called Congress into a special session and delivered to the National Legislature an address in which Adams appears at his best.

The "refusal [by the Directory] . . . to receive him [Pinckney] until we had acceded to their demands without discussion and without investigation, is to treat us neither as allies nor as friends, nor as a sovereign state," said the President; who continued: —

"The speech of the President [Barras] discloses sentiments more alarming than the refusal of a minister [Pinckney], because more dangerous to our independence and union. . . .

"It evinces a disposition to separate the people of the United States from the government, to persuade them that they have different affections, principles and interests from those of their fellow citizens whom they themselves have chosen to manage their com-

[1] See Barras's speech in *Am. St. Prs., For. Rel.*, ii, 12.
[2] See Allen: *Naval War with France*, 31–33.

mon concerns and thus to produce divisions fatal to our peace.

"Such attempts ought to be repelled with a decision which shall convince France and the world that we are not a degraded people, humiliated under a colonial spirit of fear and sense of inferiority, fitted to be the miserable instruments of foreign influence, and regardless of national honor, character, and interest.

"I should have been happy to have thrown a veil over these transactions if it had been possible to conceal them; but they have passed on the great theatre of the world, in the face of all Europe and America, and with such circumstances of publicity and solemnity that they cannot be disguised and will not soon be forgotten. They have inflicted a wound in the American breast. It is my sincere desire, however, that it may be healed."

Nevertheless, so anxious was President Adams for peace that he informed Congress: "I shall institute a fresh attempt at negotiation. . . . If we have committed errors, and these can be demonstrated, we shall be willing to correct them; if we have done injuries, we shall be willing on conviction to redress them; and equal measures of justice we have a right to expect from France and every other nation." [1]

Adams took this wise action against the judgment of the Federalist leaders,[2] who thought that, since the outrages upon American commerce had been

[1] Adams, Message to Congress, May 16, 1797; Richardson, i, 235–36; also, *Works: Adams*, ix, 111–18.

[2] Gibbs, ii, 171–72.

committed by France and the formal insult to our Minister had been perpetrated by France, the advances should come from the offending Government. Technically, they were right; practically, they were wrong. Adams's action was sound as well as noble statesmanship.

Thus came about the extraordinary mission, of which Marshall was a member, to adjust our differences with the French Republic. The President had taken great care in selecting the envoys. He had considered Hamilton, Jefferson, and Madison,[1] for this delicate and fateful business; but the two latter, for reasons of practical politics, would not serve, and without one of them, Hamilton's appointment was impossible. Pinckney, waiting at Amsterdam, was, of course, to head the commission. Finally Adams's choice fell on John Marshall of Virginia and Francis Dana, Chief Justice of the Supreme Court of Massachusetts; and these nominations were confirmed by the Senate.[2]

But Dana declined,[3] and, against the unanimous advice of his Cabinet,[4] Adams then nominated Elbridge Gerry, who, though a Republican, had, on account of their personal relations, voted for Adams for President, apologizing, however, most humbly to Jefferson for having done so.[5]

No appointment could have better pleased that unrivaled politician. Gerry was in general agree-

[1] Hamilton proposed Jefferson or Madison. (Hamilton to Pickering, March 22, 1797; Lodge: *Cabot*, 101.)

[2] *Works:* Adams, ix, 111–18.   [3] *Ib.*

[4] Gibbs, i, 467, 469, and footnote to 530–31.

[5] Austin: *Gerry*, ii, 134–35.

ment with Jefferson and was, temperamentally, an easy instrument for craft to play upon. When Gerry hesitated to accept, Jefferson wrote his "dear friend" that "it was with infinite joy to me that you were yesterday announced to the Senate" as one of the envoys; and he pleaded with Gerry to undertake the mission.[1]

The leaders of the President's party in Congress greatly deplored the selection of Gerry. "No appointment could . . . have been more injudicious," declared Sedgwick.[2] "If, sir, it was a desirable thing to distract the mission, a fitter person could not, perhaps, be found. It is ten to one against his agreeing with his colleagues," the Secretary of War advised the President.[3] Indeed, Adams himself was uneasy about Gerry, and in a prophetic letter sought to forestall the very indiscretions which the latter afterwards committed.

"There is the utmost necessity for harmony, complaisance, and condescension among the three envoys, and unanimity is of great importance," the President cautioned Gerry. "It is," said Adams, "my sincere desire that an accommodation may take place; but our national faith, and the honor of our government, cannot be sacrificed. You have known enough of the unpleasant effects of disunion among ministers to convince you of the necessity of avoiding it, like a rock or quicksand. . . . It is prob-

---

[1] Jefferson to Gerry, June 21, 1797; *Works: Ford*, viii, 314. This letter flattered Gerry's vanity and nullified Adams's prudent advice to him given a few days later. (See *infra*.)

[2] Sedgwick to King, June 24, 1797; King, ii, 193.

[3] McHenry to Adams, in Cabinet meeting, 1797; Steiner, 224.

General Marshall took leave of me last night and sails to day, in **The Grace** Captain Willis for Amsterdam. He is a plain Man, very sensible, cautious, guarded, learned in the Laws of Nations — I think you will be pleased with him. — You will arrive in Amsterdam as soon or sooner than he will. The Sec. of State will send you all the Document you may want.

I am, dear sir with best wishes for your pleasant Voyage, Successful Negotiation and glorious return, your friend John Adams

Mr Gerry

PART OF LETTER OF JULY 17, 1797, FROM JOHN ADAMS TO ELBRIDGE GERRY DESCRIBING JOHN MARSHALL
(Facsimile)

able there will be manœuvres practiced to excite
jealousies among you." [1]

Forty-eight days after Marshall took ship at
Philadelphia, he arrived at The Hague.[2] The long
voyage had been enlivened by the sight of many
vessels and the boarding of Marshall's ship three
times by British men-of-war.

"Until our arrival in Holland," Marshall writes
Washington, "we saw only British & neutral vessels. This added to the blockade of the dutch fleet in
the Texel, of the french fleet in Brest & of the spanish fleet in Cadiz, manifests the entire dominion
which one nation [Great Britain] at present possesses over the seas.

"By the ships of war which met us we were three
times visited & the conduct of those who came on
board was such as wou'd proceed from general orders
to pursue a system calculated to conciliate America.

"Whether this be occasion'd by a sense of justice
& the obligations of good faith, or solely by the
hope that the perfect contrast which it exhibits to
the conduct of France may excite keener sensations

[1] Adams to Gerry, July 8, 1797; *Works:* Adams, viii, 547–48.
Nine days later the President again admonishes Gerry. While expressing confidence in him, the President tells Gerry that "Some
have expressed . . . fears of an unaccommodating disposition [in
Gerry] and others of an obstinacy that will risk great things to secure small ones.

"Some have observed that there is, at present, a happy and perfect harmony among all our ministers abroad, and have expressed apprehension that your appointment might occasion an interruption of
it." (Adams to Gerry, July 17, 1797; *ib.*, 549.)

[2] Marshall took the commission and instructions of John Quincy
Adams as the American Minister to Prussia (*Writings, J. Q. A.:* Ford,
ii, footnote to 216), to which post the younger Adams had been appointed by Washington because of his brilliant "Publicola" essays.

at that conduct, its effects on our commerce is the same." [1]

It was a momentous hour in French history when the Virginian landed on European soil. The French elections of 1797 had given to the conservatives a majority in the National Assembly, and the Directory was in danger. The day after Marshall reached the Dutch Capital, the troops sent by Bonaparte, that young eagle, his pinions already spread for his imperial flight, achieved the revolution of the 18th Fructidor (4th of September); gave the ballot-shaken Directory the support of bayonets; made it, in the end, the jealous but trembling tool of the youthful conqueror; and armed it with a power through which it nullified the French elections and cast into prison or drove into exile all who came under its displeasure or suspicion.

With Lodi, Arcola, and other laurels upon his brow, the Corsican already had begun his astonishing career as dictator of terms to Europe. The native Government of the Netherlands had been replaced by one modeled on the French system; and the Batavian Republic, erected by French arms, had become the vassal and the tool of Revolutionary France.

Three days after his arrival at The Hague, Marshall writes his wife of the safe ending of his voyage and how "very much pleased" he is with Pinckney, whom he "immediately saw." They were waiting "anxiously" for Gerry, Marshall tells her. "We

[1] Marshall, to Washington, The Hague, Sept. 15, 1797; Washington MSS., Lib. Cong. See citations *ib.*, *infra*. (Sparks MSS., *Proc. Mass. Hist. Soc.*, lxvi; also *Amer. Hist. Rev.*, ii, no. 2, Jan., 1797.)

shall wait a week or ten days longer & shall then proceed on our journey [to Paris]. You cannot conceive (yes you can conceive) how these delays perplex & mortify me. I fear I cannot return until the spring & that fear excites very much uneasiness & even regret at my having ever consented to cross the Atlantic. I wish extremely to hear from you & to know your situation. My mind clings so to Richmond that scarcely a night passes in which during the hours of sleep I have not some interesting conversation with you or concerning you."

Marshall tells his "dearest Polly" about the appearance of The Hague, its walks, buildings, and "a very extensive wood adjoining the city which extends to the sea," and which is "the pride & boast of the place." "The society at the Hague is probably very difficult, to an American it certainly is, & I have no inclination to attempt to enter into it. While the differences with France subsist the political characters of this place are probably unwilling to be found frequently in company with our countrymen. It might give umbrage to France." Pinckney had with him his wife and daughter, "who," writes Marshall, "appears to be about 12 or 13 years of age. Mrs. Pinckney informs me that only one girl of her age has visited her since the residence of the family at the Hague.[1] In fact we seem to have no communication but with Americans, or those who are employed by America or who have property in our country."

[1] Pinckney and his family had been living in Holland for almost seven months. (Pinckney to Pickering, Feb. 8, 1797; *Am. St. Prs., For. Rel.*, ii, 10.)

While at The Hague, Marshall yields, as usual, to his love for the theater, although he cannot understand a word of the play. "Near my lodgings is a theatre in which a french company performs three times a week," he tells his wife. "I have been frequently to the play & tho' I do not understand the language I am very much amused at it. The whole company is considered as having a great deal of merit but there is a Madame de Gazor who is considered as one of the first performers in Paris who bears the palm in the estimation of every person."

Marshall narrates to his wife the result of the *coup d'état* of September 4. "The Directory," he writes, "with the aid of the soldiery have just put in arrest the most able & leading members of the legislature who were considered as moderate men & friends of peace. Some conjecture that this event will so abridge our negotiations as probably to occasion my return to America this fall. A speedy return is my most ardent wish but to have my return expedited by the means I have spoken of is a circumstance so calamitous that I deprecate it as the greatest of evils. Remember me affectionately to our friends & kiss for me our dear little Mary. Tell the boys how much I expect from them & how anxious I am to see them as well as their beloved mother. I am my dearest Polly unalterably your

"J Marshall." [1]

[1] Marshall to his wife, The Hague, Sept. 9, 1797, MS. Marshall's brother had been in The Hague July 30, but had gone to Berlin. Vans Murray to J. Q. Adams, July 30, 1797; *Letters:* Ford, 358. Apparently the brothers did not meet, notwithstanding the critical state of the Fairfax contract.

The theaters and other attractions of The Hague left Marshall plenty of time, however, for serious and careful investigations. The result of these he details to Washington. The following letter shows not only Marshall's state of mind just before starting for Paris, but also the effect of European conditions upon him and how strongly they already were confirming Marshall's tendency of thought so firmly established by every event of his life since our War for Independence: —

"Tho' the face of the country [Holland] still exhibits a degree of wealth & population perhaps unequal'd in any other part of Europe, its decline is visible. The great city of Amsterdam is in a state of blockade. More than two thirds of its shipping lie unemploy'd in port. Other seaports suffer tho' not in so great a degree. In the meantime the requisitions made [by the French] upon them [the Dutch] are enormous. . . .

"It is supposed that France has by various means drawn from Holland about 60,000,000 of dollars. This has been paid, in addition to the national expenditures, by a population of less than 2,000,000. . . . Not even peace can place Holland in her former situation. Antwerp will draw from Amsterdam a large portion of that commerce which is the great source of its wealth; for Antwerp possesses, in the existing state of things, advantages which not even weight of capital can entirely surmount."

Marshall then gives Washington a clear and striking account of the political happenings among the Dutch under French domination: —

"The political divisions of this country & its uncertainty concerning its future destiny must also have their operation. . . .

"A constitution which I have not read, but which is stated to me to have contain'd all the great fundamentals of a representative government, & which has been prepar'd with infinite labor, & has experienc'd an uncommon length of discussion was rejected in the primary assemblies by a majority of nearly five to one of those who voted. . . .

"The substitute wish'd for by its opponents is a legislature with a single branch having power only to initiate laws which are to derive their force from the sanction of the primary assemblies. I do not know how they wou'd organize it. . . . It is remarkable that the very men who have rejected the form of government propos'd to them have reëlected a great majority of the persons who prepar'd it & will probably make from it no essential departure. . . . It is worthy of notice that more than two thirds of those entitled to suffrage including perhaps more than four fifths of the property of the nation & who wish'd, as I am told, the adoption of the constitution, withheld their votes. . . .

"Many were restrain'd by an unwillingness to take the oath required before a vote could be receiv'd; many, disgusted with the present state of things, have come to the unwise determination of revenging themselves on those whom they charge with having occasion'd it by taking no part whatever in the politics of their country, & many seem to be indifferent to every consideration not immediately connected with their particular employments."

Holland's example made the deepest impression on Marshall's mind. What he saw and heard fortified his already firm purpose not to permit America, if he could help it, to become the subordinate or ally of any foreign power. The concept of the American people as a separate and independent Nation unattached to, unsupported by, and unafraid of any other country, which was growing rapidly to be the passion of Marshall's life, was given fresh force by the humiliation and distress of the Dutch under French control.

"The political opinions which have produc'd the rejection of the constitution," Marshall reasons in his report to Washington, "& which, as it wou'd seem, can only be entertain'd by intemperate & ill inform'd minds unaccustom'd to a union of the theory & practice of liberty, must be associated with a general system which if brought into action will produce the same excesses here which have been so justly deplor'd in France.

"The same materials exist tho' not in so great a degree. They have their clubs, they have a numerous poor & they have enormous wealth in the hands of a minority of the nation."

Marshall interviewed Dutch citizens, in his casual, indolent, and charming way; and he thus relates to Washington the sum of one such conversation: —

"On my remarking this to a very rich & intelligent merchant of Amsterdam & observing that if one class of men withdrew itself from public duties

& offices it wou'd immediately be succeeded by another which wou'd acquire a degree of power & influence that might be exercis'd to the destruction
of those who had retir'd from society, he replied that
the remark was just, but that they relied on France
for a protection from those evils which she had herself experienc'd. That France wou'd continue to require great supplies from Holland & knew its situation too well to permit it to become the prey of
anarchy.

"That Holland was an artificial country acquired
by persevering industry & which cou'd only be pre-
serv'd by wealth & order. That confusion & anarchy
wou'd banish a large portion of that wealth, wou'd
dry up its sources & wou'd entirely disable them
from giving France that pecuniary aid she so much
needed. That under this impression very many who
tho' friends to the revolution, saw with infinite mortification french troops garrison the towns of Holland, wou'd now see their departure with equal
regret.

"Thus, they willingly relinquish national independence for individual safety. What a lesson to
those who wou'd admit foreign influence into the
United States!"

Marshall then narrates the events in France which
followed the *coup d'état* of September 4. While this
account is drawn from rumors and newspapers and
therefore contains a few errors, it is remarkable on
the whole for its general accuracy. No condensation
can do justice to Marshall's review of this period
of French history in the making. It is of first im-

portance, also, as disclosing his opinions of the Government he was so soon to encounter and his convictions that unrestrained liberty must result in despotism.

"You have observed the storm which has been long gathering in Paris," continues Marshall. "The thunderbolt has at length been launch'd at the heads of the leading members of the legislature & has, it is greatly to be fear'd, involv'd in one common ruin with them, the constitution & liberties of their country. . . . Complete & impartial details concerning it will not easily be obtained as the press is no longer free. The journalists who had ventur'd to censure the proceedings of a majority of the directory are seiz'd, & against about forty of them a sentence of transportation is pronounced.

"The press is plac'd under the superintendence of a police appointed by & dependent on the executive. It is supposed that all private letters have been seiz'd for inspection.

"From some Paris papers it appears, that on the first alarm, several members of the legislature attempted to assemble in their proper halls which they found clos'd & guarded by an arm'd force. Sixty or seventy assembled at another place & began to remonstrate against the violence offer'd to their body, but fear soon dispersed them.

"To destroy the possibility of a rallying point the municipal administrations of Paris & the central administration of the seine were immediately suspended & forbidden by an arrêté of the directoire, to assemble themselves together.

"Many of the administrators of the departments through France elected by the people, had been previously remov'd & their places filled by persons chosen by the directory. . . .

"The fragment of the legislature convok'd by the directory at L'Odéon & L' école de santé, hasten'd to repeal the law for organizing the national guards, & authoriz'd the directory to introduce into Paris as many troops as shou'd be judg'd necessary. The same day the liberty of the press was abolish'd by a line, property taken away by another & personal security destroy'd by a sentence of transportation against men unheard & untried.

"All this," sarcastically remarks Marshall, "is still the triumph of liberty & of the constitution."

Although admitting his lack of official information, Marshall "briefly" observes that: "Since the election of the new third, there were found in both branches of the legislature a majority in favor of moderate measures & apparently, wishing sincerely for peace. They have manifested a disposition which threaten'd a condemnation of the conduct of the directory towards America, a scrutiny into the transactions of Italy, particularly those respecting Venice & Genoa, an enquiry into the disposition of public money & such a regular arrangement of the finances as wou'd prevent in future those dilapidations which are suspected to have grown out of their disorder. They [French conservatives] have sought too by their laws to ameliorate the situation of those whom terror had driven out of France, & of those priests who had committed no offense."

Marshall thus details to Washington the excuse of the French radicals for their severe treatment of the conservatives: —

"The cry of a conspiracy to reëstablish royalism was immediately rais'd against them [conservatives]. An envoy was dispatched to the Army of Italy to sound its disposition. It was represented that the legislature was hostile to the armies, that it withheld their pay & subsistence, that by its opposition to the directory it encourag'd Austria & Britain to reject the terms of peace which were offer'd by France & which but for that opposition wou'd have been accepted, & finally that it had engag'd in a conspiracy for the destruction of the constitution & the republic & for the restoration of royalty.

"At a feast given to the armies of Italy to commemorate their fellow soldiers who had fallen in that country the Generals address'd to them their complaints, plainly spoke of marching to Paris to support the directory against the councils & received from them addresses manifesting the willingness of the soldiers to follow them.

"The armies also addressed the directory & each other, & addresses were dispatched to different departments. The directory answer'd them by the stronge[st] criminations of the legislature. Similar proceedings were had in the army of the interior commanded by Gen! Hoche. Detachments were mov'd within the limits prohibited by the constitution, some of which declar'd they were marching to Paris 'to bring the legislature to reason.'"

Here follows Marshall's story of what then hap-

pened, according to the accounts which were given
him at The Hague: —

"Alarm'd at these movements the council of five
hundred call'd on the directory for an account of
them. The movement of the troops within the constitutional circle was attributed to accident & the
discontents of the army to the faults committed by
the legislature who were plainly criminated as conspirators against the army & the republic.

"This message was taken up by Tronçon in the
council of antients & by Thibideau in the council of
five hundred. I hope you have seen their speeches.
They are able, & seem to me entirely exculpated the
legislature.

"In the mean time the directory employed itself
in the removal of the administrators of many of the
departments & cantons & replacing those whom the
people had elected by others in whom it cou'd confide, and in the removal generally of such officers
both civil & military as cou'd not be trusted to make
room for others on whom it cou'd rely.

"The legislature on its part, pass'd several laws
to enforce the constitutional restrictions on the
armies & endeavored to organize the national guards.
On this latter subject especially Pichegru, great &
virtuous I believe in the cabinet as in the field, was
indefatigable. We understand that the day before
the law for their organization wou'd have been carried into execution the decisive blow was struck."

Marshall now relates, argumentatively, the facts as
he heard them in the Dutch Capital; and in doing so,
reveals his personal sentiments and prejudices: —

"To support the general charge of conspiracy in favor of royalty I know of no particular facts alledged against the arrested Members except Pichegru & two or three others. . . . Pichegru is made in the first moment of conversation to unbosom himself entirely to a perfect stranger who had only told him that he came from the Prince of Conde & cou'd not exhibit a single line of testimonial of any sort to prove that he had ever seen that Prince or that he was not a spy employ'd by some of the enemies of the General.

"This story is repel'd by Pichegru's character which has never before been defil'd. Great as were the means he possess'd of personal aggrandizement he retir'd clean handed from the army without adding a shilling to his private fortune. It is repel'd by his resigning the supreme command, by his numerous victories subsequent to the alleged treason, by its own extreme absurdity & by the fear which his accusers show of bringing him to trial according to the constitution even before a tribunal they can influence & overawe, or of even permitting him to be heard before the prostrate body which is still term'd the legislature & which in defiance of the constitution has pronounc'd judgment on him.

"Yet this improbable & unsupported tale seems to be receiv'd as an established truth by those who the day before [his] fall bow'd to him as an idol. I am mortified as a man to learn that even his old army which conquer'd under him, which ador'd him, which partook of his fame & had heretofore not join'd their brethren in accusing the legislature, now

unite in bestowing on him the heaviest execrations
& do not hesitate to pronounce him a traitor of the
deepest die."

Irrespective of the real merits of the controversy,
Marshall tells Washington that he is convinced that
constitutional liberty is dead or dying in France:—

"Whether this conspiracy be real or not," he says,
"the wounds inflicted on the constitution by the
three directors seem to me to be mortal. In opposition to the express regulations of the constitution the
armies have deliberated, the result of their delibera-
tions addressed to the directory has been favorably
received & the legislature since the revolution has
superadded its thanks.

"Troops have been marched within those limits
which by the constitution they are forbidden to
enter but on the request of the legislature. The directory is forbidden to arrest a member of the legislature unless in the very commission of a criminal
act & then he can only be tried by the high court, on
which occasion forms calculated to protect his person from violence or the prejudice of the moment are
carefully prescrib'd.

"Yet it has seized, by a military force, about fifty
leading members not taken in a criminal act & has
not pursued a single step mark'd out by the constitution. The councils can inflict no penalty on their
own members other than reprimand, arrest for
eight & imprisonment for three days. Yet they have
banished to such places as the directory shall chuse
a large portion of their body without the poor formality of hearing a defense.

"The legislature shall not exercise any judiciary power or pass any retrospective law. Yet it has pronounc'd this heavy judgment on others as well as its own members & has taken from individuals property which the law has vested in them."

Marshall is already bitter against the Directory because of its violation of the French Constitution, and tells Washington: —

"The members of the directory are personally secur'd by the same rules with those of the legislature. Yet three directors have depriv'd two of their places, the legislature has then banished them without a hearing & has proceeded to fill up the alledg'd vacancies. Merlin late minister of justice & François de Neufchatel have been elected.

"The constitution forbids the house of any man to be entered in the night. The orders of the constituted authorities can only be executed in the day. Yet many of the members were seiz'd in their beds.

"Indeed, sir, the constitution has been violated in so many instances that it wou'd require a pamphlet to detail them. The detail wou'd be unnecessary for the great principle seems to be introduc'd that the government is to be administered according to the will of the nation."

Marshall now indulges in his characteristic eloquence and peculiar method of argument: —

"Necessity, the never to be worn out apology for violence, is alledg'd — but cou'd that necessity go further than to secure the persons of the conspirators? Did it extend to the banishment of the printers & to the slavery of the press? If such a necessity did exist it was created by the disposition of the people at large & it is a truth which requires no demonstration that if a republican form of government cannot be administered by the general will, it cannot be administered against that will by an army."

Nevertheless, hope for constitutional liberty in France lingers in his heart in spite of this melancholy recital.

"After all, the result may not be what is apprehended. France possesses such enormous power, such internal energy, such a vast population that she may possibly spare another million & preserve or reacquire her liberty. Or, the form of the government being preserved, the independence of the legislature may be gradually recover'd.

"With their form of government or resolutions we have certainly no right to intermeddle, but my regrets at the present state of things are increased by an apprehension that the rights of our country will not be deem'd so sacred under the existing system as they wou'd have been had the legislature preserved its legitimate authority." [1]

Washington's reply, which probably reached Marshall some time after the latter's historic letter to Talleyrand in January, 1798,[2] is informing. He "prays for a continuance" of such letters and hopes he will be able to congratulate Marshall "on the favorable conclusion of your embassy. . . . To predict the contrary might be as unjust as it is im-

[1] Marshall to Washington, The Hague, Sept. 15, 1797; *Amer. Hist. Rev.*, ii, no. 2, Jan., 1897; and MS., Lib. Cong.

[2] See *infra*, next chapter.

politic, and therefore," says Washington, "mum —
on that topic. Be the issue what it may," he is sure
"that nothing which justice, sound reasoning, and
fair representation would require will be wanting to
render it just and honorable." If so, and the mission
fails, "then the eyes of all who are not willfully
blind .... will be fully opened." The Directory
will have a rude awakening, if they expect the Republicans to support France against America in the
"dernier ressort. . . . For the mass of our citizens
require no more than to understand a question to
decide it properly; and an adverse conclusion of the
negotiation will effect this." Washington plainly
indicates that he wishes Marshall to read his letter
between the lines when he says: "I shall dwell very
little on European politics ... because this letter may
pass through many hands." [1]

Gerry not arriving by September 18, Marshall and
Pinckney set out for Paris, "proceeding slowly in the
hope of being overtaken" by their tardy associate.
From Antwerp Marshall writes Charles Lee, then
Attorney-General, correcting some unimportant
statements in his letter to Washington, which, when
written, were "considered as certainly true," but
which "subsequent accounts contradict." [2] Down-
heartedly he says: —

[1] Washington to Marshall, Dec. 4, 1797; *Writings:* Ford, xiii,
432–34.
[2] To justify the violence of the 18th Fructidor, the Directory asserted that the French elections, in which a majority of conservatives
and anti-revolutionists were returned and General Pichegru chosen
President of the French Legislature, were parts of a royal conspiracy
to destroy liberty and again place a king upon the throne of France.
In these elections the French liberals, who were not in the army, did not

"Our insulted injured country has not before it
the most flattering prospects. There is no circumstance calculated to flatter us with the hope that our
negotiations will terminate as they ought to do.
. . . We understand that all is now quiet in France,
the small show of resistance against which Napoleon
march'd is said to have dispersed on hearing of his
movement."

He then describes the celebration in Antwerp of
the birth of the new French régime: —

"To-day being the anniversary of the foundation
of the Republic, was celebrated with great pomp
by the military at this place. Very few indeed of the

vote; while all conservatives, who wished above all things for a stable
and orderly government of law and for peace with other countries,
flocked to the polls.

Among the latter, of course, were the few Royalists who still remained in France. Such, at least, was the view Marshall took of this
episode. To understand Marshall's subsequent career, too much weight
cannot be given this fact and, indeed, all the startling events in France
during the six historic months of Marshall's stay in Paris.

But Marshall did not take into account the vital fact that the
French soldiers had no chance to vote at this election. They were
scattered far and wide — in Italy, Germany, and elsewhere. Yet
these very men were the soul of the Revolutionary cause. And the
private soldiers were more enraged by the result of the French elections than their generals — even than General Augereau, who was
tigerish in his wrath.

They felt that, while they were fighting on the battlefield, they had
been betrayed at the ballot box. To the soldiers of France the revolution of the 18th Fructidor was the overthrow of their enemies
in their own country. The army felt that it had answered with loyal
bayonets a conspiracy of treasonable ballots. It now seems probable that the soldiers and officers of the French armies were right in
this view.

Pinckney was absurdly accused of interfering in the elections in
behalf of the "Royalist Conspiracy." (Vans Murray to J. Q. Adams,
April 3, 1798; *Letters: Ford*, 391.) Such a thing, of course, was perfectly impossible.

inhabitants attended the celebration. Everything
in Antwerp wears the appearance of consternation
and affright.

"Since the late revolution a proclamation has been
published forbidding any priest to officiate who has
not taken the oath prescribed by a late order. No
priest at Antwerp has taken it & yesterday commenced the suspension of their worship.

"All the external marks of their religion too with
which their streets abound are to be taken down.
The distress of the people at the calamity is almost as great as if the town was to be given up to
pillage." [1]

Five days after leaving Antwerp, Marshall and
Pinckney arrived in the French Capital. The Paris
of that time was still very much the Paris of Riche-
lieu, except for some large buildings and other im-
provements begun by Louis XIV. The French metropolis was in no sense a modern city and bore
little resemblance to the Paris of the present day.
Not until some years afterward did Napoleon as
Emperor begin the changes which later, under Napoleon III, transformed it into the most beautiful
city in the world. Most of its ancient interest, as
well as its mediæval discomforts, were in existence
when Marshall and Pinckney reached their destination.

The Government was, in the American view, incredibly corrupt, and the lack of integrity among the
rulers was felt even among the people. "The venal-

[1] Marshall to Lee, Antwerp, Sept. 22, 1797; MS., New York
Pub. Lib.

ity is such," wrote Gouverneur Morris, in 1793, "that if there be no traitor it is because the enemy has not common sense." [1] And again: "The . . . administration is occupied in acquiring wealth." [2] Honesty was unknown, and, indeed, abhorrent, to most of the governing officials; and the moral sense of the citizens themselves had been stupefied by the great sums of money which Bonaparte extracted from conquered cities and countries and sent to the treasury at Paris. Time and again the Republic was saved from bankruptcy by the spoils of conquest; and long before the American envoys set foot in Paris the popular as well as the official mind had come to expect the receipt of money from any source or by any means.

The bribery of ministers of state and of members of the Directory was a matter of course; [3] and weaker countries paid cash for treaties with the arrogant Government and purchased peace with a price. During this very year Portugal was forced to advance a heavy bribe to Talleyrand and the Directory before the latter would consent to negotiate concerning a treaty; and, as a secret part of the compact, Portugal was required to make a heavy loan to France. It was, indeed, a part of this very Portuguese money with which the troops were

---

[1] Gouverneur Morris to Washington, Feb., 1793; Morris, ii, 37. While Morris was an aristocrat, thoroughly hostile to democracy and without sympathy with or understanding of the French Revolution, his statements of facts have proved to be generally accurate. (See Lyman: *Diplomacy of the United States*, i, 352, on corruption of the Directory.)

[2] Morris to Pinckney, Aug. 13, 1797; Morris, ii, 51.

[3] Loliée: *Talleyrand and His Times*, 170-71.

brought to Paris for the September revolution of
1797.[1]

Marshall and Pinckney at once notified the French
Foreign Office of their presence, but delayed present-
ing their letters of credence until Gerry should join
them before proceeding to business. A week passed;
and Marshall records in his diary that every day the
waiting envoys were besieged by "Americans whose
vessels had been captured & condemned. By appeals & other dilatory means the money had been
kept out of the hands of the captors & they were now
waiting on expenses in the hope that our [the envoys'] negotiations might relieve them."[2] A device, this, the real meaning of which was to be made
plain when the hour should come to bring it to bear
on the American envoys.

Such was the official and public atmosphere in
which Marshall and Pinckney found themselves on
their mission to adjust, with honor, the differences
between France and America: a network of unoffi-
cial and secret agents was all about them; and at its
center was the master spider, Talleyrand. The un-
frocked priest had been made Foreign Minister under
the Directory in the same month and almost the day
that Marshall embarked at Philadelphia for Paris.
It largely was through the efforts and influence of
Madame de Staël [3] that this prince of intriguers was

[1] King to Secretary of State, Dispatch no. 54, Nov. 18, 1897;
King, ii, 243.
[2] Marshall's Journal, official copy, Pickering Papers, Mass. Hist.
Soc., 1.
[3] Loliée: *Talleyrand and His Times*, 147; and Blennerhassett:
Talleyrand, ii, 256–57.

able to place his feet upon this first solid step of his amazing career.

Talleyrand's genius was then unknown to the world, and even the Directory at that time had no inkling of his uncanny craft. To be sure, his previous life had been varied and dramatic and every page of it stamped with ability; but in the tremendous and flaming events of that tragic period he had not attracted wide attention. Now, at last, Talleyrand had his opportunity.

Among other incidents of his life had been his exile to America. For nearly two years and a half he had lived in the United States, traveling hither and yon through the forming Nation. Washington as President had refused to receive the expelled Frenchman, who never forgave the slight. In his journey from State to State he had formed a poor opinion of the American people. "If," he wrote, "I have to stay here another year I shall die." [1]

The incongruities of what still was pioneer life, the illimitable forests, the confusion and strife of opinion, the absence of National spirit and general purpose, caused Talleyrand to look with contempt upon the wilderness Republic. But most of all, this future master spirit of European diplomacy was impressed with what seemed to him the sordid, money-grubbing character of the American people. Nowhere did he find a spark of that idealism which had achieved our independence; and he concluded that gold was the American god. [2]

---

[1] Talleyrand to Mme. de Staël, quoted in McCabe: *Talleyrand*, 137.
[2] *Memoirs of Talleyrand:* Broglie's ed., i, 179–82; also see McCabe's

Fauchet's disclosures [1] had caused official Paris to measure the American character by the same yardstick that Talleyrand applied to us, when, on leaving our shores, he said: "The United States merit no more consideration than Genoa or Genève."[2]

The French Foreign Minister was not fairly established when the American affair came before him. Not only was money his own pressing need, but to pander to the avarice of his master Barras and the other corrupt members of the Directory was his surest method of strengthening his, as yet, uncertain official position. Such were Talleyrand's mind, views, and station, when, three days after Gerry's belated arrival, the newly installed Minister received the American envoys informally at his house, "where his office was held." By a curious freak of fate, they found him closeted with the Portuguese Minister from whom the very conditions had been exacted which Talleyrand so soon was to attempt to extort from the Americans.

It was a striking group — Talleyrand, tall and thin of body, with pallid, shrunken cheeks and slumberous eyes, shambling forward with a limp, as,

summary in his *Talleyrand*, 136–38. Talleyrand was greatly impressed by the statement of a New Jersey farmer, who wished to see Bingham rather than President Washington because he had heard that Bingham was "so wealthy. . . . Throughout America I met with a similar love of money," says Talleyrand. (*Memoirs of Talleyrand:* Broglie's ed., i, 180.) In this estimate of American character during that period, Talleyrand did not differ from other travelers, nor, indeed, from the opinion of most Americans who expressed themselves upon this subject. (See vol. I, chaps. VII, and VIII, of this work.)

[1] Talleyrand as quoted in Pickering to King, Nov. 7, 1798; *Pickering:* Pickering, ii, 429.

[2] *Am. St. Prs., For. Rel.*, ii, 158.

with halting speech,[1] he coldly greeted his diplomatic visitors; Gerry, small, erect, perfectly attired, the owl-like solemnity of his face made still heavier by his long nose and enormous wig; Pinckney, handsome, well-dressed, clear-eyed, of open countenance;[2] and Marshall, tall, lean, loose-jointed, carelessly appareled, with only his brilliant eyes to hint at the alert mind and dominant personality of the man.

Talleyrand measured his adversaries instantly. Gerry he had known in America and he weighed with just balance the qualities of the Massachusetts envoy; Pinckney he also had observed and feared nothing from the blunt, outspoken, and transparently honest but not in the least subtle or far-seeing South Carolinian; the ill-appearing Virginian, of whom he had never heard, Talleyrand counted as a cipher. It was here that this keen and cynical student of human nature blundered.

Marshall and Talleyrand were almost of an age,[3] the Frenchman being only a few months older than his Virginia antagonist. The powers of neither were known to the other, as, indeed, they were at that time unguessed generally by the mass of the people, even of their own countries.

A month after Talleyrand became the head of French Foreign Affairs, Rufus King, then our Min-

---

[1] *Memoirs of Talleyrand* : Stewarton, ii, 10.

[2] Pinckney was the only one of the envoys who could speak French. He had received a finished education in England at Westminster and Oxford and afterward had studied in France at the Royal Military College at Caen.

[3] Marshall and Talleyrand were forty-two years of age, Pinckney fifty-one, and Gerry fifty-three.

Maillard Del.

Bocourt Sculp.

TALLEYRAND

ister at London, as soon as he had heard of the appointment of the American envoys, wrote Talleyrand a conciliatory letter congratulating the French diplomat upon his appointment. King and Talleyrand had often met both in England and America.

"We have been accustomed," writes King, "to converse on every subject with the greatest freedom"; then, assuming the frankness of friendship, King tries to pave the way for Marshall, Pinckney, and Gerry, without mentioning the latter, however. "From the moment I heard that you had been named to the Department of Foreign Affairs," King assures Talleyrand, "I have felt a satisfactory Confidence that the Cause of the increasing Misunderstanding between us would cease, and that the overtures mediated by our Government would not fail to restore Harmony and Friendship between the two Countries."[1]

King might have saved his ink. Talleyrand did not answer the letter; it is doubtful whether he even read it. At any rate, King's somewhat amateurish effort to beguile the French Foreign Minister by empty words utterly failed of its purpose.

The Americans received cold comfort from Talleyrand; he was busy, he said, on a report on Franco-American affairs asked for by the Directory; when he had presented it to his superiors he would, he said, let the Americans know "what steps were to follow." Talleyrand saw to it, however, that the envoys received "cards of hospitality" which had been

[1] King to Talleyrand, London, Aug. 3, 1797; King, ii, 206–08.

denied to Pinckney. These saved the Americans at least from offensive attentions from the police.[1]

Three days later, a Mr. Church, an American-born French citizen, accompanied by his son, called on Gerry, but found Marshall, who was alone. From Thomas Paine, Church had learned of plans of the Directory concerning neutrals which, he assured Marshall, "would be extremely advantageous to the United States." "Do not urge your mission now," suggested Church — the present was "a most unfavorable moment." Haste meant that "all would probably be lost." What were these measures of the Directory? asked Marshall. Church was not at liberty to disclose them, he said; but the envoys' "true policy was to wait for events."

That night came a letter from the author of "Common Sense." "This letter," Marshall records, "made very different impressions on us. I thought it an insult which ought to be received with that coldness which would forbid the repetition of it. Mr. Gerry was of a contrary opinion." Marshall insisted that the Directory knew of Paine's letter and would learn of the envoys' answer, and that Pinckney, Gerry, and himself must act only as they knew the American Government would approve. It was wrong, said he, and imprudent to lead the Directory to expect anything else from the envoys; and Paine's "aspersions on our government"

---

[1] *Am. St. Prs., For. Rel.*, ii, 158; Marshall's Journal, Official Copy; MS., Mass. Hist. Soc., 2. The envoys' dispatches to the Secretary of State were prepared by Marshall, largely, from his Journal. Citations will be from the dispatches except when not including matter set out exclusively in Marshall's Journal.

should be resented.[1] So began the break between Marshall and Gerry, which, considering the characters of the two men, was inevitable.

Next, Talleyrand's confidential secretary confided to Major Mountflorence, of the American Consulate, that the Directory would require explanations of President Adams's speech to Congress, by which they were exasperated. The Directory would not receive the envoys, he said, until the negotiations were over; but that persons would be appointed "to treat with" the Americans, and that these agents would report to Talleyrand, who would have "charge of the negotiations." [2] Mountflorence, of course, so advised the envoys.

Thus the curtain rose upon the melodrama now to be enacted — an episode without a parallel in the history of American diplomacy. To understand what follows, we must remember that the envoys were governed by careful, lengthy, and detailed instructions to the effect that "no blame or censure be directly, or indirectly, imputed to the United States"; that in order not to "wound her [France] feelings or to excite her resentment" the negotiations were to be on the principles of the British Treaty; "that no engagement be made inconsistent with . . . any prior treaty"; that "no restraint on our lawful commerce with any other nation be admitted"; that nothing be done "incompatible with the complete sovereignty and independence of the United States in matters of policy, commerce, and government";

[1] Marshall's Journal, Oct. 11, 2–4.
[2] *Am. St. Prs., For. Rel.*, ii, 8–11, and 158. Fulwar Skipwith was consul; but Mountflorence was connected with the office.

and "*that no aid be stipulated in favor of France during the present war.*" [1]

We are now to witness the acts in that strange play, known to American history as the X. Y. Z. Mission, as theatrical a spectacle as any ever prepared for the stage. Indeed, the episode differs from a performance behind the footlights chiefly in that in this curious arrangement the explanation comes after the acting is over. When the dispatches to the American Government, which Marshall now is to write, were transmitted to Congress, diplomatic prudence caused the names of leading characters to be indicated only by certain letters of the alphabet. Thus, this determining phase of our diplomatic history is known to the present day as "The X. Y. Z. Affair."

---

[1] *Am. St. Prs., For. Rel.*, ii, 157. Italics are mine.

CHAPTER VII .

FACING TALLEYRAND

Society is divided into two classes; the shearers and the shorn. We should always be with the former against the latter. (Talleyrand.)

To lend money to a belligerent power is to relinquish our neutrality. (Marshall.)

DIPLOMATICALLY Marshall and his associates found themselves marooned. Many and long were their discussions of the situation. "We have had several conversations on the extraordinary silence of the Government concerning our reception," writes Marshall in his Journal. "The plunder of our commerce sustains no abatements, the condemnations of our vessels are press'd with ardor . . . our reception is postponed in a manner most unusual & contemptuous.

"I urge repeatedly that we ought, in a respectful communication to the Minister [Talleyrand] . . . to pray for a suspension of all further proceedings against American vessels until the further order of the Directory. . . .

"We have already permitted much time to pass away, we could not be charged with precipitation, & I am willing to wait two or three days longer but not more. . . . The existing state of things is to France the most beneficial & the most desirable, but to America it is ruinous. I therefore urge that in a few days we shall lay this interesting subject before the Minister." [1]

[1] Marshall's Journal, Oct. 15, 4–5.

Marshall tells us that Gerry again opposed action, holding that for the envoys to act would "irritate the [French] Government." The Directory "might take umbrage." [1] Besides, declared Gerry, France was in a quandary what to do and "any movement on our part" would relieve her and put the blame on the envoys. "But," records Marshall, "in the address I propose I would say nothing which could give umbrage, & if, as is to be feared, France is determined to be offended, she may quarrel with our answer to any proposition she may make or even with our silence." Pinckney agreed with Marshall; but they yielded to Gerry in order to "preserve unanimity." [2]

Tidings soon arrived of the crushing defeat of the Dutch fleet by the British; and on the heels of this came reports that the Directory were ready to negotiate with the Americans.[3] Next morning, and four days after the mysterious intimations to the Ameri-

---

[1] Paris made an impression on the envoys as different as their temperaments. Vans Murray records the effect on Gerry, who had written to his friends in Boston of "how handsomely they [the envoys] were received in Paris and how hopeful he is of settlement! ! !"

"Good God — he has mistaken the lamps of Paris for an illumination on his arrival," writes our alarmed Minister at The Hague, "and the salutations of fisherwomen for a procession of chaste matrons hailing the great Pacificator! . . . His foible is to mistake things of common worldly politeness for deference to his rank of which he rarely loses the idea. . . . Gerry is no more fit to enter the labyrinth of Paris as a town — alone — than an innocent is, much less formed to play a game with the political genius of that city . . . without some very steady friend at his elbow. . . . Of all men in America he is . . . the least qualify'd to play a part in Paris, either among the men or the women — he is too virtuous for the last — too little acquainted with the world and himself for the first." (Vans Murray to J. Q. Adams, April 13, 1798; *Letters:* Ford, 394.)

[2] Marshall's Journal, 5.   [3] *Ib.,* Oct. 17, 6.

can envoys from Talleyrand through his confidential
secretary, a Parisian business man called on Pinckney and told him that a Mr. Hottenguer,[1] "a native of Switzerland who had been in America," [2] and
"a gentleman of considerable credit and reputation," would call on Pinckney. Pinckney had met
Hottenguer on a former occasion, probably at The
Hague. That evening this cosmopolitan agent of
financiers and foreign offices paid the expected visit.
After a while Hottenguer "whispered . . . that he
had a message from Talleyrand." Into the next room
went Pinckney and his caller. There Hottenguer
told Pinckney that the Directory were "exceedingly
irritated" at President Adams's speech and that
"they should be softened."

Indeed, the envoys would not be received, said
Hottenguer, unless the mellowing process were applied to the wounded and angry Directory. He was
perfectly plain as to the method of soothing that
sore and sensitive body — "money" for the pockets
of its members and the Foreign Minister which
would be "at the disposal of M. Talleyrand."
Also a loan must be made to France. Becoming
still more explicit, Hottenguer stated the exact
amount of financial salve which must be applied
in the first step of the healing treatment required
from our envoys — a small bribe of one million
two hundred thousand livres [about fifty thousand
pounds sterling, or two hundred and fifty thousand
dollars].

[1] Probably the same Hottenguer who had helped Marshall's
brother negotiate the Fairfax loan in Amsterdam. (*Supra*, chap. IV.)
[2] Marshall's Journal, Oct. 17, 6.

"It was absolutely required," reports Marshall, "that we should . . . pay the debts due by contract from France to our citizens . . . pay for the spoliations committed on our commerce . . . & make a considerable loan. . . . Besides this, added Mr. Hottenguer, there must be something for the pocket . . . for the private use of the Directoire & Minister under the form of satisfying claims which," says Marshall, "did not in fact exist." [1]

Pinckney reported to his colleagues. Again the envoys divided as to the course to pursue. "I was decidedly of opinion," runs Marshall's chronicle, "& so expressed myself, that such a proposition could not be made by a nation from whom any treaty, short of the absolute surrender of the independence of the United States was to be expected, but that if there was a possibility of accommodation, to give any countenance whatever to such a proposition would be certainly to destroy that possibility because it would induce France to demand from us terms to which it was impossible for us to accede. I therefore," continues Marshall, "thought we ought, so soon as we could obtain the whole information, to treat the terms as inadmissible and without taking any notice of them to make some remonstrance to the minister on our situation & on that of our countrymen." Pinckney agreed with Marshall; Gerry dissented and declared that "the whole negotiation . . . would be entirely broken off if such an answer was given as I [Marshall] had hinted & there would be a war between the two

[1] *Am. St. Prs., For. Rel.*, ii, 158; Marshall's Journal, 6–7.

nations." At last it was decided to get Hottenguer's proposition in writing.[1]

When Pinckney so informed Hottenguer, the latter announced that he had not dealt "immediately with Talleyrand but through another gentleman in whom Talleyrand had great confidence." Hottenguer had no objection, however, to writing out his "suggestions," which he did the next evening.[2] The following morning he advised the envoys that a Mr. Bellamy, "the confidential friend of M. Talleyrand," would call and explain matters in person. Decidedly, the fog was thickening. The envoys debated among themselves as to what should be done.

"I again urg'd the necessity of breaking off this indirect mode of procedure," testifies Marshall; but "Mr. Gerry reprobated precipitation, insisted on further explanations as we could not completely understand the scope & object of the propositions & conceiv'd that we ought not abruptly object to them." Marshall and Pinckney thought "that they [Talleyrand's demands] were beyond our powers & . . . amounted to a surrender of the independence of our country." [3] But Gerry had his way and the weaving of the spider's web went on.

Two hours after candlelight that evening Hottenguer and Bellamy entered Marshall's room where the three Americans were waiting for them; and Bellamy was introduced as "the confidential friend of M. Talleyrand," of whom Hottenguer had told

---

[1] Marshall's Journal, 7–8.   [2] *Am. St. Prs., For. Rel.*, ii, 158.
[3] Marshall's Journal, Oct. 20, 8–9.

the envoys. Bellamy was, says Marshall, "a genevan now residing in Hamburg but in Paris on a visit." [1] He went straight to the point. Talleyrand, he confided to the envoys, was "a friend of America . . . the kindness and civilities he had personally received in America" had touched his heart; and he was burning to "repay these kindnesses." But what could this anxious friend of America do when the cruel Directory were so outraged at the American President's address to Congress that they would neither receive the envoys nor authorize "Talleyrand to have any communications with" them.

Bellamy pointed out that under these circumstances Talleyrand could not, of course, communicate directly with the envoys; but "had authorized" him to deal with them "and to promise" that the French Foreign Minister would do his best to get the Directory to receive the Americans if the latter agreed to Talleyrand's terms. Nevertheless, Bellamy "stated explicitly and repeatedly that he was clothed with no authority" — he was not a diplomat, he said, but only the trusted friend of Talleyrand. He then pointed out the passages from Adams's address [2] which had so exasperated the French rulers and stated what the envoys must do to make headway.

The American envoys, asserted Bellamy, must make "a formal disavowal in writing . . . that . . . the speech of the Citizen President," Barras, was "not offensive" to America; must offer "reparation" for President Adams's address; must affirm

---

[1] Marshall's Journal, Oct. 20, 8-9.   [2] *Supra*, 226.

that the decree of the Directory,[1] which Adams had denounced, was not "contrary to the treaty of 1778"; must state "in writing" the depredations on American trade "by the English and French privateers," and must make "a formal declaration" that Adams in his speech to Congress had not referred to the French Government or its agents: if all this were done "the French Republic is disposed to renew their old-time relations with America" by a new treaty which should place France "with respect to the United States exactly on the same footing as they [the United States] should be with England." But, said Bellamy, there must be a secret article of this new treaty providing for a loan from America to France.[2]

Impossible as these terms were, the whole business must be preceded by a bribe. "I will not disguise from you," said Bellamy, "that this situation being met, the essential part of the treaty remains to be adjusted. . . . *You must pay money — you must pay a great deal of money.*" Little was said about the two hundred and fifty thousand dollars bribe; "that," declare the envoys' dispatches to the American Secretary of State, "being completely understood on all sides to be required for the officers of the government, and, therefore, needing no further explanation." When all these conditions were complied with, said Bellamy, "M. Talleyrand trusted that, by his influence with the Directory, he could prevail

---

[1] Directing the capture of enemy goods on American ships, thus nullifying the declaration in the Franco-American Treaty that "free bottoms make free goods."

[2] *Am. St. Prs., For. Rel.,* ii, 159.

on the government to receive" the Americans. For
two hours the talk ran on. Before Talleyrand's
agents left, the anxiously hospitable Gerry invited
them to breakfast the next morning.

Into consultation once more went the envoys. "I
pressed strongly," writes Marshall in his Journal,
"the necessity of declaring that the propositions were
totally inadmissible" and that "it was derogatory
from the honor and wounded the real interests of
our country to permit ourselves, while unacknowl-
edg'd, to carry on this clandestine negotiation with
persons who produced no evidence of being authoriz'd by the Directoire or the Minister to treat
with us. Mr. Gerry was quite of a contrary opinion
& the old beaten ground about precipitation &c. was
trodden once again. Gen'l Pinckney advocated decidedly the same opinions with myself & we determined that the next morning should positively put
an end to these conferences." [1]

"On our retiring," continues Marshall's narrative,
"Mr. Gerry began to propose further delays & that
we shou'd inform them [Talleyrand's go-betweens]
that we wou'd take their propositions into consideration — I improperly interrupted him & declared
that I wou'd not consent to any proposition of the
sort, that the subject was already considered & that
so far as my voice wou'd go I wou'd not permit it
to be supposed longer that we cou'd deliberate on
such propositions as were made to us."

Pinckney agreed with Marshall; but, for harmony's sake, Marshall finally said that he would

[1] Marshall's Journal, Oct. 20, 10. *Am. St. Prs., For. Rel.*, ii, 159.

return to America to "consult our government" on this express condition only — "that France should previously and immediately suspend all depredations upon American commerce." For once, Gerry assented and a letter was written accordingly.[1]

Hottenguer was prompt in his engagement to breakfast with Gerry the next morning; but Bellamy did not come till ten o'clock, explaining that he had been closeted with Talleyrand. Bellamy was much depressed; the Directory, he declared, would not receive the envoys until the latter had disavowed President Adams's speech, *unless* they "could find the means to change their [the Directory's] determination in this particular." What were such "means?" asked the envoys. "I am not authorized to state them," said Bellamy. "You must search for them and propose them yourselves."

Still, Bellamy, merely as an individual, was willing to suggest such "means." It was money, he explained. The "Directory were jealous of their own honor and the honor of the nation"; they demanded the same treatment formerly accorded to the King; and their "honor must be maintained in the manner required" unless "the envoys substituted . . . something perhaps more valuable, and that was money."[2]

It was all so simple, according to Bellamy. All that the envoys had to do was to buy thirty-two million florins of Dutch inscriptions at twenty shillings to the pound. "It was certain," he assured

---

[1] Marshall's Journal, Oct. 21, 10–11.
[2] *Am. St. Prs., For. Rel.*, ii, 159–60.

the Americans, "that after a time the Dutch Government would repay . . . the money, so that America would ultimately lose nothing" and everybody would be happy. But even if the envoys made the loan in this way, the bribe of two hundred and fifty thousand dollars must be paid in addition. Thereupon the envoys handed him the letter which Marshall had prepared the night before, which stated that they had no power to make a loan, but could send one of their number to America for consultation and instruction.

Bellamy was "disappointed" and at once modified his language. Why did the envoys treat the money proposition as coming from the Directory? It was only his own personal suggestion. Then "what has led to our present conversation?" asked the envoys. Pinckney recalled Hottenguer's first visit and the latter confirmed Pinckney's account.

Upon the envoys stating the differences between France and America, to settle which was the purpose of their mission, and gently resenting the demands made upon them, Bellamy became excited. The envoys' conduct was not to be borne, he exclaimed; let them beware of the resentment of France. They "could not help it," answered the envoys — the Directory must look after France; the envoys must look after the United States.

Bellamy was "in despair." What a provincial view these Americans took of a diplomatic negotiation! They must broaden their horizon. They must acquire worldly wisdom. They must remember "the respect which the Directory required"; they must realize that that august body "would exact as much as was paid to the ancient kings." The envoys would not be received without it; that was flat, Bellamy informed them; and "he seemed to shudder at the consequences."

Marshall and Pinckney simply would not see the point. But Gerry was a man of the world who could understand European diplomacy. Marshall declared that the envoys were there to adjust international differences. If, however, France "would make war," then, said they: "We regret the unavoidable necessity of defending ourselves." [1]

For a little while Talleyrand's leeches dropped away from the perplexed Americans. Marshall reported to Washington French conditions as he had observed them up to that time. He confirms to the former President the American report that French agriculture had been improved "in the course of the present war": —

"In that part of the country through which I have passed the evidences of plenty abound. The whole earth appears to be in cultivation & the harvests of the present year appear to be as productive as the fields which yield them are extensive.

"I am informed that every part of the country exhibits the same aspect. If this be the fact, there will probably remain, notwithstanding the demands of the armies, a surplus of provisions."

Marshall briefly but clearly analyzes the economic and commercial outcome of the war: —

"Manufactures have declined in the same ratio

[1] *Am. St. Prs., For. Rel.*, ii, 159–60.

that the cultivation of the soil has increas'd. War has been made upon the great manufacturing towns & they are in a considerable degree destroy'd. With manufactures France does not supply herself fully from her internal resources.

"Those of Britain flow in upon her notwithstanding the most severe prohibitory laws. The port of Rotterdam is purposely left open by the English & their goods are imported by the Dutch under Prussian and other neutral colors. They are smuggled in great quantities into France.

"Peace, then, will find this [French] nation entirely competent to the full supply of her colonies with provisions and needing manufactures to be imported for her own consumption. . . . France can take from America tobacco & raw cotton she can supply us with wines, brandies & silks."

Marshall then makes a searching commentary on French politics.

"The existing political state of France is connected with certain internal & powerfully operating causes by which it has been & will continue to be greatly influenc'd. Not the least of these is the tenure by which property is held.

"In the course of the revolution it is believed that more than half the land of France has become national.[1] Of this a very considerable proportion has been sold at a low rate.

"It is true that much of it belonged to those who have fallen under the Guillotine or who have been termed emigrants. Among the emigrants are many

[1] By "national" lands, Marshall refers to the confiscated estates.

whose attachment to their country has never been shaken; & what is remarkable, among them are many who were never out of France. The law upon this subject is worthy of attention.

"Any two persons, no matter what their reputation, may, to some authority, I believe the municipality of the district, write & subscribe against any person whatever a charge, that such person is an emigrant, on receipt of which the person so charg'd is without further investigation inscribed on the list of emigrants.

"If the person so inscribed be afterwards apprehended while his name remains on the list, the trial, as I understand, is, not of the fact of emigration, but of the identity of the persons, & if this identity be established, he is instantly fusiller'd[shot]. The law is either rightly executed or permitted to be relax'd, as the occasion or the temper of the times may direct.

"During intervals of humanity some disposition has been manifested to permit the return of those who have never offended, who have been banished by a terror which the government itself has reprobated, & to permit in case of arrestation, an investigation of the fact of emigration as well as of the identity of the person accus'd.

"There is too a great deal of property which has been sold as national but which in truth was never so, & which may be reclaimed by the original proprietors.

"In this state the acquirers of national property are of course extremely suspicious. They form a vast proportion of the population of France. They are not only important in consequence of their numbers, but in consequence of their vigor, their activity & that unity of interest which produces a unity of effort among them.

"The armies too have been promised a milliard. This promise rests upon the national property for its performance. The effect of these circumstances cannot escape your observation. Classes of citizens are to be disfranchised against the next election."

Marshall and Pinckney, at this early stage of Talleyrand's financial-diplomatic intrigue, were so disgusted that they were on the point of "returning to America immediately." The continuance of French depredations on the high seas caused Marshall to write to Washington as follows: —

"The captures of our vessels seem to be only limited by the ability to capture. That ability is increasing, as the government has let out to hardy adventurers the national frigates. Among those who plunder us, who are most active in this infamous business, & most loud in vociferating criminations equally absurd and untrue, are some unprincipled apostates who were born in America.

"These sea rovers by a variety of means seem to have acquired great influence in the government.

"This influence will be exerted to prevent an accommodation between the United States & France and to prevent any regulations which may intercept the passage of the spoils they have made on our commerce, to their pockets. The government I believe is too well disposed to promote their views. At present it seems to me to be radically hostile to our country.

"I cou'd wish to form a contrary opinion, but to do so I must shut my eyes on every object which presents itself to them & fabricate in my own mind non-existing things, to be substituted for realities, & to form the basis of my creed.

"Might I be permitted to hazard an opinion it wou'd be the Atlantic only can save us, & that no consideration will be sufficiently powerful to check the extremities to which the temper of this government will carry it, but an apprehension that we may be thrown into the arms of Britain."

Although the Treaty of Campo Formio had been signed on the 17th of October, Paris had not yet heard of it. This treaty marked Bonaparte as the most constructive diplomat, as well as the foremost captain, of the age, for such he had already proved himself to be. A week later, when Marshall wrote the above letter to Washington (October 24, 1797), he reported that "The negotiations with the Emperor of Austria are said not to have been absolutely broken off. Yesterday it was said that peace with him was certain. Several couriers have arrived lately from Buonaparte & the national debt rose yesterday from seven to ten livres in the hundred. Whether this is founded on a real expectation of peace with Austria or is the mere work of stock jobbers is not for me to decide."

But three days afterward (October 27) the news reached Paris; and Marshall adds this postscript: "The definitive peace is made with the Emperor.

You will have seen the conditions. Venice has experienced the fate of Poland. England is threatened with an invasion." [1]

The thunders of cannon announcing Bonaparte's success were still rolling through Paris when Talleyrand's plotters again descended upon the American envoys. Bellamy came and, Pinckney and Gerry being at the opera, saw Marshall alone. The triumph of Bonaparte was his theme. The victorious general was now ready to invade England, announced Bellamy; but "concerning America not a syllable was said." [2]

Already Talleyrand, sensitive as any hawk to coming changes in the political weather, had begun to insinuate himself into the confidence of the future conqueror of Europe, whose diplomatic right arm he so soon was to become. The next morning the thrifty Hottenguer again visits the envoys. Bonaparte's success in the negotiations of Campo Formio, which sealed the victories of the French arms, has alarmed Hottenguer, he declares, for the success of the American mission.

Why, he asks, have the Americans made no proposition to the Directory? That haughty body "were becoming impatient and would take a decided course in regard to America" if the envoys "could not soften them," exclaims Talleyrand's solicitous messenger. Surely the envoys can see that Bonaparte's treaty with Austria has changed everything,

[1] Marshall to Washington, Paris, Oct. 24 (postscript, 27th), 1797; *Amer. Hist. Rev.*, Jan., 1897, ii, 301–03; also, Washington MSS., Lib. Cong.; or Sparks MSS., Mass. Hist. Soc.

[2] Marshall's Journal, Oct. 26, 12.

and that therefore the envoys themselves must change accordingly.

Exhibiting great emotion, Hottenguer asserts that the Directory have determined "that all nations should aid them [the French], or be considered and treated as enemies." Think, he cries, of the "power and violence of France." Think of the present danger the envoys are in. Think of the wisdom of "softening the Directory." But he hints that "the Directory might be made more friendly." Gain time! Gain time! Give the bribe, and gain time! the wily agent advises the Americans. Otherwise, France may declare war against America.

That would be most unfortunate, answer the envoys, but assert that the present American "situation was more ruinous than a declared war could be"; for now American "commerce was floundering unprotected." In case of war "America would protect herself."

"You do not speak to the point," Hottenguer passionately cries out; "it is money; it is expected that you will offer money."

"We have given an answer to that demand," the envoys reply.

"No," exclaims Hottenguer, "you have not! What is your answer?"

"It is no," shouts Pinckney; "no; not a sixpence!"

The persistent Hottenguer does not desist. He tells the envoys that they do not know the kind of men they are dealing with. The Directory, he insists, disregard the justice of American claims; care nothing even for the French colonies; "consider themselves as perfectly invulnerable" from the United States. Money is the only thing that will interest such terrible men. The Americans, parrying, ask whether, even if they give money, Talleyrand will furnish proofs that it will produce results. Hottenguer evades the question. A long discussion ensues.

Pay the bribe, again and again urges the irritated but tenacious go-between. Does not your Government "know that nothing is to be obtained here without money?"

"Our Government had not even suspected such a state of things," declare the amazed Americans.

"Well," answers Hottenguer, "there is not an American in Paris who could not have given that information. . . . Hamburgh and other states of Europe were obliged to buy peace . . . nothing could resist" the power of France; let the envoys think of "the danger of a breach with her." [1]

Thus far Pinckney mostly had spoken for the envoys. Marshall now took up the American case. Few utterances ever made by him more clearly reveal the mettle of the man; and none better show his conception of the American Nation's rights, dignity, and station among the Governments of the world.

"I told him [Hottenguer]," writes Marshall, "that . . . no nation estimated her [France's] power more highly than America or wished more to be on amicable terms with her, but that one object was still dearer to us than the friendship of France which was our national independence. That America had taken a neutral station. She had a right to take it. No

[1] *Am. St. Prs., For. Rel.*, ii, 161–62.

CHARLES COTESWORTH PINCKNEY

nation had a right to force us out of it. That to lend
. . . money to a belligerent power abounding in every
thing requisite for war but money was to relinquish
our neutrality and take part in the war. To lend this
money under the lash & coercion of France was to
relinquish the government of ourselves & to submit
to a foreign government imposed on us by force,"
Marshall declared. "That we would make at least
one manly struggle before we thus surrendered our
national independence.

"Our case was different from that of the minor
nations of Europe," he explained. "They were unable to maintain their independence & did not expect
to do so. America was a great, & so far as concerned
her self-defense, a powerful nation. She was able to
maintain her independence & must deserve to lose it
if she permitted it to be wrested from her. France &
Britain have been at war for near fifty years of the
last hundred & might probably be at war for fifty
years of the century to come."

Marshall asserted that "America has no motives
which could induce her to involve herself in those
wars and that if she now preserved her neutrality &
her independence it was most probable that she
would not in future be afraid as she had been for four
years past — but if she now surrendered her rights of
self government to France or permitted them to be
taken from her she could not expect to recover them
or to remain neutral in any future war." [1]

[1] Marshall's Journal, Oct. 27, 16–17. This statement of the American case by Marshall is given in the dispatches, which Marshall prepared as coming from the envoys generally. (See *Am. St. Prs., For.
Rel.*, ii, 161–62.)

For two hours Talleyrand's emissary pleads, threatens, bullies, argues, expostulates. Finally, he departs to consult with his fellow conspirator, or to see Talleyrand, the master of both. Thus ran the opening dialogue between the French bribe procurers and the American envoys. Day after day, week after week, the plot ran on like a play upon the stage. "A Mr. Hauteval whose fortune lay in the island of St. Domingo" called on Gerry and revealed how pained Talleyrand was that the envoys had not visited him. Again came Hauteval, whom Marshall judged to be the only one of the agents "solicitous of preserving peace."

Thus far the envoys had met with the same request, that they "call upon Talleyrand at private hours." Marshall and Pinckney said that, "having been treated in a manner extremely disrespectful" to their country, they could not visit the Minister of Foreign Affairs "in the existing state of things . . . unless he should expressly signify his wish" to see them "& would appoint a time & place." But, says Marshall, "Mr. Gerry having known Mr. Talleyrand in Boston considered it a piece of personal respect to wait on him & said that he would do so." [1]

Hottenguer again calls to explain how anxious Talleyrand was to serve the envoys. Make "one more effort," he urges, "to enable him to do so." Bonaparte's daring plan for the invasion of England was under way and Hottenguer makes the most of this. "The power and haughtiness of France," the inevitable destruction of England, the terrible con-

[1] Marshall's Journal, Oct. 23, 11-12.

sequences to America, are revealed to the Americans. "Pay by way of fees" the two hundred and fifty thousand dollar bribe, and the Directory would allow the envoys to stay in Paris; Talleyrand would then even consent to receive them while one of them went to America for instructions.[1]

Why hesitate? It was the usual thing; the Portuguese Minister had been dealt with in similar fashion, argues Hottenguer. The envoys counter by asking whether American vessels will meanwhile be restored to their owners. They will not, was the answer. Will the Directory stop further outrages on American commerce, ask the envoys? Of course not, exclaims Hottenguer. We do "not so much regard a little money as [you] said," declare the envoys, "although we should hazard ourselves by giving it but we see only evidences of the most extreme hostility to us." Thereupon they go into a long and useless explanation of the American case.

Gerry's visit to his "old friend" Talleyrand was fruitless; the Foreign Minister would not receive him.[2] Gerry persisted, nevertheless, and finally found the French diplomat at home. Talleyrand demanded the loan, and held a new decree of the Directory before Gerry, but proposed to withhold it for a week so that the Americans could think it over. Gerry hastened to his colleagues with the news. Marshall and Pinckney told Hauteval to inform Talleyrand "that unless there is a hope that the Directory itself might be prevailed upon by reason to

[1] *Am. St. Prs., For. Rel.*, ii, 163; Marshall's Journal, Oct. 29, 21–22.
[2] Marshall's Journal, Oct. 23, 12.

alter its arrêté, we do not wish to suspend it for an instant." [1]

The next evening, when Marshall and Pinckney were away from their quarters, Bellamy and Hottenguer called on Gerry, who again invited them to breakfast. This time Bellamy disclosed the fact that Talleyrand was now intimately connected with Bonaparte and the army in Italy. Let Gerry ponder over that! "The fate of Venice was one which might befall the United States," exclaimed Talleyrand's mouthpiece; and let Gerry not permit Marshall and Pinckney to deceive themselves by expecting help from England — France could and would attend to England, invade her, break her, force her to peace. Where then would America be? Thus for an hour Bellamy and Hottenguer worked on Gerry. [2]

Far as Talleyrand's agents had gone in trying to force the envoys to offer a bribe of a quarter of a million dollars, to the Foreign Minister and Directory, they now went still further. The door of the chamber of horrors was now opened wide to the stubborn Americans. Personal violence was intimated; war was threatened. But Marshall and Pinckney refused to be frightened.

The Directory, Talleyrand, and their emissaries, however, had not employed their strongest resource. "Perhaps you believe," said Bellamy to the envoys, "that in returning and exposing to your countrymen the unreasonableness of the demands of this government, you will unite them in their resistance to those

---

[1] Marshall's Journal, Oct. 28, 18–19.
[2] *Am. St. Prs., For. Rel.*, ii, 163.

demands. You are mistaken; you ought to know
that the diplomatic skill of France and the means she
possesses in your country are sufficient to enable
her, with the French party in America,[1] to throw
the blame which will attend the rupture of the
negotiations on the federalists, as you term yourselves, but on the British party as France terms
you. And you may assure yourselves that this will
be done." [2]

Thus it was out at last. This was the hidden card
that Talleyrand had been keeping back. And it was
a trump. Talleyrand managed to have it played
again by a fairer hand before the game was over.
Yes, surely; here was something to give the obstinate
Marshall pause. For the envoys knew it to be true.
There was a French party in America, and there
could be little doubt that it was constantly growing
stronger.[3] Genêt's reception had made that plain.
The outbursts throughout America of enthusiasm
for France had shown it. The popular passion exhibited, when the Jay Treaty was made public, had
proved it. Adams's narrow escape from defeat had
demonstrated the strength of French sympathy in
America.

[1] "Infinite pains have been taken there [in France] to spread universally the idea that there are, in America, only two parties, the one
entirely devoted to France and the other to England." (J. Q. Adams
to his father, The Hague, July 2, 1797; *Writings, J. Q. A.*: Ford,
ii, 181.)

[2] Marshall's Journal, Oct. 30, 25–26; *Am. St. Prs., For. Rel.*, 164.

[3] "The French were extremely desirous of seeing Mr. Jefferson
President; . . . they exerted themselves to the utmost in favor of his
election [in 1796]; . . . they made a great point of his success." (Harper to his Constituents, Jan. 5, 1797; *Bayard Papers*: Donnan, 25;
and see *supra*, chaps. I, II, III, and IV, of this volume.)

A far more dangerous circumstance, as well known
to Talleyrand as it was to the envoys, made the
matter still more serious—the democratic societies,
which, as we have seen, had been organized in great
numbers throughout the United States had pushed
the French propaganda with zeal, system, and ability; and were, to America, what the Jacobin Clubs
had been to France before their bloody excesses.
They had already incited armed resistance to the
Government of the United States.[1] Thorough information of the state of things in the young country
across the ocean had emboldened Barras, upon taking leave of Monroe, to make a direct appeal to the
American people in disregard of their own Government, and, indeed, almost openly against it. The
threat, by Talleyrand's agents, of the force which
France could exert in America, was thoroughly
understood by the envoys. For, as we have seen,
there was a French party in America — "a party,"
as Washington declared, "determined to advocate
French measures under *all* circumstances." [2] It was
common knowledge among all the representatives
of the American Government in Europe that the
French Directory depended upon the Republican
Party in this country. "They reckon . . . upon
many friends and partisans among us," wrote the
American Minister in London to the American
Minister at The Hague.[3]

The Directory even had its particular agents in
the United States to inflame the American people

---

[1] See *supra*, chap. III, 86 *et seq.*
[2] Washington to King, June 25, 1797; King, ii, 194.
[3] King to Murray, March 31, 1798; *ib.*, 294.

against their own Government if it did not yield to French demands. Weeks before the President, in 1797, had called Congress in special session on French affairs, "the active and incessant manœuvres of French agents in" America made William Smith think that any favorable action of France "will drive the great mass of knaves & fools back into her [France's] arms," notwithstanding her piracies upon our ships.[1]

On November 1 the envoys again decided to "hold no more indirect intercourse with" Talleyrand or the Directory. Marshall and Pinckney told Hottenguer that they thought it "degrading our country to carry on further such an indirect intercourse"; and that they "would receive no propositions" except from persons having "acknowledged authority." After much parrying, Hottenguer again unparked the batteries of the French party in America.

He told Marshall and Pinckney that "intelligence had been received from the United States, that if Colonel Burr and Mr. Madison had constituted the Mission, the difference between the two nations would have been accommodated before this time." Talleyrand was even preparing to send a memorial to America, threatened Hottenguer, complaining that the envoys were "unfriendly to an accommodation with France."

The insulted envoys hotly answered that Talleyrand's "correspondents in America took a good deal on themselves when they undertook to say how the Directory would have received Colonel Burr and

[1] Smith to King, Philadelphia, April 3, 1797; King, ii, 165.

Mr. Madison"; and they defied Talleyrand to send a memorial to the United States.[1]

Disgusted with these indirect and furtive methods, Marshall insisted on writing Talleyrand on the subject that the envoys had been sent to France to settle. "I had been for some time extremely solicitous" that such a letter should be sent, says Marshall. "It appears to me that for three envoys extraordinary to be kept in Paris thirty days without being received can only be designed to degrade & humiliate their country & to postpone a consideration of its just & reasonable complaints till future events in which it ought not to be implicated shall have determined France in her conduct towards it. Mr. Gerry had been of a contrary opinion & we had yielded to him but this evening he consented that the letter should be prepared." [2]

Nevertheless Gerry again objected.[3] At last the Paris newspapers took a hand. "It was now in the power of the Administration [Directory]," says Marshall, "to circulate by means of an enslaved press precisely those opinions which are agreeable to itself & no printer dares to publish an examination of them."

"With this tremendous engine at its will, it [the Directory] almost absolutely controls public opinion on every subject which does not immediately affect the interior of the nation. With respect to its designs against America it experiences not so much difficulty as . . . would have been experienced had not

[1] *Am. St. Prs., For. Rel.*, ii, 163–64.
[2] Marshall's Journal, Nov. 4, 31.   [3] *Ib.*, 31.

our own countrymen labored to persuade them that
our Government was under a British influence." [1]

On November 3, Marshall writes Charles Lee:
"When I clos'd my last letter I did not expect to
address you again from this place. I calculated on
being by this time on my return to the United States.
. . . My own opinion is that France wishes to retain
America in her present situation until her negotiation with Britain, which it is believed is about to
recommence, shall have been terminated, and a
present absolute rupture with America might encourage England to continue the war and peace with
England . . . will put us more in her [France's]
power. . . . Our situation is more intricate and difficult than you can believe. . . . The demand for
money has been again repeated. The last address
to us . . . concluded . . . that the French party in
America would throw all the blame of a rupture on
the federalists. . . . We were warned of the fate of
Venice. All these conversations are preparing for a
public letter but the delay and the necessity of writing only in cypher prevents our sending it by this
occasion. . . . I wish you could . . . address the
Minister concerning our reception. We despair of
doing anything. . . . Mr. Putnam an American citizen has been arrested and sent to jail under the pretext of his cheating frenchmen. . . . This . . . is a
mere pretext. It is considered as ominous toward
Americans generally. He like most of them is a
creditor of the [French] government." [2]

[1] Marshall's Journal, Nov. 8, 33.
[2] Marshall to Lee, Nov. 3, 1797; MS., Lib. Cong. Lee was Attorney-General. Marshall's letter was in cipher.

Finally the envoys sent Talleyrand the formal request, written by Marshall,[1] that the Directory receive them. Talleyrand ignored it. Ten more days went by. When might they expect an answer? inquired the envoys. Talleyrand parried and delayed. "We are not yet received," wrote the envoys to Secretary of State Pickering, "and the condemnation of our vessels . . . is unremittingly continued. Frequent and urgent attempts have been made to inveigle us again into negotiations with persons not officially authorized, of which the obtaining of money is the basis; but we have persisted in declining to have any further communication relative to diplomatic business with persons of that description." [2]

Anxious as Marshall was about the business of his mission, which now rapidly was becoming an intellectual duel between Talleyrand and himself, he was far more concerned as to the health of his wife, from whom he had heard nothing since leaving America. Marshall writes her a letter full of apprehension, but lightens it with a vague account of the amusements, distractions, and dissipations of the French Capital.

"I have not, since my departure from the United States," Marshall tells his wife, "received a single letter from you or from any one of my friends in America. Judge what anxiety I must feel concerning you. I do not permit myself for a moment to suspect that you are in any degree to blame for this. I am sure you have written often to me but unhappily for

---

[1] Marshall to Lee, Nov. 7, 8, 9, 10, and 11; MS., Lib. Cong.
[2] *Am. St. Prs., For. Rel.*, ii, 166.

me your letters have not found me. I fear they will
not. They have been thrown over board or intercepted. Such is the fate of the greater number of the
letters addressed by Americans to their friends in
France, such I fear will be the fate of all that may
be address'd to me.

"In my last letter I informed you that I counted
on being at home in March. I then expected to
have been able to leave this country by christmas
at furthest & such is my impatience to see you &
my dear children that I had determined to risk a
winter passage." He asks his wife to request Mr.
Wickham to see that one of Marshall's law cases
"may ly till my return. I think nothing will prevent
my being at the chancery term in May.

"Oh God," cries Marshall, "how much time &
how much happiness have I thrown away! Paris
presents one incessant round of amusement & dissi-
pation but very little I believe even for its inhabitants of that society which interests the heart. Every
day you may see something new magnificent & beautiful, every night you may see a spectacle which
astonishes & enchants the imagination. The most
lively fancy aided by the strongest description cannot equal the reality of the opera. All that you can
conceive & a great deal more than you can conceive
in the line of amusement is to be found in this gay
metropolis but I suspect it would not be easy to find
a friend.

"I would not live in Paris," Marshall tells his
"dearest Polly" "[if I could] . . . be among the
wealthiest of its citizens. I have changed my lodg-

ing much for the better. I liv'd till within a few
days in a house where I kept my own apartments
perfectly in the style of a miserable old bachelor
without any mixture of female society. I now have
rooms in the house of a very accomplished a very
sensible & I believe a very amiable Lady whose temper, very contrary to the general character of her
country women, is domestic & who generally sits
with us two or three hours in the afternoon.

"This renders my situation less unpleasant than
it has been but nothing can make it eligible. Let me
see you once more & I . . . can venture to assert that
no consideration would induce me ever again to consent to place the Atlantic between us. Adieu my
dearest Polly. Preserve your health & be happy as
possible till the return of him who is ever yours."[1]

The American Minister in London was following
anxiously the fortunes of our envoys in Paris, and
gave them frequent information and sound advice.
Upon learning of their experiences, King writes
that "I will not allow myself yet to despair of
your success, though my apprehensions are greater
than my hopes." King enclosed his Dispatch number 52 to the American Secretary of State, which
tells of the Portuguese Treaty and the decline of
Spain's power in Paris.[2]

In reply, Pinckney writes King, on December 14,
that the Directory "are undoubtedly hostile to our
Government, and are determined, if possible, to

[1] Marshall to his wife, Paris, Nov. 27, 1797; MS.
[2] King to Pinckney, Marshall, and Gerry, Nov. 15, 1797; enclosing
Dispatch no. 52 to Pinckney; King, ii, 240–41. See *ib.*, 245; and
Dec. 9, 1797; *ib.*, 247.

effectuate a change in our administration, and to oblige our present President [Adams] to resign," and further adds that the French authorities contemplate expelling from France "every American who could not prove" that he was for France and against America.

"Attempts," he continues, "are made to divide the Envoys and with that view some civilities are shown to Mr. G.[erry] and none to the two others [Marshall and Pinckney]. . . . The American Jacobins here pay him [Gerry] great Court." [1] The little New Englander already was yielding to the seductions of Talleyrand, and was also responsive to the flattery of a group of unpatriotic Americans in Paris who were buttering their own bread by playing into the hands of the Directory and the French Foreign Office.

Marshall now beheld a stage of what he believed was the natural development of unregulated democracy. Dramatic events convinced him that he was witnessing the growth of license into absolutism. Early in December Bonaparte arrived in Paris. Swiftly the Conqueror had come from Rastadt, traveling through France *incognito*, after one of his lightning-flash speeches to his soldiers reminding them of "the Kings whom you have vanquished, the people upon whom you have conferred liberty." The young general's name was on every tongue.

Paris was on fire to see and worship the hero. But Bonaparte kept aloof from the populace. He made himself the child of mystery. The future Emperor of

[1] Pinckney to King, Paris, Dec. 14, 1797; King, ii, 259-60.

the French, clad in the garments of a plain citizen, slipped unnoticed through the crowds. He would meet nobody but scholars and savants of world renown. These he courted; but he took care that this fact was known to the people. In this course he continued until the stage was set and the cue for his entrance given.

Finally the people's yearning to behold and pay homage to their soldier-statesman becomes a passion not to be denied. The envious but servile Directory yield, and on December 10, 1797, a splendid festival in Bonaparte's honor is held at the Luxembourg. The scene flames with color: captured battle-flags as decorations; the members of the Directory appareled as Roman Consuls; foreign ministers in their diplomatic costumes; officers in their uniforms; women brilliantly attired in the height of fashion.[1] At last the victorious general appears on the arm of Talleyrand, the latter gorgeously clad in the dress of his high office; but Bonaparte, short, slender, and delicate, wearing the plainest clothes of the simplest citizen.

Upon this superb play-acting John Marshall looked with placid wonder. Here, then, thought this Virginian, who had himself fought for liberty on many a battlefield, were the first fruits of French revolutionary republicanism. Marshall beheld no

---

[1] Talleyrand, who gave the fête, wrote: "I spared no trouble to make it brilliant and attractive; although in this I experienced some difficulty on account of the vulgarity of the directors' wives who, of course, enjoyed precedence over all other ladies." (*Memoirs of Talleyrand:* Broglie's ed., i, 197; also see Sloane: *Life of Napoleon*, ii, 20; and Lanfrey: *Life of Napoleon*, i, 254–57.)

devotion here to equal laws which should shield all men, but only adoration of the sword-wielder who was strong enough to rule all men. In the fragile, eagle-faced little warrior,[1] Marshall already saw the man on horseback advancing out of the future; and in the thunders of applause he already heard the sound of marching armies, the roar of shotted guns, the huzzas of charging squadrons.

All this was something that Jefferson had not seen. Jefferson's sojourn in France had been at the time when the French Revolution was just sprouting; and he foresaw only that beautiful idealism into which the glorious dreamers of the time fondly imagined the Revolution would flower.

But Marshall was in Paris after the guillotine had done its work; when corruption sat in the highest places of government; and when military glory in the name of liberty had become the deity of the people. So where Jefferson expected that the roses of peace would bloom, Marshall saw clusters of bayonets, as the fruitage of the French Revolution.

[1] "At first sight he [Bonaparte] seemed . . . to have a charming face, so much do the halo of victory, fine eyes, a pale and almost consumptive look, become a young hero." (*Memoirs of Talleyrand:* Broglie's ed., i, 196.)

CHAPTER VIII .

THE AMERICAN MEMORIAL

Separated far from Europe, we mean not to mingle in her quarrels. (Marshall.)

A fraudulent neutrality is no neutrality at all. (Marshall.)

We have a very considerable party in America who are strongly in our interest. (Madame de Villette.)

FOUR days after the festival of triumph to Bonaparte, Talleyrand's agents resumed their work. The sordid scenes were repeated, but their monotony was broken. Now the lady of the plot appeared upon the scene. In the long, vexed, and fruitless days of their stay in Paris, the American envoys, it seems, were not without the solace and diversion of the society of the French Capital.

Among the attractive feminine acquaintances they made, one was undoubtedly an agent of the French Foreign Office. Madame de Villette was one of the most engaging women in the French Capital.[1] Cultivated, brilliant, and altogether charming, she made herself particularly agreeable to the American envoys. She and Marshall became especially good

---

[1] *Am. St. Prs., For. Rel.*, ii, 167. This lady was "understood to be Madame de Villette, the celebrated Belle and Bonne of Voltaire." (Lyman: *Diplomacy of the United States*, ii, footnote to 336.) Lyman says that "as to the lady an intimation is given that that part of the affair was not much to the credit of the Americans." (And see Austin: *Gerry*, ii, footnote to 202.) Madame de Villette was the widow of a Royalist colonel. Her brother, an officer in the King's service, was killed while defending Marie Antoinette. Robespierre proscribed Madame de Villette and she was one of a group confined in prison awaiting the guillotine, of whom only a few escaped. (*Ib.*)

friends; but Madame de Villette ventured no diplomatic suggestions to him, notwithstanding his easy good nature. She was far too good a judge of character to commit that indiscretion. So was Talleyrand, who by this time had begun to appreciate Marshall's qualities. But Pinckney, hearty, handsome man of the world, but without Marshall's penetration and adroitness, was another matter. Gerry the intriguers could already count upon; and only one other member of the commission was necessary to their ends. Perhaps Pinckney might be won over by this captivating Frenchwoman. On some occasion Madame de Villette approached him: —

"Why will you not lend us money?" said she to Pinckney. "If you were to make us a loan, all matters will be adjusted. When you were contending for your Revolution we lent you money." Pinckney pointed out the differences — that America had *requested* a loan of France, and France now *demanded* a loan of America. "Oh, no," said she. "We do not make a demand; we think it more delicate that the offer should come from you; but M. Talleyrand has mentioned to me (who am surely not in his confidence) the necessity of your making us a loan, and I know that he has mentioned it to two or three others; and that you have been informed of it; and I will assure you that, if you remain here six months longer, you will not advance a single step further in your negotiations without a loan."

If that is so, bluntly answered Pinckney, the envoys might as well leave at once. "Why," exclaimed Talleyrand's fair agent, "that might possibly lead to a rupture, which you had better avoid; for we have a very considerable party in America who are strongly in our interest." [1]

The fox-like Talleyrand had scented another hole by which he might get at his elusive quarry. "Every man has his price" was his doctrine; and his experience hitherto had proved it sound. He found that the brilliant Paris adventurer, Beaumarchais, had a lawsuit against the State of Virginia. Beaumarchais had won this suit in the lower court and it was now pending on appeal. John Marshall was his attorney.[2] Here, then, thought Talleyrand, was the way to reach this unknown quantity in his problem.

On December 17, Marshall, happening into Gerry's

[1] *Am. St. Prs., For. Rel.*, ii, 167.

[2] Beaumarchais was one of the most picturesque figures of that theatrical period. He is generally known to-day only as the author of the operas, *The Barber of Seville* and the *Marriage of Figaro.* His suit was to recover a debt for supplies furnished the Americans during the Revolution. Silas Deane, for our Government, made the original contract with Beaumarchais. In addition to the contest before the courts, in which Marshall was Beaumarchais's attorney, the matter was before Congress three times during the claimant's life and, through his heirs, twice after his death. In 1835 the case was settled for 800,000 francs, which was nearly 2,500,000 francs less than Alexander Hamilton, in an investigation, ordered by Congress, found to be due the Frenchman; and 3,500,000 livres less than Silas Deane reported that America owed Beaumarchais.

Arthur Lee, Beaumarchais's enemy, to whom Congress in 1787 left the adjustment, had declared that the Frenchman owed the United States two million francs. This prejudiced report was the cause of almost a half-century of dispute, and of gross injustice. (See Loménie: *Beaumarchais et son temps;* also, Channing, iii, 283, and references in the footnote; and Perkins: *France in the American Revolution.* Also see Henry to Beaumarchais, Jan. 8, 1785; Henry, iii, 264, in which Henry says: "I therefore feel myself gratified in seeing, as I think, ground for hope that yourself, and those worthy and suffering of ours in your nation, who in so friendly a manner advanced their money and goods when we were in want, will be satisfied that nothing has been omitted which lay in our power towards paying them.")

apartment, found Bellamy there. Beaumarchais had given a dinner to Marshall and his fellow envoys, from which Bellamy had been kept by a toothache. The envoys had returned Beaumarchais's courtesy; and he had retired from this dinner "much indisposed." [1] Since then Marshall had not seen his client. Bellamy casually remarked that he had not known, until within a short time, that Marshall was the attorney for Beaumarchais, who, he said, had very high regard for his Virginia attorney.

Marshall, his lawyer's instincts at once aroused, told Bellamy that Beaumarchais's case was of very great magnitude and that he was deeply interested in it. Whereupon, in a low tone, spoken aside for his ear only, Bellamy told Marshall that, in case the latter won the suit, Beaumarchais would "sacrifice £50,000 Sterling of it as the private gratification" demanded by the Directory and Talleyrand, "so that the gratification might be made without any actual loss to the American government." Marshall rejected this offer and informed Pinckney of it. [2]

Marshall's character is revealed by the entry he promptly made in his Journal. "Having been originally the Counsel of Mr. de Beaumarchais, I had determined & so I informed Genl. Pinckney, that I would not by my voice establish any argument in his favor, but that I would positively oppose any admission of the claim of any French citizen if not accompanied with the admission of claims of the American

1 Marshall's Journal, ii, Dec. 17, 36.
2 *Am. St. Prs., For. Rel.*, ii, 167; Marshall's Journal, Dec. 17, 36–37.

citizens to property captured and condemned for
want of a Rôle d'équipage." [1]

Bellamy then urged upon Gerry his plan of the
Marshall-Beaumarchais arrangement. Talleyrand
had been entertaining Gerry privately, and the flattered New Englander again wished to call on the
French Minister, "to return the civility" by inviting
Talleyrand to dinner.[2] To Talleyrand, then, went
Gerry in company with Bellamy and asked the
Foreign Minister to dine with him. Then Gerry
tediously reviewed the situation, concluding in a
manner that must have amused the bored Talleyrand: He would rather see the envoys depart for
some city in another nation, said Gerry, until the
Directory would receive them, than to stay in Paris
under the circumstances.

Gerry was sure that the French diplomat was
alarmed by this stern threat. "M. Talleyrand appeared to be uneasy at this declaration," he told
his colleagues. Still, Talleyrand avoided "saying
a word on it"; but he did say that Bellamy's representations "might always be relied on." Talleyrand
declared that he would go further; he would himself write out his propositions. This he proceeded to
do, held the writing before Gerry's eyes and then
burned it; after this performance Talleyrand said
he would dine with Gerry "the decade [ten days]
after the present." [3]

---

[1] Marshall's Journal, Dec. 17, 38. The "Rôle d'équipage" was a
form of ship's papers required by the French Government which it
was practically impossible for American masters to furnish; yet,
without it, their vessels were liable to capture by French ships under
one of the many offensive decrees of the French Government.

[2] Marshall's Journal, Dec. 17, 38.   [3] Am. St. Prs., For. Rel., ii, 168.

Meanwhile, however, Gerry dined with the Foreign Minister. It was not a merry function. Aside from his guest of honor, the French Minister also had at his board Hottenguer, Bellamy, and Hauteval. Gerry could not speak French and Hauteval acted as translator. It must have been a pallid feast; the brilliant, witty, accomplished Talleyrand, man of the world, *bon vivant*, and lover of gayety; the solemn, dull, and rigid Gerry; the three trained French agents, one of them, as interpreter, the only means of general communication.[1] On rising from the table, Hottenguer at once brought up the question of the bribe. Would the envoys now give it? Had they the money ready? Gerry answered no![2]

Talleyrand, by now the mouthpiece of the rising Bonaparte, had proposed terms of peace to Great Britain; "the price was a Bribe of a Million Sterling to be divided among Directors, Ministers, and others. Talleyrand's Department was to share one hundred thousand Pounds Sterling." The British Government declined.[3]

King in London hastens to inform his American diplomatic associates in Paris of this offer, and cautions the envoys to act in concert. To Pinckney, King writes in cipher his anxiety about Gerry, whose integrity King had hoped would "overcome a miserable vanity and a few little defects of character . . .

[1] This account in the dispatches is puzzling, for Talleyrand spoke English perfectly.

[2] *Am. St. Prs., For. Rel.*, ii, 230.

[3] King to Secretary of State (in cipher) London, Dec. 23, 1797; King, ii, 261. King to Pinckney, Marshall, and Gerry, Dec. 23, 1797; *ib.*, 263.

which I now fear have been discovered by those who will be assiduous to turn them to mischief."

From the same source Pinckney is warned: "You must not appear to suspect what you may really know; . . . you must . . . save him [Gerry] and, in doing so, prevent the Division that would grow out of a Schism in your Commission." Gerry will be all right, thinks King, "unless Pride shall be put in opposition to Duty, or Jealousy shall mislead a mind neither ingenuous nor well organized, but habitually suspicious, and, when assailed by personal vanity, inflexible." [1]

Pinckney informs King of the situation in Paris on December 27, declaring "that we ought to request our Passports and no longer exhibit to the World the unprecedented Spectacle of three Envoys Extraordinary from a free and independent nation, in vain soliciting to be heard." [2]

Marshall now insists that the American case be formally stated to the French Government. Gerry at last agrees.[3] Marshall, of course, prepares this vastly important state paper. For two weeks he works over the first half of this historic document. "At my request Genl. Pinckney & Mr. Gerry met in my room & I read to them the first part of a letter to the Minister of Exterior Relations which consisted of a justification of the American Government," [4] he relates in his Journal.

Over the last half of the American case, Marshall

[1] King to Pinckney (in cipher) London, Dec. 24, 1797; King, ii, 263–64.

[2] Pinckney to King, Dec. 27, 1797; King, ii, 266–67.

[3] Marshall's Journal, Dec. 18, 1797, 38.   [4] *Ib.*, Jan. 2, 1798, 39.

spends seven days. "The Second part of the letter to the Minister of Exterior Relations, comprehending the claims of the United States upon France, being also prepared, I read it to Genl Pinckney & Mr. Gerry." Both sections of Marshall's letter to Talleyrand were submitted to his colleagues for suggestions.[1]

It was hard work to get Gerry to examine and sign the memorial. "I had so repeatedly pressed Mr. Gerry," notes Marshall, "on the subject of our letter prepared for the Minister of Exterior Relations & manifested such solicitude for its being so completed as to enable us to send it, that I had obviously offended. Today I have urged that subject and for the last time." [2] Two days later Marshall chronicles that "Mr. Gerry finished the examination of our letter to the Minister of Exterior Relations." [3] A week later the letter, translated and signed, is delivered to Talleyrand.[4]

Upon this memorial were based future and successful American negotiations,[5] and the statement by Marshall remains to this day one of the ablest state papers ever produced by American diplomacy.

Marshall reminds Talleyrand of the frequent and open expressions of America's regard for France, given "with all the ardor and sincerity of youth." These, he says, were considered in America "as evidencing a mutual friendship, to be as durable as the republics themselves." Unhappily the scene changed, says Marshall, and "America looks around in vain

---

[1] Marshall's Journal, Jan. 2 and 10, 39.
[2] Ib., Jan. 22, 40.   [3] Ib., 40.   [4] Ib., Jan. 31.
[5] The Ellsworth mission. (See infra, chap. XII.)

for the ally or the friend." He pictures the contrast in the language and conduct of the French Government with what had passed before, and says that the French charge of American partiality toward Great Britain is unfounded.

Marshall then reviews the international situation and makes it so plain that America could not take part in the European wars, that even Talleyrand was never able to answer the argument. "When that war [began] which has been waged with such unparalleled fury," he writes, "which in its vast vicissitudes of fortune has alternately threatened the very existence of the conflicting parties, but which, in its progress, has surrounded France with splendor, and added still more to her glory than to her territory," America found herself at peace with all the belligerent Powers; she was connected with some of them by treaties of amity and commerce, and with France by a treaty of alliance.

But these treaties, Marshall points out, did not require America to take part in this war. "Being bound by no duty to enter into the war, the Government of the United States conceived itself bound by duties, the most sacred, to abstain from it." Upon the ground that man, even in different degrees of social development, is still the natural friend of man, "the state of peace, though unstipulated by treaty," was the only course America could take. "The laws of nature" enjoined this, Marshall announces; and in some cases "solemn and existing engagements ... require a religious observance" of it.[1]

[1] *Am. St. Prs., For. Rel.*, ii, 169.

Such was the moral ground upon which Marshall built his argument, and he strengthened it by practical considerations. "The great nations of Europe," he writes, "either impelled by ambition or by existing or supposed political interests, peculiar to themselves, have consumed more than a third of the present century in wars." The causes that produced this state of things "cannot be supposed to have been entirely extinguished, and humanity can scarcely indulge the hope that the temper or condition of man is so altered as to exempt the next century from the ills of the past. Strong fortifications, powerful navies, immense armies, the accumulated wealth of ages, and a full population, enable the nations of Europe to support those wars." [1]

Problems of this character, Marshall explains, must be solved by European countries, not by the United States. For, "encircled by no dangerous Powers, they [the Americans] neither fear, nor are jealous of their neighbors," says Marshall, "and are not, on that account, obliged to arm for their own safety." He declares that America, separated from Europe "by a vast and friendly ocean," has "no motive for a voluntary war," but "the most powerful reasons to avoid it." [2]

America's great and undefended commerce, made necessary by her then economic conditions, would be, Marshall contends, the "immediate and certain victim" of engaging in European wars; and he then demonstrates the disastrous results to America of departing from her policy of Neutrality.

[1] *Am. St. Prs., For. Rel.*, ii, 169–70.   [2] *Ib.*, 170.

The immense and varied resources of the United States can only be used for self-defense, reasons the Virginia lawyer. "Neither the genius of the nation, nor the state of its own finances admit of calling its citizens from the plough but to defend their own liberty and their own firesides."

He then points out that, in addition to the moral wrong and material disaster of America's taking part in France's wars, such a course means the launching into the almost boundless ocean of European politics. It implies "contracting habits of national conduct and forming close political connections which must have compromitted the future peace of the nation, and have involved it in all the future quarrels of Europe."

Marshall then describes the "long train of armies, debts, and taxes, checking the growth, diminishing happiness, and perhaps endangering the liberty of the United States, which must have followed." And all this for what? Not to fulfill America's treaties; "not to promote her own views, her own objects, her own happiness, her own safety; but to move as a satellite around some other greater planet, whose laws she must of necessity obey." [1]

"It was believed," he declares, "that France would derive more benefit from the Neutrality of America than from her becoming a party in the war." Neutrality determined upon, he insists that "increased motives of honor and of duty commanded its faithful observance. . . . A fraudulent neutrality is no neutrality at all. . . . A . . . nation which would

---

[1] *Am. St. Prs., For. Rel.*, ii, 170.

be admitted to its privileges, should also perform the duties it enjoins."

If the American Government, occupying a neutral position, had granted "favors unstipulated by treaty, to one of the belligerent Powers which it refused to another, it could no longer have claimed the immunities of a situation of which the obligations were forgotten; it would have become a party to the war as certainly as if war had been openly and formally declared, and it would have added to the madness of wantonly engaging in such a hazardous conflict, the dishonor of insincere and fraudulent conduct; it would have attained, circuitously, an object which it could not plainly avow or directly pursue, and would have tricked the people of the United States into a war which it would not venture openly to declare."

Then follows this keen thrust which Talleyrand could not evade: "It was a matter of real delight to the government and people of America," suavely writes Marshall, "to be informed that France did not wish to interrupt the peace they [the American people] enjoyed."

Marshall then makes a sudden and sharp attack memorable in the records of diplomatic dueling. He calls attention to the astounding conduct of the French Minister on American soil immediately after the American Government had proclaimed its Neutrality to the world and had notified American citizens of the duties which that Neutrality enjoined. In polite phrase he reminds Talleyrand of Genêt's assumption of "the functions of the government to which he was deputed, . . . although he was not even acknowledged as a minister or had reached the authority which should inspect his credentials."

But, notwithstanding this, says Marshall, "the American Government resolved to see in him [Genêt] only the representative of a republic to which it was sincerely attached" and "gave him the same warm and cordial reception which he had experienced from its citizens without a single exception from Charleston to Philadelphia."

Two paragraphs follow of fulsome praise of France, which would seem to have been written by Gerry, who insisted on revising the memorial.[1] But in swift contrast Marshall again throws on the screen the indefensible performances of the French Minister in America and the tolerance with which the American Government treated them. "In what manner would France have treated any foreign minister, who should have dared to so conduct himself toward this republic? . . . In what manner would the American Government have treated him [Genêt] had he been the representative of any other nation than France?"

No informed man can doubt the answer to these questions, says Marshall. "From the Minister of France alone could this extraordinary conduct be borne with temper." But "to have continued to bear it without perceiving its extreme impropriety would have been to have merited the contempt" of the world and of France herself. "The Government of the United States did feel it," declares Marshall, but did not attribute Genêt's misconduct to the French Nation. On the contrary, the American Government

[1] Marshall's Journal, 39; also see Austin: *Gerry*, ii, chap. VI.

"distinguished strongly between the [French] Government and its Minister," and complained "in the language of a friend afflicted but not irritated." Genêt's recall "was received with universal joy" in America, "as a confirmation that his . . . conduct was attributable only to himself"; and "not even the publication of his private instructions could persuade the American Government to ascribe any part of it to this [French] republic." [1]

Marshall further points out "the exertions of the United States to pay up the arrearages" of their debt to France; America's "disinterested and liberal advances to the sufferers of St. Domingo . . . whose recommendation was that they were Frenchmen and unfortunate"; and other acts of good-will of the American Government toward the French Republic.

He then makes a characteristically clear and convincing argument upon the points at issue between France and America. France complained that one article of the Jay Treaty provided that in case of war the property of an enemy might be taken by either out of the ships of the other; whereas, by the Treaty of 1778 between France and America, neither party should take out of the vessels of the other the goods of its enemy. France contended that this was a discrimination against her in favor of Great Britain. Marshall shows that this provision in the Jay Treaty was merely the statement of the existing law of nations, and that therefore the Jay Treaty gave no new rights to Great Britain.

Marshall reminds Talleyrand that any two na-

[1] *Am. St. Prs., For. Rel.,* ii, 170–71.

tions by treaty have the power to alter, as to their mutual intercourse, the usages prescribed by international law; that, accordingly, France and America had so changed, as between themselves, the law of nations respecting enemy's goods in neutral bottoms. He cites the ordinance of France herself in 1744 and her long continued practice under it; and he answers so overwhelmingly the suggestion that the law of nations had not been changed by the rules laid down by the "Armed Neutrality" of the Northern Powers of Europe in the war existing at the time of that confederation, that the resourceful Talleyrand made no pretense of answering it.

The stipulation in the Franco-American Treaty of "protecting the goods of the enemy of either party in the vessels of the other, and in turn surrendering its own goods found in the vessels of the enemy," extended, Marshall insists, to no other nation except to France and America; and contends that this could be changed only by further specific agreements between those two nations.

Marshall wishes "that the principle that neutral bottoms shall make neutral goods" were universally established, and declares that that principle "is perhaps felt by no nation on earth more strongly than by the United States." On this point he is emphatic, and reiterates that "no nation is more deeply interested in its establishment" than America. "It is an object they [the United States] have kept in view, and which, if not forced by violence to abandon it, they will pursue in such manner as their own judgment may dictate as being best calculated to attain it."

"But," he says, "the wish to establish a principle is essentially different from a determination that it is already established. . . . However solicitous America might be to pursue all proper means, tending to obtain for this principle the assent of any or all of the maritime Powers of Europe, she never conceived the idea of attaining that consent by force." [1] "The United States will only arm to defend their own rights," declares Marshall; "neither their policy nor their interests permit them to arm, in order to compel a surrender of the rights of others."

He then gives the history of the Jay Treaty, and points out that Jay's particular instructions not to preserve peace with Great Britain, "nor to receive compensations for injuries sustained, nor security against their future commission, at the expense of the smallest of its [America's] engagements to France," [2] were incorporated in the treaty itself, in the clause providing that "nothing in this treaty shall, however, be construed or operate contrary to former and existing public treaties with other sovereignties or states." [3] So careful, in fact, was America to meet the views of France that "previous to its ratification" the treaty was submitted to the French Minister to the United States, who did not even comment on the article relating to enemy's goods in neutral bottoms, but objected only to that enlarging the list of contraband; [4] and the American Government went to extreme lengths to meet the views of

[1] *Am. St. Prs., For. Rel.*, ii, 172.
[2] *Ib.*, 173. [3] *Ib.* [4] *Ib.*

the French Minister, who finally appeared to be satisfied.

The articles of contraband enumerated in the Jay Treaty, to which the French Government objected, says Marshall, were contraband by the laws of nations and so admitted by France herself in her treaties with other countries.[1]

Answering the charge that in the treaty the United States had agreed that more articles should be contraband than she had in compacts with other Powers, Marshall explains that "the United States, desirous of liberating commerce, have invariably seized every opportunity which presented itself to diminish or remove the shackles imposed on that of neutrals. In pursuance of this policy, they have on no occasion hesitated to reduce the list of contraband, as between themselves and any nation consenting to such reduction. Their preëxisting treaties have been with nations as willing as themselves to change this old rule." But these treaties leave other governments, who do not accept the American policy, "to the law which would have governed had such particular stipulation never been made" — that is, to the law of nations.

Great Britain declined to accept this American view of the freedom of the seas; and, therefore, America was forced to leave that nation where it had found her on the subject of contraband and freedom of ocean-going commerce. Thus, contends Marshall, the Jay Treaty "has not added to the catalog of contraband a single article . . . ceded no

[1] *Am. St. Prs., For. Rel.*, ii, 175.

privilege . . . granted no right," nor changed, in the most minute circumstance, the preëxisting situation of the United States in relation either to France or to Great Britain. Notwithstanding these truths, "the Government of the United States has hastened to assure its former friend [France], that, if the stipulations between them are found oppressive in practice, it is ready to offer up those stipulations a willing sacrifice at the shrine of friendship." [1]

Stating the general purposes of the United States, Marshall strikes at the efforts of France to compel America to do what France wishes and in the manner that France wishes, instead of doing what American interests require and in the manner America thinks wisest.

The American people, he asserts, "must judge exclusively for themselves how far they will or ought to go in their efforts to acquire new rights or establish new principles. When they surrender this privilege, they cease to be independent, and they will no longer deserve to be free. They will have surrendered into other hands the most sacred of deposits — the right of self-government; and instead of approbation, they will merit the contempt of the world." [2]

Marshall states the economic and business reasons why the United States, of all countries, must depend upon commerce and the consequent necessity for the Jay Treaty. He tartly informs Talleyrand that in doing so the American Government was "transacting a business exclusively its own." Marshall denies the insinuation that the negotiations of the

[1] *Am. St. Prs., For. Rel.,* ii, 175.　　[2] *Ib.,* 176.

Jay Treaty had been unusually secret, but sarcastically observes that "it is not usual for nations about to enter into negotiations to proclaim to others the various objects to which those negotiations may possibly be directed. Such is not, nor has it ever been, the principle of France." To suppose that America owed such a duty to France, "is to imply a dependence to which no Government ought willingly to submit." [1]

Marshall then sets forth specifically the American complaints against the French Government,[2] and puts in parallel columns the words of the Jay Treaty to which the French objected, and the rules which the French Directory pretended were justified by that treaty. So strong is Marshall's summing up of the case in these portions of the American memorial that it is hard for the present-day reader to see how even the French Directory of that lawless time could have dared to attempt to withstand it, much less to refuse further negotiations.

Drawing to a conclusion, Marshall permits a lofty sarcasm to lighten his weighty argument. "America has accustomed herself," he observes, "to perceive in France only the ally and the friend. Consulting the feelings of her own bosom, she [America] has believed that between republics an elevated and refined friendship could exist, and that free nations were capable of maintaining for each other a real and permanent affection. If this pleasing theory, erected with so much care, and viewed with so much delight, has been impaired by experience, yet the hope con-

[1] *Am. St. Prs., For. Rel.*, ii, 177.   [2] *Ib.*, 178.

tinues to be cherished that this circumstance does not necessarily involve the opposite extreme." [1]

Then, for a moment, Marshall indulges his eloquence: "So intertwined with every ligament of her heart have been the cords of affection which bound her to France, that only repeated and continued acts of hostility can tear them asunder." [2]

Finally he tells Talleyrand that the American envoys, "searching only for the means of effecting the objects of their mission, have permitted no personal considerations to influence their conduct, but have waited, under circumstances beyond measure embarrassing and unpleasant, with that respect which the American Government has so uniformly paid to that of France, for permission to lay before you, citizen Minister, these important communications with which they have been charged." But, "if no such hope" remains, "they [the envoys] have only to pray that their return to their own country may be facilitated." [3]

But Marshall's extraordinary power of statement and logic availed nothing with Talleyrand and the Directory. "I consider Marshall, whom I have heard speak on a great subject,[4] as one of the most powerful reasoners I ever met with either in public or in print," writes William Vans Murray from The Hague, commenting on the task of the envoys. "Reasoning in such cases will have a fine effect in America, but to depend upon it in Europe is really to place Quixote with Ginés de Passamonte and among

---

[1] *Am. St. Prs., For. Rel.*, ii, 181.   [2] *Ib.*, 181–82.   [3] *Ib.*, 182.
[4] British Debts cases. (See vol. I, chap. v.)

the men of the world whom he reasoned with, and so sublimely, on their way to the galleys. They answer him, with you know stones and blows, though the Knight is an *armed* as well as an eloquent Knight." [1]

The events which had made Marshall and Pinckney more resolute in demanding respectful treatment had made Gerry more pliant to French influence. "Mr. Gerry is to see Mr. Talleyrand the day after to-morrow. Three appointments have been made by that gentleman," Marshall notes in his Journal, "each of which Mr. Gerry has attended and each of which Mr. Talleyrand has failed to attend; nor has any apology for these disappointments been thought necessary." [2] Once more Gerry waits on Talleyrand, who remains invisible. [3] And now again Beaumarchais appears. The Directory issues more and harsher decrees against American commerce. Marshall's patience becomes finite. "I prepared to-day a letter to the Minister remonstrating against the decree, . . . subjecting to confiscation all neutral vessels having on board any article coming out of England or its possessions." The letter closes by "requesting our passports." [4]

Marshall's memorial of the American case remained unread. One of Talleyrand's many secretaries asked Gerry "what it contained? (for they could not take the trouble to read it) and he added

---

[1] Murray to J. Q. Adams, Feb. 20, 1798, *Letters:* Ford, 379. Murray thought Marshall's statement of the American case "unanswerable" and "proudly independent." (*Ib.*, 395.) Contrast Murray's opinion of Marshall with his description of Gerry, *supra*, chap. VII, 258, and footnote.

[2] Marshall's Journal, Jan. 31, 1798, 40.

[3] *Ib.*, Feb. 2.   [4] *Ib.*, Feb. 2, 41.

ELBRIDGE GERRY

that such long letters were not to the taste of the French Government who liked a short address coming straight to the point." [1] Gerry, who at last saw Talleyrand, "informed me [Marshall] that communications & propositions had been made to him by that Gentleman, which he [Gerry] was not at liberty to impart to Genl Pinckney or myself." Upon the outcome of his secret conferences with Talleyrand, said Gerry, "probably depended peace or war." [2]

Gerry's "communication necessarily gives birth to some very serious reflections," Marshall confides to his Journal. He recalls the attempts to frighten the envoys "from our first arrival" — the threats of "a variety of ills . . . among others with being ordered immediately to quit France," none of them carried out; "the most haughty & hostile conduct . . . towards us & our country and yet . . . an unwillingness . . . to profess the war which is in fact made upon us." [3]

A French agent, sent by the French Consul-General in America, just arrived in Paris, "has probably brought with him," Marshall concludes, "accurate details of the state of parties in America. . . . I should think that if the French Government continues its hostility and does not relax some little in its hauteur its party in the United States will no longer support it. I suspect that some intelligence of this complexion has been received . . . whether she [France] will be content to leave us our Independence if she can neither cajole or frighten us

---

[1] Marshall's Journal, Feb. 3, 42.
[2] Ib., Feb. 4, 42.   [3] Ib., 42–43, 46.

out of it or will even endeavor to tear it from us by
open war there can be no doubt of her policy in one
respect — she will still keep up and cherish, if it be
possible, . . . her party in the United States." Whatever course France takes, Marshall thinks will be
"with a view to this her primary object."

Therefore, reasons Marshall, Talleyrand will maneuver to throw the blame on Pinckney and himself if the mission fails, and to give Gerry the credit
if it succeeds. "I am led irresistibly by this train
of thought to the opinion that the communication
made to Mr. Gerry in secret is a proposition to furnish passports to General Pinckney and myself and
to retain him for the purpose of negotiating the differences between the two Republics." This would
give the advantage to the French party in any
event.

"I am firmly persuaded of his [Talleyrand's] unwillingness to dismiss us while the war with England
continues in its present uncertain state. He believed
that Genl Pinckney and myself are both determined
to remain no longer unless we can be accredited."
Gerry had told Marshall that he felt the same way;
"but," says Marshall, "I am persuaded the Minister
[Talleyrand] does not think so. He would on this
account as well as on another which has been the
base of all propositions for an accommodation [the
loan and the bribe] be well pleased to retain only one
minister and to chuse that one [Gerry]." [1]

Marshall and Pinckney decided to let Gerry go his
own gait. "We shall both be happy if, by remaining

[1] Marshall's Journal, Feb. 4, 42–45.

without us, Mr. Gerry can negotiate a treaty which shall preserve the peace without sacrificing the independence of our country. We will most readily offer up all personal considerations as a sacrifice to appease the haughtiness of this Republic." [1]

Marshall gave Gerry the letter on the decree and passport question "and pressed his immediate attention to it." But Gerry was too excited by his secret conferences with Talleyrand to heed it. Time and again Gerry, bursting with importance, was closeted with the Foreign Minister, hinting to his colleagues that he held peace or war in his hand. Marshall bluntly told him that Talleyrand's plan now was "only to prevent our taking decisive measures until the affairs of Europe shall enable France to take them. I have pressed him [Gerry] on the subject of the letter concerning the Decree but he has not yet read it." [2]

Talleyrand and Gerry's "private intercourse still continues," writes Marshall on February 10. "Last night after our return from the Theatre Mr. Gerry told me, just as we were separating to retire each to his own apartment, that he had had in the course of the day a very extraordinary conversation with" a clerk of Talleyrand. It was, of course, secret. Marshall did not want to hear it. Gerry said he could tell his colleagues that it was on the subject of money. Then, at last, Marshall's restraint gave way momentarily and his anger, for an instant, blazed. Money proposals were useless; Talleyrand was playing with the Americans, he declared. "Mr. Gerry was

[1] Marshall's Journal, Feb. 5, 45–46.   [2] *Ib.*, Feb. 6 and 7, 46.

a little warm and the conversation was rather unpleasant. A solicitude to preserve harmony restrained me from saying all I thought." [1]

Money, money, money! Nothing else would do! Gerry, by now, was for paying it. No answer yet comes to the American memorial delivered to Talleyrand nearly three weeks before. Marshall packs his belongings, in readiness to depart. An unnamed person [2] calls on him and again presses for money; France is prevailing everywhere; the envoys had better yield; why resist the inevitable, with a thousand leagues of ocean between them and home? Marshall answers blandly but crushingly.

Again Talleyrand's clerk sees Gerry. The three Americans that night talk long and heatedly. Marshall opposes any money arrangement; Gerry urges it "very decidedly"; while Pinckney agrees with Marshall. Gerry argues long about the horrors of war, the expense, the risk. Marshall presents the justice of the American cause. Gerry reproaches Marshall with being too suspicious. Marshall patiently explains, as to a child, the real situation. Gerry again charges Marshall and Pinckney with undue suspicion. Marshall retorts that Gerry "could not answer the argument but by misstating it." The evening closes, sour and chill. [3]

The next night the envoys once more endlessly

---

[1] Marshall's Journal, Feb. 10, 47–48.

[2] Undoubtedly Beaumarchais. Marshall left his client's name blank in his Journal, but Pickering, on the authority of Pinckney, in the official copy, inserted Beaumarchais's name in later dates of the Journal.

[3] Marshall's Journal, Feb. 26, 52–60.

debate their course. Marshall finally proposes that they shall demand a personal meeting with Talleyrand on the real object of the mission. Gerry stubbornly dissents and finally yields, but indulges in long and childish discussion as to what should be said to Talleyrand, confusing the situation with every word.[1] Talleyrand fixes March 2 for the interview.

The following day Marshall accidentally discovers Gerry closeted with Talleyrand's clerk, who came to ask the New Englander to attend Talleyrand "in a particular conversation." Gerry goes, but reports that nothing important occurred. Then it comes out that Talleyrand had proposed to get rid of Marshall and Pinckney and keep Gerry. Gerry admits it. Thus Marshall's forecast made three weeks earlier [2] is proved to have been correct.

At last, for the first time in five months, the three envoys meet Talleyrand face to face. Pinckney opens and Talleyrand answers. Gerry suggests a method of making the loan, to which Talleyrand gives qualified assent. The interview seems at an end. Then Marshall comes forward and states the American case. There is much parrying for an hour.[3]

The envoys again confer. Gerry urges that their instructions permit them to meet Talleyrand's demands. He goes to Marshall's room to convince the granite-like Virginian, who would not yield. "I told him," writes Marshall, "that my judgment was not

[1] Marshall's Journal, Feb. 27, 61-67.

[2] *Ib.*, Feb. 28, 67-68. See *supra*, 312.

[3] *Am. St. Prs., For. Rel.*, ii, 186-87; Marshall's Journal, March 2, 68-72.

more perfectly convinced that the floor was wood or that I stood on my feet and not on my head than that our instructions would not permit us to make the loan required." [1] Let Gerry or Marshall or both together return to America and get new instructions if a loan must be made.

Two days later, another long and absurd discussion with Gerry occurs. Before the envoys go to see Talleyrand the next day, Gerry proposes to Marshall that, with reference to President Adams's speech, the envoys should declare, in any treaty made, "that the complaints of the two governments had been founded in mistake." Marshall hotly retorts: "With my view of things, I should tell an absolute lye if I should say that our complaints were founded in mistake. He [Gerry] replied hastily and with warmth that he wished to God, I would propose something which was accommodating: that I would propose nothing myself and objected to every thing which he proposed. I observed that it was not worth while to talk in that manner: that it was calculated to wound but not to do good: that I had proposed every thing which in my opinion was calculated to accommodate differences on just and reasonable grounds. He said that . . . to talk about justice was saying nothing: that I should involve our country in a war and should bring it about in such a manner, as to divide the people among themselves. I felt a momentary irritation, which I afterwards regretted, and told Mr. Gerry that I was not accustomed to such language and did

[1] Marshall's Journal, March 3, 74.

not permit myself to use it with respect to him or his opinions."

Nevertheless, Marshall, with characteristic patience, once more begins to detail his reasons. Gerry interrupts — Marshall "might think of him [Gerry] as I [he] pleased." Marshall answers moderately. Gerry softens and "the conversation thus ended." [1]

Immediately after the bout between Marshall and Gerry the envoys saw Talleyrand for a third time. Marshall was dominant at this interview, his personality being, apparently, stronger even than his words. These were strong enough — they were, bluntly, that the envoys could not and would not accept Talleyrand's proposals.

A week later Marshall's client, Beaumarchais, called on his American attorney with the alarming news that "the effects of all Americans in France were to be Sequestered." Pay the Government money and avoid this fell event, was Beaumarchais's advice; he would see Talleyrand and call again. "Mr. Beaumarchais called on me late last evening," chronicles Marshall. "He had just parted from the Minister. He informed me that he had been told confidentially . . . that the Directory were determined to give passports to General Pinckney and myself but to retain Mr. Gerry." But Talleyrand would hold the order back for "a few days to give us time to make propositions conforming to the views of the Government," which "if not made Mr. Talleyrand would be compelled to execute the order."

[1] Marshall's Journal, March 6, 79–81.

"I told him," writes Marshall, "that if the proposition . . . was a loan it was perfectly unnecessary to keep it [the order] up [back] a single day: that the subject had been considered for five months" and that the envoys would not change; "that for myself, if it were impossible to effect the objects of our mission, I did not wish to stay another day in France and would as cheerfully depart the next day as at any other time." [1]

Beaumarchais argued and appealed. Of course, France's demand was not just — Talleyrand did not say it was; but "a compliance would be useful to our country [America]." "France," said Beaumarchais, "thought herself sufficiently powerful to give the law to the world and exacted from all around her money to enable her to finish successfully her war against England."

Finally, Beaumarchais, finding Marshall flint, "hinted" that the envoys themselves should propose which one of them should remain in France, Gerry being the choice of Talleyrand. Marshall countered. If two were to return for instructions, the envoys would decide that for themselves. If France was to choose, Marshall would have nothing to do with it.

"General Pinckney and myself and especially me," said Marshall, "were considered as being sold to the English." Beaumarchais admitted "that our positive refusal to comply with the demands of France was attributed principally to me who was considered as entirely English. . . . I felt some little

[1] Marshall's Journal, 82-88; *Am. St. Prs., For. Rel.*, ii, 187-88.

resentment and answered that the French Government thought no such thing; that neither the government nor any man in France thought me English: but they knew I was not French: they knew I would not sacrifice my duty and the interest of my country to any nation on earth, and therefore I was not a proper man to stay, and was branded with the epithet of being English: that the government knew very well I loved my own country exclusively, and it was impossible to suppose any man who loved America, fool enough to wish to engage her in a war with France if that war was avoidable."

Thus Marshall asserted his purely American attitude. It was a daring thing to do, considering the temper of the times and the place where he then was. Even in America, at that period, any one who was exclusively American and, therefore, neutral, as between the European belligerents, was denounced as being British at heart. Only by favoring France could abuse be avoided. And to assert Neutrality in the French Capital was, of course, even more dangerous than to take this American stand in the United States.

But Beaumarchais persisted and proposed to take passage with his attorney to America; not on a public mission, of course (though he had hinted at wishing to "reconcile" the two governments), but merely "to testify," writes Marshall, "to the moderation of my conduct and to the solicitude I had uniformly expressed to prevent a rupture with France."

Beaumarchais "hinted very plainly," continues Marshall, "at what he had before observed that

means would be employed to irritate the people of
the United States against me and that those means
would be successful. I told him that I was much
obliged to him but that I relied entirely on my conduct itself for its justification and that I felt no sort
of apprehension for consequences, as they regarded
me personally; that in public life considerations of
that sort never had and never would in any degree
influence me. We parted with a request, on his part,
that, whatever might arise, we would preserve the
most perfect temper, and with my assuring him of
my persuasion that our conduct would always manifest the firmness of men who were determined, and
never the violence of passionate men."

"I have been particular," concludes Marshall, "in
stating this conversation, because I have no doubt of
its having been held at the instance of the Minister
[Talleyrand] and that it will be faithfully reported to
him. I mentioned to-day to Mr. Gerry that the Government wished to detain him and send away General Pinckney and myself. He said he would not
stay; but I find I shall not succeed in my efforts
to procure a Serious demand of passports for Mr.
Gerry and myself." [1]

During his efforts to keep Gerry from dangerously compromising the American case, and while
waiting for Talleyrand to reply to his memorial,
Marshall again writes to Washington a letter giving a survey of the war-riven and intricate European situation. He tells Washington that, "before
this reaches you it will be known universally in

[1] Marshall's Journal, March 13, 87-93.

America [1] that scarcely a hope remains of" honorable adjustment of differences between France and
America; that the envoys have not been and will not
be "recognized" without "acceding to the demands
of France . . . for money — to be used in the
prosecution of the present war"; that according to
"reports," when the Directory makes certain that
the envoys "will not add a loan to the mass of
American property already in the hands of this
[French] government, they will be ordered out of
France and a nominal [formally declared] as well as
actual war will be commenc'd against the United
States." [2]

Marshall goes on to say that his "own opinion has
always been that this depends on the state of war
with England"; the French are absorbed in their
expected attack on Great Britain; "and it is perhaps justly believed that on this issue is stak'd the
independence of Europe and America." He informs
Washington of "the immense preparations for an
invasion" of England; the "numerous and veteran
army lining the coast"; the current statement that
if "50,000 men can be" landed "no force in England will be able to resist them"; the belief that "a
formidable and organized party exists in Britain,
ready, so soon as a landing shall be effected, to rise
and demand a reform"; the supposition that England then "will be in . . . the situation of the bata-

[1] This would seem to indicate that Marshall knew that his famous
dispatches were to be published.

[2] France was already making "actual war" upon America; the
threat of formally declaring war, therefore, had no terror for Marshall.

vian and cisalpine republics and that its wealth, its
commerce, and its fleets will be at the disposition
of this [French] government."

But, he continues, "this expedition is not without its hazards. An army which, arriving safe, would
sink England, may itself be . . . sunk in the channel.
. . . The effect of such a disaster on a nation already
tir'd of the war and groaning under . . . enormous
taxation" and, intimates Marshall, none too warm
toward the "existing arrangements . . . might be
extremely serious to those who hold the reins of government" in France. Many intelligent people therefore think, he says, that the "formidable military
preparations" for the invasion of England "cover
and favor secret negotiations for peace." This view
Marshall himself entertains.

He then briefly informs Washington of Bonaparte's arrangement with Austria and Prussia which
will "take from England, the hope of once more
arming" those countries "in her favor," "influence
the secret [French] negotiations with England,"
and greatly affect "Swisserland." Marshall then
gives an extended account of the doings and purposes of the French in Switzerland, and refers to
revolutionary activities in Sardinia, Naples, and
Spain.

But notwithstanding the obstacles in its way, he
concludes that "the existing [French] government
. . . needs only money to enable it to effect all its
objects. A numerous brave and well disciplined
army seems to be devoted to it. The most military
and the most powerful nation on earth [the French]

is entirely at its disposal.[1] Spain, Italy, and Holland, with the Hanseatic towns, obey its mandates."

But, says he, it is hard to "procure funds to work this vast machine. Credit being annihilated . . . the enormous contributions made by foreign nations," together with the revenue from imposts, are not enough to meet the expenses; and, therefore, "France is overwhelmed with taxes. The proprietor complains that his estate yields him nothing. Real property pays in taxes nearly a third of its produce and is greatly reduc'd in its price." [2]

While Marshall was thus engaged in studying French conditions and writing his long and careful report to Washington, Talleyrand was in no hurry to reply to the American memorial. Indeed, he did not answer until March 18, 1798, more than six weeks after receiving it. The French statement reached Marshall and Pinckney by Gerry's hands, two days after its date. "Mr. Gerry brought in, just before dinner, a letter from the Minister of exterior relations," writes Marshall, "purporting to be an answer to our long memorial criminating in strong terms our government and ourselves, and proposing that two of us should go home leaving for the negotiation the person most acceptable to France. The person is not named but no question is entertained that Mr. Gerry is alluded to. I read the letter and gave it again to Mr. Gerry." [3]

[1] Here Marshall contradicts his own statement that the French Nation was tired of the war, groaning under taxation, and not "universally" satisfied with the Government.

[2] Marshall to Washington, Paris, March 8, 1798; *Amer. Hist. Rev.*, Jan., 1897, ii, 303; also MS., Lib. Cong.

[3] Marshall's Journal, March 20, 93.

The next day the three envoys together read Talleyrand's letter. Gerry protests that he had told the French Foreign Minister that he would not accept Talleyrand's proposal to stay, "That," sarcastically writes Marshall, "is probably the very reason why it was made." Talleyrand's clerk calls on Gerry the next morning, suggesting light and innocent duties if he would remain. No, theatrically exclaims Gerry, I "would sooner be thrown into the Seine." [1] But Gerry remained.

It is impossible, without reading Talleyrand's answer in full, to get an idea of the weak shiftiness to which that remarkable man was driven in his reply to Marshall. It was, as Pinckney said, "weak in argument, but irritating and insulting in style." [2] The great diplomat complains that the Americans have "claimed the right to take cognizance of the validity of prizes carried into the ports of the United States by French cruisers"; that the American Government permitted "any vessels to put into the ports of the United States after having captured the property of ships belonging to French citizens"; that "a French corvette had anchored at Philadelphia and was seized by the Americans"; and that the Jay Treaty was hostile to France.

But his chief complaint was with regard to the American newspapers which, said Talleyrand, "have since the treaty redoubled the invectives and calumnies against the [French] republic, and against her

---

[1] Marshall's Journal, March 22, 95.

[2] Murray to J. Q. Adams, April 3, 1798, quoting Pinckney; *Letters:* Ford, 391.

principles, her magistrates, and her envoys"; [1] and of the fact that the American Government might have, but did not, repress "pamphlets openly paid for by the Minister of Great Britain" which contained "insults and calumnies." So far from the American Government stopping all this, snarls Talleyrand, it encouraged "this scandal in its public acts" and, through its President, had denounced the French Directory as endeavoring to propagate anarchy and division within the United States.

Talleyrand then openly insults Marshall and Pinckney by stating that it was to prevent the restoration of friendship that the American Government had sent "to the French republic persons whose opinions and connections are too well known to hope from them dispositions sincerely conciliatory." Appealing directly to the French party in the United States, he declares that he "does not hesitate to believe that the American nation, like the French nation, sees this state of affairs with regret, and does not consider its consequences without sorrow. He apprehends that the American people will not commit a mistake concerning the prejudices with which it has been desired to inspire them against an allied people, nor concerning the engagements which it seems to be wished to make them contract to the detriment of an alliance, which so powerfully contributed to place them in the rank of nations, and to support them in it; and that they

---

[1] The exact reverse was true. Up to this time American newspapers, with few exceptions, were hot for France. Only a very few papers, like Fenno's *Gazette of the United States*, could possibly be considered as unfriendly to France at this point. (See *supra*, chap. I.)

will see in these new combinations the only dangers their prosperity and importance can incur." [1]

Finally, with cynical effrontery, Talleyrand actually proposes that Gerry alone shall conduct the negotiations. "Notwithstanding the kind of prejudice which has been entertained with respect to them [the envoys], the Executive Directory is disposed to treat with that one of the three, whose opinions, presumed to be more impartial, promise, in the course of explanations, more of that reciprocal confidence which is indispensable." [2]

Who should answer Talleyrand? Marshall, of course. "It was agreed ... that I should ... prepare an answer ... in which I should state that no one of the ministers could consent to remain on a business committed to all three." [3] In the discussion leading to this decision, "I," writes Marshall, "was perfectly silent." Again Dutrimond, a clerk of Talleyrand's, calls on Gerry, but sees Marshall instead, Gerry being absent.

Dutrimond's advice to Marshall is to leave France. The truth is, he declares, that his chief must order the envoys out of France "in three days at farthest." But spare them Gerry; let him remain — all this in polite terms and with plausible argument. "I told him," relates Marshall, "that personally nothing could be more desirable to me than to return immediately to the United States."

Then go on your own initiative, urges Talleyrand's clerk. Marshall grows evasive; for he wishes the

---

[1] *Am. St. Prs., For. Rel.*, ii, 190–91.   [2] *Ib.*, 191.
[3] Marshall's Journal, March 22, 95.

Directory to order his departure. A long talk ensues. Dutrimond leaves and Gerry returns. Marshall relates what had passed. "To prevent war I will stay," exclaims Gerry. "I made no observation on this," dryly observes Marshall in his Journal.[1]

Beaumarchais again tries his luck with Marshall, who replies that he will go home by "the direct passage to America" if he can get safe-conduct, "tho' I had private business of very considerable consequence in England." [2] Otherwise, declares Marshall, "I should embark immediately for England." That would never do, exclaims Beaumarchais; it would enrage the Directory and subject Marshall to attacks at home. Marshall remarks that he prefers to sail direct, although he knows "that the captains of privateers had received orders to cruise for us . . . and take us to the West Indies." [3]

Beaumarchais sees Talleyrand and reports that the Foreign Minister is horrified at the thought of Marshall's returning by way of England; it would "irritate this government" and delay "an accommodation"; it would blast Marshall's reputation; the Directory "would immediately publish . . . that I was gone to England to receive the wages I had earned by breaking off the treaty with France," Marshall records of the representations made to him.

"I am entitled to safe conduct," cries Marshall; and "the calumny threatened against myself is too contemptible to be credited for a moment by those

[1] Marshall's Journal, March 22, 95–97.   [2] The Fairfax purchase.
[3] Marshall's Journal, March 23, 99.

who would utter it." I "despise" it, exclaims the insulted Virginian.[1] Thus back and forth went this fantastic dance of corrupt diplomacy and cautious but defiant honesty.

At the long last, the interminable Gerry finished his review of Marshall's reply to Talleyrand and made a lengthy and unctuous speech to his colleagues on the righteousness of his own motives. Pinckney, intolerably bored and disgusted, told Gerry what he thought of him. The New Englander peevishly charged Marshall and Pinckney with concealing their motives.

"It is false, sir," shouted Pinckney. Gerry, he said, was the one who had concealed from his colleagues, not only his purposes, but his clandestine appointments with Talleyrand. Pinckney rode Gerry hard, "and insisted in plain terms on the duplicity which had been practiced [by Gerry] upon us both." The latter ridiculously explained, evaded, and, in general, acted according to the expectation of those who warned Adams against his appointment. Finally, however, Marshall's reply was signed by all three and sent to Talleyrand.[2]

The calmness, dignity, and conclusiveness of Marshall's rejoinder can be appreciated only by reading the entire document. Marshall begins his final statement of the American case and refutation of the French claims by declaring what he had stated before, that the American envoys "are ready to consider and to compensate the injury, if the American Government has given just cause of complaint to

[1] Marshall's Journal, March 29, 99–100.   [2] Ib., April 3, 102–07.

that of France"; and points out that the negotiations which the American envoys had sought fruitlessly for six months, if taken up even now, would "demonstrate the sincerity of this declaration." [1] This offer Marshall repeats again and again.

Before taking up Talleyrand's complaints in detail, he states that if the envoys cannot convince Talleyrand that the American Government is not in the wrong on a single point Talleyrand mentions, the envoys will prove their good faith; and thus, with an offer to compensate France for any wrong, "a base for an accommodation" is established. Every grievance Talleyrand had made is then answered minutely and at great length. History, reason, evidence, march through these pages like infantry, cavalry, and artillery going to battle. Marshall's paper was irresistible. Talleyrand never escaped from it.

In the course of it there is a passage peculiarly applicable to the present day. Answering Talleyrand's complaints about newspapers, Marshall says: —

"The genius of the Constitution, and the opinions of the people of the United States, cannot be overruled by those who administer the Government. Among those principles deemed sacred in America, . . . there is no one . . . more deeply impressed on the public mind, than the liberty of the press. That this liberty is often carried to excess, that it has sometimes degenerated into licentiousness, is seen and lamented; but the remedy has not been discovered. Perhaps it is an evil inseparable from the good with

[1] *Am. St. Prs., For. Rel.*, ii, 191.

which it is allied; perhaps it is a shoot which cannot
be stripped from the stalk, without wounding vitally
the plant from which it is torn."

At any rate, declares Marshall, there is, in America, no redress for "the calumnies and invectives" of
the press except "legal prosecution in courts which
are alike open to all who consider themselves as injured. Without doubt this abuse of a valuable privilege is [a] matter of peculiar regret when it is extended to the Government of a foreign nation." It
never is so extended "with the approbation of the
Government of the United States." But, he goes on
to say, this is unavoidable "especially on points respecting the rights and interests of America, . . . in
a nation where public measures are the results of
public opinion."

This practice of unrestricted criticism was not
directed toward France alone, Marshall assures
Talleyrand; "it has been lavished still more profusely on its [France's] enemies and has even been
bestowed, with an unsparing hand, on the Federal
[American] Government itself. Nothing can be more
notorious than the calumnies and invectives with
which the wisest measures and most virtuous characters of the United States have been pursued and
traduced [by American newspapers]." It is plain,
therefore, that the American Government cannot
influence the American press, the excesses of which
are, declares Marshall, "a calamity incident to the
nature of liberty."

He reminds Talleyrand that "the same complaint
might be urged on the part of the United States.

You must well know what degrading and unworthy calumnies against their Government, its principles, and its officers, have been published to the world by French journalists and in French pamphlets." Yet America had not complained of "these calumnies, atrocious as they are. . . . Had not other causes, infinitely more serious and weighty, interrupted the harmony of the two republics, it would still have remained unimpaired and the mission of the undersigned would never have been rendered necessary."[1]

Marshall again briefly sums up in broad outline the injuries which the then French Government had inflicted upon Americans and American property, and finally declares: "It requires no assurance to convince, that every real American must wish sincerely to extricate his country from the ills it suffers, and from the greater ills with which it is threatened; but all who love liberty must admit that it does not exist in a nation which cannot exercise the right of maintaining its neutrality."

Referring to Talleyrand's desire that Gerry remain and conduct the negotiations, Marshall remarks that the request "is not accompanied by any assurances of receding from those demands of money heretofore made the consideration on which alone the cessation of hostility on American commerce could be obtained." No one of the three American envoys had power to act alone, he maintains. In spite of neglect and insult Marshall still hopes that negotiations may begin; but if that is impossible, he asks for passports and safe-conduct.

[1] *Am. St. Prs., For. Rel.*, ii, 196.

Marshall made his final preparations for sailing, in order, he says, "that I might be in readiness to depart so soon as the will of the government should be signified to me." He was so hurried, he declares, that "I could not even lay in a moderate stock of wine or send my foul linen to be washed." [1] The now inescapable Beaumarchais saw Marshall again and told him that Talleyrand said that "I [Marshall] was no foreign minister; that I was to be considered as a private American citizen, to obtain my passport in the manner pursued by all others through the Consul . . . I must give my name, stature, age, complexion, &c., to our Consul."

Marshall answered with much heat. Beaumarchais conferred with Talleyrand, taking Marshall's side. Talleyrand was obdurate and said that "he was mistaken in me [Marshall]; that I prevented all negotiation and that so soon as I was gone the negotiation would be carried on; that in America I belonged to the English faction, which universally hated and opposed the French faction; that all I sought for was to produce a rupture in such a manner as to throw the whole blame on France." Marshall replied that Talleyrand "endeavored to make our situation more unpleasant than his orders required, in order to gratify his personal feelings," and he flatly refused to leave until ordered to go. [2]

Finally Marshall and Pinckney received their

---

[1] This would seem to dispose of the story that Marshall brought home enough "very fine" Madeira to serve his own use, supply weddings, and still leave a quantity in existence three quarters of a century after his return. (*Green Bag*, viii, 486.)

[2] Marshall's Journal, April 10 and 11, 1798, 107–14.

passports. Pinckney, whose daughter was ill and could leave France at that time only at the risk of her life, had serious difficulty in getting permission to stay in the south of France. On April 24, Marshall sailed for home. It is characteristic of the man that, notwithstanding his humiliating experiences and the failure of the mission, he was neither sour nor depressed. He had made many personal friends in Paris; and on taking ship at Bordeaux he does not forget to send them greetings, singling out Madame de Villette for a gay message of farewell. "Present me to my friends in Paris," he writes the American Consul-General at the French Capital, "& have the goodness to say to Madam Vilette in my name & in the handsomest manner, every thing which respectful friendship can dictate. When you have done that You will have rendered not quite half justice to my sentiments." [1]

Gerry, to whom Pinckney and Marshall did not even bid farewell,[2] remained in Paris, "extremely miserable." [3] Infinitely disgusted, Pinckney writes King that Gerry, "as I suspected, is resolved to remain here," notwithstanding Pinckney's "warm remonstrances with him on the bad consequences ... of such conduct and on the impropriety of" his secret "correspondence with Talleyrand under injunction not to communicate it to his colleagues." Pinckney says: "I have made great sacrifices of my feelings to preserve union; but in vain. I never met

[1] Marshall to Skipwith, Bordeaux, April 21, 1798; MS., Pa. Hist. Soc.

[2] Murray to J. Q. Adams, April 24, 1798; *Letters:* Ford, 399.

[3] Same to same, May 18, 1798; *ib.*, 407.

with a man of less candour and so much duplicity as Mr. Gerry. General Marshall is a man of extensive ability, of manly candour, and an honest heart." [1]

[1] Pinckney to King, Paris, April 4, 1798, enclosed in a letter to Secretary of State, April 16, 1798; Pickering MSS., Mass. Hist. Soc.

CHAPTER IX·

THE TRIUMPHANT RETURN

The present crisis is the most awful since the days of Vandalism. (Robert Troup.)

Millions for defense but not one cent for tribute. (Toast at banquet to Marshall.)

We shall remain free if we do not deserve to be slaves. (Marshall to citizens of Richmond.)

What a wicked use has been made of the X. Y. Z. dish cooked up by Marshall. (Jefferson.)

WHILE Talleyrand's drama of shame was enacting in Paris, things were going badly for the American Government at home. The French party in America, with whose wrath Talleyrand's male and female agents had threatened our envoys, was quite as powerful and aggressive against President Adams as the French Foreign Office had been told that it was.[1]

Notwithstanding the hazard and delay of ocean travel,[2] Talleyrand managed to communicate at least once with his sympathizers in America, whom he told that the envoys' "pretensions are high, that possibly no arrangement may take place, but that there will be no declaration of war by France." [3]

Jefferson was alert for news from Paris. "We have still not a word from our Envoys. This long silence (if they have been silent) proves things are not going on very roughly. If they have not been silent,

[1] See summary in McMaster, ii, 374.

[2] Six copies of the dispatches of the American envoys to the Secretary of State were sent by as many ships, so that at least one of them might reach its destination.

[3] Jefferson to Madison, Jan. 25, 1798; *Works:* Ford, viii, 259.

it proves their information, if made public, would check the disposition to arm." [1] He had not yet received the letter written him March 17, by his agent, Skipwith. This letter is abusive of the Administration of Washington as well as of that of Adams. Marshall was "one of the declaiming apostles of Jay's Treaty"; he and Pinckney courted the enemies of the Revolutionary Government; and Gerry's "paralytic mind" was "too weak" to accomplish anything. [2]

The envoys' first dispatches, sent from Paris October 22, 1797, reached Philadelphia on the night of March 4, 1798. [3] These documents told of the corrupt French demands and machinations. The next morning President Adams informed Congress of their arrival. [4] Two weeks later came the President's startling message to Congress declaring that the envoys could not succeed "on terms compatible with the safety, the honor, or the essential interests of the nation" and "exhorting" Congress to prepare for war. [5]

The Republicans were dazed. White hot with anger, Jefferson writes Madison that the President's "insane message . . . has had great effect. Exultation on the one side & a certainty of victory; while

---

[1] Jefferson to Madison, Feb. 15, 1798; *Works:* Ford, viii, 368.

[2] Skipwith to Jefferson, Paris, March 17, 1798; Gibbs, ii, 160.

[3] *Am. St. Prs., For. Rel.,* ii, 152, 157, 159, 161, 166.

[4] *Ib.* The President at this time communicated only the first dispatch, which was not in cipher. It merely stated that there was no hope that the envoys would be received and that a new decree directed the capture of all neutral ships carrying any British goods whatever. (*Ib.,* 157.)

[5] *Ib.,* 152; Richardson, i, 264; and *Works:* Adams, ix, 156.

the other [Republican] is petrified with astonishment." [1] The same day he tells Monroe that the President's "almost insane message" had alarmed the merchants and strengthened the Administration; but he did not despair, for the first move of the Republicans "will be a call for papers [the envoys' dispatches]. [2] In Congress the battle raged furiously; "the question of war & peace depends now on a toss of cross & pile," [3] was Jefferson's nervous opinion.

But the country itself still continued French in feeling; the Republicans were gaining headway even in Massachusetts and Connecticut; Jefferson expected the fall elections to increase the Republican strength in the House; petitions against war measures were pouring into Congress from every section; the Republican strategy was to gain time. Jefferson thought that "the present period, . . . of two or three weeks, is the most eventful ever known since that of 1775." [4]

The Republicans, who controlled the House of Representatives, demanded that the dispatches be made public: they were sure that these papers would not justify Adams's grave message. If the President should refuse to send Congress the papers it would demonstrate, said the "Aurora," that he "suspects the popularity of his conduct if exposed to public view. . . . If he thinks he has done right, why should he be afraid of letting his measures be known?" Let

[1] Jefferson to Madison, March 21, 1798; *Works:* Ford, viii, 386.
[2] Jefferson to Monroe, March 21, 1798; *ib.*, 388–89.
[3] Jefferson to Madison, March 29, 1798; *ib.*, 392.
[4] Jefferson to Pendleton, April 2, 1798; *ib.*, 394–97.

the representatives of the people see "*the whole* of the papers . . . a *partial* communication would be worse than none." [1]

Adams hesitated to reveal the contents of the dispatches because of "a regard for the *personal safety* of the Commissioners and an apprehension of the effect of a disclosure upon our future diplomatic intercourse." [2] High Federalist business men, to whom an intimation of the contents of the dispatches had been given, urged their publication. "We wish much for the papers if they can with propriety be made public" was Mason's reply to Otis. "The Jacobins want them. And in the name of God let them be gratified; it is not the first time they have wished for the means of their destruction." [3]

Both Federalists who were advised and Republicans who were still in the dark now were gratified in their wish to see the incessantly discussed and mysterious message from the envoys. The effect on the partisan maneuvering was as radical and amusing as it is illuminative of partisan sincerity. When, on April 3, the President transmitted to Congress the dispatches thus far received, the Republicans instantly altered their tactics. The dispatches did not show that the negotiations were at an end, said the "Aurora"; it was wrong, therefore, to publish them — such a course might mean war. Their publication was a Federalist trick to discredit the Republican Party; and anyway Talleyrand was

[1] *Aurora*, April 3, 1798.

[2] Otis to Mason, March 22, 1798; Morison, i, 90.

[3] Jonathan Mason to Otis, March 30, 1798; *ib.*, 93. And see the valuable New England Federalist correspondence of the time in *ib.*

a monarchist, the friend of Hamilton and King. So raged and protested the Republican organ.[1]

Troup thus reports the change: The Republicans, he says, "were very clamorous for the publication [of the dispatches] until they became acquainted with the intelligence communicated. From that moment they opposed publication, and finally they carried a majority against the measure. The Senate finding this to be the case instantly directed publication."[2] The President then transmitted to Congress the second dispatch which had been sent from Paris two weeks after the first. This contained Marshall's superb memorial to Talleyrand. It was another blow to Republican hopes.

The dispatches told the whole story, simply yet with dramatic art. The names of Hottenguer, Bellamy, and Hauteval were represented by the letters X, Y, and Z,[3] which at once gave to this picturesque episode the popular name that history has adopted. The effect upon public opinion was instantaneous and terrific.[4] The first result, of course, was felt in Congress. Vice-President Jefferson now thought it his "duty to be silent."[5] In the House the Republi-

[1] *Aurora*, April 7, 1798. A week later, under the caption, "The Catastrophe," the *Aurora* began the publication of a series of ably written articles excusing the conduct of the French officials and condemning that of Marshall and Pinckney.

[2] Troup to King, June 3, 1798; King, ii, 329. Ten thousand copies of the dispatches were ordered printed and distributed at public expense. Eighteen hundred were sent to Virginia alone. (Pickering to Marshall, July 24, 1798; Pickering MSS., Mass. Hist. Soc.) This was the beginning of the printing and distributing of public documents by the National Government. (Hildreth, ii, 217.)

[3] Pickering's statement, April 3, 1798; *Am. St. Prs.*, ii, 157.

[4] Jefferson to Madison, April 5, 1798; *Works:* Ford, viii, 398.   [5] *Ib.*

cans were "thunderstruck."[1] Many of their boldest leaders left for home; others went over openly to
the Federalists.[2] Marshall's disclosures "produced
such a shock on the republican mind, as has never
been seen since our independence," declared Jefferson.[3] He implored Madison to write for the public
an analysis of the dispatches from the Republican
point of view.[4]

After recovering from his "shock" Jefferson tried
to make light of the revelations; the envoys had
"been assailed by swindlers," he said, "but that the
Directory knew anything of it is neither proved nor
probable." Adams was to blame for the unhappy
outcome of the mission, declared Jefferson; his
"speech is in truth the only obstacle to negotiation."[5] Promptly taking his cue from his master,
Madison asserted that the publication of the dispatches served "more to inflame than to inform the
country." He did not think Talleyrand guilty — his
"conduct is scarcely credible. I do not allude to its
depravity, which, however heinous, is not without
example. Its unparalleled stupidity is what fills me
with astonishment."[6]

The hot-blooded Washington exploded with anger.
He thought "the measure of infamy was filled" by
the "profligacy . . . and corruption" of the French

---

[1] Pickering to Jay, April 9, 1798; *Jay:* Johnston, iv, 236.

[2] Jefferson to Madison, April 26, 1798; *Works:* Ford, viii, 411.
Among the Republicans who deserted their posts Jefferson names
Giles, Nicholas, and Clopton.

[3] Jefferson to Madison, April 6, 1798; *ib.*, 403.

[4] *Ib.*, April 12, 1798; *ib.*, 404.

[5] Jefferson to Carr, April 12, 1798; *Works:* Ford, viii, 405–06.

[6] Madison to Jefferson, April 15, 1798; *Writings:* Hunt, vi, 315.

Directory; the dispatches ought "to open the eyes of the blindest," but would not "change . . . the *leaders* of the opposition unless there shou'd appear a manifest desertion of the followers." [1] Washington believed the French Government "capable [of] any thing bad" and denounced its "outrageous conduct . . . toward the United States"; but he was even more wrathful at the "inimitable conduct of its partisans [in America] who aid and abet their measures." He concluded that the Directory would modify their defiant attitude when they found "the spirit and policy of this country rising with resistance and that they have falsely calculated upon support from a large part of the people thereof." [2]

Then was heard the voice of the country. "The effects of the publication [of the dispatches] . . . on the people . . . has been prodigious. . . . The leaders of the opposition . . . were astonished & confounded at the profligacy of their beloved friends the French." [3] In New England, relates Ames, "the Jacobins [Republicans] were confounded, and the trimmers dropt off from the party, like windfalls from an apple tree in September." [4] Among all classes were observed "the most magical effects"; so "irresistible has been the current of public opinion . . . that . . . it has broken down the opposition in Congress." [5] Jefferson mournfully informed Madison that "the spirit kindled up in the towns is wonder-

---

[1] Washington to Pickering, April 16, 1798; *Writings:* Ford, xiii, 495.
[2] Washington to Hamilton, May 27, 1798; *ib.*, xiv, 6–7.
[3] Sedgwick to King, May 1, 1798; King, ii, 319.
[4] Ames to Gore, Dec. 18, 1798; *Works:* Ames, i, 245–46.
[5] Troup to King, June 3, 1798; King, ii, 329.

ful. . . . Addresses . . . are pouring in offering life &
fortune." [1] Long afterwards he records that the
French disclosures "carried over from us a great
body of the people, real republicans & honest men,
under virtuous motives." [2] In New England, especially, the cry was for "open and deadly war with
France." [3] From Boston Jonathan Mason wrote
Otis that "war for a time we must have and our
fears . . . are that . . . you [Congress] will rise without a proper *climax*. . . . We pray that decisive
orders may be given and that accursed Treaty [with
France] may be annulled. . . . The time is now
passed, when we should fear giving offense. . . . The
yeomanry are not only united but spirited." [4]

Public meetings were held everywhere and "addresses from all bodies and descriptions of men"
poured "like a torrent on the President and both
Houses of Congress." [5] The blood of Federalism was
boiling. "We consider the present crisis as the most
awful since the days of Vandalism," declared the
ardent Troup. [6] "Yankee Doodle," "Stony Point,"
"The President's March," supplanted in popular
favor "Ça ira" and the "Marseillaise," which had
been the songs Americans best loved to sing.

[1] Jefferson to Madison, May 3, 1797; *Works:* Ford, viii, 413.
[2] Jefferson to Monroe, March 7, 1801; *ib.*, ix, 203.
[3] Higginson to Pickering, June 26, 1798; Pickering MSS., Mass.
Hist. Soc.
[4] Jonathan Mason to Otis, May 28, 1798; Morison, i, 95–96.
[5] Troup to King, June 3, 1798; King, ii, 329.
[6] *Ib.*, 330; and see letters of Bingham, Lawrence, and Cabot to
King, *ib.*, 331–34. From the newspapers of the time, McMaster has
drawn a brilliant picture of the thrilling and dramatic scenes which
all over the United States marked the change in the temper of the
people. (McMaster, ii, 376 *et seq.*),

The black cockade, worn by patriots during the Revolutionary War, suddenly took the place of the French cockade which until the X. Y. Z. disclosures had decorated the hats of the majority in American cities. The outburst of patriotism produced many songs, among others Joseph Hopkinson's "Hail Columbia!" ("The President's March"), which, from its first presentation in Philadelphia, caught the popular ear. This song is of historic importance, in that it expresses lyrically the first distinctively National consciousness that had appeared among Americans. Everywhere its stirring words were sung. In cities and towns the young men formed American clubs after the fashion of the democratic societies of the French party.

> "Hail, Columbia! happy land!
> Hail, ye heroes! heaven-born band!
> Who fought and bled in Freedom's cause," —

sang these young patriots, and "Hail, Columbia!" chanted the young women of the land.[1] On every hilltop the fires of patriotism were signaling devotion and loyalty to the American Government.

Then came Marshall. Unannounced and unlooked for, his ship, the Alexander Hamilton, had sailed into New York Harbor after a voyage of fifty-three days from Bordeaux.[2] No one knew of his coming. "General Marshall arrived here on Sunday last. His arrival was unexpected and his stay with us was very short. I have no other apology to make,"

[1] "Hail Columbia exacts not less reverence in America than the Marseillaise Hymn in France and Rule Britannia in England." (Davis, 128.)

[2] Norfolk (Va.) *Herald*, June 25, 1798.

writes Troup, "for our not giving him a public demonstration of our love and esteem." [1] Marshall hurried on to Philadelphia. Already the great memorial to Talleyrand and the brilliantly written dispatches were ascribed to his pen, and the belief had become universal that the Virginian had proved to be the strong and resourceful man of the mission.

On June 18, 1798, he entered the Capital, through which, twenty years before, almost to a day, he had marched as a patriot soldier on the way to Monmouth from Valley Forge. Never before had any American, excepting only Washington, been received with such demonstration. [2] Fleets of carriages filled with members of Congress and prominent citizens, and crowds of people on horseback and on foot, went forth to meet him.

"The concourse of citizens . . . was immense." Three corps of cavalry "in full uniform" gave a warlike color to the procession which formed behind Marshall's carriage six miles out from Philadelphia. "The occasion cannot be mentioned on which so prompt and general a muster of the cavalry ever before took place." When the city was reached, the church bells rang, cannon thundered, and amid "the shouts of the exulting multitudes" Marshall was "escorted through the principal streets to the city Tavern." The leading Federalist newspaper, the "Gazette of the United States," records that, "even in the Northern Liberties, [3] where the demons

[1] Troup to King, June 23, 1798; King, ii, 349.

[2] Even Franklin's welcome on his first return from diplomatic service in England did not equal the Marshall demonstration.

[3] A strenuously Republican environ of Philadelphia.

of anarchy and confusion are attempting to organize treason and death, repeated shouts of applause were given as the cavalcade approached and passed along." [1] The next morning O'Ellers Tavern was thronged with Senators and Representatives and "a numerous concourse of respectable citizens" who came to congratulate Marshall. [2]

The "Aurora" confirms this description of its Federalist rival; but adds bitterly: "What an occasion for rejoicing! Mr. Marshall was sent to France for the *ostensible* purpose, at least, of effecting an amicable accommodation of differences. He returns without having accomplished that object, and on his return the Tories rejoice. This certainly looks as if they did not wish him to succeed. . . . Many pensive and melancholy countenances gave the glare of parade a gloom much more suited to the occasion, and more in unison with the feelings of Americans. Well may they despond: For tho' the patriotic Gerry may succeed in settling the differences between the two countries — it is too certain that his efforts can be of no avail when the late conduct of our administration, and the unprecedented intemperance of our chief executive magistrate is known in Europe." [3]

Jefferson watched Marshall's home-coming with keen anxiety. "We heard of the arrival of Marshall at New York," he writes, "and I concluded to stay & see whether that circumstance would produce any

[1] *Gazette of the United States*, June 20, 1798; see also Claypoole's *American Daily Advertiser*, Wednesday, June 20, 1798.

[2] *Gazette of the United States*, June 21, 1798.

[3] *Aurora*, June 21, 1798; and see *ib.*, June 20.

new projects. No doubt he there received more than
hints from Hamilton as to the tone required to be
assumed. . . . Yet I apprehend he is not hot enough
for his friends."

With much chagrin he then describes what happened when Marshall reached Philadelphia: "M.
was received here with the utmost éclat. The Secretary of State & many carriages, with all the city
cavalry, went to Frankfort to meet him, and on his
arrival here in the evening, the bells rung till late
in the night, & immense crowds were collected to
see & make part of the shew, which was circuitously
paraded through the streets before he was set down
at the city tavern." But, says Jefferson, "all this
was to secure him [Marshall] to their [the Administration's] views, that he might say nothing which
would expose the game they have been playing.[1]
Since his arrival I can hear nothing directly from
him."

Swallowing his dislike for the moment, Jefferson
called on Marshall while the latter was absent from
the tavern. "Thomas Jefferson presents his compliments to General Marshall" ran the card he left.
"He had the honor of calling at his lodgings twice
this morning, but was so $\overset{\wedge}{un}$lucky as to find that he
was out on both occasions. He wished to have
expressed in person his regret that a pre-engagement
for to-day which could not be dispensed with,
would prevent him the satisfaction of dining in
company with General Marshall, and therefore begs
leave to place here the expressions of that respect

[1] Jefferson to Madison, June 21, 1798; *Works:* Ford, viii, 439–40.

which in company with his fellow citizens he bears him." [1]

Many years afterwards Marshall referred to the adding of the syllable "un" to the word "lucky" as one time, at least, when Jefferson came near telling the truth.[2] To this note Marshall returned a reply as frigidly polite as Jefferson's: —

"J. Marshall begs leave to accompany his respectful compliments to Mr. Jefferson with assurances of the regret he feels at being absent when Mr. Jefferson did him the honor to call on him.

"J. Marshall is extremely sensible to the obliging expressions contained in Mr. Jefferson's polite billet of yesterday. He sets out to-morrow for Winchester & would with pleasure charge himself with any commands of Mr. Jefferson to that part of Virginia."[3]

Having made his report to the President and Secretary of State, Marshall prepared to start for Virginia. But he was not to leave without the highest compliment that the Administration could, at that time, pay him. So gratified were the President, Cabinet, and Federalist leaders in Congress with Marshall's conduct in the X. Y. Z. mission, and so high their opinion of his ability, that Adams tendered him the appointment to the place on the Supreme Bench,[4] made vacant by the death of Justice Wilson. Marshall promptly declined. After applying to the Fairfax indebtedness all the money which he

---

[1] General Marshall at O'Eller's Hotel, June 23, 1798; Jefferson MSS., Lib. Cong.

[2] *Green Bag*, viii, 482–83.

[3] Marshall to Jefferson; Jefferson MSS., Lib. Cong.

[4] Pickering to Marshall, Sept. 20, 1798; Pickering MSS., Mass. Hist. Soc.

might receive as compensation for his services in the French mission, there would still remain a heavy balance of obligation; and Marshall must devote all his time and strength to business.

On the night before his departure, the members of Congress gave the hero of the hour the historic dinner at the city's principal tavern, "as an evidence of their affection for his person and their gratified approbation of the patriotic firmness with which he sustained the dignity of his country during his important mission." One hundred and twenty enthusiastic men sat at the banquet table.

The Speaker of the National House, the members of the Cabinet, the Justices of the Supreme Court, the Speaker of the Pennsylvania State Senate, the field officers of the army, the Right Reverend Bishops Carroll and White, "and other distinguished public characters attended." Toasts "were drank with unbounded plaudits" and "many of them were encored with enthusiasm." High rose the spirit of Federalism at O'Eller's Tavern in Philadelphia that night; loud rang Federalist cheers; copiously flowed Federalist wine.

"Millions for Defense but not a cent for Tribute!" was the crowning toast of that jubilant evening. It expressed the spirit of the gathering; out over the streets of Philadelphia rolled the huzzas that greeted it. But its unknown author[1] "builded bet-

---

[1] This sentiment has been ascribed to General C. C. Pinckney, Marshall's colleague on the X. Y. Z. mission. But it was first used at the Philadelphia banquet to Marshall. Pinckney's nearest approach to it was his loud, and wrathful, " No! not a sixpence!" when Hottenguer made one of his incessant demands for money. (See *supra*, 273.)

ter than he knew." He did more than flatter Marshall and bring the enthusiastic banqueters, wildly shouting, to their feet: he uttered the sentiment of the Nation. "Millions for Defense but not a cent for Tribute" is one of the few historic expressions in which Federalism spoke in the voice of America. Thus the Marshall banquet in Philadelphia, June 18, 1798, produced that slogan of defiant patriotism which is one of the slowly accumulating American maxims that have lived.

After Marshall retired from the banquet hall, the assemblage drank a final toast to "The man whom his country delights to Honor." [1]

[1] Claypoole's *American Daily Advertiser*, Wednesday, June 20, 1798; Pa. Hist. Soc. The toasts drank at this dinner to Marshall illustrate the popular spirit at that particular moment. They also furnish good examples of the vocabulary of Federalism at the period of its revival and only two years before its annihilation by Jefferson's new party: —

" 1. The United States — 'free, sovereign & independent.'

" 2. The people and the Government — 'one and indivisible.'

" 3. The President — ' some other hand must be found to sign the ignominious deed' that would surrender the sovereignty of his Country.

" 4. General Washington — 'His name a rampart & the Knowledge that he lives a bulwark against mean and secret enemies of his Country's Peace.'

" 5. General Pinckney. ''T is not in mortals to command success: He has done more — deserved it.'

" 6. The Officers & Soldiers of the American Army. 'May glory be their Theme, Victory their Companion, & Gratitude & Love their Rewards.'

" 7. The Navy of the United States. 'May its infant efforts, like those of Hercules, be the Presage of its future Greatness.'

" 8. The Militia. 'May they never cease to combine the Valor of the Soldier with the Virtues of the Citizen.'

" 9. The Gallant Youth of America. 'May they disdain to hold as Tenants at Will, the Independence inherited from their ancestors.'

"10. The Heroes who fell in the Revolutionary War. 'May their memory never be dishonored by a surrender of the Freedom purchased with their Blood.'

Marshall was smothered with addresses, congratulations, and every variety of attention from public bodies and civic and military organizations. A committee from the Grand Jury of Gloucester County, New Jersey, presented the returned envoy a laudatory address. His answer, while dignified, was somewhat stilted, perhaps a trifle pompous. The Grand Jury compliment was, said Marshall, "a sweet reward" for his "exertions." The envoys wished, above all things, for peace, but felt "that not even peace was to be purchased at the price of national independence." [1]

The officers of a militia brigade delivered to Marshall a eulogy in which the war note was clear and dominant. Marshall answered that, desirable as peace is, it "ought not to have been bought by dishonor and national degradation"; and that the resort to the sword, for which the militia officers declared themselves ready, made Marshall "feel with an elevated pride the dignity and grandeur of the American character." [2]

"11. The American Eagle. 'May it regard with disdain the crowing of the Gallic cock.'

"12. Union & Valour — infallible Antidotes against diplomatic skill.

"13. 'Millions for Defense but not a cent for Tribute.'

"14. The first duties of a good citizen — Reverence for the Laws and Respect for the Magistracy.

"15. Agriculture & Commerce — A Dissolution of whose partnership will be the Bankruptcy of both.

"16. The Constitution — 'Esto Perpetua.'

"After General Marshall Retired: —

"General Marshall — The man whom his country delights to Honor." (*Ib.*, June 25, 1798.)

[1] Claypoole's *American Daily Advertiser*, Monday, June 25, 1798; and *Gazette of the United States*, Saturday, June 23, 1798.

[2] *Ib.*, June 25, 1798; and June 23, 1798.

The day before Marshall's departure from Philadelphia the President, addressing Congress, said: "I congratulate you on the arrival of General Marshall . . . at a place of safety where he is justly held in honor. . . . The negotiation may be considered at an end. *I will never send another Minister to France without assurances that he will be received, respected, and honored as the representative of a great, free, powerful, and independent nation.*" [1] Bold and defiant words expressive of the popular sentiment of the hour; but words which were to be recalled later by the enemies of Adams, to his embarrassment and to the injury of his party. [2]

"Having heard that Mrs. Marshall is in Winchester I shall immediately set out for that place," [3] Marshall writes Washington. His departure from the Capital was as spectacular as his arrival. He "was escorted by detachments of cavalry," says the "Aurora." "Certainly nothing less was due considering the distinguished services which he has rendered by his mission — he has acquired some knowledge of the French language," [4] sneers that partisan newspaper in good Republican fashion. When Marshall approached Lancaster he was met by companies of "cavalry and uniformed militia" which escorted him into the town, where he was "welcomed by the discharges of artillery and the ringing of bells." [5]

[1] Adams to Congress, June 21, 1798; *Works: Adams,* ix, 158; and Richardson, i, 266. Italics are mine.

[2] *Infra,* chap. XII.

[3] Marshall to Washington, June 22, 1798; MS., Lib. Cong.

[4] *Aurora,* June 30, 1798.

[5] *Gazette of the United States,* June 28, 1797.

His journey throughout Pennsylvania and Virginia, repeating scenes of his welcome at Philadelphia and Lancaster, ended at Richmond. There, among his old neighbors and friends, the demonstrations reached their climax. A long procession of citizens went out to meet him. Again rang the cheers, again the bells pealed, again the cannon thundered. And here, to his townsmen and friends, Marshall, for the first time, publicly opened his heart and told, with emotion, what had befallen in France. In this brief speech the Nationalist and fighting spirit, which appears in all his utterances throughout his entire life, flashes like a sword in battle.

Marshall cannot express his "emotions of joy" which his return to Richmond has aroused; nor "paint the sentiments of affection and gratitude towards" his old neighbors. Nobody, he assures his hearers, could appreciate his feelings who had not undergone similar experiences.

The envoys, far from their country with no news from their Government, were in constant anxiety, says Marshall. He tells of their trials, of how they had discharged their duty, of his exultation over the spirit America was now displaying. "I rejoice that I was not mistaken in the opinion I had formed of my countrymen. I rejoice to find, though they know how to estimate, and therefore seek to avoid the horrors and dangers of war, yet they know also how to value the blessings of liberty and national independence. Peace would be purchased at too high a price by bending beneath a foreign yoke" and such a peace would be but brief; for "the nation thus submitting would be soon involved in the quarrels of its master. . . . We shall remain free if we do not deserve to be slaves."

Marshall compares the governments of France and America. To one who, like himself, is so accustomed to real liberty that he "almost considers it as the indispensable companion of man, a view of [French] despotism," though "borrowing the garb usurping the name of freedom," teaches "the solid safety and real security" existing in America. The loss of these "would poison . . . every other joy." Without them "freemen would turn with loathing and disgust from every other comfort of life." To preserve them, "all . . . difficulties ought to be encountered."

Stand by "the government of your choice," urges Marshall; its officials are from the people, "subject in common with others to the laws they make," and must soon return to the popular body "whose destiny involves their own and in whose ruin they must participate." This is always a good rule, but "it is peculiarly so in a moment of peril like the present" when "want of confidence in our government . . . furnishes. . . a foreign real enemy [France] those weapons which have so often been so successfully used." [1]

The Mayor, Recorder, Aldermen, and Common Council of Richmond presented Marshall with an address of extravagant praise. "If reason and argument . . . if integrity, candor, and the pure spirit of conciliation" had met like qualities in France, "smiling peace would have returned along with you." But if Marshall had not brought peace, he

[1] *Columbian Centinel*, Boston, Sept. 22, 1798.

had warned America against a government "whose touch is death." Perhaps he had even preserved "our excellent constitution and . . . our well earned liberties." In answer Marshall said that he reciprocated the "joy" of his "fellow citizens, neighbors, and ancient friends" upon his return; that they were right in thinking honorable peace with France was impossible; and warned them against "the countless dangers which lurk beneath foreign attachments."[1]

Marshall had become a national hero. Known before this time, outside of his own State, chiefly to the eminent lawyers of America, his name now became a household word in the remotest log cabins of Kentucky and Tennessee, as well as in the residences of Boston and New York. "Saving General Washington, I believe the President, Pinckney, and Marshall are the most popular characters now in our country," Troup reported to King in London.[2]

For the moment, only one small cloud appeared upon the horizon of Marshall's popularity; but a vicious flash blazed from it. Marshall went to Fredericksburg on business and attended the little theater at that place. The band of the local artillery company furnished the music. A Philadelphia Federalist, who happened to be present, ordered them to play "The President's March" ("Hail, Columbia!"). Instantly the audience was in an uproar. So violent did they become that "a considerable riot took place." Marshall was openly insulted. Nor did their hostility subside with Marshall's departure.

[1] Norfolk (Va.) *Herald*, Aug. 30, 1798.

[2] Troup to King, Nov. 16, 1798; King, ii, 465; and see same to same, July 10, 1798; *ib.*, 363.

"The inhabitants of Fredericksburg waited," in anxious expectation, for an especially hated Federalist Congressman, Harper of South Carolina, to pass through the town on his way home, with the intention of treating him even more roughly.[1]

With this ominous exception, the public demonstrations for Marshall were warmly favorable. His strength with the people was greater than ever. By the members of the Federal Party he was fairly idolized. This, the first formal party organization in our history, was, as we have seen, in sorry case even under Washington. The assaults of the Republicans, directed by Jefferson's genius for party management, had all but wrecked the Federalists. That great party general had out-maneuvered his adversaries at every point and the President's party was already nearing the breakers.

The conduct of the French mission and the publication of Marshall's dispatches and letters to Talleyrand saved the situation for the moment. Those whom Jefferson's consummate skill had won over to the Republican Party returned by thousands to their former party allegiance.[2]

Congress acted with belated decision. Our treaty with France was abrogated; non-intercourse laws passed; a provisional army created; the Navy Department established; arsenals provided; the building of warships directed. For a season our National machinery was permitted to work with vigor and effectiveness.

---

[1] Carey's *United States Recorder*, Aug. 16, 1798.
[2] McMaster, ii, 380–85; Hildreth, v, 203 *et seq.*

The voices that were wont to declaim the glories of French democracy were temporarily silent. The people, who but yesterday frantically cheered the "liberté, égalité, fraternité" of Robespierre and Danton, now howled with wrath at mention of republican France. The pulpit became a tribune of military appeal and ministers of the gospel preached sermons against American "Jacobins." [1] Federalist orators had their turn at assailing "despotism" with rhetoric and defending "liberty" with eloquence; but the French Government was now the international villain whom they attacked.

"The struggle between Liberty and Despotism, Government and Anarchy, Religion and Atheism, has been gloriously decided. . . . France has been foiled, and America is free. The elastick veil of Gallick perfidy has been rent, . . . the severing blow has been struck." Our abrogation of the treaty with France was "the completion of our Liberties, the acme of our Independence . . . and . . . emancipated us from the oppressive friendship of an ambitious, malignant, treacherous ally." That act evidenced "our nation's manhood"; our Government was now "an Hercules, who, no longer amused with the coral and bells of 'liberty and equality' . . . no longer willing to trifle at the *distaff* of a 'Lady Negociator,' boldly invested himself in the *toga virilis*." [2] Such was the language of the public platform; and private expressions of most men were even less restrained.

[1] McMaster, ii, 380–85.
[2] "Oration of Robert Treat Paine to Young Men of Boston," July 17, 1799; in *Works of Robert Treat Paine*, ed. 1812, 301 *et seq.*

Denouncing "the Domineering Spirit and boundless ambition of a nation whose Turpitude has set
all objections, divine & human, at naught," [1] Washington accepted the appointment as Commander-in-
Chief of the newly raised army. "Huzza! Huzza!
Huzza! How transporting the fact! The great, the
good, the aged WASHINGTON has said 'I am ready
again to go with my fellow citizens to the field of
battle in defense of the Liberty & Independence
of my Country,'" ran a newspaper announcement,
typically voicing the popular heart.[2]

To Marshall's brother James, who had offered his
services as an aide-de-camp, Washington wrote that
the French "(although *I* conceive them capable of
anything that is unjust or dishonorable)" will not
"attempt a serious invasion of this country" when
they learn of "the preparation which [we] are making to receive them." They have "made calculations on false ground" in supposing that Americans
would not "support Independence and the Government of their country *at every hazard*." Nevertheless, "the highest possible obligation rests upon the
country to be prepared for the event as the most
effective means to avert the evil." [3] Military preparations were active and conspicuous: On July 4,
New York City "resembles a camp rather than a
commercial port," testifies Troup.[4]

[1] Washington to Murray, Aug. 10, 1798; *Writings:* Ford, xiv, 72.
[2] Norfolk (Va.) *Herald*, July 10, 1798.
[3] Washington to Jas. Marshall, July 18, 1798; MS., N.Y. Pub. Lib.
And see Washington to Murray, Aug. 10, 1798; *Writings:* Ford, xiv,
71. "I . . . hope that . . . when the Despots of France find how much
they . . . have been deceived by their partisans *among us*, . . . that
an appeal to arms . . . will be . . . unnecessary." (*Ib.*)
[4] Troup to King, July 10, 1798; King, ii, 362.

The people for the moment believed, with Marshall and Washington, that we were on the brink of war; had they known what Jefferson knew, their apprehension would have been still keener. Reporting from Paris, the French partisan Skipwith tells Jefferson that, from motives of "commercial advantage and aggrandisement" as well as of "vengeance," France will probably fall upon America. "Yes sir, the moment is come that I see the fortunes, nay, independence, of my country at hazard, and in the hands of the most gigantic nation on earth. . . . Already, the language of planting new colonies upon the . . . Mississippi is the language of Frenchmen here." [1] Skipwith blames this predicament upon Adams's character, speech, and action and upon Marshall's and Pinckney's conduct in Paris; [2] and advises Jefferson that "war may be prevented, and our country saved" by "modifying or breaking" the Jay Treaty and lending money to France. [3]

Jefferson was frantic with disappointment and anger. Not only did he see the Republican Party, which he had built up with such patience and skill, going to pieces before his very eyes; but the prospect of his election to the Presidency as the successor of Adams, which until then appeared to be inviting, now jeopardized if not made hopeless. With his almost uncanny understanding of men, Jefferson laid all this to Marshall; and, from the moment of his fellow Virginian's arrival from France, this captain of the popular cause began that open and malignant

[1] Skipwith to Jefferson, March 17, 1798; Gibbs, ii, 158.
[2] *Supra*, chap. VIII.
[3] Skipwith to Jefferson, March 17, 1798; Gibbs, ii, 158.

warfare upon Marshall which ended only with Jefferson's last breath.

At once he set out to repair the havoc which Marshall's work had wrought in his party. This task was made the harder because of the very tactics which Jefferson had employed to increase the Republican strength. For, until now, he had utilized so thoroughly the deep and widespread French sentiment in America as his immediate party weapon, and made so emphatic the French issue as a policy of party tactics, that, in comparison, all other issues, except the central one of States' Rights, were secondary in the public mind at this particular time.

The French propaganda had gone farther than Jefferson, perhaps, intended it to go. "They [the French] have been led to believe by their agents and Partisans amongst *us*," testifies Washington, "that we are a divided people, that the latter are opposed to their own Government." [1] At any rate, it is certain that a direct connection, between members of what the French politicians felt themselves justified in calling "the French party" in America and the manipulators of French public opinion, existed and was made use of. This is shown by the effect in France of Jefferson's famous letter to Mazzei of April 24, 1796.[2] It is proved by the amazing fact that Talleyrand's answer to the memorial of the envoys was published in the Jeffersonian organ, the "Aurora," before Adams had transmitted that document to Congress, if not indeed before the President himself

[1] Washington to Adams, July 4, 1798; *Writings:* Ford, xiv, 15–19.
[2] See *infra*, chap. XII.

had received from our envoys Talleyrand's reply to Marshall's statement of the American case.[1]

Jefferson took the only step possible to a party leader. He sought to minimize the effect of the disclosures revealed in Marshall's dispatches. Writing to Peter Carr, April 12, 1798, Jefferson said: "You will perceive that they [the envoys] have been assailed by swindlers, whether with or without the participation of Talleyrand is not very apparent. . . . That the Directory knew anything of it is neither proved nor probable." [2] On June 8, 1798, Jefferson wrote to Archibald Stuart: "It seems fairly presumable that the douceur of 50,000 Guineas mentioned in the former dispatches was merely from X. and Y. as not a word is ever said by Talleyrand to our envoys nor by them to him on the subject." [3] Thus Jefferson's political desperation caused him to deny facts which were of record, for the dispatches show, not only that Talleyrand had full knowledge of the disgraceful transaction, but also that he originated and directed it.

The efforts of the Republicans to sneer away the envoys' disclosures awakened Washington's bitter sarcasm. The Republicans were " thunder-stricken . . . on the publication of the dispatches from our envoys," writes he, "but the contents of these dispatches are now resolved by them into harmless chitchat — mere trifles — less than was or ought to have been expected from the misconduct of the Adminis-

---

[1] See Marshall (1st ed.), v, footnote to 743; Hildreth, v, 218; also McMaster, ii, 390.

[2] Jefferson to Carr, April 12, 1798; *Works:* Ford, viii, 405.

[3] Jefferson to Stuart, June 8, 1798; *ib.*, 436.

tration of this country, and that it is better to
submit to such chastisement than to hazard greater
evils by shewing futile resentment." [1]

Jefferson made no headway, however, in his attempts to discredit the X. Y. Z. revelations. Had the
Federalists stopped with establishing the Navy Department and providing for an army, with Washington at its head; had they been content to build ships
and to take other proper measures for the National
defense, Adams's Administration would have been
saved, the Federalist Party kept alive for at least
four years more, the Republican Party delayed in its
recovery and Jefferson's election to the Presidency
made impossible. Here again Fate worked, through
the blindness of those whose day had passed, the
doom of Federalism. The Federalists enacted the
Alien and Sedition Laws and thus hastened their
own downfall.

Even after this legislation had given him a new,
real, and irresistible "issue," Jefferson still assailed
the conduct of Marshall and Pinckney; he was resolved that not a single Republican vote should be
lost. Months later he reviews the effect of the X.
Y. Z. disclosures. When the envoys were appointed,
he asserts, many "suspected . . . from what was
understood of their [Marshall's and Pinckney's] dispositions," that the mission would not only fail,
but "widen the breach and provoke our citizens to
consent to a war with" France "& union with England." While the envoys were in Paris the Adminis-

[1] Washington to McHenry, May, 1798; *Writings:* Ford, xiii, footnote to 495.

tration's hostile attitude toward France alarmed
the people; "meetings were held . . . in opposition
to war"; and the "example was spreading like a
wildfire."

Then "most critically for the government [Admin-
istration]," says Jefferson, "the dispatches . . . prepared by . . . Marshall, with a view to their being
made public, dropped into their laps. It was truly
a God-send to them & they made the most of it.
Many thousands of copies were printed & dispersed
gratis, at the public expense; & the zealots for war
co-operated so heartily, that there were instances of
single individuals who printed & dispersed 10. or
12,000 copies at their own expense. The odiousness
of the corruption supposed in those papers excited a
general & high indignation among the people."

Thus, declares Jefferson, the people, "unexperi-
enced in such maneuvers," did not see that the whole
affair was the work of "private swindlers" unauthorized by "the French government of whose participation there was neither proof nor probability." So
"the people . . . gave a loose [tongue] to" their
anger and declared "their honest preference of war
to dishonor. The fever was long & successfully kept
up and . . . war measures as ardently crowded." [1]

Jefferson's deep political sagacity did not under-
estimate the revolution in the thought and feelings
of the masses produced by the outcome of the
French mission; and he understood, to a nicety,
the gigantic task which must be performed to
reassemble and solidify the shattered Republican

[1] Jefferson to Gerry, Jan. 26, 1799; *Works: Ford*, ix, 21-22.

ranks. For public sentiment was, for the time being, decidedly warlike. "We will pay tribute to no nation; . . . We shall water our soil with our blood . . . before we yield," [1] was Troup's accurate if bombastic statement of the popular feeling.

When the first ship with American newspapers containing the X. Y. Z. dispatches reached London, they were at once "circulated throughout Europe," [2] and "produced everywhere much sensation favorable to the United States and hostile to France." [3] The intimates of Talleyrand and the Directory were "disappointed and chagrined. . . . Nothing can exceed the rage of the apostate Americans, who have so long misrepresented and disgraced their country at Paris." [4] From the first these self-expatriated Americans had flattered Gerry and sent swarms of letters to America about the good intentions of the Directory.[5]

American diplomatic representatives abroad were concerned over Gerry's whimsical character and conduct. "Gerry is yet in Paris! . . . I . . . fear . . . that man's more than infantine weakness. Of it you cannot have an idea, unless you had seen him here [The Hague] and at Paris. Erase all the two lines above; it is true, but it is cruel. If they get hold of him they will convert him into an innocent baby-engine against the government." [6]

[1] Troup to King, July 10, 1798; King, ii, 363.

[2] King to Hamilton, London, July 14, 1798; *ib.*, 365.

[3] Smith to Wolcott, Lisbon, Aug. 14, postscript Aug. 17, 1798; Gibbs, ii, 120.

[4] King to Troup, July 31, 1798; King, ii, 377.

[5] King to Pickering, July 19, 1798; *ib.*, 370.

[6] Murray to J. Q. Adams, June 8, 1787; *Letters:* Ford, 416.

And now Gerry, with whom Talleyrand had been amusing himself and whose conceit had been fed by American partisans of France in Paris, found himself in sorry case. Talleyrand, with cynical audacity, in which one finds much grim humor, peremptorily demands that Gerry tell him the names of the mysterious "X., Y., and Z." With comic self-abasement, the New Englander actually writes Talleyrand the names of the latter's own agents whom Gerry had met in Talleyrand's presence and who the French Minister personally had informed Gerry were dependable men.

The Federalists made the most of Gerry's remaining in Paris. Marshall told them that Gerry had "suffered himself to be wheedled in Paris."[1] "I . . . rejoice that I voted against his appointment,"[2] declared Sedgwick. Cabot denounced Gerry's "course" as "the most dangerous that cou'd have been taken."[3] Higginson asserted that "those of us who knew him [Gerry] regretted his appointment and expected mischief from it; but he has conducted himself worse than we had anticipated."[4] The American Minister to Great Britain, bitterly humiliated, wrote to Hamilton that Gerry's "answer to Talleyrand's demands of the names of X, Y, and Z, place him in a more degraded light than I ever believed it possible that he or any other American citizen could be exhibited."[5] And Thomas Pinckney

---

[1] Troup to King, July 10, 1798; King, ii, 363.
[2] Sedgwick to King, July 1, 1798; ib., 353.
[3] Cabot to King, July 2, 1798; ib., 353.
[4] Higginson to Wolcott, Sept. 11, 1798; Gibbs, ii, 107.
[5] King to Hamilton, London, July 14, 1798; King, ii, 365.

feared "that to want of [Gerry's] judgment . . . may
be added qualities of a more criminal nature." [1]

Such sentiments, testifies Pickering, were common
to all "the public men whom I had heard speak of
Mr. G."; Pinckney, Gerry's colleague, tells his
brother that he "never met with a man *so destitute of
candour and so full of deceit as Mr. Gerry*," and that
this opinion was shared by Marshall.[2] Troup wrote:
"We have seen and read with the greatest contempt
the correspondence between Talleyrand and Mr.
Gerry relative to Messrs. X. Y. and Z. . . . I can
say nothing honorable to [of] him [Gerry]. De
mortuis nil nisi bonum is a maxim as applicable to
him as if he was in his grave." [3] Washington gave
his opinion with unwonted mildness: "Nothing can
excuse his [Gerry's] *secret* negotiations . . . I fear
. . . that *vanity* which may have led him into the
mistake — & consciousness of being *duped* by the
Diplomatic skill of our good and magnanimous
Allies are too powerful for a weak mind to overcome." [4]

Marshall was on tenter-hooks for fear that Gerry
would not leave France before the Directory got
wind "of the present temper" of the American
people, and would hint to Gerry "insidious propositions . . . not with real pacific views but for the
purpose of dividing the people of this country and

[1] Thomas Pinckney to King, July 18, 1798; King, ii, 369.
[2] Pickering to King, Sept. 15, 1798, quoting Pinckney; *ib.*, 414.
Italics are Pinckney's.
[3] Troup to King, Oct. 2, 1798; *ib.*, 432–33.
[4] Washington to Pickering, Oct. 26, 1798; *Writings:* Ford, xiv,
121.

separating them from their government." [1] The
peppery Secretary of State grew more and more
intolerant of Gerry. He tells Marshall that
"Gerry's correspondence with Talleyrand about
W.[2] X. Y. and Z: . . . is the finishing stroke to his
conduct in France, by which he has dishonoured
and injured his country and sealed his own indelible
disgrace." [3]

Marshall was disgusted with the Gerry-Talley-
rand correspondence about the names of "X. Y. Z.,"
and wrote Pickering of Gerry's dinner to Talleyrand at which Hottenguer, Bellamy, and Hauteval
were present and of their corrupt proposition to
Gerry in Talleyrand's presence.[4] Pickering urged
Marshall to write "a short history of the mission of the envoys extraordinary," and asked permission to show Marshall's journal to President
Adams.[5]

Marshall is "unwilling," he says, "that my hasty
journal, which I had never even read over until I
received it from you, should be shown to him. This
unwillingness proceeds from a repugnance to give
him the vexation which I am persuaded it would give
him." Nevertheless, Adams did read Marshall's
Journal, it appears; for Cabot believed that "the
reading of Marshall's journal has compelled the

---

[1] Marshall to Pickering, Aug. 11, 1798; Pickering MSS., Mass.
Hist. Soc.

[2] Beaumarchais.

[3] Pickering to Marshall, Sept. 4, 1798; Pickering MSS., Mass.
Hist. Soc.

[4] Marshall to Secretary of State, Sept. 15, 1798; *ib.*

[5] Pickering to Marshall, Oct. 19, 1798; *ib.*

P[resident] to . . . acquiesce in the unqualified condemnation of Gerry." [1]

On his return to America, Gerry writes a turgid letter defending himself and exculpating Talleyrand and the Directory. The Secretary of State sends Gerry's letter to Marshall, declaring that Gerry "ought to be impeached." [2] It "astonishes me," replies Marshall; and while he wishes to avoid altercation, he thinks "it is proper for me to notice this letter," and encloses a communication to Gerry, together with a "certificate," stating the facts of Gerry's now notorious dinner to Talleyrand. [3]

Marshall is especially anxious to avoid any personal controversy at the particular moment; for, as will presently appear, he is again running for office. He tells Pickering that the Virginia Republicans are "perfectly prepared" to use Gerry in any way "which can be applied to their purposes"; and are ready "to receive him into their bosoms or to drop him entirely as he may be French or American." He is so exasperated, however, that he contemplates publishing the whole truth about Gerry, but adds: "I have been restrained from doing so by my having as a punishment for some unknown sins, consented to be nam'd a candidate for the ensuing election to Congress." [4]

Finding himself so violently attacked in the press, Marshall says: "To protect myself from the vexation of these newspaper altercations . . . I wish if it be

[1] Cabot to King, April 26, 1798; King, iii, 9.
[2] Pickering to Marshall, Nov. 5, 1798; Pickering MSS.
[3] Marshall to Pickering, Nov. 12, 1798; ib.
[4] See next chapter.

possible to avoid appearing in print myself." Also
he makes the excuse that the courts are in session,
and that "my absence has plac'd my business in
such a situation as scarcely to leave a moment
which I can command for other purposes." [1]

A week later Marshall is very anxious as to what
course Gerry intends to take, for, writes Marshall, publications to mollify public opinion toward
France and to irritate it against England "and to
diminish the repugnance to pay money to the
French republic are appearing every day." [2]

The indefatigable Republican chieftain had been
busily inspiring attacks upon the conduct of the
mission and particularly upon Marshall. "You
know what a wicked use has been made of the . . .
X. Y. Z. dish cooked up by Marshall, where the
swindlers are made to appear as the French government," wrote Jefferson to Pendleton. "Art and
industry combined have certainly wrought out of
this business a wonderful effect on the people."
But "now that Gerry comes out clearing the French
government of that turpitude, . . . the people will
be disposed to suspect they have been duped."

Because Marshall's dispatches "are too volumi-
nous for them [the people] and beyond their reach"
Jefferson begs Pendleton to write a pamphlet "re-
capitulating the whole story . . . short, simple &
levelled to every capacity." It must be "so concise
as omitting nothing material, yet may be printed

---

[1] Marshall to Pickering, Oct. 15, 1798; Pickering MSS., Mass. Hist.
Soc.

[2] Marshall to Pickering, Oct. 22, 1798; ib., Mass. Hist. Soc., xxiii,
251.

in handbills." Jefferson proposes to "print & dis-
perse 10. or 20,000 copies" [1] free of postage under
the franks of Republican Congressmen.

Pickering having referred scathingly to the Gerry-
Talleyrand dinner, Gerry writes the President, to
deny Marshall's account of that function. Marshall
replies in a personal letter to Gerry, which, considering Marshall's placid and unresentful nature, is a
very whiplash of rebuke; it closes, however, with
the hope that Gerry "will think justly of this subject and will thereby save us both the pain of an
altercation I do so wish to avoid." [2]

A few months later Marshall, while even more
fixed than ever in his contempt for Gerry, is mel-
lower in expressing it. "I am grieved rather than
surprised at Mr. Gerry's letter," he writes.[3] So
ended the only incident in Marshall's life where
he ever wrote severely of any man. Although the
unfriendliness between Jefferson and himself grew
through the years into unrelenting hatred on both
sides, Marshall did not express the intensity of
his feeling. While his courage, physical and moral,
was perfect, he had no stomach for verbal en-
counters. He could fight to the death with arms
or arguments; but personal warfare by tongue or
pen was beyond or beneath him. Marshall simply
could not scold or browbeat. He was incapable of
participating in a brawl.

Soon after reaching Richmond, the domestic

[1] Jefferson to Pendleton, Jan. 29, 1799; *Works:* Ford, ix, 27–28.

[2] Marshall to Pickering, November 12, 1798; Pickering MSS.,
Mass. Hist. Soc.

[3] Marshall to Secretary of State, Feb. 19, 1799; *ib.*

Marshall again shines out sunnily in a letter to his wife at Winchester, over the Blue Ridge. He tells his "dearest Polly" that although a week has passed he has "scarcely had time to look into any business yet, there are so many persons calling every hour to see me. ... The hot and disagreeable ride" to Richmond had been too much for him, but "if I could only learn that you were entirely restored I should be happy. Your Mama & friends are in good health & your Mama is as cheerful as usual except when some particular conversation discomposes her.

"Your sweet little Mary is one of the most fascinating little creatures I ever beheld. She has improved very much since I saw her & I cannot help agreeing that she is a substitute for her lovely sister. She talks in a way not easily to be understood tho she comprehends very well everything that is said to her & is the most coquettish little prude & the most prudish little coquet I ever saw. I wish she was with you as I think she would entertain you more than all the rest of your children put together.

"Poor little John[1] is cutting teeth & of course is sick. He appeared to know me as soon as he saw me. He would not come to me, but he kept his eyes fixed on me as on a person he had some imperfect recollection of. I expect he has been taught to look at the picture & had some confused idea of a likeness. He is small & weakly but by no means an ugly child. If as I hope we have the happiness to raise him I

---

[1] Marshall's fourth child, born January 15, 1798, during Marshall's absence in France.

trust he will do as well as the rest. Poor little fellow, the present hot weather is hard on him cutting teeth, but great care is taken of him & I hope he will do well.

"I hear nothing from you my dearest Polly but I will cherish the hope that you are getting better & will indulge myself with expecting the happiness of seeing you in october quite yourself. Remember my love to give me this pleasure you have only to take the cold bath, to use a great deal of exercise, to sleep tranquilly & to stay in cheerful company. I am sure you will do everything which can contribute to give you back to yourself & me. This hot weather must be very distressing to you — it is to everybody — but it will soon be colder. Let me know in time everything relative to your coming down. Farewell my dearest Polly. I am your ever affectionate

"J. MARSHALL." [1]

On taking up his private business, Marshall found himself hard-pressed for money. Payments for the Fairfax estate were overdue and he had no other resources with which to meet them but the money due him upon his French mission. "The disarrangement," he writes to the Secretary of

[1] Marshall to his wife, Richmond, Aug. 18, 1798; MS. Mrs. Marshall remained in Winchester, where her husband had hurried to see her after leaving Philadelphia. Her nervous malady had grown much worse during Marshall's absence. Mrs. Carrington had been "more than usual occupied with my poor sister Marshall . . . who fell into a deep melancholy. Her husband, who might by his usual tenderness (had he been here) have dissipated this frightful gloom, was long detained in France. . . . The malady increased." (Mrs. Carrington to Miss C[airns], 1800; Carrington MSS.)

State, "produc'd by my absence and the dispersion of my family oblige me to make either sales which I do not wish or to delay payments of money which I ought not to delay, unless I can receive from the treasury. This state of things obliges me to apply to you and to ask whether you can furnish me either with an order from the Secretary of the Treasury on Colo. Carrington or with your request to him to advance money to me. The one or the other will be sufficient." [1]

Pickering writes Marshall that Carrington can safely advance him the needed cash. "I will lose no time to place the balance in your hands," [2] says Pickering, upon the receipt of Marshall's statement of his account with the Government.

The total amount paid Marshall for his eleven months' absence upon the French mission was $19,963.97,[3] which, allowing five thousand dollars for his expenses — a generous estimate — was considerably more than three times as much as Marshall's annual income from his law practice. It was an immense sum, considering the compensation of public officials at that period — not much less than the annual salaries of the President and his entire Cabinet; more than the total amount annu-

[1] Marshall to Pickering, August 11, 1798; Pickering MSS., Mass. Hist. Soc., xxiii, 33.

[2] Pickering to Marshall, Sept. 4, 1798; ib.

[3] Archives, State Department. Thirty-five hundred dollars was placed at Marshall's disposal when he sailed for France, five hundred dollars in specie and the remainder by letter of credit on governments and European bankers. (Marshall to Secretary of State, July 10, 1797; Pickering MSS. Also Archives, State Department.) He drew two thousand dollars more when he arrived at Philadelphia on his return (June 23; ib.), and $14,463.97 on Oct. 13 (ib.).

ally paid to the justices of the Supreme Court. Thus, for the time being, the Fairfax estate was saved.

It was still necessary, however, if he, his brother, and brother-in-law, were to discharge the remaining payments, that Marshall should give himself to the business of making money — to work much harder than ever he had done before and than his natural inclinations prompted. Therefore, no more of unremunerative public life for him — no more waste of time in the Legislature. There never could, of course, come another such "God-send," to use Marshall's phrase as reported by Jefferson,[1] as the French mission; and few public offices, National or State, yielded so much as he could make in the practice of his profession. Thus financial necessity and his own desire settled Marshall in the resolve, which he believed nothing ever could shake, to give the remainder of his days to his personal and private business. But Fate had her own plans for John Marshall and again overruled what he believed to be his fixed and unalterable purpose.

[1] The "Anas"; *Works:* Ford, i, 355.

CHAPTER X.

CANDIDATE FOR CONGRESS

Of the three envoys, the conduct of General Marshall alone has been entirely satisfactory. (Adams.)

In heart and sentiment, as well as by birth and interest, I am an American. We should make no political connection with any nation on earth. (Marshall to constituents.)

Tell Marshall I love him because he felt and acted as a Republican and an American. (Patrick Henry.)

In the congressional campaign of 1798–99, the Federalists of the Richmond District were without a strong candidate. The one they had put up lacked that personal popularity which then counted for as much in political contests as the issues involved. Upon Marshall's return from France and his enthusiastic reception, ending with the Richmond demonstration, the Federalist managers pressed Marshall to take the place of the candidate then running, who, indeed, was anxious to withdraw in his favor. But the returned envoy refused, urged the Federalist then standing to continue his candidacy, and pledged that he would do all in his power to secure his election.

Finally Washington asked Marshall to come to see him. "I received an invitation from General Washington," writes Marshall in his account of this important event, "to accompany his nephew . . . on a visit to Mount Vernon." [1]

[1] Marshall to Paulding, April 4, 1835; *Lippincott's Magazine* (1868), ii, 624–25.

When Bushrod Washington wrote that Marshall accepted the invitation, the General was extremely gratified. "I learnt with much pleasure . . . of General Marshall's intention to make me a visit," he writes his nephew. "I wish it of all things; and it is from the ardent desire I have to see him that I have not delayed a moment to express it. . . . The crisis is most important. . . . The temper of the people in this state . . . is so violent and outrageous that I wish to converse with General Marshall and yourself on the elections which must soon come." [1] Washington says that when his visitors arrive the matter of the fictitious Langhorne letter will also be taken up "and we will let General Marshall into the whole business and advise with him thereon." [2]

To Mount Vernon, therefore, Marshall and his

[1] Washington to Bushrod Washington, Aug. 27, 1798; *Writings:* Ford, xiv, 75.

[2] *Ib.* In September, 1797, when Marshall was absent on the X. Y. Z. mission, Washington received a letter from one "John Langhorne" of Albemarle County. Worded with skillful cunning, it was designed to draw from the retired President imprudent expressions that could be used against him and the Federalists. It praised him, denounced his detractors, and begged him to disregard their assaults. (Langhorne to Washington, Sept. 25, 1797; *Writings:* Sparks, xi, 501.) Washington answered vaguely. (Washington to Langhorne, Oct. 15, 1797; *Writings:* Ford, xiii, 428–30.) John Nicholas discovered that the Langhorne letter had been posted at Charlottesville; that no person of that name lived in the vicinity; and that Washington's answer was called for at the Charlottesville post-office (where Jefferson posted and received letters) by a person closely connected with the master of Monticello. It was suspected, therefore, that Jefferson was the author of the fictitious letter. The mystery caused Washington much worry and has never been cleared up. (See Washington to Nicholas, Nov. 30, 1797; *ib.*, footnote to 429–30; to Bushrod Washington, March 8, 1798; *ib.*, 448; to Nicholas, March 8, 1798; *ib.*, 449–50.) It is not known what advice Marshall gave Washington when the latter asked for his opinion; but from his lifelong conduct in such matters and his strong repugnance to personal disputes, it is probable that Marshall advised that the matter be dropped.

companion journeyed on horseback. For convenience in traveling, they had put their clothing in the same pair of saddle-bags. They arrived in a heavy rain and were "drenched to the skin." Unlocking the saddle-bags, the first article they took out was a black bottle of whiskey. With great hilarity each charged this to be the property of the other. Then came a thick twist of tobacco, some corn bread, and finally the worn apparel of wagoners; at some tavern on the way their saddle-bags had become exchanged for those of drivers. The rough clothes were grotesque misfits; and when, clad in these, his guests presented themselves, Washington, roaring with laughter, expressed his sympathy for the wagoners when they, in turn, discovered the exchange they had made with the lawyers.[1] In such fashion began the conference that ended in John Marshall's candidacy for Congress in the vital campaign of 1798–99.

This was the first time, so far as is known, that Marshall had visited Washington at his Potomac home. No other guest except Washington's nephew seems to have been present at this conference, so decisive of Marshall's future. The time was September, 1798, and the conversations were held on the broad piazza,[2] looking out upon the river, with the new Capitol almost within sight. There, for "four or five days," his old commander used all his influence to induce Marshall to become the Federalist candidate.

"General Washington urged the importance of the crisis," writes Marshall in describing the cir-

[1] Paulding: *Washington*, ii, 191–92. [2] Marshall to Paulding, *supra*.

cumstance; "every man," insisted Washington, "who could contribute to the success of sound opinions was required by the most sacred duty to offer his services to the public." Marshall doubted his "ability to do any good. I told him that I had made large pecuniary engagements which required close attention to my profession and which would distress me should the emoluments derived from it be abandoned."

Marshall told of his promise to the Federalist candidate who was then making his campaign for election. Washington declared that this candidate still would withdraw in Marshall's favor; but Marshall remained unshaken. Finally Washington gave his own conduct as an example. Marshall thus describes the final appeal which his old leader made to him: "He had withdrawn from office with a declaration of his determination never again, under any circumstances, to enter public life. No man could be more sincere in making that declaration, nor could any man feel stronger motives for adhering to it. No man could make a stronger sacrifice than he did in breaking a resolution, thus publicly made, and which he had believed to be unalterable. Yet I saw him," continues Marshall, "in opposition to his public declaration, in opposition to his private feelings, consenting, under a sense of duty, to surrender the sweets of retirement, and again to enter the most arduous and perilous station which an individual could fill. My resolution yielded to this representation." [1]

[1] Marshall to Paulding, *supra*. This letter was in answer to one from Paulding asking Marshall for the facts as to Washington's part in inducing Marshall to run for Congress.

There is a tradition that, at one point in the conference, Marshall, becoming offended by Washington's insistence, which, runs the story, took the form of a peremptory and angrily expressed command, determined to leave so early in the morning that his host would have no opportunity to press the matter further; but, Washington noting Marshall's irritation and anticipating his purpose, was on the piazza when his departing guest appeared at dawn, and there made the final appeal which won Marshall's reluctant consent.

Marshall felt that he was making a heavy personal sacrifice; it meant to him the possible loss of the Fairfax estate. As we have seen, he had just declined appointment to the Supreme Bench [1] for this very reason, and this place later was given to Bushrod Washington, largely on Marshall's advice. [2] Adams had been reluctant to give Marshall up as one of the Associate Justices of the Supreme Court; "General Marshall or Bushrod Washington will succeed Judge Wilson," wrote the President to his Secretary of State [3] nearly three months after the first tender of the place to Marshall in Philadelphia. Later on the President again returned to Marshall.

"I still think that General Marshall ought to be preferred," he wrote. "Of the three envoys, the conduct of Marshall alone has been entirely satisfactory, and ought to be marked by the most decided approbation of the public. He has raised the

[1] Pickering to Marshall, Sept. 20, 1798; Pickering MSS., Mass. Hist. Soc.

[2] Ib.

[3] Adams to Pickering, Sept. 14, 1798; *Works: Adams*, viii, 595.

American people in their own esteem, and, if the
influence of truth and justice, reason and argument
is not lost in Europe, he has raised the consideration
of the United States in that quarter of the world.
... If Mr. Marshall should decline, I should next
think of Mr. [Bushrod] Washington." [1]

Washington's appeal to Marshall's patriotism and
sense of duty, however, outbalanced the weighty
financial reasons which decided him against becoming an Associate Justice of the Supreme Court.
Thus, against his desire, he found himself once more
in the hurly-burly of partisan politics. But this
time the fight which he was forced to lead was to
be desperate, indeed.

The moment Marshall announced his candidacy
he became the center of Republican attack in Virginia. The virulence of the campaign against him
was so great that it has become a tradition; and while
scarcely any of the personal assaults, which appeared
in print, are extant, they are known to have been
ruthless, and utterly unrestrained both as to the
charges made and the language used in making
them.

In his scurrilous review of Adams's Administration, which Adams properly denounced as "a Mass
of Lyes from the first page to the last," [2] John
Wood repeats the substance of some of the attacks
which, undoubtedly, were launched against Marshall
in this bitter political conflict. "John Marshall,"
says Wood, "was an improper character in several

[1] Adams to Pickering, Sept. 26, 1798; *Works: Adams*, viii, 597.
[2] Adams to Rush, June 25, 1807; *Old Family Letters*, 152.

respects; his principles of aristocracy were well known. Talleyrand, when in America, knew that this man was regarded as a royalist and not as a republican, and that he was abhorred by most honest characters." [1]

The abuse must have been very harsh and unjust; for Marshall, who seldom gave way to resentment, complained to Pickering with uncharacteristic temper. "The whole malignancy of Anti-federalism," he writes, "not only in the district, where it unfortunately is but too abundant, but throughout the State, has become uncommonly active and considers itself as peculiarly interested in the reëlection of the old member [Clopton].

"The Jacobin presses, which abound with us and only circulate within the State, teem with publications of which the object is to poison still further the public opinion and which are level'd particularly at me. Anything written by me on the subject of French affairs wou'd be ascrib'd to me, whether it appear'd with or without my signature and wou'd whet and sharpen up the sting of every abusive scribbler who had vanity enough to think himself a writer because he cou'd bestow personal abuse and cou'd say things as malignant as they are ill founded." [2]

---

[1] Wood, 260. Wood's book was " suppressed" by Aaron Burr, who bought the plates and printer's rights. It consists of dull attacks on prominent Federalists. Jefferson's friends charged that Burr suppressed it because of his friendship for the Federalist leaders. (See Cheetham's letters to Jefferson, Dec. 29, 1801, Jan. 30, 1802, *Proceedings*, Mass. Hist. Soc. (April and May, 1907) 51–58.) Soon afterward Jefferson began his warfare on Burr.

[2] Marshall to Pickering, Oct. 15, 1798; Pickering MSS., Mass.

The publication of the American envoys' dispatches from France, which had put new life into the Federalist Party, had also armed that decaying organization with enough strength to enact the most imprudent measures that its infatuated leaders ever devised. During June and July, 1798, they had succeeded in driving through Congress the famous Alien and Sedition Laws.[1]

The Alien Act authorized the President to order out of the country all aliens whom he thought "dangerous" or "suspected" of any "treasonable or secret machination against the government" on pain of imprisonment not to exceed three years and of being forever afterwards incapacitated from becoming citizens of the United States. But if the alien could prove to the satisfaction of the President that he was not dangerous, a presidential "license" might be granted, permitting the alien to remain in the United States as long as the President saw fit and in such place as he might designate. If any expelled alien returned without permission he was to be imprisoned as long as the President thought "the public safety may require."

The Sedition Act provided penalties for the crime of unlawful combination and conspiracy against the Government;[2] a fine not exceeding two thousand dollars and imprisonment not exceeding two years

Hist. Soc. This campaign was unusually acrimonious everywhere. "This Electioneering is worse than the Devil." (Smith to Bayard, Aug. 2, 1798; *Bayard Papers:* Donnan, 69.)

[1] See Statutes at Large, 566, 570, 577, for Alien Acts of June 18, June 25, and July 6, and *ib.*, 196, for Sedition Law of July 14, 1798.

[2] This section was not made a campaign issue by the Republicans.

for any person who should write, print, publish, or
speak anything "false, scandalous and malicious"
against the Government, either House of Congress,
or the President "with intent to defame" the Government, Congress, or the President, or "to bring
them or either of them into contempt or disrepute;
or to excite against them or either or any of them
the hatred of the good people of the United States,
or to stir up sedition within the United States."

When Jefferson first heard of this proposed stupid
legislation, he did not object to it, even in his intimate letters to his lieutenant Madison.[1] Later, however, he became the most ferocious of its assailants.
Hamilton, on the other hand, saw the danger in the
Sedition Bill the moment a copy reached him: "There
are provisions in this bill . . . highly exceptionable,"
he wrote. "I hope sincerely the thing may not be
hurried through. Let us not establish a tyranny.
Energy is a very different thing from violence."[2]
When Madison got the first inkling of the Alien Bill,
he wrote to Jefferson that it "is a monster that must
forever disgrace its parents."[3]

As soon as the country learned what the Alien and
Sedition Laws contained, the reaction against the
Federalist Party began. In vain did the Federalists
plead to the people, as they had urged in the debate
in Congress, that these laws were justified by events;
in vain did they point out the presence in America of

[1] Jefferson to Madison, May 10, 1798; *Works:* Ford, viii, 417; and
to Monroe, May 21, 1798; *ib.*, 423. Jefferson's first harsh word was to
Madison, June 7, 1798; *ib.*, 434.

[2] Hamilton to Wolcott, June 29, 1798; *Works:* Lodge, x, 295.

[3] Madison to Jefferson, May 20, 1798; *Writings:* Hunt, vi, 320.

large numbers of foreigners who were active and bitter against the American Government; in vain did they read to citizens the abuse published in newspapers against the Administration and cite the fact that the editors of these libelous sheets were aliens.[1]

The popular heart and instinct were against these crowning blunders of Federalism. Although the patriotic wave started by Marshall's return and the X. Y. Z. disclosures was still running strong, a more powerful counter-current was rising. "Liberty of the press," "freedom of speech," "trial by jury" at once became the watchwords and war-cries of Republicanism. On the hustings, in the newspapers, at the taverns, the Alien and Sedition Laws were denounced as unconstitutional — they were null and void — no man, much less any State, should obey or respect them.

The Alien Law, said its opponents, merged the Judicial and the Executive Departments, which the Constitution guaranteed should be separate and distinct; the Sedition Act denied freedom of speech, with which the Constitution expressly forbade Congress to interfere; both struck at the very heart of liberty — so went the Republican argument and appeal.[2]

In addition to their solid objections, the Republicans made delirious prophecies. The Alien and Sedition Laws were, they asserted, the beginning of mon-

---

[1] For the Federalists' justification of the Alien and Sedition Laws see Gibbs, ii, 78 *et seq.*

[2] As a matter of fact, the anger of Republican leaders was chiefly caused by their belief that the Alien and Sedition Laws were aimed at the Republican Party as such, and this, indeed, was true.

archy, the foundation of absolutism. The fervid
Jefferson indulged, to his heart's content, in these
grotesque predictions: "The alien & sedition laws are
working hard," declared the great Republican. Indeed, he thought them only "an experiment on the
American mind to see how far it will bear an avowed
violation of the constitution. If this goes down, we
shall immediately see attempted another act of Congress declaring that the President shall continue in
office during life, reserving to another occasion the
transfer of the succession to his heirs, and the establishment of the Senate for life. . . . That these things
are in contemplation, I have no doubt; nor can I be
confident of their failure, after the dupery of which our
countrymen have shewn themselves susceptible." [1]

Washington was almost as extravagant on the
other side. When an opponent of the Alien and Sedition Acts asked him for his opinion of them, he advised his questioner to read the opposing arguments
"and consider to what lengths a certain description
of men in our country have already driven and seem
resolved further to drive matters" and then decide
whether these laws are not necessary, against those
"who acknowledge no allegiance to this country, and
in many instances are sent among us . . . for the
express purpose of poisoning the minds of our people,
— and to sow dissensions among them, in order to
alienate their affections from the government of
their choice, thereby endeavoring to dissolve the
Union." [2]

[1] Jefferson to S. T. Mason, Oct. 11, 1798; *Works:* Ford, viii, 450.
[2] Washington to Spotswood, Nov. 22, 1798; *Writings:* Ford, xiv,
121–22.

Washington thought that the ferocious Republican attack on the Alien and Sedition Laws was but a cunning maneuver of politicians, and this, indeed, for the moment at least, seems to have been the case. "The Alien and Sedition Laws are now the desiderata of the Opposition. . . . But any thing else would have done, — and something there will always be, for them to torture; and to disturb the public mind with their unfounded and ill favored forebodings" was his pessimistic judgment.[1]

He sent "to General Marshall Judge Addison's charge to the grand juries of the county courts of the Fifth Circuit of the State of Pennsylvania. . . . This charge is on the liberty of speech and of the press and is a justification of the sedition and alien laws. But," wrote Washington, "I do not believe that . . . it . . . or . . . any other writing will produce the least change in the conduct of the leaders of the opposition to the measures of the general government. They have points to carry from which no reasoning, no consistency of conduct, no absurdity can divert them. If, however, such writings should produce conviction in the mind of those who have hitherto placed faith in their assertions, it will be a fortunate event for this country." [2]

[1] Washington to Murray, Dec. 26, 1798; *Writings:* Ford, xiv, 132.
[2] Washington to Bushrod Washington, Dec. 31, 1798; *ib.*, 135–36. Judge Addison's charge was an able if intemperate interpretation of the Sedition Law. The Republican newspapers assailed and ridiculed this very effectively in the presidential campaign of 1800. "Alexander Addison has published in a volume a number of his *charges* to juries — and *precious* charges they are — brimstone and saltpetre, assifœtida and train oil." (*Aurora*, Dec. 6, 1800. See Chief Justice Ellsworth's comments upon Judge Addison's charge in Flanders, ii, 193.)

Marshall had spoken in the same vein soon after his arrival at Richmond. "The people . . . are pretty right as it respects France," he reports to the Secretary of State. The Republican criticisms of the X. Y. Z. mission "make so little impression that I believe France will be given up and the attack upon the government will be supported by the alien and sedition laws. I am extremely sorry to observe that here they are more successful and that these two laws, especially the sedition bill, are viewed by a great many well meaning men, as unwarranted by the constitution.

"I am entirely persuaded that with many the hate of Government of our country is implacable and that if these bills did not exist the same clamor would be made by them on some other account, but," truthfully and judicially writes Marshall, "there are also many who are guided by very different motives, and who tho' less noisy in their complaints are seriously uneasy on this subject." [1]

The Republicans pressed Marshall particularly hard on the Alien and Sedition Laws, but he found a way to answer. Within a few days after he had become the Federalist candidate, an anonymous writer, signing himself "Freeholder," published in the Richmond newspapers an open letter to Marshall asking him whether he was for the Constitution; whether the welfare of America depended on a foreign alliance; whether a closer connection with Great Britain was desirable; whether the Administration's

[1] Marshall to Pickering, Aug. 11, 1798; Pickering MSS., Mass. Hist. Soc.

conduct toward France was wise; and, above all, whether Marshall was "an advocate of the alien and sedition bills or in the event of your election will you use your influence to obtain a repeal of these laws?"

In printing Marshall's answers to "Freeholder," the "Times and Virginia Advertiser" of Alexandria remarked: "Mr. John Marshall has offered as a candidate for a representative in the next Congress. He has already begun his electioneering campaign. The following are answers to some queries proposed to him. Whether the queries were propounded with a view of discovering his real sentiments, or whether they were published by one of his friends to serve electioneering purposes, is immaterial: — The principles Mr. Marshall professes to possess are such as influence the conduct of every real American." [1]

A week later Marshall published his answers. "Every citizen," says he, "has a right to know the political sentiments of a candidate"; and besides, the candidate wishes everybody to know his "real principles" and not "attribute" to him "those with which active calumny has . . . aspersed" him. In this spirit Marshall answers that "in heart and sentiment, as well as by birth and interest," he is "an American; attached to the . . . Constitution . . . which will preserve us if we support it firmly."

He is, he asserts, against any alliance, "offensive or defensive," with Great Britain or "any closer connection with that nation than already exists. . . .

---

[1] Oct. 11, 1798. The questions of "Freeholder" were, undoubtedly, written with Marshall's knowledge. Indeed a careful study of them leads one to suspect that he wrote or suggested them himself.

No man in existence is more decidedly opposed to
such an alliance or more fully convinced of the evils
that would result from it." Marshall declares that
he is for American neutrality in foreign wars; and
cites his memorial to Talleyrand as stating his views
on this subject.

"The whole of my politics respecting foreign nations, are reducible to this single position: . . . Commercial intercourse with all, but political ties with
none . . . buy as cheap and sell as dear as possible
. . . never connect ourselves politically with any
nation whatever."

He disclaims the right to speak for the Administration, but believes it to have the same principles. If
France, while at war with Great Britain, should also
make war on America, "it would be madness and
folly" not to secure the "aid of the British fleets to
prevent our being invaded"; but, not even for that,
would he "make such a sacrifice as . . . we should
make by forming a permanent political connection
with . . . any nation on earth."

Marshall says that he believes the Administration's
policy as regards France to have been correct, and
necessary to the maintenance "of the neutrality and
independence of our country." Peace with France
was not possible "without sacrificing those great
objects," for "the primary object of France is . . .
dominion over others." The French accomplish
this purpose by "immense armies on their part
and divisions among . . . those whom they wish to
subdue."

Marshall declares that he is "not an advocate of

the Alien and Sedition Bills," and, had he been in Congress, "certainly would have opposed them," although he does not "think them fraught with all those mischiefs ascribed to them." But he thinks them "useless . . . calculated to create unnecessary discontents and jealousies"; and that, too, "at a time when our very existence as a nation may depend on our union."

He believes that those detested laws "would never have been enacted" if they had been opposed on these principles by a man not suspected of intending to destroy the government or being hostile to it." The effort to repeal them "will be made before he can become a member of Congress"; if it fails and is renewed after he takes his seat, he "will obey the voice of his constituents." He thinks, however, it will be unwise to revive the Alien and Sedition Acts which are, by their own terms, about to expire; and Marshall pledges that he will "indisputably oppose their revival." [1]

Upon Marshall as their favorite candidate for Congress, the eyes of the Federalist leaders in other States were focused. They were particularly anxious and uncertain as to his stand on the Alien and Sedition Laws; for he seems to have privately expressed, while in Philadelphia on his return from France, a mild disapproval of the wisdom and political expe-

---

[1] The *Times and Virginia Advertiser*, Alexandria, Virginia, October 11, 1798. This paper, however, does not give "Freeholder's" questions. The *Columbian Centinel*, Boston, October 20, 1798, prints both questions and answers, but makes several errors in the latter. The correct version is given in Appendix III, *infra*, where "Freeholder's" questions and Marshall's answers appear in full.

diency of this absurd legislation. His answers to
"Freeholder" were therefore published everywhere.
When the New England Federalists read them in
the "Columbian Centinel" of Saturday, October
20, most of them were as hot against Marshall as
were the rabid Virginia Republicans.

Ames whetted his rhetoric to razor edge and
slashed without mercy. He describes Republican
dismay when Marshall's dispatches were published:
"The wretches [Republicans] looked round, like
Milton's devils when first recovering from the
stunning force of their fall from Heaven, to see
what new ground they could take." They chose,
says Ames, "the alien and sedition bills, and the
land tax" with which to arouse discontent and revive their party. So "the implacable foes of the
Constitution — foes before it was made, while it was
making, and since — became full of tender fears
lest it should be violated by the alien and sedition
laws."

The Federalists, complained Ames, "are forever
hazarding the cause by heedless and rash conces-
sions. John Marshall, with all his honors in blossom
and bearing fruit, answers some newspaper queries
unfavorably to these laws. . . . No correct man, —
no incorrect man, even, — whose affections and
feelings are wedded to the government, would give
his name to the base opposers of the law. . . . This
he has done. Excuses may palliate, — future zeal in
the cause may partially atone, — but his character
is done for. . . . Like a man who in battle receives
an ounce ball in his body — it may heal, it lies too

deep to be extracted. . . . There let it lie. False Federalists, or such as act wrong from false fears, should be dealt hardly by, if I were Jupiter Tonans. . . . The moderates [like Marshall] are the meanest of cowards, the falsest of hypocrites." [1] Theodore Sedgwick declared that Marshall's "mysterious & unpardonable" conduct had aided "french villainy" and that he had "degraded himself by a mean & paltry electioneering trick." [2]

At first, the Republicans praised Marshall's stand; and this made the New England Federalists frantic. Cabot, alone, defended Marshall in the press, although not over his own name and only as a matter of party tactics. He procured some one to write to the "Columbian Centinel" under the name of "A Yankee Freeholder." This contributor tried to explain away Marshall's offense.

"General Marshall is a citizen too eminent for his talents, his virtues and his public services, to merit so severe a punishment as to [receive the] applause of disorganizers [Republicans]." He should be saved from the "admiration of the *seditious*" — that much was due to Marshall's "spirit, firmness and eloquence" in the contest with "the Despots of *France*." As "drowning men would catch at straws" so "the eagle-eyed and disheartened sons of faction" had "with forlorn and desperate . . . avidity . . . seized on " Marshall's answers to "Freeholder."

And no wonder; for "even *good men* have stood

[1] Ames to Gore, Dec. 18, 1798; *Works:* Ames, i, 245–47.
[2] Sedgwick to Pickering, Oct. 23, 1798; Pickering MSS., Mass. Hist. Soc.

appalled, at observing a man whom they so highly
venerate soliciting votes at the expense of principles which they deem sacred and inviolable." "Yankee Freeholder" therefore proposes "to vindicate
General MARSHALL."

Marshall was the only Richmond Federalist who
could be elected; he "patriotically" had consented
to run only because of "the situation and danger of
his country at this moment." Therefore "it was
absolutely necessary to take all the ordinary steps"
to succeed. This "may appear extraordinary . . . to
those who are only acquainted with the delicacy of
New England elections where *personal* solicitation
is the Death-warrant to success"; but it was "not
only pardonable but necessary . . . in the Southern
States."

"Yankee Freeholder" reminded his readers that
"Calumny had assailed General MARSHALL, in
common with other men of merit." Virginia newspapers had "slandered him"; politicians had called
him "*Aristocrat, Tory,* and *British Agent.* All this
abuse . . . would infallibly have rendered him popular in *New-England*" — but not so in "*Virginia,*"
where there were "too many ignorant, ill-informed
and inflamed minds."

Therefore, "it became necessary that General
MARSHALL should explicitly exhibit his political
creed." After all, his answers to "Freeholder" were
not so bad — he did not assail the constitutionality
of the Alien and Sedition Laws. "If Gen. MARSHALL
thought them unconstitutional or dangerous to liberty, would he" be content merely to say they were

unnecessary? "Would a man of General MAR-
SHALL's force of reasoning, simply denominate *laws
useless*," if he thought them unconstitutional? "No
— the idea is too absurd to be indulged. . . . Time
and General MARSHALL's conduct will hereafter
prove that I am not mistaken in my opinion of his
sentiments." [1]

Cabot's strategy had little effect on New England, which appeared to dislike Virginia with a curious intolerance. The Essex County politician, nevertheless, stood by his guns; and six months later thus
reassures King: "I am ready to join you as well as
Ames in reprobating the publication of Marshall's
sentiments on the Sedition & Alien Acts, but I still
adhere to my first opinion that Marshall ought not
to be attacked in the Newspapers, nor too severely
condemned anywhere, because Marshall has not yet
learned his whole lesson, but has a mind & disposition which can hardly fail to make him presently an
accomplished (political) Scholar & a very useful
man.

"Some allowance too should be made," contends
Cabot, "for the influence of the Atmosphere of
Virginia which doubtless makes every one who
breathes it visionary &, upon the subject of Free
Govt., incredibly credulous; but it is certain that
Marshall at Phila. would become a most powerful
auxiliary to the cause of order & good Govt., &
therefore we ought not to diminish his fame which
wou'd ultimately be a loss to ourselves." [2]

[1] *Columbian Centinel* (Boston), Oct. 24, 1798.
[2] Cabot to King, April 26, 1799; King, iii, 9.

The experienced practical politician, Sedgwick, correctly judged that "Freeholder's" questions to Marshall and Marshall's answers were an "electioneering trick." But Pickering stoutly defended Marshall upon this charge. "I have not met with one good federalist, who does not regret his answers to the Freeholder; but I am sorry that it should be imagined to be an 'electioneering trick.' ... General Marshall is incapable of doing a dishonorable act." Only Marshall's patriotism had induced him to accept the French mission, said the Secretary of State.[1] Nothing but "the urging of friends ... overcame his reluctance to come to Congress. ... A man of untainted honor," had informed Pickering that "Marshall is a *Sterling fellow*." [2]

The Federalists' complaints of him continued to be so strong and widespread, however, that they even reached our legations in Europe: "I too have lamented that John Marshall, after such a mission particularly, should lend himself thus against a law which the French Jacobinism in the United States had forced government to adopt. M[arshall] *before,* was not, that we ever heard of, one of us." [3]

Toward the end of October Marshall gives his private opinion of the Virginia Republicans and their real motives, and foretells the Virginia Resolutions. "The real french party of this country

[1] This was not true. The Fairfax embarrassment, alone, caused Marshall to go to France in 1797.

[2] Pickering to Sedgwick, Nov. 6, 1798; Pickering MSS., Mass. Hist. Soc.

[3] Murray to J. Q. Adams, March 22, 1799; *Letters:* Ford, 530. Murray had been a member of Congress and a minor Federalist politician. By "us" he means the extreme Federalist politicians.

again begins to show itself," he writes. "There are very many indeed in this part of Virginia who speak of our own government as an enemy infinitely more formidable and infinitely more to be guarded against than the French Directory. Immense efforts are made to induce the legislature of the state which will meet in Dec'r to take some violent measure which may be attended with serious consequences. I am not sure that these efforts will entirely fail. It requires to be in this part of Virginia to know the degree of irritation which has been excited and the probable extent of the views of those who excite it."[1]

The most decent of the attacks on Marshall were contained in a series of open letters first published in the "Aurora"[2] and signed "Curtius."

"You have long been regarded," writes Curtius, "as the leader of that party in this State" which has tried "by audacious efforts to erect a monarchy or aristocracy upon the ruins of our free constitution. The energy of your mind and the violence of your zeal have exalted you to this bad eminence." If you had "employed your talents in defense of the people . . . your history would have been read in a nation's eyes."

"The publication of your dispatches and the happy exercise of diplomatic skill has produced a momentary delusion and infatuation in which an opposition to the administration is confounded with hostility to the government and treason to the country. . . . The execrations and yells against French

[1] Marshall to Pickering, Oct. 22, 1798; Pickering MSS., Mass. Hist. Soc.

[2] Adams: *Gallatin*, 212.

cruelty and French ambition, are incessantly kept up by the hirelings of Great Britain and the enemies of liberty."

But, he cries, "the vengeance of an oppressed and insulted people is almost as terrible as the wrath of Heaven"; and, like a true partisan, Curtius predicts that this is about to fall on Marshall. Why, he asks, is Marshall so vague on the constitutionality of the Alien and Sedition Laws?[1] "Notwithstanding the magnitude . . . of your talents, you are ridiculously awkward in the arts of dissimulation and hypocrisy. . . . It is painful to attack . . . a man whose talents are splendid and whose private character is amiable"; but "sacred duties . . . to the cause of truth and liberty require it." Alas for Marshall! "You have lost forever," Curtius assures him, "the affection of a nation and the applause of a world. In vain will you pursue the thorny and rugged path that leads to fame."[2]

But while "monarchist," "aristocrat," "British

[1] "Freeholder" had not asked Marshall what he thought of the constitutionality of these laws.

[2] Thompson: *The Letters of Curtius*. John Thompson of Petersburg was one of the most brilliant young men that even Virginia ever produced. See Adams: *Gallatin*, 212, 227. There is an interesting resemblance between the uncommon talents and fate of young John Thompson and those of Francis Walker Gilmer. Both were remarkably intellectual and learned; the characters of both were clean, fine, and high. Both were uncommonly handsome men. Neither of them had a strong physical constitution; and both died at a very early age. Had John Thompson and Francis Walker Gilmer lived, their names would have been added to that wonderful list of men that the Virginia of that period gave to the country.

The intellectual brilliancy and power, and the lofty character of Thompson and Gilmer, their feeble physical basis and their early passing seem like the last effort of that epochal human impulse which produced Henry, Madison, Mason, Jefferson, Marshall, and Washington.

agent," "enemy of free speech," "destroyer of trial
by jury" were among the more moderate epithets
that filled the air from Republican lips; and "anar-
chist," "Frenchman," "traitor," "foe of law and
order," "hater of government" were the milder of
the counter-blasts from the Federalists, all this was
too general, scattered, and ineffective to suit the
leader of the Republican Party. Jefferson saw that
the growing popular rage against the Alien and
Sedition Laws must be gathered into one or two
concentrated thunderbolts and thus hurled at the
heads of the already quaking Federalists.

How to do it was the question to which Jefferson
searched for an answer. It came from the bravest,
most consistent, most unselfish, as well as one of the
very ablest of Republicans, John Taylor "of Caroline," Virginia. In a letter to Jefferson concerning the
Alien and Sedition Laws, this eminent and disinterested radical suggested that "*the right of the State
governments to expound the constitution* might possibly
be made the basis of a movement towards its amendment. If this is insufficient the people in state conventions are incontrovertibly the contracting parties
and, possessing the infringing rights, may proceed
by orderly steps to attain the object." [1]

So was planted in Jefferson's mind the philosophy
of secession. In that fertile and receptive soil it grew
with magic rapidity and bore fatal fruit. Within two
months after he received Taylor's letter, Jefferson
wrote the historic resolutions which produced a situ-

[1] Taylor to Jefferson, June 25, 1798; as quoted in *Branch Historical Papers*, ii, 225. See entire letter, *ib.*, 271–76.

ation that, a few years afterward, called forth Marshall's first great constitutional opinion, and, not many decades later, gave the battle-cry that rallied heroic thousands to armed resistance to the National Government.[1] On October 5, 1798, Nicholas writes Jefferson that he has delivered to "Mr. John Breckenridge a copy of the resolutions that you sent me."[2] They were passed by the Legislature of Kentucky on November 14, 1798; and the tremendous conflict between Nationality and States' Rights, which for so long had been preparing, at last was formally begun.[3] Jefferson's "Kentucky Resolutions" declared that parts of the Alien and Sedition Laws were "altogether void and of no effect."[4] Thus a State

[1] For an excellent treatment of the Kentucky and Virginia Resolutions see Von Holst: *Constitutional History of the United States*, i, chap. iv.

[2] Nicholas to Jefferson, Oct. 5, 1798; quoted by Channing in "Kentucky Resolutions of 1798"; *Amer. Hist. Rev.*, xx, no. 2, Jan., 1915, 333–36.

[3] Writing nearly a quarter of a century later, Jefferson states that Nicholas, Breckenridge, and he conferred on the matter; that his draft of the "Kentucky Resolutions" was the result of this conference; and that he "strictly required" their "solemn assurance" that no one else should know that he was their author. (Jefferson to Breckenridge, Dec. 11, 1821; *Works:* Ford, viii, 459–60.)

Although this letter of Jefferson is positive and, in its particulars, detailed and specific, Professor Channing has demonstrated that Jefferson's memory was at fault; that no such conference took place; and that Jefferson sent the resolutions to Nicholas, who placed them in the hands of Breckenridge for introduction in the Kentucky Legislature; and that Breckenridge and Nicholas both thought that the former should not even see Jefferson, lest the real authorship of the resolutions be detected. (See "The Kentucky Resolutions": Channing, in *Amer. Hist. Rev.*, xx, no. 2, Jan., 1915, 333–36.)

[4] See Jefferson's "Rough Draught" and "Fair Copy" of the Kentucky Resolutions; and the resolutions as the Kentucky Legislature passed them on Nov. 10, 1798; *Works:* Ford, viii, 458–79. See examination of Marshall's opinion in Marbury *vs.* Madison, vol. iii of this work.

asserted the "right" of any or all States to annul and overthrow a National law.

As soon as Kentucky had acted, Jefferson thus writes Madison: "I enclose you a copy of the draught of the Kentucky resolves. I think we should distinctly affirm all the important principles they contain so as to hold that ground in future, and leave the matter in such a train as that we may not be committed absolutely to push the matter to extremities, & yet may be free to push as far as events will render prudent." [1]

Madison accordingly drew the resolutions adopted by the Legislature of Virginia, December 21, 1798. While declaring the Alien and Sedition Laws unconstitutional, the Virginia Resolutions merely appealed to the other States to "co-operate with this state in maintaining unimpaired the authority, rights, and liberties reserved to the states respectively or to the people." [2]

The Legislature promptly adopted them and would gladly have approved far stronger ones. "The leaders . . . were determined upon the overthrow of the General Government; and if no other measure would effect it, that they would risk it upon the chance of war. . . . Some of them talked of 'seceding from the Union.'" [3] Iredell writes his wife: "The General Assembly of Virginia are pursuing steps which directly lead to a civil war; but there is a respectable minority struggling in defense of

[1] Jefferson to Madison, Nov. 17, 1798; *Works:* Ford, viii, 457.

[2] *Writings:* Hunt, vi, 326–31.

[3] Davie to Iredell, June 17, 1799; quoting from a Virginia informant — very probably Marshall; McRee, ii, 577.

the General Government, and the Government itself is fully prepared for anything they can do, resolved, if necessary, to meet force with force." [1]
Marshall declared that he "never saw such intemperance as existed in the V[irginia] Assembly." [2]

Following their defiant adoption of Madison's
resolutions, the Republican majority of the Legislature issued a campaign pamphlet, also written by
Madison,[3] under the form of an address to the people. The "guardians of State Sovereignty would be
perfidious if they did not warn" the people "of
encroachments which . . . may" result in "usurped
power"; the State Governments would be "precipi-
tated into impotency and contempt" in case they
yielded to such National laws as the Alien and Sedition Acts; if like "infractions of the Federal Compact" were repeated "until the people arose . . . in
the majesty of their strength," it was certain that
"the way for a revolution would be prepared."

The Federalist pleas "to disregard usurpation
until foreign danger shall have passed" was "an artifice which may be forever used," because those who
wished National power extended "can ever create
national embarrassments to soothe the people to
sleep whilst that power is swelling, silently, secretly
and fatally."

Such was the Sedition Act which "commits the
sacrilege of arresting reason; . . . punishes without
trial; . . . bestows on the President despotic powers

---

[1] Iredell to Mrs. Iredell; Jan. 24, 1799; McRee, ii, 543.
[2] Murray to J. Q. Adams, April 1, 1799; quoting Marshall to Sykes,
Dec. 18, 1798; *Letters:* Ford, 534.
[3] *Writings:* Hunt, vi, 332–40.

. . . which was never expected by the early friends of
the Constitution." But now "Federal authority is
deduced by implication" by which "the states will
be stript of every right reserved." Such "tremendous pretensions . . . inflict a death wound on the
Sovereignty of the States." Thus wrote the same
Madison who had declared that nothing short of a
veto by the National Government on "any and
every act of the states" would suffice. There was,
said Madison's campaign document, no "specified
power" in the National Government "embracing a
right against freedom of the press" — that was a
"constitutional" prerogative of the States.

"Calumny" could be redressed in the State courts;
but "usurpation can only be controuled by the act
of society [revolution]." Here Madison quotes *ver-
batim* and in italics from Marshall's second letter to
Talleyrand in defense of the liberty of the press,
without, however, giving Marshall credit for the
language or argument.[1] Madison's argument is characteristically clear and compact, but abounds in
striking phrases that suggest Jefferson.[2]

This "Address" of the Virginia Legislature was
aimed primarily at Marshall, who was by far the
most important Federalist candidate for Congress
in the entire State. It was circulated at public expense and Marshall's friends could not possibly get
his views before the people so authoritatively or so
widely. But they did their best, for it was plain that

[1] For Marshall's defense of the liberty of the press, quoted by
Madison, see *supra*, chap. VIII.

[2] Address of the General Assembly to the People of the Commonwealth of Virginia, Journal, H.D. (Dec., 1798), 88–90.

Madison's Jeffersonized appeal, so uncharacteristic of that former Nationalist, must be answered. Marshall wrote the reply [1] of the minority of the Legislature, who could not "remain silent under the unprecedented" attack of Madison. "Reluctantly," then, they "presented the present crisis plainly before" the people.

"For . . . national independence . . . the people of united America" changed a government by the British King for that of the Constitution. "The will of the majority produced, ratified, and conducts" this constitutional government. It was not perfect, of course; but "the best rule for freemen . . . in the opinion of our ancestors, was . . . that . . . of obedience to laws enacted by a majority of" the people's representatives.

Two other principles "promised immortality" to this fundamental idea: power of amendment and frequency of elections. "Under a Constitution thus formed, the prosperity of America" had become "great and unexampled." The people "bemoaned foreign war" when it "broke out"; but "they did not possess even a remote influence in its termination." The true American policy, therefore, was in the "avoiding of the existing carnage and the continuance of our existing happiness." It was for this reason that Washington, after considering everything, had proclaimed American Neutrality. Yet Genêt had "appealed" to the people "with acrimony" against the Government. This was resented

---

[1] Sedgwick to Hamilton, Feb. 7, 1799; *Works: Hamilton*, vi, 392–93; and to King, March 20, 1799; *King*, ii, 581. And Murray to J. Q. Adams, April 5, 1799; *Letters: Ford*, 536.

"for a while only" and "the fire was rekindled as occasion afforded fuel."

Also, Great Britain's "unjustifiable conduct . . . rekindled our ardor for hostility and revenge." But Washington, averse to war, "made his last effort to avert its miseries." So came the Jay Treaty by which "peace was preserved with honor."

Marshall then reviews the outbursts against the Jay Treaty and their subsidence. France "taught by the bickerings of ourselves . . . reëchoed American reproaches with French views and French objects"; as a result "our commerce became a prey to French cruisers; our citizens were captured" and British outrages were repeated by the French, our "former friend . . . thereby committing suicide on our national and individual happiness."

Emulating Washington, Adams had twice striven for "honorable" adjustment. This was met by "an increase of insolence and affront." Thus America had "to choose between submission . . . and . . . independence. What American," asks Marshall, "could hesitate in the option?" And, "the choice being made, self-preservation commanded preparations for self-defense . . . — the fleet, . . . an army, a provision for the removal of dangerous aliens and the punishment of seditious citizens." Yet such measures "are charged with the atrocious design of creating a monarchy . . . and violating the constitution." Marshall argues that military preparation is our only security.

"Upon so solemn an occasion what curses would be adequate," asks Marshall, "to the supineness of our government, if militia were the only resort for safety, against the invasion of a veteran army, flushed with repeated victories, strong in the skill of its officers, and led by distinguished officers?" He then continues with the familiar arguments for military equipment.

Then comes his attack on the Virginia Resolutions. Had the criticisms of the Alien and Sedition Laws "been confined to ordinary peaceable and constitutional efforts to repeal them," no objection would have been made to such a course; but when "general hostility to our government" and "proceedings which may sap the foundations of our union" are resorted to, "duty" requires this appeal to the people.

Marshall next defends the constitutionality of these acts. "Powers necessary for the attainment of all objects which are general in their nature, which interest all America" and "can only be obtained by the coöperation of the whole . . . would be naturally vested in the government of the whole." It is obvious, he argues, that States must attend to local subjects and the Nation to general affairs.

The power to protect "the nation from the intrigues and conspiracies of dangerous aliens; . . . to secure the union from their wicked machinations, . . . which is essential to the common good," belongs to the National Government in the hands of which "is the force of the nation and the general power of protection from hostilities of every kind." Marshall then makes an extended argument in support of his Nationalist theory. Occasionally he employs almost the exact language which, years afterwards, appears in those constitutional opinions from the Supreme Bench that have given him his lasting fame. The doctrine of implied powers is expounded with all of his peculiar force and clearness, but with some overabundance of verbiage. In no writing or spoken word, before he became Chief Justice of the United States, did Marshall so extensively state his constitutional views as in this unknown paper.[1]

The House of Delegates, by a vote of 92 against 52,[2] refused to publish the address of the minority along with that of the majority. Thereupon the Federalists printed and circulated it as a campaign document. It was so admired by the supporters of the Administration in Philadelphia that, according to the untrustworthy Callender, ten thousand copies were printed in the Capital and widely distributed.[3]

Marshall's authorship of this paper was not popularly known; and it produced little effect. Its tedious length, lighted only by occasional flashes of eloquence, invited Republican ridicule and derision. It contained, said Callender, "such quantities of words . . . that you turn absolutely tired"; it abounded in "barren tautology"; some sentences were nothing more than mere "assemblages of syllables"; and "the hypocritical canting that so strongly marks it corresponds very well with the dispatches of X. Y. and Z."[4]

Marshall's careful but over-elaborate paper was

[1] Address of the Minority: Journal, H.D. (Dec., 1798), 88–90. Also printed as a pamphlet. Richmond, 1798.

[2] Journal, H.D. (1799), 90.

[3] Callender: *Prospect Before Us*, 91.   [4] *Ib.*, 112 *et seq.*

not, therefore, generally read. But the leading Federalists throughout the country were greatly pleased. The address was, said Sedgwick, "a masterly performance for which we are indebted to the pen of General Marshall, who has, by it, in some measure atoned for his pitiful electioneering epistle." [1]

When Murray, at The Hague, read the address, he concluded that Marshall was its author: "He may have been weak enough to declare *against* those laws that *might* be against the *policy* or necessity, etc., etc., etc., yet sustain their constitutionality. . . . I *hope* J. Marshall did write the Address." [2]

The Republican appeal, unlike that of Marshall, was brief, simple, and replete with glowing catchwords that warmed the popular heart and fell easily from the lips of the multitude. And the Republican spirit was running high. The Virginia Legislature provided for an armory in Richmond to resist "encroachments" of the National Government.[3] Memorials poured into the National Capital.[4] By February "the tables of congress were loaded with petitions against" the unpopular Federalist legislation.[5]

Marshall's opinion of the motives of the Republican leaders, of the uncertainty of the campaign, of the real purpose of the Virginia Resolutions, is frankly set forth in his letter to Washington acknowl-

[1] Sedgwick to King, March 20, 1799; King, ii, 581.
[2] Murray to J. Q. Adams, April 5, 1799; *Letters:* Ford, 536.
[3] Mordecai, 202; also Sedgwick to King, Nov. 15, 1799; King, iii, 147–48.
[4] Jefferson to Pendleton, Feb. 14, 1799; *Works:* Ford, ix, 46; and to Madison, Jan. 30, 1799; *ib.*, 31.
[5] Jefferson to Bishop James Madison, Feb. 27, 1799; *ib.*, 62.

edging the receipt of Judge Addison's charge: "No
argument," wrote Marshall, "can moderate the
leaders of the opposition. . . . However I may regret
the passage of one of the acts complained of [Sedition
Law] I am firmly persuaded that the tempest has not
been raised by them. Its cause lies much deeper and
is not easily to be removed. Had they [Alien and
Sedition Laws] never been passed, other measures
would have been selected. An act operating on the
press in any manner, affords to its opposers arguments which so captivate the public ear, which so
mislead the public mind that the efforts of reason"
are unavailing.

Marshall tells Washington that "the debates were
long and animated" upon the Virginia Resolutions
"which were substantiated by a majority of twenty-
nine." He says that "sentiments were declared and
. . . views were developed of a very serious and
alarming extent. . . . There are men who will hold
power by any means rather than not hold it; and who
would prefer a dissolution of the union to a continuance of an administration not of their own party.
They will risk all ills . . . rather than permit that
happiness which is dispensed by other hands than
their own."

He is not sure, he says, of being elected; but adds,
perhaps sarcastically, that "whatever the issue . . .
may be I shall neither reproach myself, nor those
at whose instance I have become a candidate, for
the step I have taken. The exertions against me by"
men in Virginia "and even from other states" are
more "active and malignant than personal consid-

erations would excite. If I fail," concludes Marshall, "I shall regret the failure more" because it will show "a temper hostile to our government . . . than of" his own "personal mortification." [1]

The Federalists were convinced that these extreme Republican tactics were the beginning of a serious effort to destroy the National Government. "The late attempt of Virginia and Kentucky," wrote Hamilton, "to unite the State Legislatures in a direct resistance to certain laws of the Union can be considered in no other light than as an attempt to change the government"; and he notes the "hostile declarations" of the Virginia Legislature; its "actual preparation of the means of supporting them by force"; its "measures to put their militia on a more efficient footing"; its "preparing considerable arsenals and magazines"; and its "laying new taxes on its citizens" for these purposes. [2]

To Sedgwick, Hamilton wrote of the "tendency of the doctrine advanced by Virginia and Kentucky to destroy the Constitution of the United States," and urged that the whole subject be referred to a special committee of Congress which should deal with the Virginia and Kentucky Resolutions and justify the laws at which they were aimed. "No pains or expense," he insisted, "should be spared to disseminate this report. . . . A little pamphlet containing it should find its way into every house in Virginia." [3]

[1] Marshall to Washington, Jan. 8, 1799; Washington MSS., Lib. Cong.

[2] Hamilton to Dayton, 1799; *Works:* Lodge, x, 330. The day of the month is not given, but it certainly was early in January. Mr. Lodge places it before a letter to Lafayette, dated Jan. 6, 1799.

[3] Hamilton to Sedgwick, Feb. 2, 1799; *Works:* Lodge, x, 340-42.

Thus the congressional campaign of 1798–99 drew to a close. Marshall neglected none of those personal and familiar campaign devices which the American electorate of that time loved so well. His enemies declared that he carried these to the extreme; at a rally in Hanover County he "threw billets into the bonfires and danced around them with his constituents"; [1] he assured the voters that "his sentiments were the same as those of Mr. Clopton [the Republican candidate]"; he "spent several thousands of dollars upon barbecues." [2]

These charges of the besotted Callender,[3] written from his cell in the jail at Richmond, are, of course, entirely untrue, except the story of dancing about the bonfire. Marshall's answers to "Freeholder" dispose of the second; his pressing need of money for the Fairfax purchase shows that he could have afforded no money for campaign purposes; and, indeed, this charge was so preposterous that even the reckless Callender concludes it to be unworthy of belief.

From the desperate nature of the struggle and the temper and political habit of the times, one might expect far harder things to have been said. Indeed, as the violence of the contest mounted to its climax, worse things were charged or intimated by word of mouth than were then put into type. Again it is the political hack, John Wood, who gives us a hint of the baseness of the slanders that were circulated; he

---

[1] This was probably true; it is thoroughly characteristic and fits in perfectly with his well-authenticated conduct after he became Chief Justice. (See vol. III of this work.)

[2] Callender: *Prospect Before Us*, 90 *et seq*.

[3] See Hildreth, v, 104, 210, 214, 340, 453–55.

describes a scandal in which Marshall and Pinckney were alleged to have been involved while in Paris, the unhappy fate of a woman, her desperate voyage to America, her persecution and sad ending.[1]

Marshall was profoundly disgusted by the methods employed to defeat him. Writing to his brother a short time before election day he briefly refers to the Republican assaults in stronger language than is to be found in any other letter ever written by him:—

"The fate of my election is extremely uncertain. The means us'd to defeat it are despicable in the extreme and yet they succeed. Nothing I believe more debases or pollutes the human mind than faction [party]." [2]

The Republicans everywhere grew more confident as the day of voting drew near. Neutrality, the Alien and Sedition Laws, the expense of the provisional army, the popular fear and hatred of a permanent military force, the high taxes, together with the reckless charges and slanders against the Federalists and the perfect discipline exacted of the Republicans by Jefferson — all were rapidly overcoming the patriotic fervor aroused by the X. Y. Z. disclosures. "The tide is evidently turning . . . from Marshall's

[1] Wood, 261–62. This canard is an example of the methods employed in political contests when American democracy was in its infancy.

[2] Marshall to his brother James M., April 3, 1799; MS. Marshall uses the word "faction" in the sense in which it was then employed. "Faction" and "party" were at that time used interchangeably; and both words were terms of reproach. (See *supra*, chap. II.) If stated in the vernacular of the present day, this doleful opinion of Marshall would read: "Nothing, I believe, more debases or pollutes the human mind than partisan politics."

PART OF LETTER FROM JOHN MARSHALL TO HIS BROTHER, DATED APRIL 3, 1799

(*Facsimile*)

romance" was the Republican commander's conclusion as the end of the campaign approached.[1]

For the first time Marshall's personal popularity
was insufficient to assure victory. But the animosity of the Republicans caused them to make a false
move which saved him at the very last. They circulated the report that Patrick Henry, the arch-
enemy of "aristocrats," was against Marshall because the latter was one of this abhorred class.
Marshall's friend, Archibald Blair, Clerk of the
Executive Council, wrote Henry of this Republican
campaign story.

Instantly both the fighter and the politician in
Henry were roused; and the old warrior, from his
retirement at Red Hill, wrote an extraordinary
letter, full of affection for Marshall and burning
with indignation at the Republican leaders. The
Virginia Resolutions meant the "dissolution" of the
Nation, wrote Henry; if that was not the purpose of
the Republicans "they have none and act *ex tempore*." As to France, "her conduct has made it to
the interest of the great family of mankind to wish
the downfall of her present government." For the
French Republic threatened to "destroy the great
pillars of all government and social life — I mean
virtue, morality, and religion," which "alone . . . is
the armour . . . that renders us invincible." Also,
said Henry, "infidelity, in its broad sense, under
the name of philosophy, is fast spreading . . . under
the patronage of French manners and principles."

Henry makes "these prefatory remarks" to

[1] Jefferson to Pendleton, April 22, 1799; *Works:* Ford, ix, 64-65.

"point out the kind of character amongst our countrymen most estimable in my [his] eyes." The ground thus prepared, Henry discharges all his guns against Marshall's enemies. "General Marshall and his colleagues exhibited the American character as respectable. France, in the period of her most triumphant fortune, beheld them as unappalled. Her threats left them as she found them. . . .

"Can it be thought that with these sentiments I should utter anything tending to prejudice General Marshall's election? Very far from it indeed. Independently of the high gratification I felt from his public ministry, he ever stood high in my esteem as a private citizen. His temper and disposition were always pleasant, his talents and integrity unquestioned.

"These things are sufficient to place that gentleman far above any competitor in the district for congress. But when you add the particular information and insight which he has gained, and is able to communicate to our public councils, it is really astonishing, that even blindness itself should hesitate in the choice. . . .

"Tell Marshall I love him, because he felt and acted as a republican, as an American. The story of the Scotch merchants and old torys voting for him is too stale, childish, and foolish, and is a French *finesse;* an appeal to prejudice, not reason and good sense. . . . I really should give him my vote for Congress, preferably to any citizen in the state at this juncture, one only excepted [Washington]." [1]

[1] Henry to Blair, Jan. 8, 1799; Henry, ii, 591–94.

Henry's letter saved Marshall. Not only was the congressional district full of Henry's political followers, but it contained large numbers of his close personal friends. His letter was passed from hand to hand among these and, by election day, was almost worn out by constant use.[1]

But the Federalist newspapers gave Henry no credit for turning the tide; according to these partisan sheets it was the "anarchistic" action of the Kentucky and Virginia Legislatures that elected Marshall. Quoting from a letter of Bushrod Washington, who had no more political acumen than a turtle, a Federalist newspaper declared: "We hear that General Marshall's election is placed beyond all doubt. I was firmly convinced that the violent measures of our Legislature (which were certainly intended to influence the election) would favor the pretensions of the Federal candidates by disclosing the views of the opposite party." [2]

Late in April the election was held. A witness of that event in Richmond tells of the incidents of the voting which were stirring even for that period of turbulent politics. A long, broad table or bench was placed on the Court-House Green, and upon it the local magistrates, acting as election judges, took their seats, their clerks before them. By the side of the judges sat the two candidates for Congress; and when an elector declared his preference for either, the favored one rose, bowing, and thanked his supporter.

[1] Henry to Blair, Jan. 8, 1799; Henry, ii, 595.
[2] *Virginia Herald* (Fredericksburg), March 5, 1799.

Nobody but freeholders could then exercise the suffrage in Virginia.[1] Any one owning one hundred acres of land or more in any county could vote, and this landowner could declare his choice in every county in which he possessed the necessary real estate. The voter did not cast a printed or written ballot, but merely stated, in the presence of the two candidates, the election officials, and the assembled gathering, the name of the candidate of his preference. There was no specified form for this announcement.[2]

"I vote for John Marshall."

"Thank you, sir," said the lank, easy-mannered Federalist candidate.

"Hurrah for Marshall!" shouted the compact band of Federalists.

"And I vote for Clopton," cried another freeholder.

"May you live a thousand years, my friend," said Marshall's competitor.

"Three cheers for Clopton!" roared the crowd of Republican enthusiasts.

Both Republican and Federalist leaders had seen to it that nothing was left undone which might bring victory to their respective candidates. The two political parties had been carefully "drilled to move together in a body." Each party had a business committee which attended to every practical detail

---

[1] This was true in most of the States at that period.

[2] This method of electing public officials was continued until the Civil War. (See John S. Wise's description of a congressional election in Virginia in 1855; Wise: *The End of An Era*, 55–56. And see Professor Schouler's treatment of this subject in his "Evolution of the American Voter"; *Amer. Hist. Rev.*, ii, 665–74.)

of the election. Not a voter was overlooked. "Sick men were taken in their beds to the polls; the halt, the lame, and the blind were hunted up and every mode of conveyance was mustered into service." Time and again the vote was a tie. No sooner did one freeholder announce his preference for Marshall than another gave his suffrage to Clopton.

"A barrel of whisky with the head knocked in," free for everybody, stood beneath a tree; and "the majority took it straight," runs a narrative of a witness of the scene. So hot became the contest that fist-fights were frequent. During the afternoon, knock-down and drag-out affrays became so general that the county justices had hard work to quell the raging partisans. Throughout the day the shouting and huzzaing rose in volume as the whiskey sank in the barrel. At times the uproar was "perfectly deafening; men were shaking fists at each other, rolling up their sleeves, cursing and swearing. . . . Some became wild with agitation." When a tie was broken by a new voter shouting that he was for Marshall or for Clopton, insults were hurled at his devoted head.

"You, sir, ought to have your mouth smashed," cried an enraged Republican when Thomas Rutherford voted for Marshall; and smashing of mouths, blacking of eyes, and breaking of heads there were in plenty. "The crowd rolled to and fro like a surging wave." [1] Never before and seldom, if ever,

[1] This account of election day in the Marshall-Clopton contest is from Munford, 208–10. For another fairly accurate but mild description of a congressional election in Virginia at this period, see Mary Johnston's novel, *Lewis Rand*, chap. iv.

since, in the history of Virginia, was any election so
fiercely contested. When this "democratic" struggle was over, it was found that Marshall had been
elected by the slender majority of 108.[1]

Washington was overjoyed at the Federalist success. He had ridden ten miles to vote for General
Lee, who was elected;[2] but he took a special delight
in Marshall's victory. He hastened to write his political protégé: "With infinite pleasure I received the
news of your Election. For the honor of the District
I wish the majority had been greater; but let us be
content, and hope, as the tide is turning, the current
will soon run strong in your favor."[3]

Toward the end of the campaign, for the purpose
of throwing into the contest Washington's personal
influence, Marshall's enthusiastic friends had published the fact of Marshall's refusal to accept the
various offices which had been tendered him by
Washington. They had drawn a long bow, though
very slightly, and stated positively that Marshall
could have been Secretary of State.[4] Marshall hastened to apologize:—

"Few of the unpleasant occurrences" of the campaign "have given me more real chagrin than this.
To make a parade of proffered offices is a vanity
which I trust I do not possess; but to boast of one
never in my power would argue a littleness of mind

[1] Henry, ii, 598.   [2] Randall, ii, 495.

[3] Washington to Marshall, May 5, 1799; *Writings:* Ford, xiv, 180.

[4] As a matter of fact, they were not far wrong. Marshall almost
certainly would have been made Secretary of State if Washington had
believed that he would accept the portfolio. (See *supra*, 147.) The
assertion that the place actually had been offered to Marshall seems
to have been the only error in this campaign story.

at which I ought to blush." Marshall tells Washington that the person who published the report "never received it directly or indirectly from me." If he had known "that such a publication was designed" he "would certainly have suppressed it." It was inspired "unquestionably . . . by a wish to serve me," says Marshall, "and by resentment at the various malignant calumnies which have been so profusely bestowed on me." [1]

Washington quickly reassured Marshall: "I am sorry to find that the publication you allude to should have given you a moment's disquietude. I can assure you it made no impression on my mind, of the tendency apprehended by you." [2]

As soon as all the election returns were in, Marshall reported to Washington that the defeat of two of the Federalist candidates for Congress was unexpected and "has reduced us to eight in the legislature of the Union"; that the Republicans maintained their "majority in the house of Delegates," which "means an antifederal senator and governor," and that "the baneful influence of a legislature hostile perhaps to the Union — or if not so — to all its measures will be kept up." [3]

Marshall's campaign attracted the attention of the whole country, and the news of his success deeply interested both Federalists and Republicans. Pickering, after writing King of the Federalist success in New York City, declared that "the other domestic

[1] Marshall to Washington, May 1, 1799; *Writings:* Ford, xiv, footnote to 180–81; also Flanders, ii, 389.

[2] Washington to Marshall, May 5, 1799; *Writings:* Ford, xiv, 180.

[3] Marshall to Washington, May 16, 1799; Washington MSS., Lib. Cong.

intelligence, still more important, is, that Genl. Marshall is elected a member of Congress for his district."[1]

Speaker Sedgwick also informed King of Marshall's election. "General Marshall you know is a member of the House of Representatives. His talents, his character and the situation he has been in, will combine to give him an influence, which will be further aided by the scene which he immediately represents. He may and probably will give a tone to the federal politics South of the Susquehannah. I well know the respect he entertains for you and for your opinions."[2]

But the Federalist leaders were none too sure of their Virginia congressional recruit. He was entirely too independent to suit the party organization. His campaign statement on the Alien and Sedition Laws angered and troubled them when it was made; and, now that Marshall was elected, his opinion on this, to the Federalists, vital subject, his admitted power of mind and character, and his weighty influence over the Southern wing of the Federalists caused serious apprehension among the party's Northern leaders. Sedgwick advises King to write Marshall on the subject of party regularity.

"I have brought this subject to your mind, that you may decide on the propriety of a communication of your sentiments to him, which you may do in season to be useful. Should he, which, indeed, I do not expect, conform his political conduct generally, to

---

[1] Pickering to King, May 4, 1799; King, iii, 13.
[2] Sedgwick to King, July 26, 1799; King, iii, 69.

what seems indicated by his public declaration relative to the alien & sedition acts, it would have been
better that his insignificant predecessor should have
been reëlected. There never has been an instance
where the commencement of a political career was
so important as is that of General Marshall." [1]

Apprehension and uncertainty as to Marshall's
course in the House was in the minds of even the
Federalist leaders who were out of the country. The
American Minister at The Hague was as much
troubled about Marshall as were the Federalist
politicians at home: "If M[arshall]'s silly declaration on the *inexpediency* of the Sedition law does not
entangle him he may be very useful." [2] But Murray was uneasy: "Marshall, I fear, comes in on
middle ground, and when a man plays the amiable
in a body like that [House of Representatives] he
cannot be counted [on], but he will vote generally
right. I was amiable the first session! It cannot
last." [3]

Jefferson, of course, was much depressed by the
Federalist congressional victories, which he felt
"are extremely to be regretted." He was especially
irritated by Marshall's election: It "marks a taint
in that part of the State which I had not expected."
He was venomous toward Henry for having helped
Marshall: "His [Henry's] apostacy, must be unac-
countable to those who do not know all the recesses
of his heart." [4]

[1] Sedgwick to King, July 26, 1799; King, iii, 69.
[2] Murray to J. Q. Adams, June 25, 1799; *Letters:* Ford, 566.
[3] Murray to J. Q. Adams, July 1, 1799; *ib.*, 568.
[4] Jefferson to Stuart, May 14, 1799; *Works:* Ford, ix, 67.

A week later, however, Jefferson decided that the
Federalist success did not mean a permanent Republican reverse. Spoils and corruption, he concluded, were the real cause of the Federalist gain.
"The Virginia congressional elections have astonished every one," he informs Tench Coxe. "This
result has proceeded from accidental combinations
of circumstances, & not from an unfavorable change
of sentiment. . . . We are not incorruptible; on the
contrary, corruption is making sensible tho' silent
progress. Offices are as acceptable here as elsewhere,
& whenever a man has cast a longing on them, a
rottenness begins in his conduct." [1]

Jefferson, with settled and burning hatred, now
puts his branding-iron on Henry: "As to the effect
of his name among the people, I have found it crum-
ble like a dried leaf the moment they become satisfied of his apostacy." [2]

During the weeks which immediately followed his
election, Marshall was busy reporting to Washington on the best men to be appointed as officers in
the provisional army; and his letters to the Commander-in-Chief show a wide and careful acquaintance with Virginians of military training, and a
delicate judgment of their qualities. [3]

By now the hated Sedition Law was justifying
the political hydrophobia which it had excited
among the Republicans. [4] All over the country men

---

[1] Jefferson to Coxe, May 21, 1799; *Works:* Ford, ix, 69–70.   [2] *Ib.*, 70.

[3] For instances of these military letters, see Marshall to Washington, June 12, 1799; Washington MSS., Lib. Cong.

[4] See Morison, i, 156–57; also Hudson: *Journalism in the United
States*, 160. Party newspapers and speakers to-day make state-

were being indicted and convicted for wholly justifiable political criticisms, — some of them trivial and
even amusing, — as well as for false and slanderous
attacks on public officers. President Adams himself
had begun to urge these prosecutions. He was particularly bitter against the "Aurora," the Republican organ, which, according to Adams, contained an
"uninterrupted stream of slander on the American
government." [1] He thought that the editor ought
to be expelled from the country.[2]

All this was more fuel to the Republican furnace.
Wicked and outrageous as were some of these prosecutions, they were not so extravagant as the
horrors which Republican politicans declared that
the Sedition Laws would bring to every fireside.

During the summer after his election Marshall
visited his father in Kentucky. Thomas Marshall
was ill, and his son's toilsome journey was solely for
the purpose of comforting him; but Jefferson could
see in it nothing but a political mission. He writes
to Wilson Cary Nicholas to prepare an answer to
the States that had opposed the Kentucky and Virginia Resolutions; but, says Jefferson, "As to the
preparing anything [myself] I must decline it, to
avoid suspicions (which were pretty strong in some
quarters on the last occasion) [the Kentucky Resolu-

ments, as a matter of course, in every political campaign much
more violent than those for which editors and citizens were fined
and imprisoned in 1799–1800. (See *ib.*, 315; and see summary from
the Republican point of view of these prosecutions in Randall, ii,
416–20.)

[1] Adams to Pickering, July 24, 1799; *Works*: Adams, ix, 3.
[2] Adams to Pickering, Aug. 1, 1799; *ib.*, 5; and same to same,
Aug. 3, 1799; *ib.*, 7.

tions]. . . . The visit of the apostle Marshall[1] to
Kentucky, excite[s] anxiety. However, we doubt
not that his poisons will be effectually counter-
worked." [2]

Jefferson's suspicions were groundless. Marshall
did not even sound public opinion on the subject.
On his return to Richmond he writes the Secretary
of State, who was the most active politician of
Adams's Cabinet, and to whom Marshall freely
opened his mind on politics, that "a visit to an aged
& rever'd Father" prevented an earlier answer to a
letter from Pickering; and, although Marshall has
much to say, not one word is written of the Kentucky and Virginia Resolutions. He is obsessed
with the French question and of the advantage the
French "party in America" may secure by the impression that France was not really hostile. "This
will enable her [France's] party in America to attack
from very advantageous ground the government of
the United States." [3]

Now came the public circumstance that made the
schism in the Federalist Party an open and remorseless feud. The President's militant declaration,
that he would "never send another minister to
France without assurances that he will [would] be
received, respected, and honored as the represent-

[1] Professor Washington, in his edition of Jefferson's *Writings*, leaves
a blank after "apostle." Mr. Ford correctly prints Marshall's name as
it is written in Jefferson's original manuscript copy of the letter.

[2] Jefferson to Wilson Cary Nicholas, Sept. 5, 1799; *Works:*
Ford, ix, 79–81.

[3] Marshall to Pickering, Aug. 25, 1799; Pickering MSS., Mass.
Hist. Soc. Marshall had not yet grasped the deadly significance of
Jefferson's States' Rights and Nullification maneuver.

ative of a great, free, powerful, and independent people,"[1] was perfectly attuned to the warlike spirit of the hour. The country rang with approval. The Federalist politicians were exultant.

Thereupon the resourceful Talleyrand wrote the Secretary of the French Legation at The Hague to intimate to Murray, the American Minister, that the French Directory would now receive a minister from the United States.[2] Murray hastened the news to Adams.[3] It was a frail assurance, indirect, irregular, unacknowledged to the world; and from men who had insulted us and who would not hesitate to repudiate Murray's statement if their purposes so required. Yet the President grasped by the forelock this possibility for peace, and, against the emphatic protest of his Cabinet, suddenly sent a second commission to try again for that adjustment which Marshall and his associates had failed to secure. It was the wisest and most unpopular act of Adams's troubled Administration.

The leading Federalist politicians were enraged. Indeed, "the whole [Federalist] party were prodigiously alarmed."[4] They thought it a national humiliation. What! said they, kiss the hand that had slapped our face! "The new embassy . . . disgusts most men here," reported Ames from New

---

[1] *Supra.*

[2] Talleyrand to Pichon, Aug. 28, and Sept. 28; *Am. St. Prs.*, ii, 241–42; Murray to Adams, Appendix of *Works:* Adams, viii. For familiar account of Pichon's conferences with Murray, see Murray's letters to J. Q. Adams, then U.S. Minister to Berlin, in *Letters:* Ford, 445, 473, 475–76; and to Pickering, *ib.*, 464.

[3] "Murray, I guess, wanted to make himself a greater man than he is by going to France," was Gallatin's shrewd opinion. Gallatin to his wife, March 1, 1799; Adams: *Gallatin*, 227–28.   [4] *Ib.*

England.[1] Cabot confirmed Ames's doleful message — "Surprise, indignation, grief, & disgust followed each other in swift succession in the breasts of the true friends of our country," he advised King.[2]

The Federalist leaders really wanted war with France, most of them as a matter of patriotism; some, undoubtedly, because war would insure party success in the approaching presidential election. Upon his return Marshall had prophesied formal declaration of hostilities from the Republic of France, when news of the dispatches reached Europe; and the war Federalists were sorely disappointed at the failure of his prediction. "Genl. Marshall unfortunately held the decided opinion that France would DECLARE war when the Dispatches should appear; and T. Sewell with other good men were so strongly impressed with the advantage of such a declaration by them that they could not be persuaded to relinquish the belief in it — I was astonished that they should have attributed to the French such miserable policy." So wrote the able and balanced Cabot.[3] That France refused to adopt "such miserable policy" as Marshall had expected was sufficiently exasperating to the war Federalists; but to meet that country three fourths of the way on the road to peace was intolerable.

"The end [peace] being a bad one all means are unwise and indefensible" was the ultra-Federalist belief.[4] Adams's second mission was, they said,

---

[1] Ames to Dwight, Feb. 27, 1799; *Works: Ames*, i, 252.
[2] Cabot to King, March 10, 1799; *King*, ii, 551.
[3] Cabot to King, Feb. 16, 1799; *ib.*, 543.
[4] Ames to Pickering, March 12, 1799; *Works: Ames*, i, 253.

party surrender to the Republicans; it was "a policy that threatens . . . to revive the Jacobin faction in our bosom." [1] Federalist members of Congress threatened to resign. "I have sacrificed as much as most men . . . to support this Govt. and root out Democracy, & French principles, but . . . I feel it to be lost and worse . . . I can & will resign if all must be given up to France," cried the enraged Tracy. [2]

These "enemies of government" had said all along that things could be arranged with France; that the X. Y. Z. disclosures were merely a Federalist plot; and that the army was a wicked and needless expense. What answer could the Federalists make to these Republican charges now? Adams's new French mission, the Federalist chieftains declared, was "a measure to *make* dangers, and to nullify resources; to make the navy without object; the army an object of popular terror." [3]

And the presidential election was coming on! To hold the situation just as it was might mean Federalist victory. Suppose events did develop a formal declaration of war with France? That would make Federalist success more certain. The country would not turn out a party in charge of the Government when cannon were roaring. Even more important, an open and avowed conflict with the "bloody Republic" would, reasoned the Federalist leaders, check the miasmic growth of French revolutionary ideas among the people.

---

[1] Ames to Pickering, Oct. 19, 1799; *ib.*, 257.
[2] Uriah Tracy to McHenry, Sept. 2, 1799; Steiner, 417.
[3] Ames to Pickering, Nov. 5, 1799; *Works: Ames*, i, 260–61.

In short, a declaration of war with France would do everything which the Federalists wished and hoped for. "Peace [with France] . . . is not desired as it should not be" [1] was their opinion of the statesmanship demanded by the times. And now Adams, without one word to the men who reluctantly had made him President,[2] had not only prevented a rupture which would have accomplished every Federalist purpose, but had delivered his party into the hands of the "Jacobins." He had robbed the Federalists of their supreme campaign "issue." "Peace with France, they think an evil and holding out the hope of it another, as it tends to chill the public fervor"; [3] and the "public fervor" surely needed no further reduction of temperature, for Federalist health.

If Adams did not wish for a formal declaration of war, at least he might have let things alone. But now! "Government will be weakened by the friends it loses and betrayed by those it will gain. It will lose . . . the friendship of the sense, and worth, and property of the United States, and get in exchange the prejudice, vice, and bankruptcy of the nation," [4] wrote Ames to Pickering. "In Resistance alone there is safety," [5] was Cabot's

---

[1] Ames to Pickering, March 12, 1799; *Works: Ames*, i, 254.

[2] "Men of principal influence in the Federal party . . . began to entertain serious doubts about his [Adams's] fitness for the station, yet . . . they thought it better to indulge their hopes than to listen to their fears, [and] . . . determined to support Mr. Adams for the Chief Magistracy." ("Public Conduct, etc., John Adams"; Hamilton: *Works:* Lodge, vii, 318.)

[3] Ames to Dwight, Feb. 27, 1799; *Works: Ames*, i, 252.

[4] Ames to Pickering, Nov. 5, 1799; *ib.*, 260.

[5] Cabot to King, March 10, 1799; *King*, ii, 552.

opinion. "The Jacobin influence is rising, and has been ever since the mission to France was determined on; . . . if a Treaty be made with France their [Republican] ascendancy will be sure"; [1] and, after that, the deluge.

The Federalist leaders felt that, even without a declaration of hostilities by Congress, they might make shift to win the approaching election. For on the sea we already were waging war on France, while formally at peace with her. Our newborn navy was taking French privateers, defeating French men-of-war, and retaliating with pike, cutlass, and broadside for the piratical French outrages upon American commerce.[2] As things stood, it was certain that this would continue until after the election, and with each glorious victory of a Truxton or a Hull, National pride and popular enthusiasm would mount higher and grow stronger. So the Federalist politicians thought that "the only negotiation compatible with our honor or our safety is that begun by Truxton in the capture of the L'Insurgente." [3]

Priceless campaign ammunition was this for the Federalist political guns. Early in the year the bilious but keen-eyed watchman on the ramparts of New England Federalism had noted the appearance of "a little patriotism, and the capture of the *Insurgente* cherishes it." [4] And now Adams's second

---

[1] Higginson to Pickering, April 16, 1800; Pickering MSS., Mass. Hist. Soc., printed in *An. Rept.*, Amer. Hist. Assn., 1896, i, 836.

[2] For an excellent summary of this important episode in our history see Allen: *Our Naval War with France.*

[3] Pickering to King, March 6, 1799; King, ii, 548–49.

[4] Ames to Pickering, March 12, 1799; *Works: Ames*, i, 254.

mission might spoil everything. "The Jacobins will
rise in consequence of this blunder," [1] was the doleful prophecy. Indeed, it was already in fulfillment
even with the utterance: "Already the Jacobins
raise their disgraced heads from the mire of contempt!" [2] The "country gentlemen" were the
hands as the business interests were the brain and
heart of the Federalist Party; "the President destroyed their influence, and ... left them prostrate
before their vindictive adversaries." [3]

The Republicans were overjoyed. Adams had
reversed himself, eaten his own words, confessed
the hypocrisy of the "infamous X. Y. Z. plot."
"This renders their [Federalists'] efforts for war
desperate, & silences all further denials of the sincerity of the French government," gleefully wrote
Jefferson. [4]

Marshall alone of the commanding Federalists,
approved Adams's action. "I presume it will afford
you satisfaction to know that a measure which
excited so much agitation here, has met the approbation of so good a judge as Mr. Marshall," Lee
reported to the President. [5] Marshall's support
cheered the harried Chief Executive. "Esteeming
very highly the opinion and character of your friend
General Marshall, I thank you for inclosing his
letter," responded Adams. [6]

[1] Ames to Dwight, Oct. 20, 1799; *ib.*, 259.
[2] Ames to Pickering, Oct. 19, 1799; *ib.*, 257.
[3] Wolcott to Ames, Aug. 10, 1800; Gibbs, ii, 403.
[4] Jefferson to Pendleton, Feb. 19, 1799; *Works:* Ford, ix, 54.
[5] Lee to Adams, March 14, 1799; *Works:* Adams, viii, 628.
[6] Adams to Lee, March 29, 1799; *ib.*, 629.

The President had done still worse. Auctioneer John Fries, a militia captain, had headed an armed mob in resistance to the National officers who were levying the National direct tax on the houses and lands of the farmers of eastern Pennsylvania. He had been finally taken prisoner, tried, and convicted of sedition and treason, and sentenced to death. Against the unanimous written advice of his Cabinet, formally tendered,[1] the President pardoned the "traitor" and "his fellow criminals." [2] And this clemency was granted at the plea of McKean, the arch-"Jacobin" of Pennsylvania,[3] without even consulting the judges of the courts in which they were twice tried and convicted.[4]

What was this, asked the Federalist leaders in dazed and angry amazement! Paralyze the arm of the law! Unloose the fingers of outraged authority from the guilty throat which Justice had clutched! What was to become of "law and order" when the Nation's head thus sanctioned resistance to both? [5] In his charge to the Federal Grand Jury, April 11, 1799, Justice Iredell declared that if "traitors" are not punished "anarchy will ride triumphant and all lovers of order, decency, truth & justice will be trampled under foot." [6]

[1] Cabinet to President, Sept. 7, 1799; *Works:* Adams, ix, 21–23; and same to same, May 20, 1799; *ib.*, 59–60.

[2] Adams to Lee, May 21, 1800; *ib.*, 60. For account of Fries's Rebellion see McMaster, ii, 435–39. Also Hildreth, v, 313.

[3] Pickering to Cabot, June 15, 1800; Lodge: *Cabot,* 275.

[4] "Public Conduct, etc., John Adams"; Hamilton: *Works:* Lodge, vii, 351–55; and see Gibbs, ii, 360–62.

[5] See Hamilton's arraignment of the Fries pardon in "Public Conduct, etc., John Adams"; *Works:* Lodge, vii, 351–55.

[6] McRee, ii, 551.

How, now, could the Federalists repel Republican
assaults on this direct tax? How, now, could they
reply to the Republican attacks upon the army to
support which the tax was provided! In pardoning
Fries, Adams had admitted everything which the
hated Jefferson had said against both tax and army.[1]
If Adams was right in pardoning Fries, then Washington was wrong in suppressing the Whiskey
Rebellion. The whole Federalist system was abandoned.[2] The very roots of the Federalist philosophy
of government and administration were torn from
their none too firm hold upon the scanty soil which
Federalist statesmen had laboriously gathered for
their nourishment. And why had Adams done this?

[1] " The Aurora, in analyzing the reasons upon which Fries, Hainy,
and Getman have been pardoned brings the President forward as,
by this act, condemning: 1. The tax law which gave rise to the insurrection; 2. The conduct of the officers appointed to collect the
tax; 3. The marshal; 4. The witnesses on the part of the United
States; 5. The juries who tried the prisoners; 6. The court, both
in their personal conduct and in their judicial decisions. In short,
every individual who has had any part in passing the law — in
endeavoring to execute it, or in bringing to just punishment those
who have treasonably violated it." (*Gazette of the United States*, reviewing bitterly the comment of the Republican organ on Adams's
pardon of Fries.)

[2] Many Federalists regretted that Fries was not executed by court-
martial. "I suppose military execution was impracticable, but if some
executions are not had, of the most notorious offenders — I shall regret the events of lenity in '94 & '99 — as giving a fatal stroke to Government. . . . Undue mercy to villains, is cruelty to all the good & virtuous. Our people in this State are perfectly astonished, that cost
must continually be incurred for insurrections in Pennsylvania for
which they say they are taxed & yet no punishment is inflicted on the
offenders. I am fatigued & mortified that our Govt. which is weak at
best, would withhold any of its strength when all its energies should
be doubled." (Uriah Tracy to McHenry, on Fries, May 6, 1799;
Steiner, 436.) And "I am in fear that something will occur to release
that fellow from merited Death." (Same to same, May 20, 1790; *ib.*)

Because, said the Federalist politicians, it was popular in Pennsylvania;[1] that was the President's motive — the same that moved him to send the new mission to France.[2]

Bending under heavy burdens of state, harassed by the politicians, Adams was enduring a private pain sharper than his public cares. His wife, the incomparable Abigail, was in Massachusetts and seriously ill. The President had left her to meet his Cabinet and dispatch the second mission to France. That done, he hastened back to the bedside of his sick wife. But the politicians made no allowances. Adams's absence "from the seat of government . . . is a source of much disgust," chronicles the ardent Troup. "It . . . has the air of an abdication."[3] A month later he records that the President "still continues at Braintree,[4] and the government, like Pope's wounded snake, drags its slow length along."[5]

Such was the condition of the country and the state of political parties when Marshall took his seat in Congress. For the Federalists, the House was a very "cave of the winds," with confusion, uncertainty, suspicion, anger, and all the disintegrating passions blowing this way and that. But the Republicans were a compact, disciplined, determined body full of spirit and purpose.

[1] "Public Conduct, etc., John Adams"; Hamilton: *Works:* Lodge, vii, 351–55.
[2] Ames to Pickering, Nov. 23, 1799; *Works:* Ames, i, 270.
[3] Troup to King, May 6, 1799; King, iii, 14.
[4] Adams's home, now Quincy, Massachusetts.
[5] Troup to King, June 5, 1799; King, iii, 34.

CHAPTER XI

INDEPENDENCE IN CONGRESS

The Constitution is not designed to secure the rights of the people of Europe or Asia or to direct proceedings against criminals throughout the universe. (Marshall.)

The whole world is in arms and no rights are respected but those that are maintained by force. (Marshall.)

Marshall is disposed to express great respect for the sovereign people and to quote their expressions as evidence of truth. (Theodore Sedgwick.)

"I HAVE been much in Company with General Marshall since we arrived in this City. He possesses great powers and has much dexterity in the application of them. He is highly & deservedly respected by the friends of Government [Federalists] from the South. In short, we can do nothing without him. I believe his intentions are perfectly honorable, & yet I do believe he would have been a more decided man had his education been on the other side of the Delaware, and he the immediate representative of that country." [1]

So wrote the Speaker of the House of Representatives after three weeks of association with the Virginia member whom he had been carefully studying. After another month of Federalist scrutiny, Cabot agreed with Speaker Sedgwick as to Marshall's qualities.

"In Congress, you see Genl. M.[arshall] is a leader. He is I think a virtuous & certainly an able man; but you see in him the faults of a Virginian. He thinks too much of that State, & he expects the

---

[1] Sedgwick to King, Dec. 29, 1799; King, iii, 163.

world will be governed according to the Rules of Logic. I have seen such men often become excellent legislators after experience has cured their errors. I hope it will prove so with Genl. M.[arshall], who seems calculated to act a great part." [1]

The first session of the Sixth Congress convened in Philadelphia on December 2, 1799. Marshall was appointed a member of the joint committee of the Senate and the House to wait upon the President and inform him that Congress was in session.[2]

The next day Adams delivered his speech to the Senators and Representatives. The subject which for the moment now inflamed the minds of the members of the President's party was Adams's second French mission. Marshall, of all men, had most reason to resent any new attempt to try once more where he had failed, and to endeavor again to deal with the men who had insulted America and spun about our representatives a network of corrupt intrigue. But if Marshall felt any personal humiliation, he put it beneath his feet and, as we have seen, approved the Ellsworth mission. "The southern federalists have of course been induced [by Marshall] to vindicate the mission, as a sincere, honest, and politic measure," wrote Wolcott to Ames.[3]

Who should prepare the answer of the House to the President's speech? Who best could perform the difficult task of framing a respectful reply which would support the President and yet not offend the rebellious Federalists in Congress? Marshall was

---

[1] Cabot to King, Jan. 20, 1800; *ib.*, 184.
[2] *Annals*, 6th Cong., 1st Sess., 187.
[3] Wolcott to Ames, Dec. 29, 1799; Gibbs, ii, 314.

selected for this delicate work. "Mr. Marshall, from the committee appointed to draught an Address in answer to the Speech of the President of the United States . . . reported same." [1] Although written in admirable temper, Marshall's address failed to please; the result was pallid.

"Considering the state of the House, it was necessary and proper that the answer to the speech should be prepared by Mr. Marshall," testifies Wolcott. "He has had a hard task to perform, and you have seen how it has been executed. The object was to unite all opinions, at least of the federalists; it was of course necessary to appear to approve the mission, and yet to express the approbation in such terms as when critically analyzed would amount to no approbation at all. No one individual was really satisfied; all were unwilling to encounter the danger and heat which a debate would produce and the address passed with silent dissent; the President doubtless understood the intention, and in his response has expressed his sense of the dubious compliment in terms inimitably obscure." [2] Levin Powell, a Federalist Representative from Virginia, wrote to his brother: "There were members on both sides that disliked that part of it [Marshall's address] where he spoke of the Mission to France." [3]

The mingled depression, excitement, and resentment among Marshall's colleagues must have been

[1] *Annals*, 6th Cong. 1st Sess., 194. The speech as reported passed with little debate.

[2] Wolcott to Ames, Dec. 29, 1799; Gibbs, ii, 314. And see McMaster, ii, 452.

[3] Levin Powell to Major Burr Powell, Dec. 11, 1799; *Branch Historical Papers*, ii, 232.

great indeed to have caused them thus to look upon his first performance in the House; for the address, which, even now, is good reading, is a strong and forthright utterance. While, with polite agreement, gliding over the controverted question of the mission, Marshall's speech is particularly virile when dealing with domestic politics. In coupling Fries's Pennsylvania insurrection with the Kentucky and Virginia Resolutions Marshall displayed as clever political dexterity as even Jefferson himself.

The address enumerates the many things for which Americans ought to thank "the benevolent Deity," and laments "that any portion of the people . . . should permit themselves, amid such numerous blessings, to *be seduced* by . . . *designing men* into an open resistance to the laws of the United States. . . . Under a Constitution where the public burdens can only be imposed by the people themselves, for their own benefit, and to promote their own objects, a hope might well have been indulged that the general interest would have been too well understood, and the general welfare too highly prized, to have produced in any of our citizens a disposition to hazard so much felicity, by the criminal effort of a part, to oppose with lawless violence the will of the whole." [1]

While it augured well that the courts and militia coöperated with "the military force of the nation" in "restoring order and submission to the laws," still, this only showed the necessity of Adams's "recommendation" that "the judiciary system"

[1] *Annals*, 6th Cong., 1st Sess., 194.

should be extended. As to the new French mission, the address "approves the pacific and humane policy" which met, by the appointment of new envoys, "the first indications on the part of the French Republic" of willingness to negotiate; and "offers up fervent prayers to the Supreme Ruler of the Universe for the success of their embassy."

Marshall declares "the present period critical and momentous. The important changes which are occurring, the new and great events which are every hour preparing . . . the spirit of war . . . prevalent in almost every nation . . . demonstrate" the need of providing "means of self-defense." To neglect this duty from "love of ease or other considerations" would be "criminal and fatal carelessness." No one could tell how the new mission would terminate: "It depends not on America alone. The most pacific temper will not ensure peace." Preparation for "national defense . . . is an . . . obvious duty. Experience the parent of wisdom . . . has established the truth . . . that . . . nothing short of the power of repelling aggression will" save us from "war or national degradation." [1]

Gregg of Pennsylvania moved to strike out the italicized words in Marshall's address to the President, but after a short debate the motion was defeated without roll-call. [2]

Wolcott gives us a clear analysis of the political situation and of Marshall's place and power in it at this particular moment: "The federal party is composed of the old members who were generally re-

[1] *Annals*, 6th Cong., 1st Sess., 194–97.   [2] *Ib.*, 194.

elected in the northern, with new members from the southern states. New York has sent an anti-federal majority; Pennsylvania has done the same; opposition principles are gaining ground in New Jersey and Maryland, and in the present Congress, the votes of these states will be fluctuating and undecided."

Nothing shows more clearly the intimate gossip of the time than the similarity of Wolcott's and Cabot's language in describing Marshall. "A number of distinguished men," continues Wolcott, "appear from the southward, who are not pledged by any act to support the system of the last Congress; these men will pay great respect to the opinions of General Marshall; he is doubtless a man of virtue and distinguished talents, but he will think much of the State of Virginia, and is too much disposed to govern the world according to rules of logic; he will read and expound the constitution as if it were a penal statute, and will sometimes be embarrassed with doubts of which his friends will not perceive the importance." [1]

Marshall headed the committee to inquire of the President when he would receive the address of the House, and on December 10, "Mr. Speaker, attended by the members present, proceeded to the President's house, to present him their Address in answer to his Speech." [2] A doleful procession the hostile, despondent, and irritated Representatives made as they trudged along Philadelphia's streets to greet the equally hostile and exasperated Chief Magistrate.

[1] Wolcott to Ames, Dec. 29, 1799; Gibbs, ii, 314.
[2] *Annals*, 6th Cong., 1st Sess., 198.

Presidential politics was much more on the minds of the members of Congress than was the legislation needed by the country. Most of the measures and practically all the debates of this remarkable session were shaped and colored by the approaching contest between the Federalists and Republicans and, personally, between Jefferson and Adams. Without bearing this fact in mind the proceedings of this session cannot be correctly understood. A mere reading of the maze of resolutions, motions, and debates printed in the "Annals" leaves one bewildered. The principal topic of conversation was, of course, the impending presidential election. Hamilton's faction of extreme Federalists had been dissatisfied with Adams from the beginning. Marshall writes his brother "in confidence" of the plots these busy politicians were concocting.

"I can tell you in confidence," writes Marshall, "that the situation of our affairs with respect to domestic quiet is much more critical than I had conjectured. The eastern people are very much dissatisfied with the President on account of the late [second] Mission to France. They are strongly disposed to desert him & push some other candidate. King or Ellsworth with one of the Pinckneys — most probably the General, are thought of.

"If they are deter'd from doing this by the fear that the attempt might elect Jefferson I think it not improbable that they will vote generally for Adams & Pinckney so as to give the latter gentleman the best chance if he gets the Southern vote to be President.

"Perhaps this ill humor may evaporate before

the election comes on — but at present it wears a very serious aspect. This circumstance is rendered the more unpleasant by the state of our finances. The impost received this year has been less productive than usual & it will be impossible to continue the present armament without another loan. Had the impost produced the sum to which it was calculated, a loan would have been unavoidable.

"This difficulty ought to have been foreseen when it was determined to execute the law for raising the army. It is now conceiv'd that we cannot at the present stage of our negotiation with France change the defensive position we have taken without much hazard.

"In addition to this many influential characters not only contend that the army ought not now to be disbanded but that it ought to be continued so long as the war in Europe shall last. I am apprehensive that our people would receive with very ill temper a system which should keep up an army of observation at the expense of the annual addition of five millions to our debt. The effect of it wou'd most probably be that the hands which hold the reins wou'd be entirely chang'd. You perceive the perplexities attending our situation.

"In addition to this there are such different views with respect to the future, such a rancorous malignity of temper among the democrats,[1] such [an ap]-

---

[1] The Federalists called the Republicans "Democrats," "Jacobins," etc., as terms of contempt. The Republicans bitterly resented the appellation. The word "Democrat" was not adopted as the formal name of a political party until the nomination for the Presidency of Andrew Jackson, who had been Jefferson's determined enemy.

parent disposition — (if the Aurora be the index of
the [mind of] those who support it) to propel us to a
war with B[ritain] & to enfold us within the embrace
of Fran[ce], [s]uch a detestation & fear of France
among others [that I] look forward with more apprehension than I have ever done to the future political
events of our country." [1]

On December 18 a rumor of the death of Washington reached the Capital. Marshall notified the
House. His grief was so profound that even the dry
and unemotional words of the formal congressional
reports express it. "Mr. Marshall," says the
"Annals" of Congress, "in a voice that bespoke the
anguish of his mind, and a countenance expressive
of the deepest regret, rose, and delivered himself as
follows: —

"Mr. Speaker: Information has just been received,
that our illustrious fellow-citizen, the Commander-
in-Chief of the American Army, and the late President of the United States, is no more!

"Though this distressing intelligence is not certain, there is too much reason to believe its truth.
After receiving information of this national calamity, so heavy and so afflicting, the House of Representatives can be but ill fitted for public business.
I move, therefore, they adjourn." [2]

The next day the news was confirmed, and Marshall thus addressed the House: —

"Mr. Speaker: The melancholy event which was

[1] Marshall to James M. Marshall, Philadelphia, Dec. 16, 1799;
MS.
[2] *Annals*, 6th Cong., 1st Sess., 203.

yesterday announced with doubt, has been rendered but too certain.

"Our WASHINGTON is no more! The Hero, the Sage, and the Patriot of America — the man on whom in times of danger every eye was turned and all hopes were placed — lives now only in his own great actions, and in the hearts of an affectionate and afflicted people.

"If, sir, it has even not been usual openly to testify respect for the memory of those whom Heaven had selected as its instrument for dispensing good to men, yet such has been the uncommon worth, and such the extraordinary incidents, which have marked the life of him whose loss we all deplore, that the American Nation,[1] impelled by the same feelings, would call with one voice for a public manifestation of that sorrow which is so deep and so universal.

"More than any other individual, and as much as to one individual was possible, has he contributed to found this our wide-spread empire,[2] and to give to the Western World its independence and its freedom.

"Having effected the great object for which he was placed at the head of our armies, we have seen him converting the sword into the plough-share, and voluntarily sinking the soldier in the citizen.

"When the debility of our federal system had become manifest, and the bonds which connected

---

[1] Marshall appears to have been the first to use the expression "the American Nation."

[2] The word "empire" as describing the United States was employed by all public men of the time. Washington and Jefferson frequently spoke of "our empire."

the parts of this vast continent were dissolving, we have seen him the Chief of those patriots who formed for us a Constitution, which, by preserving the Union, will, I trust, substantiate and perpetuate those blessings our Revolution had promised to bestow.

"In obedience to the general voice of his country, calling on him to preside over a great people, we have seen him once more quit the retirement he loved, and in a season more stormy and tempestuous than war itself, with calm and wise determination, pursue the true interests of the Nation, and contribute, more than any other could contribute, to the establishment of that system of policy which will, I trust, yet preserve our peace, our honor and our independence.

"Having been twice unanimously chosen the Chief Magistrate of a free people, we see him, at a time when his re-election with the universal suffrage could not have been doubted, affording to the world a rare instance of moderation, by withdrawing from his high station to the peaceful walks of private life. However the public confidence may change, and the public affections fluctuate with respect to others, yet with respect to him they have in war and in peace, in public and in private life, been as steady as his own firm mind, and as constant as his own exalted virtues.

"Let us, then, Mr. Speaker, pay the last tribute of respect and affection to our departed friend — let the Grand Council of the Nation display those sentiments which the Nation feels. For this purpose

I hold in my hand some resolutions which I will take the liberty to offer to the House." [1]

The resolutions offered by Marshall declared that: —

"The House of Representatives of the United States, having received intelligence of the death of their highly valued fellow-citizen, GEORGE WASHINGTON, General of the Armies of the United States, and sharing the universal grief this distressing event must produce, *unanimously resolve:* —

"1. That this House will wait on the President of the United States, in condolence of this national calamity.

"2. That the Speaker's chair be shrouded with black, and that the members and officers of the House wear mourning during the session.

"3. That a joint committee of both Houses be appointed to report measures suitable to the occasion, and expressive of the profound sorrow with which Congress is penetrated on the loss of a citizen, first in war, first in peace, and first in the hearts of his countrymen." [2]

Thus it came about that the designation of Washington as "First in war, first in peace, and first in the hearts of his countrymen" was attributed to Marshall. But Marshall's colleague, Henry Lee, was the author of these words. Marshall's refusal to allow history to give him the credit for this famous description is characteristic. He might easily have accepted that honor. Indeed, he found it difficult to make the public believe that he did not originate

[1] *Annals,* 6th Cong., 1st. Sess., 203-04.   [2] *Ib.,* 204.

this celebrated phraseology. He presented the resolutions; they stand on the record in Marshall's name; and, for a long time, the world insisted on ascribing them to him.

In a last effort to make history place the laurels on General Lee, where they belong, Marshall, three years before his death, wrote the exact facts: —

"As the stage passed through Philadelphia," says Marshall, "some passenger mentioned to a friend he saw in the street the death of General Washington. The report flew to the hall of Congress, and I was asked to move an adjournment. I did so.

"General Lee was not at the time in the House. On receiving the intelligence which he did on the first arrival of the stage, he retired to his room and prepared the resolutions which were adopted with the intention of offering them himself.

"But the House of Representatives had voted on my motion, and it was expected by all that I on the next day announce the lamentable event and propose resolutions adapted to the occasion.

"General Lee immediately called on me and showed me his resolutions. He said it had now become improper for him to offer them, and wished me to take them. As I had not written anything myself and was pleased with his resolutions which I entirely approved, I told him I would offer them the next day when I should state to the House of Representatives the confirmation of the melancholy intelligence received the preceding day. I did so.

"You will see the fact stated in a note to the pref-

ace of the Life of Washington on p. [441] v. [2] and
again in a note to the 5th vol. p. 765. Whenever the
subject has been mentioned in my presence," Marshall adds in a postscript, "I have invariably stated
that the resolution was drawn by General Lee and
have referred to these notes in the Life of Washington." [1]

During the first session Marshall was incessantly
active, although his work was done with such ease
that he gave to his colleagues the impression of indolence. Few questions came before the House on
which he did not take the floor; and none, apparently, about which he did not freely speak his mind
in private conversation. The interminable roll-calls
of the first session show that Marshall failed to vote
only six times.[2] His name is prominent throughout
the records of the session. For example, the Republicans moved to amend the army laws so that enlist-
ments should not exempt non-commissioned officers
and privates from imprisonment for debt. Marshall
spoke against the motion, which was defeated.[3] He
was appointed chairman of a special committee to
bring in a bill for removing military forces from election places and "preventing their interference in
elections." Marshall drew this measure, reported

[1] Marshall to Charles W. Hannan, of Baltimore, Md., March 29,
1832; MS., N.Y. Pub. Lib.; also Marshall, ii, 441.

[2] These were: On the bill to enable the President to borrow money
for the public (*Annals*, 6th Cong., 1st Sess., 632); a bill for the re-
lief of Rhode Island College (*ib.*, 643); a salt duty bill (*ib.*, 667); a
motion to postpone the bill concerning the payment of admirals (*ib.*,
678); a bill on the slave trade (*ib.*, 699–700); a bill for the additional
taxation of sugar (*ib.*, 705).

[3] *Ib.*, 521–22.

it to the House, where it passed, only to be defeated in the Senate.[1]

Early in the session Marshall was appointed chairman of the committee to report upon the cession by Connecticut to the United States of that priceless domain known as the Western Reserve. He presented the committee report recommending the acceptance of the lands and introduced the bill setting out the terms upon which they could be taken over.[2] After much debate, which Marshall led, Gallatin fighting by his side, the bill was passed by a heavy majority.[3]

Marshall's vote against abrogating the power of the Governor of the Territory of the Mississippi to prorogue the Legislature;[4] his vote for the resolution that the impertinence of a couple of young officers to John Randolph at the theater did not call "for the interposition of this House," on the ground of a breach of its privileges;[5] his vote against that part of the Marine Corps Bill which provided that any officer, on the testimony of two

---

[1] *Annals*, 6th Cong., 1st Sess., *House*, 522–23, 527, 626; *Senate*, 151.

[2] *Ib.*, 633–34.

[3] *Ib.*, 662. See *ib.*, Appendix II, 495, 496. Thus Marshall was the author of the law under which the great "Western Reserve" was secured to the United States. The bill was strenuously resisted on the ground that Connecticut had no right or title to this extensive and valuable territory.

[4] *Ib.*, 532. On this vote the *Aurora* said: "When we hear such characters as General Lee calling it *innovation* and *speculation* to withhold from the Executive magistrate the dangerous and unrepublican power of *proroguing* and dissolving a legislature at his pleasure, what must be the course of our reflections? When we see men like General Marshall voting for such a principle in a Government of a portion of the American people is there no cause for alarm?" (*Aurora*, March 20, 1800.)

[5] *Annals*, 6th Cong., 1st Sess., 504–06.

witnesses, should be cashiered and incapacitated forever from military service for refusing to help arrest any member of the service who, while on shore, offended against the person or property of any citizen,[1] are fair examples of the level good sense with which Marshall invariably voted.

On the Marine Corps Bill a debate arose so suddenly and sharply that the reporter could not record it. Marshall's part in this encounter reveals his military bent of mind, the influence of his army experience, and his readiness in controversy, no less than his unemotional sanity and his disdain of popular favor if it could be secured only by sacrificing sound judgment. Marshall strenuously objected to subjecting the Marine Corps officers to trial by jury in the civil courts; he insisted that courts-martial were the only tribunals that could properly pass on their offenses. Thereupon, young John Randolph of Roanoke, whose pose at this particular time was extravagant hostility to everything military, promptly attacked him. The incident is thus described by one who witnessed the encounter "which was incidentally and unexpectedly started and as suddenly and warmly debated": —

"Your representative, Mr. Marshall, was the principal advocate for *letting the power remain with courts martial and for withholding it from the courts of law*. In the course of the debate there was some warmth and personality between him and Mr. Randolph, in consequence of the latter charging the former with adopting opinions, and using argu-

[1] *Annals*, 6th Cong., 1st Sess., 623–24.

ments, which went to sap the mode of trial by jury.

"Mr. Marshall, with leave, rose a third time, and exerted himself to repel and invalidate the deductions of Mr. Randolph, who also obtained permission, and defended the inference he had drawn, by stating that Mr. Marshall, in the affair of Robbins,[1] had strenuously argued against the jurisdiction of the American courts, and had contended that it was altogether an *Executive* business; that in the present instance he strongly contended that the business ought not to be left with the civil tribunals, but that it ought to be transferred to military tribunals, and thus the trial by jury would be lessened and frittered away, and insensibly sapped, at one time by transferring the power to the Executive, and at another to the military departments; and in other ways, as occasions might present themselves. The debate happened so unexpectedly that the shorthand man did not take it down, although its manner, its matter, and its tendency, made it more deserving of preservation, than most that have taken place during the session."[2]

Marshall's leadership in the fight of the Virginia Revolutionary officers for land grants from the National Government, strongly resisted by Gallatin and other Republican leaders, illustrates his unfailing support of his old comrades. Notwith-

---

[1] See *infra*, 458 *et seq.*

[2] "Copy of a letter from a gentleman in Philadelphia, to his friend in Richmond, dated 13th March, 1800," printed in *Virginia Gazette and Petersburg Intelligencer*, April 1, 1800.

standing the Republican opposition, he was victorious by a vote of more than two to one.[1]

But Marshall voted to rebuke a petition of "free
men of color" to revive the slave-trade laws, the
fugitive from justice laws, and to take "such measures as shall in due course" free the slaves.[2] The
debate over this resolution is important, not only
as explaining the vote of Marshall, who came from
Virginia and was himself a slaveholder, as were
Washington and Jefferson, but also as showing the
mind of the country on slavery at that particular
time.

Marshall's colleague, General Lee, said that the
petition "contained sentiments . . . highly improper
. . . to encourage."[3] John Rutledge of South Carolina exclaimed: "They now tell the House these
people are in slavery — I thank God they are! if
they were not, dreadful would be the consequences.
. . . Some of the states would never have adopted
the Federal form of government if it had not been
secured to them that Congress never would legislate on the subject of slavery."[4]

Harrison Gray Otis of Massachusetts was much
disgusted by the resolution, whose signers "were
incapable of writing their names or of reading the
petitions"; he "thought those who did not possess
that species of property [slaves] had better leave the
regulation of it to those who were cursed with it."
John Brown of Rhode Island "considered [slaves]
as much personal property as a farm or a ship. . . .

[1] *Annals*, 6th Cong., 1st Sess., 668–69.
[2] *Ib.*, 229.   [3] *Ib.*, 231.   [4] *Ib.*, 230–32.

We want money; we want a navy; we ought therefore to use the means to obtain it. . . . Why should
we see Great Britain getting all the slave trade to
themselves; why may not our country be enriched
by that lucrative traffic?" [1] Gabriel Christie of
Maryland hoped the petition would "go under the
table instead of upon it." [2] Mr. Jones of Georgia
thought that the slaves "have been immensely bene-
fited by coming amongst us." [3]

Finally, after two days of debate, in which the
cause of freedom for the blacks was almost unsupported, Samuel Goode of Virginia moved: "That the
parts of the said petition which invite Congress to
legislate upon subjects from which the General Government is precluded by the Constitution have a
tendency to create disquiet and jealousy, and ought
therefore to receive the pointed disapprobation of
this House." [4] On this motion, every member but
one, including John Marshall, voted aye. George
Thacher, a Congregationalist preacher from Massachusetts, alone voted nay. [5] Such, in general, and
in spite of numerous humanitarian efforts against
slavery, was American sentiment on that subject at
the dawn of the nineteenth century. [6]

Five subjects of critical and historic importance
came before the session: the Federalists' Disputed
Elections Bill; the Republican attack on the pro-

---

[1] *Annals*, 6th Cong., 1st Sess., 233.   [2] *Ib.*, 234.

[3] *Ib.*, 235.   [4] *Ib.*, 240.   [5] *Ib.*, 245.

[6] Concerning a similar effort in 1790, Washington wrote: "The
memorial of the Quakers (and a very *malapropos* one it was) has at
length been put to sleep, and will scarcely awake before the year
1808." (Washington to Stuart, March 28, 1790; *Writings:* Ford, xi,
474.)

visional army raised for the probable emergency of war with France; the Republican attack on the Executive power in the Jonathan Robins case; the Republican onslaught upon the Alien and Sedition Laws; and the National Bankruptcy Bill. In each of these Marshall took a leading and determining part.

Early in the session (January 23) the Republicans brought up the vexed question of the Sedition Law. A resolution to repeal the obnoxious section of this measure was presented on January 29, and after a hot debate was adopted by the close vote of 50 to 48. Marshall voted for the repeal and against his own party.[1] Had he voted with his party, the Republican attack would have failed. But no pressure of party regularity could influence Marshall against his convictions, no crack of the party whip could frighten him.

Considering the white heat of partisan feeling at the time, and especially on the subject of the Alien and Sedition Laws; considering, too, the fact that these offensive acts were Administration measures; and taking into account the prominence as a Federalist leader which Marshall had now achieved, his vote against the reprobated section of the Sedition Law was a supreme act of independence of political ties and party discipline. He had been and still was the only Federalist to disapprove, openly, the Alien and Sedition Laws.[2] "To make a little saving for our friend Marshall's address," Chief Justice Ells-

---

[1] *Annals*, 6th Cong., 1st Sess., Resolution and debate, ii, 404–19.
[2] Bassett, 260.

worth sarcastically suggested that, in case of the repeal of the Sedition Law, "the preamble . . . should
read thus: 'Whereas the increasing danger and depravity of the present time require that the law
against seditious practices *should be restored to its
full rigor,* therefore,' etc." [1]

From the point of view of its probable effect on
Marshall's political fortunes, his vote appeared to
spell his destruction, for it practically left him outside
of either party. He abhorred the doctrine of State
Sovereignty which Jefferson now was making the
rallying-point of the Republican Party; he believed,
quite as fervently as had Washington himself, that
the principle of Nationality alone could save the
Republic. So Marshall could have no hopes of any
possible future political advancement through the
Republican Party.

On the other hand, his vote against his own party
on its principal measure killed Marshall's future as
a Federalist in the opinion of all the politicians of his
time, both Federal and Republican. [2] And we may
be certain that Marshall saw this even more clearly
than did the politicians, just as he saw most things
more clearly than most men.

But if Marshall's vote on the Sedition Law was
an act of insubordination, his action on the Disputed
Elections Bill was nothing short of party treason.
This next to the last great blunder of the Federalists
was in reality a high-handed attempt to control
the coming presidential election, regardless of the

---

[1] Ellsworth to Pickering, Dec. 12, 1798; Flanders, ii, 193.

[2] Adams: *Gallatin,* 211. And see Federalist attacks on Marshall's
answers to "Freeholder," *supra.*

votes of the people. It was aimed particularly at the anticipated Republican presidential majority in Pennsylvania which had just elected a Republican Governor over the Federalist candidate.

On January 3, Senator Ross of Pennsylvania, the defeated Federalist candidate for Governor of that State, offered a resolution that a committee should be appointed to consider a law "for deciding disputed elections of President and Vice-President . . . and . . . the legality or illegality of the votes given for those officers in the different states." In a brief but pointed debate, the Republicans insisted that such a law would be unconstitutional.

The Federalist position was that, since the Constitution left open the manner of passing upon votes, Congress had the power to regulate that subject and ought to provide some method to meet anticipated emergencies. Suppose, said Senator Ross, that "persons should claim to be Electors who had never been *properly* appointed [elected], should their vote be received? Suppose they should vote for a person to be President who had not the age required by the Constitution or who had not been long enough a citizen of the United States or for two persons who were both citizens of the same State? . . . What situation would the country be in if such a case was to happen?"[1]

So lively was the interest and high the excitement that Marshall did not go to Richmond when his fifth child was born on February 13, 1800.[2] He spoke in

---

[1] *Annals*, 6th Cong., 1st Sess., 29.
[2] James Keith Marshall.

the House February 12, and was appointed on an important committee February 13.[1]

On February 14, the bill was reported to the Senate. Five days later the Republican organ, the "Aurora," made shift to get a copy of the measure,[2] and printed it in full with a bold but justifiable attack upon it and the method of its origin.[3] On March 28, the bill passed the Senate by a strict party vote.[4] It provided that a "Grand Committee," consisting of six Senators and six Representatives elected by ballot and the Chief Justice of the Supreme Court, should take charge of the certificates of electoral votes immediately after they had been opened and read in the presence of Congress.

This Grand Committee was to be given power to send for papers and persons and, in secret session, to consider and *determine* all questions concerning the election. Had bribery been employed, had force been used, had threats or intimidation, persuasion or cajolery polluted the voters? — the Grand Committee was to decide these questions; it was to declare what electoral votes should be counted; it was to throw out electoral votes which it thought to be tainted or improper; and the report of this Grand Committee was to be final and conclusive. In short,

[1] *Annals*, 6th Cong., 1st Sess., 520, 522.

[2] At this period the Senate still sat behind closed doors and its proceedings were secret.

[3] *Annals*, 6th Cong., 1st Sess., 105. This led to one of the most notably dramatic conflicts between the Senate and the press which has occurred during our history. For the prosecution of William Duane, editor of the *Aurora*, see *ib.*, 105, 113-19, 123-24. It was made a campaign issue, the Republicans charging that it was a Federalist plot against the freedom of the press. (See *Aurora*, March 13 and 17, 1800.)

[4] *Ib.*, 146.

it was to settle absolutely the Presidency; from its decree there was to be no appeal.[1]

On March 31, this bill reached the House. While no action was taken on it for more than two weeks, it was almost the sole topic of conversation among the members. In these cloak-room talks, Marshall, to the intense disgust and anger of the Federalist leaders, was outspoken against this attempt to seize the Presidency under the forms of a National law.

Two weeks later Marshall expressed his opinion on the floor. He thought that "some salutary mode" to guard against election frauds and to settle disputed presidential contests should be adopted; but he did not think that the Senate should appoint the chairman of the Grand Committee, and he objected especially to the finality of its authority.[2] He moved that these portions of the bill be stricken out and offered a substitute.[3]

Opposed as he was to the measure as it came from the Senate, he nevertheless was against its indefinite postponement and so voted.[4] His objections were to the autocratic and definitive power of the Grand Committee; with this cut from the measure, he was in favor of a joint committee of the House and Senate to examine into alleged election frauds and illegalities. The Senate bill was referred to a special committee of the House,[5] which reported a measure in accordance with Marshall's

---

[1] For a review of this astonishing bill, see McMaster, ii, 462–63, and Schouler, i, 475.

[2] *Annals*, 6th Cong., 1st Sess., 670.

[3] Marshall's substitute does not appear in the *Annals*.

[4] *Annals*, 6th Cong., 1st Sess., 674.   [5] *Ib.*, 678.

views.[1] After much debate and several roll-calls, the bill, as modified by Marshall, passed the House.[2]

Marshall's reconstruction of the Senate's Disputed Elections Bill killed that measure. It no longer served the purpose of the Federalist presidential conspiracy. By a strict party vote, the Senate disagreed with the House amendments;[3] and on the day before adjournment, the bill was finally disposed of by postponement.[4]

Thus did Marshall destroy the careful plans for his party's further control of the National Government, and increase the probability of the defeat of his friend, John Adams, and of the election of his enemy, Thomas Jefferson. Had not Marshall interfered, it seems certain that the Disputed Elections Bill would have become a law. If it had been enacted, Jefferson's election would have been impossible. Once again, as we shall see, Marshall is to save the political life of his great and remorseless antagonist.

Yet Jefferson had no words of praise for Marshall. He merely remarks that "the bill . . . has undergone much revolution. Marshall made a dexterous manœuver; he declares against the constitutionality of the Senate's bill, and proposes that the right of decision of their grand committee should be controllable by the *concurrent* vote of the two houses of congress; but to stand good if not rejected by a concurrent vote. You will readily estimate the amount of this sort of controul." [5]

[1] *Annals*, 6th Cong., 1st Sess., 691–92.   [2] *Ib.*, 687–710.
[3] *Ib.*, 179.   [4] *Ib.*, 182.
[5] Jefferson to Livingston, April 30, 1800; *Works*: Ford, ix, 132.

The party leaders labored hard and long with Marshall while the Disputed Elections Bill was before the House. Speaker Sedgwick thus describes the Federalist plot and the paralyzing effect of Marshall's private conversations with his fellow members: "Looking forward to the ensuing election," writes the disgusted Speaker, "it was deemed indispensable to prescribe a mode for canvassing the votes, provided there should be a dispute. There being no law in the state [Pennsylvania], the governor had declined, and the jacobins [Republicans] propagated the report . . . that he would return their votes. A bill was brought into the Senate & passed, wisely & effectually providing against the evil, by the constitution of a committee with ultimate powers of decision.

"Mr. Marshall in the first place called in question the constitutional powers of the legislature to delegate such authority to a Committee. On this question I had a long conversation with him, & he finally confessed himself (for there is not a more candid man on earth) to be convinced.

"He then resorted to another ground of opposition. He said the people having authorized the members to decide, personally, all disputes relative to those elections, altho' the power was not indelegable, yet he thought, in its nature, it was too delicate to be delegated, until experience had demonstrated that great inconveniences would attend its exercise by the Legislature; altho' he had no doubt such would be the result of the attempt.

"This objection is so attenuated and unsubstantial as to be hardly perceivable by a mind so merely practical as mine. He finally was convinced that it was so and abandoned it.

"In the mean time, however, he had dwelt so much, in conversation, on these subjects that he had dissipated our majority, and it never could again be compacted. The consequence was that the bill was lost." [1]

Marshall's most notable performance while in Congress was his effort in the celebrated Jonathan Robins case — "a speech," declares that capable and cautious critic, Henry Adams, "that still stands without a parallel in our Congressional debates." [2] In 1797 the crew of the British ship Hermione mutinied, murdered their officers, took the ship to a Spanish port, and sold it. One of the murderers was Thomas Nash, a British subject. Two years later, Nash turned up at Charleston, South Carolina, as the member of a crew of an American schooner.

On the request of the British Consul, Nash was seized and held in jail under the twenty-seventh article of the Jay Treaty. Nash swore that he was not a British subject, but an American citizen, Jonathan Robins, born in Danbury, Connecticut, and impressed by a British man-of-war. On overwhelming evidence, uncontradicted except by Nash, that the accused man was a British subject and a murderer, President Adams requested Judge Bee, of the United States District Court of South Carolina, to

[1] Sedgwick to King, May 11, 1800; King, iii, 237–38.
[2] Adams: *Gallatin*, 232.

deliver Nash to the British Consul pursuant to the article of the treaty requiring the delivery.[1]

Here was, indeed, a campaign issue. The land rang with Republican denunciation of the President. What servile truckling to Great Britain! Nay, more, what a crime against the Constitution! Think of it! An innocent American citizen delivered over to British cruelty. Where now were our free institutions? When President Adams thus surrendered the Connecticut "Yankee," Robins, he not only prostituted patriotism, showed himself a tool of British tyranny, but also usurped the functions of the courts and struck a fatal blow at the Constitution. So shouted Republican orators and with immense popular effect.

The fires kindled by the Alien and Sedition Laws did not heat to greater fervency the public imagination. Here was a case personal and concrete, flaming with color, full of human appeal. Jefferson took quick party advantage of the incident. "I think," wrote he, "no circumstance since the establishment of our government has affected the popular mind more. I learn that in Pennsylvania it had a great effect. I have no doubt the piece you inclosed will run through all the republican papers, & carry the question home to every man's mind." [2]

"It is enough to call a man an *Irishman*, to make it *no murder* to pervert the law of nations and to degrade national honor and character. . . . Look at what has been done in the case of *Jonathan*

---

[1] United States *vs.* Nash *alias* Robins, Bee's *Reports*, 266.
[2] Jefferson to Charles Pinckney, Oct. 29, 1799; *Works:* Ford, ix, 87.

Robbins," [*sic*] exclaimed the "Aurora." "A British lieutenant who never saw him until he was prisoner at Charleston swears his name is Thomas Nash." So "The man is hanged!" [1]

For the purposes of the coming presidential campaign, therefore, the Robins affair was made the principal subject of Republican congressional attack on the Administration. On February 4, the House requested the President to transmit all the papers in the case. He complied immediately.[2] The official documents proved beyond a doubt that the executed sailor had not been an American citizen, but a subject of the British King and that he had committed murder while on board a British vessel on the high seas.

The selectmen of Danbury, Connecticut, certified that no such person as Jonathan Robins nor any family of the name of Robins ever had lived in that town. So did the town clerk. On the contrary, a British naval officer, who knew Nash well, identified him.[3]

Bayard, for the Federalists, took the aggressive and offered a resolution to the effect that the President's conduct in the Robins case "was conformable to the duty of the Government and to . . . the 27th article of the Treaty . . . with Great Britain." [4]

Forced to abandon their public charge that the Administration had surrendered an innocent Ameri-

---

[1] *Aurora*, Feb. 12, 1800.   [2] *Annals*, 6th Cong., 1st Sess., 511.
[3] *Ib.*, 515–18. Nash himself confessed before his execution that he was a British subject as claimed by the British authorities and as shown by the books of the ship Hermione.
[4] *Ib.*, 526.

can citizen to British cruelty,[1] the Republicans based their formal assault in Congress upon the ground that the President had disobeyed the laws, disregarded the Constitution, and taken upon himself the discharge of duties and functions which belonged exclusively to the courts. They contended that, even if Nash were guilty, even if he were not an American citizen, he should, nevertheless, have been tried by a jury and sentenced by a court.

On February 20, Livingston of New York offered the Republican resolutions to this effect. Not only was the President's conduct in this serious business a "dangerous interference of the Executive with judicial decisions," declared the resolution, but the action of the court in granting the President's request was "a sacrifice of the Constitutional independence of the judicial power and exposes the administration thereof to suspicion and reproach." [2]

The House decided to consider the Livingston resolutions rather than those offered by Bayard, the Federalists to a man supporting this method of meeting the Republicans on the ground which the latter, themselves, had chosen. Thus the question of constitutional power in the execution of treaties came squarely before the House, and the great debate was on.[3] For two weeks this notable discussion continued. The first day was frittered away on questions of order.

The next day the Republicans sought for delay [4]

---

[1] The Republicans, however, still continued to urge this falsehood before the people and it was generally believed to be true.

[2] *Annals*, 6th Congress, 1st Sess., 532–33.

[3] *Ib.*, 541–47.   [4] *Ib.*, 548.

— there were not sufficient facts before the House, they said, to justify that body in passing upon so grave a question. The third day the Republicans proposed that the House should request the President to secure and transmit the proceedings before the South Carolina Federal Court on the ground that the House could not determine the matter until it had the court proceedings.[1]

Marshall's patience was exhausted. He thought this procrastinating maneuver a Republican trick to keep the whole matter open until after the coming presidential campaign,[2] and he spoke his mind sharply to the House.

"Let gentlemen recollect the nature of the case," exclaimed Marshall; "the President of the United States is charged by this House with having violated the Constitution and laws of his country, by having committed an act of dangerous interference with a judicial decision — he is so charged by a member of this House. Gentlemen were well aware how much the public safety and happiness depended on a well or a misplaced confidence in the Executive.

"Was it reasonable or right," he asked, "to receive this charge — to receive in part the evidence in support of it — to receive so much evidence as almost every gentleman declared himself satisfied with, and to leave the charge unexamined, hanging over the head of the President of the United States . . . how long it was impossible to say, but certainly long enough to work a very bad effect? To him it

[1] *Annals*, 6th Cong., 1st Sess., 558.
[2] This, in fact, was the case.

seemed of all things the most unreasonable and unjust; and the mischief resulting therefrom must be
very great indeed."

The House ought to consider the evidence it
already had; if, on such examination, it appeared
that more was needed, the matter could then be
postponed. And, in any event, why ask the President to send for the court proceedings? The House
had as much power to procure the papers as the
President had. "Was he [the President] to be a
menial to the House in a business wherein himself
was seriously charged?"[1]

Marshall was aroused. To his brother he thus
denounces the tactics of the Republicans: "Every
stratagem seems to be used to give to this business
an undue impression. On the motion to send for
the evidence from the records of South Carolina
altho' it was stated & prov'd that this would
amount to an abandonment of the enquiry during
the present session & to an abandonment under circumstances which would impress the public mind
with the opinion that we really believed Mr. Livingston's resolutions maintainable; & that the record
could furnish no satisfaction since it could not contain the parol testimony offered to the Judge & further that it could not be material to the President
but only to the reputation of the Judge what the
amount of the testimony was, yet the debate took
a turn as if we were precipitating a decision without
enquiry & without evidence."[2]

[1] *Annals*, 6th Cong., 1st Sess., 565.
[2] Marshall to James M. Marshall, Feb. 28, 1800; MS.

This Republican resolution was defeated. So was another by Gallatin asking for the papers in the case of William Brigstock, which the Republicans claimed was similar to that of Jonathan Robins. Finally the main question came on. For two hours Gallatin made an ingenious argument in support of the Livingston resolutions.[1]

The next day, March 7, Marshall took the floor and made the decisive speech which put a period to this partisan controversy. He had carefully revised his argument,[2] and it is to this prevision, so unlike Marshall's usual methods, that we owe the perfection of the reporter's excellent transcript of his performance. This great address not only ended the Republican attack upon the Administration, but settled American law as to Executive power in carrying out extradition treaties. Marshall's argument was a mingling of impressive oratory and judicial finality. It had in it the fire of the debater and the calmness of the judge.

It is the highest of Marshall's efforts as a public speaker. For many decades it continued to be published in books containing the masterpieces of American oratory as one of the best examples of the art.[3] It is a landmark in Marshall's career and a monument in the development of the law of the land. They go far who assert that Marshall's address is

[1] *Annals*, 6th Cong., 1st Sess., 595–96.

[2] Pickering to James Winchester, March 17, 1800; Pickering MSS., Mass. Hist. Soc. Also Binney, in Dillon, iii, 312.

[3] See Moore: *American Eloquence*, ii, 20–23. The speech also appears in full in *Annals*, 6th Cong., 1st Sess., 596–619; in Benton: *Abridgment of the Debates of Congress ;* in Bee's *Reports*, 266; and in the Appendix to Wharton: *State Trials*, 443.

a greater performance than any of the speeches of
Webster, Clay, Sumner, or other American orators
of the first class; and yet so perfect is this speech
that the commendation is not extreme.

The success of a democratic government, said
Marshall, depended not only on its right administration, but also on the public's right understanding
of its measures; public opinion must be "rescued
from those numerous prejudices which . . . sur-
round it." Bayard and others had so ably defended
the Administration's course that he would only
"reëstablish" and "confirm" what they had so well
said.

Marshall read the section of the Jay Treaty under
which the President acted: This provided, said he,
that a murderer of either nation, fleeing for "asylum" to the other, when charged with the crime,
and his delivery demanded on such proof as would
justify his seizure under local laws if the murder
had been committed in that jurisdiction, must be
surrendered to the aggrieved nation. Thus Great
Britain had required Thomas Nash at the hands
of the American Government. He had committed
murder on a British ship and escaped to America.

Was this criminal deed done in British jurisdiction? Yes; for "the jurisdiction of a nation extends
to the whole of its territory, and to its own citizens
in every part of the world. . . . The nature of civil
union" involves the "principle" that "the laws of a
nation are rightfully obligatory on its own citizens
in every situation where those laws are really extended to them."

This "is particularly recognized with respect to
the fleets of a nation on the high seas." By "the
opinion of the world . . . a fleet at sea is within the
jurisdiction of the nation to which it belongs," and
crimes there committed are punishable by that nation's laws. This is not contradicted by the right of
search for contraband, as Gallatin had contended,
for "in the sea itself no nation has any jurisdiction,"
and a belligerent has a right to prevent aid being
carried to its enemy. But, as to its crew, every ship
carried the law of its flag.

Marshall denied that the United States had jurisdiction, concurrent or otherwise, over the place of
the murder; "on the contrary, no nation has any
jurisdiction at sea but over its own citizens or vessels or offenses against itself." Such "jurisdiction
. . . is personal, reaching its own citizens only";
therefore American authority "cannot extend to a
murder committed by a British sailor on board a
British frigate navigating the high seas." There is no
such thing as "common [international] jurisdiction"
at sea, said Marshall; and he exhaustively illustrated
this principle by hypothetical cases of contract,
dueling, theft, etc., upon the ocean. "A common
jurisdiction . . . at sea . . . would involve the power
of punishing the offenses . . . stated." Piracy was
the one exception, because "against all and every
nation . . . and therefore punishable by all alike."
For "a pirate . . . is an enemy of the human race."

Any nation, however, may by statute declare an
act to be piratical which is not so by the law of nations; and such an act is punishable only by that

particular state and not by other governments. But an act universally recognized as criminal, such as robbery, murder, and the like, "is an offense against the community of nations."

The Republican contention was that murder and robbery (seizure of ships) constituted piracy "by the law of nations," and that, therefore, Nash should have been indicted and tried by American authority as a pirate; whereas he had been delivered to Great Britain as a criminal against that nation.

But, said Marshall, a single act does not necessarily indicate piratical intent unless it "manifests general hostility against the world"; if it shows an "intention to rob generally, then it is piracy." If, however, "it be merely mutiny and murder in a vessel with the intention of delivering it up to the enemy, it" is "an offense against a single nation and not piracy." It was only for such murder and "not piracy" that "Nash was delivered." And, indisputably, this was covered by the treaty. Even if Nash had been tried and acquitted for piracy, there still would have remained the crime of murder over which American courts had no jurisdiction, because it was not a crime punishable by international law, but only by the law of the nation in whose jurisdiction the crime was committed, and to which the criminal belonged.

American law and American courts could not deal with such a condition, insisted Marshall, but British law and courts could and the treaty bound America to deliver the criminal into British hands. "It was an act to which the American Nation was bound by a most solemn compact." For an American court to have convicted Nash and American authorities to have executed him "would have been murder"; while for them to have "acquitted and discharged him would have been a breach of faith and a violation of national duty."

It was plain, then, said he, that Nash should have been delivered to the British officers. By whom? The Republicans insisted that this authority was in the courts. Marshall demonstrated that the President alone could exercise such power. It was, he said, "a case for Executive and not for judicial decision." The Republican resolutions declared that the judicial power extends to *all* questions arising under the Constitution, treaties, and laws of the United States; but the Constitution itself provided that the judicial power extends only to all cases "*in law and equity*" arising under the Constitution, laws, and treaties of the United States.

"The difference was material and apparent," said Marshall. "A case in law or equity was a term well understood and of limited signification. It was a controversy between parties which had taken a shape for judicial decision. If the judicial power extended to every question under the Constitution, it would involve almost every subject proper for Legislative discussion and decision; if to every question under the laws and treaties of the United States, it would involve almost every subject on which the Executive could act. The division of power . . . could exist no longer, and the other departments would be swallowed up in the Judiciary."

The Constitution did not confer on the Judiciary "any political power whatever." The judicial power covered only cases where there are "parties to come into court, who can be reached by its process and bound by its power; whose rights admit of ultimate decision by a tribunal to which they are bound to submit." Such a case, said Marshall, "may arise under a treaty where the rights of individuals acquired or secured by a treaty are to be asserted or defended in court"; and he gave examples. "But the judicial power cannot extend to political compacts; as the establishment of the boundary line between American and British Dominions . . . or the case of the delivery of a murderer under the twenty-seventh article of our present Treaty with Britain. . . .

"The clause of the Constitution which declares that 'the trial of all crimes . . . shall be by jury'" did not apply to the decision of a case like that of Robins. "Certainly this clause . . . cannot be thought obligatory on . . . the whole world. It is not designed to secure the rights of the people of Europe or Asia or to direct and control proceedings against criminals throughout the universe. It can, then, be designed only to guide the proceedings of our own courts" in cases "to which the jurisdiction of the nation may rightfully extend." And the courts could not "try the crime for which Thomas Nash was delivered up to justice." The sole question was "whether he should be delivered up to a foreign tribunal which was alone capable of trying and punishing him." A provision for the trial of crimes in the courts of the United States is clearly "not a provision for the surrender to a foreign Government of an offender against that Government."

If the murder by Nash were a crime, it is one "not provided for by the Constitution"; if it were not a crime, "yet it is the precise case in which his surrender was stipulated by treaty" which the President, alone, must execute. That in the Executive decision "judicial questions" must also be determined, argued nothing; for this often must be the case, as, for instance, in so simple and ordinary matter as issuing patents for public lands, or in settling whether vessels have been captured within three miles of our coasts, or in declaring the legality of prizes taken by privateers or the restoration of such vessels — all such questions, of which these are familiar examples, are, said Marshall, "questions of political law proper to be decided by the Executive and not by the courts."

This was the Nash case. Suppose that a murder were "committed within the United States and the murderer should seek an asylum in Great Britain!" The treaty covered such a case; but no man would say "that the British courts should decide" it. It is, in its nature, a National demand made upon the Nation. The parties are two nations. They cannot come into court to litigate their claims, nor can a court decide on them. "Of consequence," declares Marshall, "the demand is not a case for judicial cognizance."

"The President is the sole organ of the nation in its external relations"; therefore "the demand of a foreign nation can only be made on him. He possesses the whole Executive power. He holds and directs the force of the nation. Of consequence, any act to be performed by the force of the nation is to be performed through him. He is charged to execute the laws. A treaty is . . . a law. He must, then, execute a treaty, where he, and he alone, possesses the means of executing it."

This, in rough outline, is Marshall's historic speech which helped to direct a new nation, groping blindly and with infinite clamoring, to a straight and safe pathway. Pickering immediately reported to Hamilton: " Mr. Marshall delivered a very luminous argument on the case, placing the 27th article of the treaty in a clear point of view and giving constructions on the questions arising out of it perfectly satisfactory, but, as it would seem, wholly unthought of when the meaning of the article was heretofore considered. His argument will, I hope, be fully and correctly published; it illustrates an important national question." [1]

The Republicans were discomfited; but they were not without the power to sting. Though Marshall had silenced them in Congress, the Republican press kept up the attack. "*Mr. Marshall* made an ingenious and *specious* defence of the administration, in relation to executive interference in the case of *Robbins*," [sic] says the "Aurora," "but he was compelled to admit, what certainly implicates both the President and Judge Bee. . . . He admitted that an American seaman was justifiable, in rescuing him-

[1] Pickering to Hamilton, March 10, 1800; Pickering MSS., Mass. Hist. Soc.

self from impressment, to put to death those who
kept him in durance. . . . Robbins [*sic*] claimed to
be an American citizen, and asserted upon his oath,
that he had been impressed and yet his claim was
not examined into by the Judge, neither did the
President *advise* and *request* that this should be a
subject of enquiry. The enquiry into his citizenship was made *after* his surrender and execution,
and the evidence exhibited has a very suspicious
aspect. . . . Town clerks may be found to certify to
anything that Timothy Pickering shall desire." [1]
Nevertheless, even the "Aurora" could not resist an
indirect tribute to Marshall, though paying it by
way of a sneer at Samuel W. Dana of Connecticut,
who ineffectually followed him.

"In the debate on *Mr. Livingston's* resolutions, on
Friday last," says the "Aurora," "Mr. Marshall
made, in the minds of some people, a very satisfactory defense of the conduct of the *President* and
Judge Bee in the case of *Jonathan Robbins* [*sic*]. Mr.
Dana, however, thought the subject exhausted, and
very *modestly* (who does not know his *modesty*) resolved with his inward man to shed a few more
rays of light on the subject; a federal judge, much
admired for his wit and humour, happened to be
present, when Mr. Dana began his flourishes.

"The judge thought the seal of conviction had
been put upon the case by Mr. Marshall, and discovered symptoms of uneasiness when our little
Connecticut Cicero displayed himself to catch Mr.
Speaker's vacant eye — 'Sir,' said the wit to a bye-

[1] *Aurora*, March 10, 1800.

stander, 'what can induce that man to rise, he is
nothing but a shakebag, and can only shake out the
ideas that have been put into the members' heads
by Mr. Marshall.'"[1]

Marshall's argument was conclusive. It is one
of the few speeches ever delivered in Congress
that actually changed votes from one party to the
other in a straight-out party fight. Justice Story
says that Marshall's speech "is one of the most
consummate juridical arguments which was ever
pronounced in the halls of legislation; . . . equally
remarkable for the lucid order of its topics, the pro-
foundness of its logic, the extent of its research,[2]
and the force of its illustrations. It may be said of
that speech . . . that it was '*Réponse sans réplique*,'
an answer so irresistible that it admitted of no
reply. It silenced opposition and settled then and
forever the points of international law on which the
controversy hinged. . . . An unequivocal demonstration of public opinion followed. The denunciations
of the Executive, which had hitherto been harsh
and clamorous everywhere throughout the land,
sunk away at once into cold and cautious whispers
only of disapprobation.

"Whoever reads that speech, even at this distance of time, when the topics have lost much of
their interest, will be struck with the prodigious

---

[1] *Aurora*, March 14, 1800.

[2] Marshall's speech on the Robins case shows some study, but not
so much as the florid encomium of Story indicates. The speeches of
Bayard, Gallatin, Nicholas, and others display evidence of much
more research than that of Marshall, who briefly refers to only two
authorities.

powers of analysis and reasoning which it displays, and which are enhanced by the consideration that the whole subject was then confessedly new in many of its aspects." [1]

The Republican leaders found their own members declaring themselves convinced by Marshall's demonstration and announcing their intentions of voting with the Administration. Gallatin, Livingston, and Randolph had hard work to hold their followers in line. Even the strongest efforts of these resourceful men would not rally all of their shattered forces. Many Republican members ignored the pleadings of their leaders and supported Marshall's position.

This is not to be wondered at, for Marshall had convinced even Gallatin himself. This gifted native of Switzerland was the Republican leader of the House. Unusually well-educated, perfectly upright, thorough in his industry, and careful in his thinking, Gallatin is the most admirable of all the characters attracted to the Republican ranks. He had made the most effective argument on the anti-Administration side in the debate over the Livingston resolutions, and had been chosen to answer Marshall's speech. He took a place near Marshall and began making notes for his reply; but soon he put his pencil and paper aside and became absorbed in Marshall's reasoning. After a while he arose, went to the space back of the seats, and paced up and down while Marshall proceeded.

When the Virginian closed, Gallatin did not come

[1] Story, in Dillon, iii, 357–58.

forward to answer him as his fellow partisans had expected. His Republican colleagues crowded around the brilliant little Pennsylvania Swiss and pleaded with him to answer Marshall's speech without delay. But Gallatin would not do it. "Answer it yourself," exclaimed the Republican leader in his quaint foreign accent; "for my part, I think it unan*swer*able," laying the accent on the *swer*.[1]

Nicholas of Virginia then tried to reply, but made no impression; Dana spoke to no better purpose, and the House ended the discussion by a vote which was admitted to be a distinctively personal triumph for Marshall. The Republican resolutions were defeated by 61 to 35, in a House where the parties were nearly equal in numbers.[2]

For once even Jefferson could not withhold his applause for Marshall's ability. "Livingston, Nicholas & Gallatin distinguished themselves on one side & J. Marshall greatly on the other," he writes in his curt account of the debate and its result.[3] And this grudging tribute of the Republican chieftain is higher praise of Marshall's efforts than the flood of eulogy which poured in upon him; Jefferson's virulence toward an enemy, and especially toward Marshall, was such that he could not see, except on rare occasions, and this was one, any merit whatever in an opponent, much less express it.

[1] Grigsby, i, 177; Adams: *Gallatin*, 232.

[2] *Annals*, 6th Cong., 1st Sess., 619.

[3] Jefferson to Madison, March 8, 1800; *Works:* Ford, ix, 121. In sending the speeches on both sides to his brother, Levin Powell, a Virginia Federalist Representative, says: "When you get to Marshall's it will be worth a perusal." (Levin Powell to Major Burr Powell, March 26, 1800; *Branch Historical Papers*, ii, 241.)

Marshall's defense of the army law was scarcely less powerful than his speech in the Robins case; and it reveals much more clearly Marshall's distinctively military temper of mind.

Congress had scarcely organized when the question came up of the reduction of the army. On this there was extended debate. Nicholas of Virginia offered a resolution to repeal the act for the provisional army of which Washington had been the Commander-in-Chief. The expense of this military establishment greatly alarmed Nicholas, who presented an array of figures on which his anxieties fed.[1] It was nonsense, he held, to keep this army law on the statute books for its effect on the negotiations with France.

Marshall promptly answered. "If it was true," said he, "that America, commencing her negotiation with her present military force would appear in the armor which she could only wear for a day, the situation of our country was lamentable indeed. If our debility was really such . . . our situation was truly desperate." There was "no cheaper mode of self-defense"; to abandon it "amounted to a declaration that we were unable to defend ourselves." It was not necessary to repeal the law entirely or to put it, "not modified," in full effect. Marshall suggested a middle ground by which "the law might be modified so as to diminish the estimated expense, without dismissing the troops already in actual service."[2]

Answering the favorite argument made by the opponents of the army, that no power can invade

---

[1] *Annals*, 6th Cong., 1st Sess., 247–50.   [2] *Ib.*, 252.

America, he asked: "What assurance have gentlemen that invasion is impracticable?" Who knows the real conditions in Europe? — the "effect of the late decisive victories of France? . . . It was by no means certain" that these had not resulted in the release of forces which she "may send across the Atlantic."

Why be precipitate? asked Marshall; by the opening of the next campaign in Europe we should have more information. Let us look the situation in the face: "We are, in fact, at war with France, though it is not declared in form"; commerce is suspended; naval battles are being fought; property is "captured and confiscated"; prisoners are taken and incarcerated. America is of "vast importance to France"; indeed, "the monopoly of our commerce in time of peace" is invaluable to both France and England "for the formation of a naval power."

The Republicans, he said, had "urged not only that the army is useless," but that we could not afford the expense of maintaining it. "Suppose this had been the language of '75!" exclaimed Marshall. "Suppose a gentleman had risen on the floor of Congress, to compare our revenues with our expenses— what would have been the result of the calculation?" It would have shown that we could not afford to strike for our independence! Yet we did strike and successfully. "If vast exertions were then made to acquire independence, will not the same exertions be now made to maintain it?"

The question was, "whether self-government and national liberty be worth the money which must be expended to preserve them?"[1] He exposed the sophistry of an expensive economy. It should never be forgotten that true economy did not content itself with inquiring into the mere saving of the present moment; it should take an enlarged view of the subject, and determine, on correct calculations, whether the consequence of a present saving might not be a much more considerable future expenditure.

Marshall admitted that the reduction of the army would certainly diminish the expense of the present year, but contended that the present saving would bear no proportion to the immense waste of blood, as well as treasure, which it might occasion.[2] "And consider," he exclaimed, "the effect the army already had produced on the mind and conduct of France. While America was humbly supplicating for peace, and that her complaints might be heard, France spurned her contemptuously and refused to enter on a discussion of differences, unless that discussion was preceded by a substantial surrender of the essential attributes of independence."

"America was at length goaded into resistance," asserted Marshall, "and resolved on the system of defense, of which the army now sought to be disbanded forms a part." What was the result? "Immediately the tone of France was changed, and she consented to treat us as an independent nation. Her depredations indeed did not cease; she continued still to bring war upon us; but although peace was not granted, the door to peace was opened."

If "a French army should be crossing the Atlantic

[1] *Annals*, 6th Cong., 1st Sess., 253–54.   [2] *Ib.*

to invade our territory," would anybody insist on disbanding our army? "Was it wise, then, to do so while such a probability existed?" In a few months we should know; and, if danger should disappear, "the army expires by the law which gave it being." Meantime the expense would be trifling.[1]

In a private letter Marshall states, with even more balance, his views of the conflicting questions of the expense involved in, and the necessity for, military equipment. He regrets that a loan is "absolutely unavoidable"; but "attention must be paid to our defenses": —

"The whole world is in arms and no rights are respected but those that [are] maintained by force. In such a state of things we dare not be totally unmindful of ourselves or totally neglectful of that military position to which, in spite of the prudence and pacific disposition of our government, we may be driven for the preservation of our liberty and national independence.

"Altho' we ought never to make a loan if it be avoidable, yet when forc'd to it much real consolation is to be deriv'd from the future resources of America. These resources, if we do not throw them away [by] dissolving the union, are invaluable. It is not to be doubted that in twenty years from this time the United States would be less burthen'd by a revenue of twenty millions than now by a revenue of ten. It is the plain & certain consequence of our increasing population & our increasing wealth. . . .

"The system of defence which has rendered this

[1] *Annals*, 6th Cong., 1st Sess., 254, 255.

measure necessary was not [only] essential to our character as an independent nation, but it has actually sav'd more money to the body of the people than has been expended & has very probably prevented either open war or such national degradation as would make us the objects of general contempt and injury.

"A bill to stop recruiting in the twelve additional regiments has been brought in and will pass without opposition. An attempt was made absolutely to disband them, but [it] was negativ'd. It has been so plainly prov'd to us that french aggression has been greatly increased, & that their contemptuous refusal even to treat with us as an independent nation has been entirely occasioned by a belief that we could not resist them; & it is so clear that their present willingness to treat is occasioned by perceiving our determination to defend ourselves, that it was thought unwise to change materially our system at the commencement of negotiation.

"In addition to this it had much weight, that we should know in a few months the facts of our negotiation & should then be able to judge whether the situation & temper of France rendered an invasion pro[bable]. Then would be the time to decide on diminishing [or] augmenting our military forces. A French 64 has it is said arrived in the west indies & three frigates expected." [1]

Although the debate dragged on and the army

[1] Marshall to Dabney, Jan. 20, 1800; MS. Colonel Charles Dabney of Virginia was commander of "Dabney's Legion" in the Revolution. He was an ardent Federalist and a close personal and political friend of Marshall.

was attacked and defended with brilliant ability, Marshall's argument remained the Gibraltar of the Administration, upon which all the assaults of the Republicans were centered unavailingly. For his army speech was never answered. Only once more during this debate did Marshall rise and then but briefly, to bring his common sense to bear upon the familiar contention that, if the country is in danger, its citizens will rise spontaneously to defend it. He said that it would be absurd to call men to arms, as had been done, and then "dismiss them before the service was performed ... merely because their zeal could be depended on" hereafter. He "hoped the national spirit would never yield to that false policy." [1]

The fourth important subject in which Marshall was a decisive influence was the National Bankruptcy Law, passed at this session of Congress. He was the second member of the committee that drafted this legislation. [2] For an entire month the committee worked on the bill and reported it on January 6, 1800. [3] After much debate, which is not given in the official reports, the bill passed the House on February 21 and the Senate March 28. [4]

While the "Annals" do not show it, we know from the testimony of the Speaker of the House that Marshall was the vital force that shaped this first National Bankruptcy Act. He was insistent that the law should not be too extensive in its provisions for the curing of bankruptcy, and it was he who

---

[1] *Annals*, 6th Cong., 1st Sess., 395–96.   [2] *Ib.*, 191.
[3] *Ib.*, 247.   [4] *Ib.*, 126; see law as passed, 1452–71.

secured the trial by jury as to the fact of bankruptcy.

"It [the Bankruptcy Law] is far from being such an one as I wished," writes Sedgwick. "The *acts* in curing bankruptcy are too restricted, and the trial of the question Bankrupt or not, by jury, will be found inconvenient, embarrassing & dilatory. The mischief was occasioned by Virginia Theory. It was the whim of General Marshall; with him a *sine qua non* of assent to the measure, & without him the bill must have been lost, for it passed the House by my casting vote."

"Besides the bankrupt bill, we have passed [only] one more of great importance," writes the Speaker of the House in a review of the work of the session.[1] Much of the Speaker's summary is devoted to Marshall. Sedgwick was greatly disappointed with the laws passed, with the exception of the Bankruptcy Bill "and one other."[2] "All the rest we have made here are, as to any permanently beneficial effects, hardly worth the parchment on which they are written. The reason of this feebleness is a real feebleness of character in the house." Sedg-

[1] Sedgwick to King, May 11, 1800; King, iii, 236.

[2] The act requiring the Secretary of the Treasury to lay before Congress at each session a report of financial conditions with his recommendations. (*Annals*, 6th Cong., 1st Sess., Appendix, 1523.) The Speaker thought this law important because it "will give splendor to the officer [Secretary of the Treasury] and respectability to the Executive Department of the Govt." (Sedgwick to King, *supra*.) Yet the session passed several very important laws, among them the act accepting the cession of the Western Reserve (*Annals*, 6th Cong., 1st Sess., Appendix, 1495–98) and the act prohibiting American citizens "or other persons residing within the United States" to engage in the slave trade between foreign countries (*ib.*, 1511–14.)

wick lays most of this at Marshall's door, and in
doing so, draws a vivid picture of Marshall the
man, as well as of Marshall the legislator: —

"Marshall was looked up to as the man whose
great and commanding genius was to enlighten &
direct the national councils. This was the general
sentiment, while some, and those of no inconsider-
able importance, calculating on his foolish declaration, relative to the alien & sedition laws, thought
him temporizing while others deemed him feeble.

"None had in my opinion justly appreciated his
character. As his character has stamped itself on the
measures of the present session, I am desirous of
letting you know how I view it.

"He is a man of a very affectionate disposition,
of great simplicity of manners and honest & honorable in all his conduct.

"He is attached to pleasures, with convivial
habits strongly fixed.

"He is indolent, therefore; and indisposed to take
part in the common business of the house.

"He has a strong attachment to popularity but
indisposed to sacrifice to it his integrity; hence it is
that he is disposed on all popular subjects to feel the
public pulse and hence results indecision and *an
expression* of doubt.

"Doubts suggested by him create in more feeble
minds those which are irremovable. He is disposed
. . . to express great respect for the sovereign people, and to quote their opinions as an evidence of
truth.

"The latter is of all things the most destructive

of personal independence & of that weight of character which a great man ought to possess.

"This gentleman, when aroused, has strong reasoning powers; they are almost unequalled. But before they are excited, he has frequently, nearly, destroyed any impression from them." [1]

Such was Marshall's work during his six months' service in Congress, the impression he made, and the estimate of him by his party friends. His "convivial habits, strongly fixed," his great good nature, his personal lovableness, were noted by his associates in the National House of Representatives quite as much as they had been observed and commented on by his fellow members in the Virginia Legislature and by his friends and neighbors in Richmond.

The public qualities which his work in Congress again revealed in brilliant light were his extraordinary independence of thought and action, his utter fearlessness, and his commanding mental power. But his personal character and daily manners applied a soothing ointment to any irritation which his official attitude and conduct on public questions created in the feelings of his associates.

So came the day of adjournment of Congress; and with it the next step which Fate had arranged for John Marshall.

[1] Sedgwick to King, May 11, 1800; King, iii, 237.

CHAPTER XII

CHIEF JUSTICE OF THE UNITED STATES

I consider General Marshall as more than a secretary — as a state conservator. (Oliver Wolcott.)

To Mr. Jefferson I have felt insuperable objections. The morals of the author of the letter to Mazzei cannot be pure. (Marshall.)

You have given an opinion in exact conformity with the wishes of your party. Come forward and defend it. (George Hay to Marshall.)

"THE P. requests Mr. McHenry's company for one minute," wrote President Adams to his Secretary of War on the morning of May 5, 1800.[1] The unsuspicious McHenry at once responded. The President mentioned an unimportant departmental matter; and then, suddenly flying into a rage, abused his astounded Cabinet adviser in "outrageous"[2] fashion and finally demanded his resignation.[3] The meek McHenry resigned. To the place thus made vacant, the harried President, without even consulting him, immediately appointed Marshall, who "as immediately declined."[4] Then Adams tendered the office to Dexter, who accepted.

And resign, too, demanded Adams of his Secretary

[1] Adams to McHenry, May 5, 1800; Steiner, 453.

[2] McHenry to John McHenry, May 20, 1800; Gibbs, ii, 348.

[3] According to McHenry, Adams's complaints were that the Secretary of War had opposed the sending of the second mission to France, had not appointed as captain a North Carolina elector who had voted for Adams, had " EULOGIZED GENERAL WASHINGTON . . . attempted to praise Hamilton," etc. (McHenry to John McHenry, May 20, 1800; Gibbs, ii, 348; and see Hamilton's "Public Conduct, etc., of John Adams"; Hamilton: *Works:* Lodge, vii, 347–49.)

[4] Gore to King, May 14, 1800; King, iii, 242–43; also Sedgwick to Hamilton, May 7, 1800; *Works:* Hamilton, vi, 437–38.

of State.[1] The doughty Pickering refused [2] — "I did not incline to accept this insidious favor," [3] he reported to Hamilton. Adams dismissed him.[4] Again the President turned to Marshall, who, deeply troubled, considered the offer. The Federalist Cabinet was broken to pieces, and a presidential election was at hand which would settle the fate of the first great political party in American history.

The campaign had already started. The political outlook was dark enough before the President's outburst; this shattering of his Cabinet was a wicked tongue of lightning from the threatening clouds which, after the flash, made them blacker still.[5]

Few Presidents have ever faced a more difficult party condition than did John Adams when, by a humiliating majority of only three votes, he was elected in 1796. He succeeded Washington; the ruling Federalist politicians looked to Hamilton as their party chieftain; even Adams's Cabinet, inherited from Washington, was personally unfriendly to the President and considered the imperious New York statesman as their supreme and real commander. "I had all the officers and half the crew always ready to throw me overboard," accurately declared Adams some years later.[6]

Adams's temperament was the opposite of Washington's, to which the Federalist leaders had so long

---

[1] Adams to Pickering, May 10, 1800; *Works: Adams,* ix, 53.
[2] Pickering to Adams, May 11, 1800; *ib.,* 54.
[3] Pickering to Hamilton, May 15, 1800; *Works:* Hamilton, vi, 443.
[4] Adams to Pickering, May 12, 1800; *Works:* Adams, ix, 55.
[5] Sedgwick to Hamilton, May 13, 1800; *Works:* Hamilton, vi, 442.
[6] Adams to Rush, March 4, 1809; *Old Family Letters,* 219.

been accustomed that the change exasperated them.[1] From the very beginning they bound his hands. The new President had cherished the purpose of calling to his aid the ablest of the Republicans, but found himself helpless. "When I first took the Chair," bitterly records Adams, "I was extremely desirous of availing myself of Mr. Madison's abilities, . . . and experience. But the violent Party Spirit of Hamilton's Friends, jealous of every man who possessed qualifications to eclipse him, prevented it. I could not do it without quarreling outright with my Ministers whom Washington's appointment had made my Masters." [2]

On the other hand, the high Federalist politicians, most of whom were Hamilton's adherents, felt that Adams entertained for their leader exactly the same sentiments which the President ascribed to them. "The jealousy which the P.[resident] has felt of H.[amilton] he now indulges toward P.[inckney], W.[olcott] & to'd *very many of their friends* who are suspected of having too much influence in the Community, & of not knowing how to appreciate his

---

[1] "There never was perhaps a greater contrast between two characters than between those of the present President & his predecessor. . . . The one [Washington] cool, considerate, & cautious, the other [Adams] headlong & kindled into flame by every spark that lights on his passions; the one ever scrutinizing into the public opinion and ready to follow where he could not lead it; the other insulting it by the most adverse sentiments & pursuits; W. a hero in the field, yet overweighing every danger in the Cabinet — A. without a single pretension to the character of a soldier, a perfect Quixotte as a statesman." (Madison to Jefferson, Feb., 1798; *Writings:* Hunt, vi, 310.) And [Adams] "always an honest man, often a wise one, but sometimes wholly out of his senses." (Madison to Jefferson, June 10, 1798; *ib.*, 325.)

[2] Adams to Rush, Aug. 23, 1805; *Old Family Letters*, 76.

[Adams's] merits. . . . The Consequence is that his ears are shut to his best real friends & open to Flatterers, to Time servers & even to some Jacobins." [1]

Adams, the scholar and statesman, but never the politician, was the last man to harmonize these differences. And Hamilton proved to be as inept as Adams.

After the President had dispatched the second mission to France, Hamilton's followers, including Adams's Cabinet, began intriguing in a furtive and vicious fashion to replace him with some other Federalist at the ensuing election. While, therefore, the President, as a personal matter, was more than justified in dismissing McHenry and Pickering (and Wolcott also [2]), he chose a fatal moment for the blow; as a matter of political strategy he should have struck sooner or not at all.

At this late hour the great party task and duty of the President was, by any and every honorable means, to unite all Federalist factions for the impending battle with the eager, powerful, and disciplined Republicans. Frank and full conference, tolerance, and conciliation, were the methods now required. These might not have succeeded, but at least they would not have irritated still more the ragged edges of party dissension. Not only did the exasperated President take the opposite course, but his manner and conduct were acid instead of ointment to the raw and angry wounds. [3]

---

[1] Cabot to King, April 26, 1799; King, iii, 8.

[2] Wolcott was as malicious as, but more cautious than, Pickering in his opposition to the President.

[3] "He [Adams] is liable to gusts of passion little short of frenzy. . . . I speak of what I have seen." (Bayard to Hamilton, Aug. 18, 1800;

This, then, was the state of the Federalist Party, the frame of mind of the President, and the distracted condition of the Cabinet, when Marshall was asked to become Secretary of State in the late spring of 1800. He was minded to refuse this high station as he had that of Secretary of War. "I incline to think Mr. Marshall will decline this office also," wrote McHenry to his brother.[1] If he accepted, he would be loyal to the President — his nature made anything else impossible. But he was the personal friend of all the Federalist leaders, who, in spite of his disapproval of the Alien and Sedition Laws and of his dissent from his party's plans in Congress, in spite, even, of his support of the President's detested second mission to France,[2] nevertheless trusted and liked him.

The President's selection of Marshall had been anticipated by the Republicans. "General Marshall . . . has been nominated to hold the station of Secretary of War," said the "Aurora," in an article heavy with abuse of Pickering. "This . . . however, is said to be but preparatory to General Marshall's appointment to succeed Mr. Pickering who is expected to resign." [3]

Works: Hamilton, vi, 457.) "He would speak in such a manner . . . as to persuade one that he was actually insane." (McHenry to John McHenry, May 20, 1800; Gibbs, ii, 347.) "Mr. Adams had conducted strangely and unaccountably." (Ames to Hamilton, Aug. 26, 1800; *Works:* Ames, i, 280.) These men were Adams's enemies; but the extreme irritability of the President at this time was noted by everybody. Undoubtedly this was increased by his distress over the illness of his wife.

[1] McHenry to John McHenry, May 20, 1800; Gibbs, ii, 347.

[2] See preceding chapter.

[3] *Aurora*, May 9, 1800; the *Aurora* had been attacking Pickering with all the animosity of partisanship.

Strangely enough the news of his elevation to the head of the Cabinet called forth only gentle criticism from the Republican press. "From what is said of Mr. Marshall," the "Aurora" thought that he was "as little likely to conciliate" France as Pickering. He "is well known to have been the disingenuous writer of all the X. Y. Z. Dispatches," which the Federalists had "confessed to be one of the best and most successful political *tricks* that was ever *played off.* . . . General Marshall's fineering and var[ni]shing capacity" was "well known," said the "Aurora." "General Marshall consequently has been nominated and appointed. . . . In genuine federal principles, General Marshall is as inflexible as Mr. Pickering; but in the negotiation with France, the General may not have imbibed so strong prejudices — and, having been one of the Envoys to that Republic, he may be supposed to be more conversant with some of the points in dispute, than Col. Pickering, and consequently to be preferred.

"We find him very well spoken of in the *reformed Gazettes of France*," continues the "Aurora," "which being now under guardianship [1] may be considered as speaking the language of the government — '*Le Bien Informé*,' after mentioning the motion Gen. M. made in announcing to Congress the death of Gen. Washington, adds — 'This is the gentleman who some time since came as Envoy from the *United States;* and who so virtuously and so spiritedly re-

[1] The French press had been quite as much under the control of the Revolutionary authorities as it was under that of Bonaparte as First Consul or even under his rule when he had become Napoleon I.

fused to fill the pockets of some of *our gentry* with Dutch inscriptions, and millions of livres.'" [1]

For nearly two weeks Marshall pondered over the President's offer. The prospect was not inviting. It was unlikely that he could hold the place longer than three quarters of a year, for Federalist defeat in the presidential election was more than probable; and it seemed certain that the head of the Cabinet would gather political cypress instead of laurel in this brief and troubled period. Marshall consulted his friends among the Federalist leaders; and, finally, accepted the proffered portfolio. Thereupon the "Aurora," quoting Pickering's statement that the office of Secretary of State "was never better filled than by General Marshall," hopes that "Gen. Marshall will take care of his *accounts*," which that Republican paper had falsely charged that Pickering had manipulated corruptly.[2]

Expressing the Republican temper the "Aurora" thus analyzes the new Federalist Cabinet: "The Secretary of the Treasury [Oliver Wolcott]" was "scarcely qualified to hold the second desk in a

[1] *Aurora*, May 27, 1800.

[2] *Ib.*, June 4, 1800; and June 17, 1800. The *Aurora* now made a systematic campaign against Pickering. It had "*substantial and damning facts*" which it threatened to publish if Adams did not subject Pickering to a "scrutiny" (*ib.*, May 21, 1800). Pickering was a "disgrace to his station" (*ib.*, May 23); several hundred thousand dollars were "unaccounted for" (*ib.*, June 4, and 17).

The attack of the Republican newspaper was entirely political, every charge and innuendo being wholly false. Adams's dismissal of his Secretary of State was not because of these charges, but on account of the Secretary's personal and political disloyalty. Adams also declared, afterwards, that Pickering lacked ability to handle the grave questions then pending and likely to arise. (*Cunningham Letters*, nos. xii, xiii, and xiv.) But that was merely a pretense.

Mercantile Counting-House"; the Attorney-General [Charles Lee] was "without talents"; the Secretary of the Navy [Benjamin Stoddert] was "a small Georgetown politician . . . cunning, gossiping, . . . of no . . . character or . . . principles"; the Secretary of War [Samuel Dexter] was no more fit for the place than "his MOTHER"; and Marshall, Secretary of State, was "more distinguished as a *rhetorician* and a *sophist* than as a *lawyer* and a *statesman* — sufficiently pliant to succeed in a corrupt court, too insincere to command respect, or confidence in a republic." However, said the "Aurora," Adams was "able to teach Mr. Marshall 'l'art diplomatique.'" [1]

Some of the Federalist leaders were not yet convinced, it appears, of Marshall's party orthodoxy. Pinckney reassures them. Writing from Virginia, he informs McHenry that "Marshall with reluctance accepts, but you may rely on his federalism, & be certain that he will not unite with Jefferson & the Jacobins." [2] Two months later even the Guy Fawkes of the Adams Cabinet declares himself more than satisfied: "If the gentlemen now in office [Marshall and Dexter] had declined," declares Wolcott, "rage, vexation & despair would probably have occasioned the most extravagant conduct [3] [on the part of the President]." After Marshall had been at the head of the Cabinet for four months, Cabot writes that "Mr. Wolcott thinks Mr. Marshall accepted the secretaryship from good motives, and

[1] *Aurora*, June 12, 1800.

[2] Pinckney to McHenry, June 10, 1800; Steiner, 460.

[3] Wolcott to Ames, Aug. 10, 1800; Gibbs, ii, 402.

with a view of preserving union, and that he and
Dexter, *by accepting*, have rendered the nation great
service; for, if they had refused, we should have had
— *Heaven alone knows whom!* He thinks, however,
as all must, that under the present chief they will be
disappointed in their hopes, and that if Jefferson is
President they will probably resign." [1]

In view of "the temper of his [Adams's] mind,"
which, asserts the unfaithful Wolcott, was "revolutionary, violent, and vindictive, . . . their [Marshall's
and Dexter's] acceptance of their offices is the best
evidence of their patriotism. . . . I consider Gen.
Marshall and Mr. Dexter as more than secretaries —
as state conservators — the value of whose services
ought to be estimated, not only by the good they do,
but by the mischief they have prevented. If I am
not mistaken, however, Gen. Marshall will find himself out of his proper element." [2]

No sooner was Marshall in the Secretary's chair
than the President hastened to his Massachusetts
home and his afflicted wife. Adams's part in directing the Government was done by correspondence. [3]
Marshall took up his duties with his characteristically serious, yet nonchalant, patience.

The National Capital had now been removed to
Washington; and here, during the long, hot summer

[1] Cabot to Gore, Sept. 30, 1800; Lodge: *Cabot*, 291.
[2] Wolcott to Ames, Aug. 10, 1800; Gibbs, ii, 401–02.
[3] Adams's correspondence shows that the shortest time for a letter
to go from Washington to Quincy, Massachusetts, was seven days,
although usually nine days were required. "Last night I received your
favor of the 4th." (Adams at Quincy to Dexter at Washington, Aug.
13, 1800; *Works:* Adams, ix, 76; and to Marshall, Aug. 14; *ib.*, 77;
and Aug. 26; *ib.*, 78; and Aug. 30; *ib.*, 80.)

of 1800, Marshall remained amidst the steaming swamps and forests where the "Federal City" was yet to be built.[1] Not till October did he leave his post, and then but briefly and on urgent private business.[2]

The work of the State Department during this period was not onerous. Marshall's chief occupation at the Capital, it would appear, was to act as the practical head of the Government; and even his political enemies admitted that he did this well. Jefferson's most partial biographer says' that "under the firm and steady lead [of Marshall and Dexter] . . . the Government soon acquired an order, system, and character which it never had before possessed."[3] Still, enough routine business came to his desk to give the new Secretary of State something to do in his own department.

Office-seeking, which had so annoyed Washington, still vexed Adams, although but few of these hornets' nests remained for him to deal with. "Your knowledge of persons, characters, and circumstances," wrote the President to Marshall concerning the applications for the office of United States Marshal for Maryland, "are so much better than mine, and my confidence in your judgment and

[1] Washington at this time was forest, swamp, and morass, with only an occasional and incommodious house. Georgetown contained the only comfortable residences. For a description of Washington at this period, see chap. I, vol. III, of this work.

[2] Marshall to Adams, Sept. 17, 1800; Adams MSS. This trip was to argue the case of Mayo vs. Bentley (4 Call, 528), before the Court of Appeals of Virginia. (See supra, chap. VI.)

[3] Randall, ii, 547. Although Randall includes Dexter, this tribute is really to Marshall who was the one dominating character in Adams's reconstructed Cabinet.

impartiality so entire, that I pray you . . . give the commission to him whom you may prefer." [1] Adams favored the son of Judge Chase; but, on the advice of Stoddert of Maryland, who was Secretary of the Navy, Marshall decided against him: "Mr. Chase is a young man who has not yet acquired the public confidence and to appoint him in preference to others who are generally known and esteem'd, might be deem'd a mere act of favor to his Father. Mr. Stoddert supposes it ineligible to accumulate, without superior pretensions, offices in the same family." [2]

Marshall generally trimmed his sails, however, to the winds of presidential preference. He undoubtedly influenced the Cabinet, in harmony with the President's wish, to concur in the pardon of Isaac Williams, convicted, under the Jay Treaty, of waging war on the high seas against Great Britain. Williams, though sailing under a French commission, was a pirate, and accumulated much wealth from his indiscriminate buccaneering. [3] But the President wrote Marshall that because of "the man's generosity to American prisoners," and "his present poverty and great distress," he desired to pardon Williams. [4]

Marshall informed the President that "repeated

[1] Adams to Marshall, July 30, 1800; *Works:* Adams, ix, 66; also Marshall to Adams, Aug. 1, Aug. 2, and July 29, 1800; Adams MSS.

[2] Marshall to Adams, July 29, 1800; Adams MSS. This cost Adams the support of young Chase's powerful father. (McHenry to John McHenry, Aug. 24, 1800; Gibbs, ii, 408.)

[3] McMaster, ii, 448.

[4] Adams to Marshall, Aug. 7, 1800; *Works:* Adams, ix, 72; and Marshall to Adams, Aug. 16, 1800; Adams MSS. Chief Justice

complaints are made to this department of the
depredations committed by the Spaniards on the
American commerce." [1] The French outrages were
continuing; indeed, our naval war with France had
been going on for months and Spain was aiding the
French. An American vessel, the Rebecca Henry,
had been captured by a French privateer. Two
Yankee sailors killed the French prize master in
recapturing the vessel, which was taken again by
another French sea rover and conveyed into a
Spanish port. The daring Americans were imprisoned and threatened with death. Marshall thought
"proper to remonstrate and to threaten retaliation
if the prisoners should be executed." [2]

The French ship Sandwich was captured by Captain Talbot, an American officer, in a Spanish port
which Spain had agreed to transfer to France.
Marshall considered this a violation of our treaty
with Spain. "I have therefore directed the Sandwich to be given up to the minister of his Catholic
Majesty," [3] he advised the President. The Spanish
Minister thanked Marshall for his "justice" and
"punctuality." [4]

But Talbot would not yield his prize; the United

Ellsworth presided at the trial of Williams, who was fairly convicted.
(Wharton: *State Trials*, 652–58.) The Republicans, however, charged
that it was another "political" conviction. It seems probable that
Adams's habitual inclination to grant the request of any one who was
his personal friend (Adams's closest friend, Governor Trumbull, had
urged the pardon) caused the President to wish to extend clemency
to Williams.

[1] Marshall to Adams, June 24, 1800; Adams MSS.
[2] Marshall to Adams, Aug. 2, 1800; *ib.*
[3] Marshall to Adams, July 26, 1800; *ib.*
[4] De Yrujo to Marshall, July 31, 1800; *ib.*

States Marshal declined to act. Marshall took "measures[1] which will," he reported to the President, "I presume occasion the delivery of this vessel, unless . . . the government has no right to interpose, so far as captors are interested." Talbot's attitude perplexed Marshall; for, wrote he, "if the Executive of the United States cannot restore a vessel captured by a national ship, in violation of the law of nations, . . . cause for war may be given by those who, of all others, are, perhaps, most apt to give it, and that department of the government, under whose orders they are plac'd will be unable to correct the mischief."[2]

· That picturesque adventurer, Bowles, whose plots and activities among the Indians had been a thorn to the National Government since the early part of Washington's Administration,[3] again became annoying. He was stirring up the Indians against the Spanish possessions in Florida and repeated his claim of having the support of Great Britain. The Spaniards eagerly seized on this as another pretext for annoying the American Government. Measures were taken to break Bowles's influence with the Indians and to suppress the adventurer's party.[4]

But, although the President was of the opinion that "the military forces . . . should join [the Span-

[1] Marshall does not state what these measures were.

[2] Marshall to Adams, Sept. 6, 1800; Adams MSS.

[3] *Am. St. Prs.*, v, *Indian Affairs*, i, 184, 187, 246. For picturesque description of Bowles and his claim of British support see Craig's report, *ib.*, 264; also, 305. Bowles was still active in 1801. (*Ib.*, 651.)

[4] Adams to Marshall, July 31, 1800; *Works: Adams*, ix, 67; Marshall to De Yrujo, Aug. 15, 1800; Adams MSS.

iards] in an expedition against Bowles," [1] Marshall
did not think "that the Spaniards require any military aid; nor," continues he, "do I suppose they
would be willing to receive it. . . . American troops
in either of the Floridas wou'd excite very much
their jealousy, especially when no specific requisition for them has been made, and when their own
force is entirely competent to the object." [2]

Liston, the British Minister, assured Marshall
that the British Government had no connection
with Bowles.[3] But, irritated by gossip and newspaper stories, he offensively demanded that Marshall "meet these insidious calumnies by a flat and
formal contradiction." [4] Without waiting for the
President's approval, Marshall quickly retorted: [5]
the "suspicions . . . were not entirely unsupported
by appearances." Newspaper "charges and sur-
mises . . . are always causes of infinite regret" to the
Government "and wou'd be prevented if the means
of prevention existed." But, said Marshall, the
British Government itself was not blameless in that
respect; "without going far back you may find examples in your own of the impunity with which a
foreign friendly nation [America] may be grossly libel'd." As to the people's hostility to Great Britain,
he tartly reminded the British Minister that "in
examining the practice of your officers employ'd in
the business of impressment, and of your courts
of Vice Admiralty, you will perceive at least some

[1] Adams to Marshall, Aug. 11, 1800; *Works:* Adams, ix, 73.
[2] Marshall to Adams, Aug. 12, 1800; Adams MSS.   [3] *Ib.*
[4] Liston to Marshall, Aug. 25, 1800; *ib.*
[5] Marshall to Adams, Sept. 6, 1800; *ib.*

of the causes, by which this temper may have been produc'd." [1]

Sweden and Denmark proposed to maintain, jointly with the United States, a naval force in the Mediterranean to protect their mutual commerce from the Barbary Powers. Marshall declined because of our treaties with those piratical Governments; and also because, "until . . . actual hostilities shall cease between" France and America, "to station American frigates in the Mediterranean would be a hazard, to which our infant Navy ought not perhaps to be exposed." [2]

Incidents amusing, pathetic, and absurd arose, such as announcements of the birth of princes, to which the Secretary of State must prepare answers; [3]

[1] Marshall to Liston, Sept. 6, 1800; Adams MSS.

[2] Marshall to J. Q. Adams, July 24, 1800; MS. It is incredible that the Barbary corsairs held the whole of Europe and America under tribute for many years. Although our part in this general submission to these brigands of the seas was shameful, America was the first to move against them. One of Jefferson's earliest official letters after becoming President was to the Bey of Tripoli, whom Jefferson addressed as "Great and Respected Friend . . . Illustrious & honored . . . whom God preserve." Jefferson's letter ends with this fervent invocation: "I pray God, very great and respected friend, to have you always in his holy keeping." (Jefferson to Bey of Tripoli, May 21, 1801; *Am. St. Prs., For. Rel.*, ii, 349.)

And see Jefferson to Bey of Tunis (Sept. 9, 1801; *ib.*, 358), in which the American President addresses this sea robber and holder of Americans in slavery, as "Great and Good Friend" and apologizes for delay in sending our tribute. In Jefferson's time, no notice was taken of such expressions, which were recognized as mere forms. But ninety years later the use of this exact expression, "Great and Good Friend," addressed to the Queen of the Hawaiian Islands, was urged on the stump and in the press against President Cleveland in his campaign for reelection. For an accurate and entertaining account of our relations with the Barbary pirates see Allen: *Our Navy and the Barbary Corsairs.*

[3] Marshall to Adams, Aug. 1, 1800; Adams MSS.

the stranding of foreign sailors on our shores, whose
plight we must relieve; [1] the purchase of jewels for
the Bey of Tunis, who was clamoring for the glitter-
ing bribes. [2]

In such fashion went on the daily routine work
of his department while Marshall was at the head of
the Cabinet.

The only grave matters requiring Marshall's attention were the perplexing tangle of the British
debts and the associated questions of British impressment of American seamen and interference
with American commerce.

Under the sixth article of the Jay Treaty a joint
commission of five members had been appointed
to determine the debts due British subjects. Two
of the Commissioners were British, two Americans,
and the fifth chosen by lot. Chance made this deciding member British also. This Commission, sitting at Philadelphia, failed to agree. The treaty
provided, as we have seen, that the United States
should pay such British debts existing at the outbreak of the Revolutionary War as the creditors
were not able to collect because of the sequestration laws and other "legal impediments," or because, during the operation of these statutes, the
debtor had become insolvent.

Having a majority of the Commission, the British
members made rules which threw the doors wide

---

[1] Marshall to Adams, June 24, 1800; Adams MSS.

[2] Marshall to Adams, Aug. 16, 1800; July 24, 1800; *Ib.* and
see Adams to Marshall, Aug. 2, and to Secretary of State, May 25;
King, iii, 243-46. The jewels were part of our tribute to the Barbary
pirates.

open.[1] "They go the length to make the United States at once the debtor for all the *outstanding* debts of British subjects contracted before the peace of 1783. . . . The amount of the claims presented exceeds nineteen millions of dollars."[2] And this was done by the British representatives with overbearing personal insolence. Aside from the injustice of the British contention, this bullying of the American members[3] made the work of the Commission all but impossible.

A righteous popular indignation arose. "The construction put upon the Treaty by the British Commissioners . . . will never be submitted to by this country. . . . The [British] demand . . . excites much ill blood."[4] The American Commissioners refused to attend further sittings of the Board. Thereupon, the British Government withdrew its members of the associate Commission sitting in London, under the seventh article of the treaty, to pass upon claims of American citizens for property destroyed by the British.

The situation was acute. It was made still sharper by the appointment of our second mission to France. For, just as France had regarded Jay's mission and treaty as offensive, so now Great Britain looked upon

[1] King to Secretary of State, Oct. 11, 1799; note to Grenville; King, iii, 129.

[2] Secretary of State to King, Feb. 5, 1799; *Am. St. Prs., For. Rel.*, ii, 383. Hildreth says that the total amount of claims filed was twenty-four million dollars. (Hildreth, v, 331; and see Marshall to King, *infra*.)

[3] Secretary of State to King, Sept. 4, 1799; *Am. St. Prs., For. Rel.*, ii, 383.

[4] Troup to King, Sept. 2, 1799; King, iii, 91.

the Ellsworth mission as unfriendly. As a way out of the difficulty, the American Government insisted upon articles explanatory of the sixth article of the Jay Treaty which would define exactly what claims the Commission should consider.[1] The British Government refused and suggested a new commission.[2]

This was the condition that faced Marshall when he became Secretary of State. War with Great Britain was in the air from other causes and the rupture of the two Commissions made the atmosphere thicker. On June 24, 1800, Marshall wrote the President that we ought "still to press an amicable explanation of the sixth article of our treaty"; perhaps during the summer or autumn the British Cabinet might feel "more favorable to an accommodation." But he "cannot help fearing that . . . the British Ministry" intends "to put such a construction on the law of nations . . . as to throw into their hands some equivalent to the probable claims of British creditors on the United States."[3]

Lord Grenville then suggested to Rufus King, our Minister at London, that the United States pay a gross sum to Great Britain in settlement of the whole controversy.[4] Marshall wondered whether this simple way out of the tangle could "afford just cause of discontent to France?"[5] Adams thought not. "We surely have a right to pay our honest debts in the

[1] Secretary of State to King, Dec. 31, 1799; *Am. St. Prs., For. Rel.,* ii, 384–85.

[2] King to Secretary of State, April 7, 1800; King, iii, 215.

[3] Marshall to Adams, June 24, 1800; Adams MSS.

[4] King to Secretary of State, April 22, 1800; King, iii, 222.

[5] Marshall to Adams, July 21, 1800; Adams MSS.

manner least inconvenient to ourselves and no foreign power has anything to do with it," said the President. Adams, however, foresaw many other difficulties;[1] but Marshall concluded that, on the whole, a gross payment was the best solution in case the British Government could not be induced to agree to explanatory articles.[2]

Thereupon Marshall wrote his memorable instructions to our Minister to Great Britain. In this, as in his letters to Talleyrand two years earlier, and in the notable one on British impressment, contraband, and freedom of the seas,[3] he shows himself an American in a manner unusual at that period. Not the least partiality does he display for any foreign country; he treats them with exact equality and demands from all that they shall deal with the American Government as a *Nation*, independent of and unconnected with any of them.[4]

The United States, writes Marshall, "can never submit to" the resolutions adopted by the British Commissioners, which put "new and injurious burthens" upon the United States "unwarranted by compact," and to which, if they had been stated in the treaty, "this Government never could and never would have assented." Unless the two Governments can "forget the past," arbitration cannot be successful; it is idle to discuss who committed the first fault, he says, when two nations are trying to adjust their differences.

[1] Adams to Marshall, Aug. 1, 1800; *Works:* Adams, ix, 68–69.
[2] Marshall to Adams, Aug. 12, 1800; Adams MSS.
[3] *Infra,* 507 *et seq.*
[4] *Am. St. Prs., For. Rel.,* ii, 386.

The American Commissioners, declares Marshall, withdrew from the Board because the hostile majority established rules under which "a vast mass of cases never submitted to their consideration" could and would be brought in against American citizens. The proceedings of the British Commissioners were not only "totally unauthorized," but "were conducted in terms and in a spirit only calculated to destroy all harmony between the two nations."

The cases which the Board could consider were distinctly and specifically stated in the fifth article of the treaty. Let the two Governments agree to an explanation, instead of leaving the matter to wrangling commissioners. But, if Minister King finds that the British Government will not agree to explanatory articles, he is authorized to substitute "a gross sum in full compensation of all claims made or to be made on this Government."

It would, of course, be difficult to agree upon the amount. "The extravagant claims which the British creditors have been induced to file," among which "are cases . . . so notoriously unfounded that no commissioners retaining the slightest degree of self-respect can establish them; . . . others where the debt has been fairly and voluntarily compromised by agreement between creditor and debtor"; others "where the money has been paid in specie, and receipts in full given"; and still others even worse, all composing that "enormous mass of imagined debt," will, says Marshall, make it hard to agree on a stated amount.[1]

[1] *Am. St. Prs., For. Rel.*, ii, 387.

The British creditors, he asserts, had been and then were proceeding to collect their debts through the American courts, and "had they not been seduced into the opinion that the trouble and expense inseparable from the pursuit of the old debts, might be avoided by one general resort to the United States, it is believed they would have been still more rapidly proceeding in the collection of the very claims, so far as they are just, which have been filed with the commissioners. They meet with no objection, either of law or fact, which are not common to every description of creditors, in every country. . . . Our judges are even liberal in their construction of the 4th article of the treaty of peace" and have shown "no sort of partiality for the debtors."

Marshall urges this point with great vigor, and concludes that, if a gross amount can be agreed upon, the American Minister must see to it, of course, that this sum is made as small as possible, not "to exceed one million sterling" in any event.[1] In a private letter, Marshall informs King that "the best opinion here is that not more than two million Dollars could justly be chargeable to the United States under the treaty." [2]

Adams was elated by Marshall's letter. "I know not," he wrote, "how the subject could have been better digested." [3]

---

[1] *Am. St. Prs., For. Rel.*, ii, 387.

[2] Marshall to Adams, Sept. 9, 1800; Adams MSS.

[3] Adams to Marshall, Sept. 18, 1800; *Works: Adams*, ix, 84. After Jefferson became President and Madison Secretary of State, King settled the controversy according to these instructions of Marshall. But the Republicans, being then in power, claimed the credit.

Almost from the exchange of ratifications of the Jay compact, impressment of American seamen by the British and their taking from American ships, as contraband, merchandise which, under the treaty, was exempt from seizure, had injured American commerce and increasingly irritated the American people.[1] The brutality with which the British practiced these depredations had heated still more American resentment, already greatly inflamed.[2]

In June, 1799, Marshall's predecessor had instructed King "to persevere . . . in denying the right of British Men of War to take from our Ships of War any men whatever, and from our merchant vessels any Americans, or foreigners, or even Englishmen."[3] But the British had disregarded the American Minister's protests and these had now been entirely silenced by the break-up of the British Debts Commissions.

Nevertheless, Marshall directed our Minister at

---

[1] Secretary of State to King, Oct. 26, 1796; King, ii, 102.

[2] For a comprehensive though prejudiced review of British policy during this period see Tench Coxe: *Examination of the Conduct of Great Britain Respecting Neutrals.* Coxe declares that the purpose and policy of Great Britain were to "monopolize the commerce of the world. . . . She denies the lawfulness of supplying and buying from her enemies, and, in the face of the world, enacts statutes to enable her own subjects to do these things. (*Ib.*, 62.) . . . She now aims at the Monarchy of the ocean. . . . Her trade is war. . . . The spoils of neutrals fill her warehouses, while she incarcerates their bodies in her floating castles. She seizes their persons and property as the rich fruit of bloodless victories over her unarmed friends." (*Ib.*, 72.)

This was the accepted American view at the time Marshall wrote his protest; and it continued to be such until the War of 1812. Coxe's book is packed closely with citations and statistics sustaining his position.

[3] Secretary of State to King, June 14, 1799; King, iii, 47; and see King to Secretary of State, July 15, 1799; *ib.*, 58–59; and King to Grenville, Oct. 7, 1799; *ib.*, 115–21.

the Court of St. James to renew the negotiations. In a state paper which, in ability, dignity, and eloquence, suggests his famous Jonathan Robins speech and equals his memorial to Talleyrand, he examines the vital subjects of impressment, contraband, and the rights of neutral commerce.

It was a difficult situation that confronted the American Secretary of State. He had to meet and if possible modify the offensive, determined, and wholly unjust British position by a statement of principles based on fundamental right; and by an assertion of America's just place in the world.

The spirit of Marshall's protest to the British Government is that America is an independent nation, a separate and distinct political entity, with equal rights, power, and dignity with all other nations [1] — a conception then in its weak infancy even in America and, apparently, not entertained by Great Britain or France. These Powers seemed to regard America, not as a sovereign nation, but as a sort of subordinate state, to be used as they saw fit for their plans and purposes.

But, asserts Marshall, "the United States do not hold themselves in any degree responsible to France or to Britain for their negotiations with the one or the other of these Powers, but are ready to make amicable and reasonable explanations with either. ... An exact neutrality ... between the belligerent Powers" is the "object of the American Government. ... Separated far from Europe, we mean not to mingle in their quarrels. ... We have avoided

[1] This complete paper is in *Am. St. Prs., For. Rel.*, ii, 486–90.

and we shall continue to avoid any . . . connections not compatible with the neutrality we profess. . . . The aggressions, sometimes of one and sometimes of another belligerent power have forced us to contemplate and prepare for war as a probable event. . . . But this is a situation of necessity, not of choice." France had compelled us to resort to force against her, but in doing so "our preference for peace was manifest"; and now that France makes friendly advances, "America meets those overtures, and, in doing so, only adheres to her pacific system."

Marshall lays down those principles of international conduct which have become the traditional American policy. Reviewing our course during the war between France and Great Britain, he says: "When the combination against France was most formidable, when, if ever, it was dangerous to acknowledge her new Government" and maintain friendly relations with the new Republic, "the American Government openly declared its determination to adhere to that state of impartial neutrality which it has ever since sought to maintain; nor did the clouds which, for a time, lowered over the fortunes of the [French] Republic, in any degree shake this resolution. When victory changed sides and France, in turn, threatened those who did not arrange themselves under her banners, America, pursuing with undeviating step the same steady course," nevertheless made a treaty with Great Britain; "nor could either threats or artifices prevent its ratification."

"At no period of the war," Marshall reminds the British Government, "has France occupied such

elevated ground as at the very point of time when
America armed to resist her: triumphant and victorious everywhere, she had dictated a peace to her
enemies on the continent and had refused one to
Britain." On the other hand, "in the reverse of her
fortune, when defeated both in Italy and on the
Rhine, in danger of losing Holland, before the victory of Massena had changed the face of the last
campaign, and before Russia had receded from the
coalition against her, the present negotiation [be-
tween America and France] was resolved on. During this pendency," says Marshall, "the state of the
war has changed, but the conduct of the United
States" has not.

"Our terms remain the same: we still pursue peace.
We still embrace it, if it can be obtained without
violating our national honor or our national faith;
but we will reject without hesitation all propositions
which may compromit the one or the other."

All this, he declares, "shows how steadily it [the
American Government] pursues its system [Neu-
trality and peace] without regarding the dangers,
from the one side or the other, to which the pursuit may be exposed. The present negotiation with
France is a part of this system, and ought, therefore,
to excite in Great Britain no feelings unfriendly to
the United States."

Marshall then takes up the British position as to
contraband of war. He declares that even under the
law of nations, "neutrals have a right to carry on
their usual commerce; belligerents have a right to
prevent them from supplying the enemy with instru-

ments of war." But the eighteenth article of the treaty itself covered the matter in express terms, and specifically enumerated certain things as contraband and also "generally whatever may serve *directly* to the equipment of vessels." Yet Great Britain had ruthlessly seized and condemned American vessels regardless of the treaty — had actually plundered American ships of farming material upon the pretense that these articles might, by some remote possibility, be used "to equip vessels." The British contention erased the word "*directly*"[1] from the express terms of the treaty. "This construction we deem alike unfriendly and unjust," he says. Such "garbling a compact ... is to substitute another agreement for that of the parties. ..."

"It would swell the list of contraband to" suit British convenience, contrary to "the laws and usages of nations. ... It would prohibit ... articles ... necessary for the ordinary occupations of men in peace" and require "a surrender, on the part of the United States, of rights in themselves unquestionable, and the exercise of which is essential to themselves. ... A construction so absurd and so odious ought to be rejected."[2]

Articles, "even if contraband," should not be confiscated, insists Marshall, except when "they are attempted to be carried to an enemy." For instance,

---

[1] At one place the word "distinctly" is used and at another the word "directly," in the *American State Papers* (ii, 487 and 488). The word "directly" is correct, the word "distinctly" being a misprint. This is an example of the inaccuracies of these official volumes, which must be used with careful scrutiny.

[2] *Am. St. Prs., For. Rel.*, ii, 488.

"vessels bound to New Orleans and laden with cargoes proper for the ordinary use of the citizens of the United States who inhabit the Mississippi and its waters ... cannot be justly said to carry those cargoes to an enemy. ... Such a cargo is not a just object of confiscation, although a part of it should also be deemed proper for the equipment of vessels, because it is not attempted to be carried to an enemy."

On the subject of blockade, Marshall questions whether "the right to confiscate vessels bound to a blockaded port ... can be applied to a place not completely invested by land as well as by sea." But waiving "this departure from principle," the American complaint "is that ports not effectually blockaded by a force capable of completely investing them, have yet been declared in a state of blockage, and vessels attempting to enter therein have been seized, and, on that account, confiscated." This "vexation ... may be carried, if not resisted, to a very injurious extent."

If neutrals submit to it, "then every port of the belligerent powers may at all times be declared in that [blockaded] state and the commerce of neutrals be thereby subjected to universal capture." But if complete blockage be required, then "the capacity to blockade will be limited by the naval force of the belligerent, and, of consequence, the mischief to neutral commerce can not be very extensive. It is therefore of the last importance to neutrals that this principle be maintained unimpaired."

The British Courts of Vice-Admiralty, says

Marshall, render "unjust decisions" in the case of captures. "The temptation which a rich neutral commerce offers to unprincipled avarice, at all times powerful, becomes irresistible unless strong and efficient restraints be imposed by the Government which employs it." If such restraints are not imposed, the belligerent Government thereby "causes the injuries it tolerates." Just this, says Marshall, is the case with the British Government.

For "the most effectual restraint is an impartial judiciary, which will decide impartially between the parties and uniformly condemn the captor in costs and damages, where the seizure has been made without probable cause." If this is not done, "indiscriminate captures will be made." If an "unjust judge" condemns the captured vessel, the profit is the captor's; if the vessel is discharged, the loss falls upon the owner. Yet this has been and still is the indefensible course pursued against American commerce.

"The British Courts of Vice Admiralty, whatever may be the case, seldom acquit and when they do, costs and damages for detention are never awarded." Marshall demands that the British Government shall "infuse a spirit of justice and respect for law into the Courts of Vice Admiralty" — this alone, he insists, can check "their excessive and irritating vexations. . . . This spirit can only be infused by uniformly discountenancing and punishing those who tarnish alike the seat of justice and the honor of their country, by converting themselves from judges into mere instruments of plunder." And Marshall broadly intimates that these courts are corrupt.

As to British impressment, "no right has been asserted to impress" Americans; "yet they are impressed, they are dragged on board British ships of war with the evidence of citizenship in their hands, and forced by violence there to serve until conclusive testimonials of their birth can be obtained." He demands that the British Government stop this lawless, violent practice "by punishing and frowning upon those who perpetrate it. The mere release of the injured, after a long course of service and of suffering, is no compensation for the past and no security for the future. . . . The United States therefore require positively that their seamen . . . be exempt from impressments." Even "alien seamen, not British subjects, engaged in our merchant service ought to be equally exempt with citizens from impressments. . . . Britain has no pretext of right to their persons or to their service. To tear them, then, from our possession is, at the same time, an insult and an injury. It is an act of violence for which there exists no palliative."

Suppose, says Marshall, that America should do the things Great Britain was doing? "Should we impress from the merchant service of Britain not only Americans but foreigners, and even British subjects, how long would such a course of injury, unredressed, be permitted to pass unrevenged? How long would the [British] Government be content with unsuccessful remonstrance and unavailing memorials?"

Or, were America to retaliate by inducing British sailors to enter the more attractive American

service, as America might lawfully do, how would
Great Britain look upon it? Therefore, concludes
Marshall, "is it not more advisable to desist from,
and to take effectual measures to prevent an acknowledged wrong, than be perseverant in that
wrong, to excite against themselves the well founded
resentment of America, and to force our Government into measures which may possibly terminate
in an open rupture?" [1]

Thus boldly and in justifiably harsh language
did Marshall assert American rights as against
British violation of them, just as he had similarly upheld those rights against French assault. Although
France desisted from her lawless practices after
Adams's second mission negotiated with Bonaparte
an adjustment of our grievances,[2] Great Britain
persisted in the ruthless conduct which Marshall and
his successors denounced until, twelve years later,
America was driven to armed resistance.

Working patiently in his stuffy office amidst the
Potomac miasma and mosquitoes during the swel-
tering months, it was Marshall's unhappy fate to
behold the beginning of the break-up of that great
party which had built our ship of state, set it upon
the waters, navigated it for twelve tempestuous
years, through the storms of domestic trouble and
foreign danger.[3] He was powerless to stay the

---

[1] *Am. St. Prs., For. Rel.*, ii, 490.   [2] *Infra*, 524.

[3] While political parties, as such, did not appear until the close of
Washington's first Administration, the Federalist Party of 1800 was
made up, for the most part, of substantially the same men and interests that forced the adoption of the Constitution and originated all
the policies and measures, foreign and domestic, of the first three
Administrations.

Federalist disintegration. Even in his home district Marshall's personal strength had turned to water, and at the election of his successor in Congress, his party was utterly crushed. "Mr. Mayo, who was proposed to succeed Gen. Marshall, lost his election by an immense majority," writes the alert Wolcott; "was grossly insulted in public by a brother-in-law of the late Senator Taylor, and was afterwards wounded by him in a duel. This is a specimen of the political influence of the Secretary of State in his own district."[1]

Marshall himself was extremely depressed. "Ill news from Virginia," he writes Otis. "To succeed me has been elected by an immense majority one of the most decided democrats[2] in the union." Upon the political horizon Marshall beheld only storm and blackness: "In Jersey, too, I am afraid things are going badly. In Maryland the full force of parties will be tried but the issue I should feel confident would be right if there did not appear to be a current setting against us of which the force is incalculable. There is a tide in the affairs of nations, of parties, and of individuals. I fear that of real Americanism is on the ebb."[3] Never, perhaps, in the history of political parties was calm, dispassionate judgment and steady courage needed more than they were now required to avert Federalist defeat.

Yet in all the States revenge, apprehension, and

[1] Wolcott to Ames, Aug. 10, 1800; Gibbs, ii, 404.

[2] During this period, the word "Democrat" was used by the Federalists as a term of extreme condemnation, even more opprobrious than the word "Jacobin." For many years most Republicans hotly resented the appellation of "Democrat."

[3] Marshall to Otis, Aug. 5, 1800; Otis MSS.

despair blinded the eyes and deranged the councils of the supreme Federalist managers.[1] The voters in the party were confused and angered by the dissensions of those to whom they looked for guidance.[2] The leaders agreed that Jefferson was the bearer of the flag of "anarchy and sedition," captain of the hordes of "lawlessness," and, above all, the remorseless antagonist of Nationalism. What should be done "by the friends of order and true liberty to keep the [presidential] chair from being occupied by an enemy [Jefferson] of both?" was the question which the distressed Federalist politicians asked one another.[3]

In May, Hamilton thought that "to support *Adams* and *Pinckney* equally is the only thing that can save us from the fangs of *Jefferson.*" [4] Yet, six days later, Hamilton wrote that "*most* of the most *influential men* of that [Federalist] party consider him [Adams] as a very *unfit* and *incapable* character. ... My mind is made up. I will never more be responsible for him by any direct support, even though the consequence should be the election of *Jefferson.* ... If the cause is to be sacrificed to a weak and perverse man, I withdraw from the party." [5]

As the summer wore on, so acrimonious grew the feeling of Hamilton's supporters toward the Presi-

[1] For a vivid review of factional causes of the Federalists' decline see Sedgwick to King, Sept. 26, 1800; King, iii, 307–10; and Ames to King, Sept. 24, 1800; *ib.*, 304.

[2] "The Public mind is puzzled and fretted. People don't know what to think of measures or men; they are mad because they are in the dark." (Goodrich to Wolcott, July 28, 1800; Gibbs, ii, 394.)

[3] Ames to Hamilton, Aug. 26, 1800; *Works:* Ames, i, 280.

[4] Hamilton to Sedgwick, May 4, 1800; *Works:* Lodge, x, 371.

[5] Same to same, May 10, 1800; *ib.*, 375.

dent that they seriously considered whether his
reëlection would not be as great a misfortune as
the success of the Republican Party.[1] Although
the Federalist caucus had agreed to support Adams
and Pinckney equally as the party's candidates for
President,[2] yet the Hamiltonian faction decided to
place Pinckney in the presidential chair.[3]

But, blindly as they groped, their failing vision was
still clear enough to discern that the small local leaders in New England, which was the strong Federalist
section of the country, were for Adams; [4] and that
everywhere the party's rank and file, though irri-

[1] "In our untoward situation we should do as well with Jefferson
for President and Mr. Pinckney Vice President as with anything we
can now expect. Such an issue of the election, if fairly produced, is
the only one that will keep the Federal Party together." (Cabot to
Wolcott, Oct. 5, 1800; Lodge: *Cabot*, 295.)

"If Mr. Adams should be reëlected, I fear our constitution would
be more injured by his unruly passions, antipathies, & jealousy, than
by the whimsies of Jefferson." (Carroll to McHenry, Nov. 4, 1800;
Steiner, 473.)

"He [Adams] has palsied the sinews of the party, and " another four
years of his administration "would give it its death wound." (Bayard to Hamilton, Aug. 18, 1800; *Works:* Hamilton, vi, 457.)

[2] McHenry to John McHenry, May 20, 1800; Gibbs, ii, 347. According to the caucus custom, two candidates were named for President, one of whom was understood really to stand for Vice-President,
the Constitution at that time not providing for a separate vote for the
latter officer.

[3] "You may rely upon my co-operation in every reasonable measure
for effecting the election of General Pinckney." (Wolcott to Hamilton, July 7, 1800; *Works:* Hamilton, vi, 447–48.)

"The affairs of this government will not only be ruined but . . . the
disgrace will attach to the federal party if they permit the re-election
of Mr. Adams." (*Ib.*) "In Massachusetts almost all the leaders of the
first class are dissatisfied with Mr. Adams and enter heartily into the
policy of supporting General Pinckney." (Hamilton to Bayard, Aug.
6, *ib.*, 452 (also in *Works:* Lodge, x, 384); and see Jefferson to Butler,
Aug. 11, 1800; *Works:* Ford, ix, 138.)

[4] Hamilton to Carroll, July 1, 1800; *Works:* Lodge, x, 378; and see
Hamilton to Bayard, Aug. 6, 1800; *ib.*, 384.

tated and perplexed, were standing by the President.
His real statesmanship had made an impression on
the masses of his party: Dayton declared that Adams
was "the most popular man in the United States." [1]
Knox assured the President that "the great body
of the federal sentiment confide implicitly in your
knowledge and virtue. . . . They will . . . cling to
you in preference to all others." [2]

— Some urged Adams to overthrow the Hamiltonian
cabal which opposed him. "Cunning half Jacobins
assure the President that he can combine the virtuous and moderate men of both parties, and that all
our difficulties are owing to an oligarchy which it is
in his power to crush, and thus acquire the general
support of the nation," [3] testifies Wolcott.

The President heeded this mad counsel. Hamilton
and his crew were not the party, said Adams; they
were only a faction and a "British faction" at that.[4]

[1] Sedgwick to Hamilton, May 7, 1800, quoting "our friend D.[ay-
ton] who is not perfectly right" (*Works:* Hamilton, vi, 437; and see
Cabot to Hamilton, Aug. 10, 1800; *ib.*, 454); also Cabot to Wolcott,
July 20, 1800; Lodge: *Cabot*, 282.)

[2] Knox to Adams, March 5, 1799; *Works:* Adams, viii, 626–27.
Knox had held higher rank than Hamilton in the Revolutionary War
and Adams had tried to place him above Hamilton in the provisional
army in 1798. But upon the demand of Washington Knox was given
an inferior rank and indignantly declined to serve. (Hildreth, v, 242–
44. And see Washington to Knox, July 16, 1798; *Writings:* Ford, xiv,
43–46.) Thereafter he became the enemy of Hamilton and the ardent
supporter of Adams.

[3] Wolcott to Ames, Dec. 29, 1799; Gibbs, ii, 315.

[4] Hamilton to Adams, Aug. 1, 1800; *Works:* Lodge, x, 382, and see
390; Ames to Wolcott, Aug. 3, 1800; Gibbs, ii, 396; Wolcott to Ames,
Dec. 29, 1799; *ib.*, 315.

The public discussion of Adams's charge of a "British faction"
against his party enemies began with the publication of a foolish letter
he had written to Coxe, in May of 1792, insinuating that Pinckney's
appointment to the British Court had been secured by "much British

He would "rip it up." [1] The justly angered President,
it appears, thought of founding a new party, an
American Party, "a constitutionalist party." [2] It
was said that the astute Jefferson so played upon
him that Adams came to think the engaging but
crafty Virginian aspired only to be and to be known
as the first lieutenant of the Massachusetts statesman. [3] Adams concluded that he could make up any
Federalist loss at the polls by courting the Republicans, whose "friendship," wrote Ames, "he seeks for
himself." [4]

But the Republicans had almost recovered from
the effect of the X. Y. Z. disclosures. "The *rabies
canina* of Jacobinism has gradually spread . . . from
the cities, where it was confined to docks and mob,
to the country," [5] was the tidings of woe that Ames
sent to Gore. The Hamiltonian leaders despaired
of the continuance of the Government and saw "a

influence." (Adams to Coxe, May, 1792; Gibbs, ii, 424.) The President gave vitality to the gossip by talking of the Hamiltonian Federalists as a "British faction." He should have charged it publicly and
formally or else kept perfectly silent. He did neither, and thus
only enraged his foe within the party without getting the advantage
of an open and aggressive attack. (See Steiner, footnote 3, to 468.)

[1] Phelps to Wolcott, July 15, 1800; relating Noah Webster's en-
dorsement of Adams's opinions; Gibbs, ii, 380.

[2] Ames to Wolcott, Aug. 3, 1800; Gibbs, ii, 396.

[3] In the summer of 1800, Jefferson dined with the President. Adams
was utterly unreserved to the Republican leader. After dinner, General Henry Lee, also a guest, remonstrated with the President, who
responded that "he believed Mr. Jefferson never had the ambition,
or desire to aspire to any higher distinction than to be his [Adams's]
first Lieutenant." (Lee to Pickering, 1802; Pickering MSS., Mass.
Hist. Soc.; also partly quoted in Gibbs, ii, 366; and see Ames to Wolcott, June 12, 1800; Gibbs, ii, 368; and to King, Sept. 24, 1800; King,
iii, 304.)

[4] Ames to Pickering, Nov. 5, 1799; *Works:* Ames, i, 261.

[5] Ames to Gore, Nov. 10, 1799; *ib.*, 265.

convulsion of revolution" as the result of "excessive democracy." [1] The union of all Federalist votes was "the only measure by which the government can be preserved." [2] But Federalist union! As well ask shattered glass to remould itself!

The harmonious and disciplined Republicans were superbly led. Jefferson combined their battle-cries of the last two years into one mighty appeal — simple, affirmative, popular. Peace, economy, "freedom of the press, freedom of religion, trial by jury, . . . no standing armies," were the issues he announced, together with the supreme issue of all, States' Rights. Upon this latter doctrine Jefferson planted all the Republican guns and directed their fire on "centralization" which, said he, would "monarchise" our Government and make it "the most corrupt on earth," with increased "stock-jobbing, speculating, plundering, office-holding, and office-hunting." [3]

The Federalists could reply but feebly. The tax-gatherer's fingers were in every man's pockets; and Adams had pardoned the men who had resisted the collectors of tribute. The increased revenue was required for the army and navy, which, thought the people, were worse than needless [4] if there were to be no war and the President's second mission made hostilities improbable (they had forgotten that this very preparation had been the principal means of

[1] Ames to Gore, Nov. 10, 1799; Ames, i, 268.

[2] Cabot to Wolcott, June 14, 1800; Lodge: *Cabot*, 274.

[3] Jefferson to Granger, Aug. 13, 1800; *Works:* Ford, ix, 138–41; and see Jefferson to Gerry, January 26, 1799; *ib.*, 17–19.

[4] "The Jacobins and the half federalists are ripe for attacking the permanent force, as expensive, and unnecessary, and dangerous to liberty." (Ames to Pickering, Oct. 19, 1799; *Works:* Ames, i, 258.)

changing the haughty attitude of France). The Alien
and Sedition Laws had infuriated the "foreign" voters[1] and alarmed thousands of American-born citizens. Even that potent bribe of free institutions, the
expectation of office, could no longer be employed
effectively with the party workers, who, testifies
Ebenezer Huntington, were going over "to Jefferson
in hopes to partake of the loaves and fishes, which
are to be distributed by the new President." [2]

The Federalist leaders did nothing, therefore, but
write letters to one another denouncing the "Jacobins" and prophesying "anarchy." "Behold France
— what is theory here is fact there." [3] Even the
tractable McHenry was disgusted with his stronger
associates. "Their conduct," said he, "is tremulous,
timid, feeble, deceptive & cowardly. They write
private letters. To whom? To each other. But they
do nothing. . . . If the party recover its pristine
energy & splendor, shall I ascribe it to such cunning,
paltry, indecisive, backdoor conduct?" [4]

[1] "In my lengthy journey through this State [Pennsylvania] I have
seen many, very many Irishmen and with very few exceptions, they
are United Irishmen, Free Masons, and the most God-provoking
Democrats on this side of Hell," who, "with the joy and ferocity of
the damned, are enjoying the mortification of the few remaining honest men and Federalists, and exalting their own hopes of preferment,
and that of their friends, in proportion as they dismiss the fears of the
gallows. . . . The Democrats are, without doubt, increasing." (Uriah
Tracy to Wolcott, Aug. 7, 1800; Gibbs, ii, 399.)

[2] Huntington to Wolcott, Aug. 6, 1800; *ib.*, 398.

[3] Ames to Wolcott, June 12, 1800; *ib.*, 369.

[4] McHenry to Wolcott, July 22, 1800; Steiner, 462. "Your very
wise political correspondents will tell you anything sooner than the
truth. For not one of them will look for anything but profound reasons
of state at the bottom of the odd superstructure of parties here. There
is nothing of the kind at the bottom." (Ames to King, Aug. 19, 1800;
King, iii, 294.)

What had become of the French mission? [1] Would
to God it might fail! That outcome might yet save
the Federalist fortunes. "If Mr. Marshall has any
[news of the second French mission] beg him to let it
out," implored Chauncey Goodrich.[2] But Marshall
had none for public inspection. The envoys' dispatches of May 17,[3] which had reached him nearly
seven weeks afterward, were perplexing. Indeed,
Marshall was "much inclined to think that . . . the
French government may be inclined to protract it
[the negotiation] in the expectation that events in
America[4] may place them on higher ground than
that which they now occupy." [5] To Hamilton, he
cautiously wrote that the dispatches contained
nothing "on which a positive opinion respecting the
result of that negotiation can be formed." [6]

But he told the President that he feared "the impression which will probably be made by the New
York Election," [7] and that European military developments might defeat the mission's purpose. He
advised Adams to consider what then should be
done. Should "hostilities against France with the
exception of their West India privateers . . . be continued if on their part a change of conduct shall be

---

[1] The Republicans were making much political capital out of the
second mission. They had "saved the country from war," they said,
by forcing Adams to send the envoys: "What a roaring and bellowing
did this excite among all the hungry gang that panted for blood only
to obtain pelf in every part of the country." (*Aurora*, March 4, 1800.)

[2] Goodrich to Wolcott, Aug. 26, 1800; Gibbs, ii, 412.

[3] *Am. St. Prs., For. Rel.*, ii, 325.

[4] Republican success in the approaching election.

[5] Marshall to Adams, July 21, 1800; Adams MSS.

[6] Marshall to Hamilton, Aug. 23, 1800; *Works:* Hamilton, vi, 460.

[7] A Republican victory.

manifest?" [1] Adams was so perturbed that he asked Marshall whether, in case the envoys returned without a treaty, Congress ought not to be asked to declare war, which already it had done in effect. For, said Adams, "the public mind cannot be held in a state of suspense; public opinion must be always a decided one whether right or not." [2]

Marshall counseled patience and moderation. Indeed, he finally informed Adams that he hoped for an adjustment: "I am greatly disposed to think," he advised the President, "that the present [French] government is much inclined to correct, at least in part, the follies of the past. Of these, none were perhaps more conspicuous or more injurious to the french nation, than their haughty and hostile conduct to neutrals. Considerable retrograde steps in this respect have already been taken, and I expect the same course will be continued." If so, "there will exist no cause for war, but to obtain compensation for past injuries"; and this, Marshall is persuaded, is not "a sufficient motive" for war. [3]

To others, however, Marshall was apprehensive: "It is probable that their [the French] late victories and the hope which many of our papers [Republican] are well calculated to inspire, that America is disposed once more to crouch at her [France's] feet may render ineffectual our endeavors to obtain peace." [4]

---

[1] Marshall to Adams, Aug. 25, 1800; Adams MSS.

[2] Adams to Marshall, Sept. 4 and 5, 1800; *Works:* Adams, ix, 80–82.

[3] Marshall to Adams, Sept. 17, 1800; Adams MSS. The "retrograde steps" to which Marshall refers were the modification of the French *arrêts* and decrees concerning attacks on our commerce.

[4] Marshall to Tinsley, Sept. 13, 1800; MS., Mass. Hist. Soc.

But the second American mission to France had dealt with Bonaparte himself, who was now First Consul. The man on horseback had arrived, as Marshall had foreseen; a statesman as well as a soldier was now the supreme power in France. Also, as we have seen, the American Government had provided for an army and was building a navy which, indeed, was even then attacking and defeating French ships. "America in arms was treated with some respect," as Marshall expresses it.[1] At any rate, the American envoys did not have to overcome the obstacles that lay in the way two years earlier and the negotiations began without difficulty and proceeded without friction.

Finally a treaty was made and copies sent to Marshall, October 4, 1800.[2] The Republicans were rejoiced; the Federalist politicians chagrined.[3] Hamilton felt that in "the general politics of the world" it "is a make-weight in the wrong scale," but he favored its ratification because "the contrary . . . would . . . utterly ruin the federal party," and "moreover it is better to close the thing where it is than to leave it to a Jacobin to do much worse."[4]

Marshall also advised ratification, although he was "far, very far, from approving"[5] the treaty.

[1] Marshall, ii, 438.

[2] *Am. St. Prs., For. Rel.*, ii, 342 *et seq.*

[3] Gunn to Hamilton, Dec. 18, 1800; *Works:* Hamilton, vi, 492; and Rutledge to Hamilton, Jan. 10, 1801; *ib.*, 511; Ames to Gore, Nov. 10, 1799; *Works:* Ames, i, 265.

[4] Hamilton to Sedgwick, Dec. 22, 1800; *Works:* Lodge, x, 397; also, to Morris, Dec. 24, 1800; *ib.*, 398.

[5] Marshall to Hamilton, Jan. 1, 1801; *Works:* Hamilton, vi, 502–03; and see Brown: *Ellsworth*, 314–15. The principal American demand was compensation for the immense spoliation of American commerce

The Federalists in the Senate, however, were resolved not to ratify it; they were willing to approve only with impossible amendments. They could not learn the President's opinion of this course; as to that, even Marshall was in the dark. "The Secretary of State knows as little of the intentions of the President as any other person connected with the government." [1] Finally the Senate rejected the convention; but it was so "extremely popular," said the Republicans, that the Federalist Senators were "frightened" to "recant." [2] They reversed their action and approved the compact. The strongest influence to change their attitude, however, was not the popularity of the treaty, but the pressure of the mercantile interests which wanted the business-destroying conflict settled. [3]

The Hamiltonian group daily became more wrathful with the President. In addition to what they considered his mistakes of policy and party blunders, Adams's charge that they were a "British faction" angered them more and more as the circulation of it spread and the public credited it. Even "General

by the French. The treaty not only failed to grant this, but provided that we should restore the French ships captured by American vessels during our two years' maritime war with France, which, though formally undeclared, was vigorous and successful. "One part of the treaty abandons all our rights, and the other part makes us the dupes of France in the game she means to play against the maritime power of England. . . . We lose our honor, by restoring the ships we have taken, and by so doing, perhaps, make an implicit acknowledgment of the injustice of our hostile operations." (Rutledge to Hamilton, Jan. 10, 1801; *Works:* Hamilton, vi, 511.)

[1] Bayard to Andrew Bayard, Jan. 26, 1801; *Bayard Papers:* Donnan, 121.

[2] Gallatin to his wife, Feb. 5, 1801; Adams: *Gallatin,* 259.

[3] *Ib.,* 254.

M[arshall] said that the hardest thing for the Federalists to bear was the charge of British influence." [1] That was just what the "Jacobins" had been saying all along. [2] "If this cannot be counteracted, our characters are the sacrifice," wrote Hamilton in anger and despair. [3] Adams's adherents were quite as vengeful against his party enemies. The rank and file of the Federalists were more and more disgusted with the quarrels of the party leaders. "I cannot describe . . . how broken and scattered your federal friends are!" lamented Troup. "We have no rallying-point; and no mortal can divine where and when we shall again collect our strength. . . . Shadows, clouds, and darkness rest on our future prospects." [4] The "Aurora" chronicles that "the disorganized state of the anti-Republican [Federalist] party . . . is scarcely describable." [5]

Marshall, alone, was trusted by all; a faith which deepened, as we shall see, during the perplexing months that follow. He strove for Federalist union, but without avail. Even the most savage of the President's party enemies felt that "there is not a man in the U. S. of better intentions [than Marshall] and he has the confidence of all good men — no man regrets more than he does the disunion which has

[1] Ames to Gore, Dec. 29, 1800; reviewing political events of the year; *Works:* Ames, i, 286–87.

[2] Hamilton to Wolcott, Aug. 3, 1800; *Works:* Lodge, x, 383; and Wolcott to Ames, Aug. 10, 1800; Gibbs, ii, 400.

[3] Hamilton to Wolcott, Sept. 26, 1800; *Works:* Lodge, x, 389 (also in Gibbs, ii, 422); and see same to same, Aug. 3, 1800; *Works:* Lodge, x, 383.

[4] Troup to King, Oct. 1, 1800; King, iii, 315.

[5] *Aurora*, May 20, 1800.

taken place and no one would do more to heal the wounds inflicted by it. In a letter . . . he says 'by union we can securely maintain our ground — without it we must sink & with us all sound correct American principle.' His efforts will . . . prove ineffectual." [1]

It seems certain, then, that Hamilton did not consult the one strong man in his party who kept his head in this hour of anger-induced madness. Yet, if ever any man needed the advice of a cool, far-seeing mind, lighted by a sincere and friendly heart, Hamilton required it then. And Marshall could and would have given it. But the New York Federalist chieftain conferred only with those who were as blinded by hate as he was himself. At last, in the midst of an absurd and pathetic confusion of counsels,[2] Hamilton decided to attack the President, and, in October, wrote his fateful and fatal tirade against Adams.[3] It was an extravaganza of party folly. It denounced Adams's "extreme egotism," "terrible jealousy," "eccentric tendencies," "violent rage";

[1] Sedgwick to King, Sept. 26, 1800; King, iii, 309.

[2] Ames to Hamilton, Aug. 26, 1800; *Works: Hamilton*, vi, 463; also Cabot to Hamilton, Aug. 21, 1800; *ib.*, 458; and Aug. 23, 1800; *ib.*, 460 (also in Lodge: *Cabot*, 284-88); and to Wolcott, Aug. 23, 1800; Lodge: *Cabot*, 288-89.

The local politicians were loyal to the President; Ames bitterly complains of "the small talk among the small politicians, about disrespect to the President, &c., &c." (Ames to Pickering, Nov. 23, 1799; *Works: Ames*, i, 272.)

[3] Hamilton to Adams, Aug. 1, 1800; *Works: Lodge*, x, 382; and same to same, Oct. 1, 1800; *ib.*, 390. Wolcott supplied most of the material and revised Hamilton's manuscript. (Wolcott to Hamilton, Oct. 1, 2, 1800; *Works: Hamilton*, vi, 470-71.) For entire attack see Hamilton: "Public Conduct and Character of John Adams"; *Works:* vii, 687-726 (also in *Works: Lodge*, vii, 309-65.)

and questioned "the solidity of his understanding."
Hamilton's screed went back to the Revolution to
discover faults in the President. Every act of his
Administration was arraigned as a foolish or wicked
mistake.

This stupid pamphlet was not to be made public,
but to be circulated privately among the Federalist
leaders in the various States. The watchful Burr
secured a copy [1] and published broadcast its bitter-
est passages. The Republican politicians shook with
laughter; the Republican masses roared with glee.[2]
The rank and file of the Federalists were dazed,
stunned, angered; the party leaders were in despair.
Thus exposed, Hamilton made public his whole
pamphlet. Although its purpose was to further the
plan to secure for Pinckney more votes than would
be given Adams, it ended with the apparent advice
to support both. Absurd conclusion! There might
be intellects profound enough to understand why it
was necessary to show that Adams was not fit to be
President and yet that he should be voted for; but
the mind of the average citizen could not fathom
such ratiocination. Hamilton's influence was irrep-
arably impaired.[3] The "Washington Federalist"

---

[1] Parton: *Burr*, 256–57; Davis: *Burr*, ii, 65 *et seq.*

[2] "This pamphlet has done more mischief to the parties concerned
than all the labors of the *Aurora!*" (Duane to Collot; Parton: *Burr*, 258.)

[3] "Our friends . . . lamented the publication. . . . Not a man . . . but
condemns it. . . . Our enemies are universally in triumph. . . . His
[Hamilton's] usefulness hereafter will be greatly lessened." (Troup to
King, Nov. 9, 1800; King, iii, 331.) "All . . . blame . . . Mr. Hamilton." (Carroll to McHenry, Nov. 4, 1800; Steiner, 476.)

Some Federalist politicians, however, observed Hamilton's wishes.
For example: "You must at all events secure to the Genr. [Pinckney] a
majority in Cong., it may there be done with *safety*, his success depends

denounced his attack as "the production of a disappointed man" and declared that Adams was "much his superior as a statesman." [1]

The campaign was a havoc of virulence. The Federalists' hatred for one another increased their fury toward the compact Republicans, who assailed their quarreling foes with a savage and unrestrained ferocity. The newspapers, whose excesses had whipped even the placid Franklin into a rage a few years before, now became geysers spouting slander, vituperation, and unsavory [2] insinuations. "The venal,

on the accomplishment of this measure. You know a friend of ours who can arrange this necessary business with the utmost perfect suavity." (Dickinson to McHenry, Oct. 7, 1800; Steiner, 471.)

Again Dickinson writes of "the absolute necessity of obtaining a *majority* (if it should only be by a *single* vote) in Cong. to favor the man who interests us most" and hopes "Hamilton's publication . . . will produce the desired effect." (Oct. 31, 1800; *ib.*, 472.)

[1] *Washington Federalist*, Nov. 29, 1800.

[2] For instance see the *Aurora's* editorial on women in the army, January 14, 1800; and see titles of imaginary books editorially suggested for use by the various Federalist leaders, especially Hamilton, Harper, and Gouverneur Morris, in *ib.*, May 10, 1800. On August 21 it described some Federalist leaders as "completely bankrupt of character as well as fortune."

Although it did not equal the extravagance of the Republican newspapers, the Federalist press was also violent. See, for instance, a satirical poem "by an Hibernian and an Alien" in the *Alexandria Advertiser*, reprinted in the *Washington Federalist* of February 12, 1801, of which the last verse runs: —

> "With J[effer]son, greatest of men,
> Our President next we will dash on.
> Republican marriages then,
> And drowning boats will be in fashion.
> Co-alitions, tri-color we'll form
> 'T wixt white Men, Mulattos, and Negroes.
> The banks of the treasury we'll storm —
> Oh! how we'll squeeze the old Quakers,
> *Philosophy is a fine thing!* "

The familiar campaign arguments were, of course, incessantly reiterated as: "The Government" cost only "FIVE MILLION dollars

servile, base and stupid"[1] "newspapers are an over-
match for any government," cried Ames. "They will
first overawe and then usurp it."[2] And Noah Webster felt that "no government can be durable . . .
under the licentiousness of the press that now dis-
graces our country."[3] Discordant Federalists and
harmonious Republicans resorted to shameful methods.[4] "Never . . . was there such an Election in
America."[5]

As autumn was painting the New England trees,
Adams, still tarrying at his Massachusetts home,
wrote Marshall to give his "sentiments as soon
as possible in writing" as to what the President
should say to Congress when it met December 3.[6]
Three days later, when his first request was not yet
halfway to Washington, Adams, apparently forgetful of his first letter, again urged Marshall to advise
him as President in regard to his forthcoming farewell address to the National Legislature.[7]

Marshall not only favored the President with his
"sentiments" — he wrote every word of the speech
which Adams delivered to Congress and sent it to

. . . before the British treaty"; now it costs "FIFTEEN MILLIONS.
Therefore every man who paid *one dollar* taxes then pays *three* dollars
now." (*Aurora*, Oct. 30, 1800.)

[1] Ames to Pickering, Nov. 5, 1799; *Works:* Ames, i, 264.

[2] Ames to Dwight, March 19, 1801; *ib.*, 294.

[3] Webster to Wolcott, June 23, 1800; Gibbs, ii, 374.

[4] The *Washington Federalist*, Jan. 12, 1801, charged that, in Virginia,
public money was used at the election and that a resolution to inquire
into its expenditures was defeated in the Legislature.

[5] Charles Pinckney to Jefferson, Oct. 12, 1800; *Amer. Hist. Rev.*, iv,
117. For election arguments and methods see McMaster, ii, 499 *et seq.*

[6] Adams to Marshall, Sept. 27, 1800; *Works:* Adams, ix, 85; and
see Graydon, footnote to 362.

[7] Adams to Marshall, Sept. 30, 1800; Adams MSS.

the distressed Chief Magistrate in such haste that he did not even make a copy.[1] This presidential address, the first ever made to Congress in Washington, was delivered exactly as Marshall wrote it, with a change of only one word "much" for "such" and the omission of an adjective "great." [2]

The address is strong on the necessity for military and naval preparation. It would be "a dangerous imprudence to abandon those measures of self-protection . . . to which . . . violence and the injustice of others may again compel us to resort. . . . Seasonable and systematic arrangements . . . for a defensive war" are "a wise and true economy." The navy is described as particularly important, coast defenses are urged, and the manufacture of domestic arms is recommended in order to "supercede the necessity of future importations." The extension of the national Judiciary is pressed as of "primary importance . . . to the public happiness." [3]

The election, at last, was over. The Republicans won, but only by a dangerously narrow margin. Indeed, outside of New York, the Federalists secured more electoral votes in 1800 than in the election of

[1] Marshall to Adams, without date; Adams MSS.

[2] Adams MSS. Marshall wrote two speeches for Adams. Both are in Marshall's handwriting. The President selected and delivered the one which appears in Adams's *Works* and in Richardson. The undelivered speech was the better, although it was written before the French treaty arrived, and was not applicable to the state of our relations with France when Congress convened. Marshall also wrote for Adams the two brief separate addresses to the Senate and the House. (*Ib.*)

[3] The original manuscripts of these speeches, in Marshall's handwriting, are in the Adams MSS. They are notable only as an evidence of Adams's confidence in Marshall at this, the most irritating period of his life.

Adams four years earlier.[1] The great constructive
work of the Federalist Party still so impressed conservative people; the mercantile and financial interests were still so well banded together; the Federalist
revival of 1798, brought about by Marshall's dispatches, was, as yet, so strong; the genuine worth of
Adams's statesmanship [2] was so generally recognized in spite of his unhappy manner, that it would
seem as though the Federalists might have succeeded
but for the quarrels of their leaders and Burr's skillful conduct of the Republican campaign in New
York.

— Jefferson and Burr each had seventy-three votes

[1] Beard: *Econ. O. J. D.*, chap. xiii.

[2] When it was certain that Adams had been defeated, "Solon," in
the *Washington Federalist* of Jan. 9, 1801, thus eulogized him: —

"The die is cast! . . . Our beloved ADAMS will now close his bright
career. . . . Immortal sage! May thy counsels continue to be our
saving Angel! Retire and receive . . . the . . . blessings of all *good*
men. . . .

"Sons of faction [party]! demagogues and high priests of anarchy,
now have you cause to triumph. Despots and tyrants! now may you
safely pronounce 'ingratitude is the common vice of all republics.
Envy and neglect are the only reward of superior merit. Calumny,
persecution and banishment are the laurels of the hoary patriot.' . . .

". . . We have to contend . . . for national existence. Magistrates
and rulers, be firm. . . . Our constitution is our last fortress. Let us
entrench it against every innovation. When this falls, our country is
lost forever."

This editorial, as well as all political matter appearing in the *Washington Federalist* during 1800–01, is important because of Marshall's
reputed influence over that paper. (See *infra*, 541.)

At news of Jefferson's success the leading Federalist journal declared that some Republicans in Philadelphia "huzzaed until they
were seized with lockjaw . . . and three hundred are now drunk
beyond hope of recovery. Gin and whiskey are said to have risen
in price 50 per cent since nine o'clock this morning. The bells have
been ringing, guns firing, dogs barking, cats meuling, children cry-
ing, and jacobins getting drunk, ever since the news of Mr. Jefferson's election arrived in this city." (*Gazette of the United States*,
Feb. 19, 1801.)

for President. Under the Constitution, as it stood at that time, the final choice for President was thus thrown into the House of Representatives.[1] By united and persistent effort, it was possible for the Federalists to elect Burr, or at least prevent any choice and, by law, give the Presidency to one of their own number until the next election. This, Jefferson advises Burr, "they are strong enough to do."[2] The Federalists saw their chance; the Republicans realized their danger.[3] Jefferson writes of the "great dismay and gloom on the republican gentlemen here and equal exultation on the federalists who openly declare they will prevent an election."[4] This "opens upon us an abyss, at which every sincere patriot must shudder."[5]

Although Hamilton hated Burr venomously, he advised the Federalist managers in Washington "to throw out a lure for him, in order to tempt him to start for the plate, and then lay the foundation of

[1] At that time, the presidential electors did not vote for a Vice-President, but only for President. The person receiving the largest number of electoral votes became President and the one for whom the second largest number of votes were cast became Vice-President. When Jefferson and Burr each had seventy-three votes for President, the election was thrown into the House of Representatives.

Thus, although, in casting their ballots for electors, the people really voted for Jefferson for President and for Burr for Vice-President, the equal number of votes received by each created a situation where it was possible to defeat the will of the people. Indeed, as appears in the text, that result was almost accomplished. It was this constitutional defect that led to the Twelfth Amendment which places the election of President and Vice-President on its present basis. (See "The Fifth Wheel in our Government"; Beveridge: *Century Magazine*, December, 1909.)

[2] Jefferson to Burr, Dec. 15, 1800; *Works:* Ford, ix, 155.

[3] "Jefferson & Burr have each 73 votes and . . . the Democrats are in a sweat." (Uriah Tracy to McHenry, Dec. 30, 1800; Steiner, 483.)

[4] Jefferson to Madison, Dec. 19, 1800; *Works:* Ford, ix, 158.

[5] Jefferson to Breckenridge, Dec. 18, 1800; *ib.*, 157.

dissension between" him and Jefferson.[1] The Federalists, however, already were turning to Burr, not according to Hamilton's unworthy suggestion, but in deadly earnest. At news of this, the fast-weakening New York Federalist chieftain became frantic. He showered letters upon the party leaders in Congress, and upon all who might have influence, appealing, arguing, persuading, threatening.[2]

But the Federalists in Congress were not to be influenced, even by the once omnipotent Hamilton. "The Federalists, almost with one Mind, from every Quarter of the Union, say elect Burr" because "they must be disgraced in the Estimation of the People if they vote for Jefferson having told Them that He was a Man without Religion, the Writer of the Letter to Mazzei, a Coward, &c., &c."[3] Hamilton's fierce warnings against Burr and his black prophecies of "the *Cataline* of America"[4] did not frighten them. They knew little of Burr, personally, and the coun-

---

[1] Hamilton to Wolcott, Dec. 16, 1800; *Works:* Lodge, x, 392.

[2] See these letters in *ib.*, 392 *et seq.*; and to Bayard, Jan. 16, 1801; *ib.*, 412 (also in *Works:* Hamilton, vi, 419, but misplaced and misdated).

[3] Hindman to McHenry, Jan. 17, 1801; Steiner, 489-90; and see Carroll to Hamilton, April 18, 1800; *Works:* Hamilton, vi, 434-35.

The *Washington Federalist*, even when the balloting was in progress, thus stimulated the members of its party in the House: "*Unworthy* will he be and consecrate his name to infamy, who . . . has hitherto opposed . . . Mr. Jefferson . . . and shall now meanly and inconsistently lend his aid to promote it [Jefferson's election]. . . . Will they confer on Mr. Jefferson the Federal suffrage in reward for the calumnies he has indiscriminately cast upon the Federal character; or will they remunerate him . . . for the very honorable epithets of *pander, to the whore of England,* '*timid men, office hunters, monocrats, speculators and plunderers*' which he has missed no opportunity to bestow upon them." (*Washington Federalist*, Feb. 12, 1801.)

[4] Hamilton to Wolcott, Dec. 17, 1800; *Works:* Lodge, x, 395.

try knew less. What was popularly known of this extraordinary man was not unattractive to the Federalists.

Burr was the son of the President of Princeton and the grandson of the celebrated Jonathan Edwards, the greatest theologian America had produced. He had been an intrepid and efficient officer in the Revolutionary War, and an able and brilliant Senator of the United States. He was an excellent lawyer and a well-educated, polished man of the world. He was a politician of energy, resourcefulness, and decision. And he was a practical man of affairs. If he were elected by Federalist votes, the fury with which Jefferson and his friends were certain to assail Burr [1] would drive that practical politician openly into their camp; and, as President, he would bring with him a considerable Republican following. Thus the Federalists would be united and strengthened and the Republicans divided and weakened.[2]

This was the reasoning which drew and bound the Federalists together in their last historic folly; and they felt that they might succeed. "It is . . . certainly within the compass of possibility that Burr

[1] Jefferson rightly attributed to Burr Republican success in the election. "He has certainly greatly merited of his country, & the Republicans in particular, to whose efforts his have given a chance of success." (Jefferson to Butler, Aug. 11, 1800; *Works:* Ford, ix, 138.)

[2] Sedgwick to Hamilton, Jan. 10, 1800; *Works:* Hamilton, vi, 511–14; Cabot to Hamilton, Aug. 10, 1800; *ib.*, 453 (also in Lodge: *Cabot*, 284); Hindman to McHenry, Jan. 17, 1801; Steiner, 489–90; Morris to Hamilton, Jan. 5, 1801; Morris, ii, 398; and same to same, Jan. 26, 1801; *ib.*, 402 (also in *Works:* Hamilton, vi, 503); Carroll to McHenry, Nov. 4, 1800; Steiner, 473–76; Rutledge to Hamilton, Jan. 10, 1801; *Works:* Hamilton, vi, 510.

may ultimately obtain nine States," writes Bayard.[1] In addition to the solid Federalist strength in the House, there were at least three Republican members, two corrupt and the other light-minded, who might by "management" be secured for Burr.[2] The Federalist managers felt that "the high Destinies . . . of this United & enlightened people are up";[3] and resolved upon the hazard. Thus the election of Burr, or, at least, a deadlock, faced the Republican chieftain.

At this critical hour there was just one man who still had the confidence of all Federalists from Adams to Hamilton. John Marshall, Secretary of State, had enough influence to turn the scales of Federalist action. Hamilton approached Marshall indirectly at first. "You may communicate this letter to *Marshall*," he instructed Wolcott, in one of his most savage denunciations of Burr.[4] Wolcott obeyed and reported that Marshall "has yet expressed no opinion."[5] Thereupon Hamilton wrote Marshall personally.

This letter is lost; but undoubtedly it was in the same vein as were those to Wolcott, Bayard, Sedgwick, Morris, and other Federalists. But Hamilton could not persuade Marshall to throw his influence to Jefferson. The most Marshall would do was to agree to keep hands off.

[1] Bayard to Andrew Bayard, Jan. 26, 1801; *Bayard Papers:* Donnan, 121.

[2] Bayard to Hamilton, March 8, 1801; *Works:* Hamilton, vi, 524.

[3] Tracy to McHenry, Jan. 15, 1801; Steiner, 488–99; and see Bayard to Andrew Bayard, Jan. 26, 1801; *supra.*

[4] Hamilton to Wolcott, Dec. 16, 1800; *Works:* Lodge, x, 392.

[5] Wolcott to Hamilton, Dec. 25, 1800; *Works:* Hamilton, vi, 498.

"To Mr. Jefferson," replies Marshall, "whose political character is better known than that of Mr. Burr, I have felt almost insuperable objections. His foreign prejudices seem to me totally to unfit him for the chief magistracy of a nation which cannot indulge those prejudices without sustaining deep and permanent injury.

"In addition to this solid and immovable objection, Mr. Jefferson appears to me to be a man, who will embody himself with the House of Representatives.[1] By weakening the office of President, he will increase his personal power. He will diminish his responsibility, sap the fundamental principles of the government, and become the leader of that party which is about to constitute the majority of the legislature. The morals of the author of the letter to Mazzei [2] cannot be pure. . . .

[1] See Chief Justice Ellsworth's statement of the conservative opinion of Jefferson. (Brown: *Ellsworth*, 324–25.)

[2] Jefferson to Mazzei, April 24, 1796; *Works:* Ford, viii, 237–41. The letter as published in America, although it had undergone three translations (from English into Italian, from Italian into French, and from French into English again), does not materially differ from Jefferson's original.

It greatly angered the Federalist leaders. Jefferson calls the Federalists "an Anglican, monarchical & aristocratical party." The Republicans had "the landed interests and men of talent"; the Federalists had "the Executive, the Judiciary," the office-holders and office-seekers — "all timid men who prefer the calm of despotism to the boisterous sea of liberty, British merchants & Americans trading on British capital, speculators & holders in the banks & public funds, a contrivance invented for the purposes of corruption," etc.

Jefferson thus refers to Washington: "It would give you a fever were I to name to you the apostates who have gone over to these heresies, men who were Samsons in the field & Solomons in the council, but who have had their heads shorn by the whore England." It was this insult to Washington which Marshall resented most bitterly.

Jefferson must have known that Mazzei would probably publish this

"Your representation of Mr. Burr, with whom I am totally unacquainted, shows that from him still greater danger than even from Mr. Jefferson may be apprehended. Such a man as you describe is more to be feared, and may do more immediate, if not greater mischief.

"Believing that you know him well, and are impartial, my preference would certainly not be for him, but I can take no part in this business. I cannot bring myself to aid Mr. Jefferson. Perhaps respect for myself should, in my present situation, deter me from using any influence (if, indeed I possessed any) in support of either gentleman.

"Although no consideration could induce me to be the Secretary of State while there was a President whose political system I believed to be at variance with my own; yet this cannot be so well known to others, and it might be suspected that a desire to be well with the successful candidate had, in some degree, governed my conduct." [1]

Marshall had good personal reasons for wishing Burr to be elected, or at least that a deadlock should be produced. He did not dream that the Chief Justiceship was to be offered to him; his law practice,

letter. Writing at Paris, in 1788, of Mazzei's appointment by the French King as "intelligencer," Jefferson said: "The danger is that he will overact his part." (Jefferson to Madison, July 31, 1788; *Works:* Ford, v, 425.)

The Republicans frankly defended the Mazzei letter; both its facts and "predictions" were correct, said the *Aurora*, which found scarcely "a line in it which does not contain something to admire for elegance of expression, striking fact, and profound and accurate penetration." (*Aurora*, May 26, 1800.)

[1] Marshall to Hamilton, January 1, 1801; *Works:* Hamilton, vi, 501–03.

neglected for three years, had passed into other hands; the head of the Cabinet was then the most important [1] office in the Government, excepting only the Presidency itself; and rumor had it that Marshall would remain Secretary of State in case Burr was chosen as Chief Magistrate. If the tie between Jefferson and Burr were not broken, Marshall might even be chosen President. [2]

"I am rather inclined to think that Mr. Burr will be preferred. . . . General Marshall will then remain in the department of state; but if Mr. Jefferson be chosen, Mr. Marshall will retire," writes Pickering. [3] But if Marshall cherished the ambition to continue as Secretary of State, as seems likely, he finally stifled it and stood aloof from the struggle. It was a decision which changed Marshall's whole life and affected the future of the Republic. Had Marshall openly worked for Burr, or even insisted upon a

---

[1] Following is a list of the annual salaries of different officers: —

President.....................................	$25,000
Vice-President...............................	5,000
Chief Justice.................................	4,000
Associate Justices............................	3,500
Attorney-General.............................	1,500
Secretary of the Treasury.....................	3,500
Secretary of State............................	3,500
Secretary of War.............................	3,000

(*Annals*, 1st Cong., 1st Sess., Appendix, 2233-38.)

[2] At the very beginning of the movement in his favor, Burr refused to encourage it. "Every man who knows me ought to know that I disclaim all competition. Be assured that the Federalist party can entertain no wish for such a change. . . . My friends would dishonor my views and insult my feelings by a suspicion that I would submit to be instrumental in counteracting the wishes and expectations of the United States. And I now constitute you my proxy to declare these sentiments if the occasion shall require." (Burr to Smith, Dec. 16, 1800; *Washington Federalist*, Dec. 31, 1800.)

[3] Pickering to King, Jan. 5, 1801; King, iii, 366.

permanent deadlock, it is reasonably certain that the Federalists would have achieved one of their alternate purposes.

Although Marshall refrained from assisting the Federalists in their plan to elect Burr, he did not oppose it. The "Washington Federalist," which was the Administration organ [1] in the Capital, presented in glowing terms the superior qualifications of Burr over Jefferson for the Presidency, three weeks after Marshall's letter to Hamilton. [2]

---

[1] See *Aurora*, Jan. 21, 1801.

[2] "Lucius," of Fredericksburg, Virginia, in the *Washington Federalist*, Jan. 21, 25, and Feb. 6, 1801.

The following extracts from the first of these articles reveal the temper and beliefs of the Federalists: "Burr never *penned* a declaration of independence; . . . but he . . . has *engraved that declaration* in *capitals* with the point of his sword: It is yet *legible* on the *walls of Quebeck*. He has *fought* for that *independency*, for which Mr. *Jefferson* only *wrote*. *He* has gallantly exposed his life in support of that declaration and for the *protection* of its *penn-man*. He has been *liberal* of his *blood, while* Mr. *Jefferson* has *only hazarded* his *ink*. . . .

"*He never shrank from the post of danger. He* is *equally fitted for* service in the *field* and in the *public counsels:* He has been *tried* in *both:* in the one we have seen him *an able and distinguished Senator;* — in the *other* a *brave* and *gallant officer*. . . .

"*Mr. Jefferson* is better qualified to give the description of a butterfly's wing or to write an essay on the bones of the Mammouth; . . . but Mr. Burr . . . in . . . knowledge . . . necessary to form the *great and enlightened statesman*, is *much superior* to Mr. Jefferson. . . .

"Mr. Burr is not . . . *consecrated* to the *French;* . . . nor has he unquenchable hatred to . . . Great Britain. Unlike the *penn-man* of the declaration he feels the *full force* of the expression, 'in *war enemies,* in *peace friends*' . . . Mr. Burr . . . will *only* consult *national honor* and *national* happiness, having no improper passions to gratify.

"Mr. Burr is . . . a friend of the Constitution . . . a friend of the commercial interests . . . the firm and decided friend of the *navy* . . . the *Eastern* States have had a President and Vice President; So have the *Southern*. It is proper that the *middle* states should also be respected. . . .

"Mr. Burr has never procured or encouraged those infamous Calumnies against those who have filled the Executive departments . . .

The Republicans said that Marshall wrote much that appeared in this newspaper.[1] If he was influential with the editor, he did not exercise his power to exclude the paper's laudation of the New York Republican leader.

It was reported that Marshall had declared that, in case of a deadlock, Congress "may appoint a Presidt. till another election is made." [2] The rumor

which we long have witnessed: Nor have those polluted *Sinks*, the Aurora, the Argus, the Press, the Richmond Examiner, and the like, poured forth their *impure* and *foetid streams* at the influence of Mr. Burr, or to subserve his vanity or his ambition.

"If Mr. Burr is elected, the *Federalists* have nothing to *fear*. . . . The vile calumniators . . . of all who have . . . supported our government, and the *foreign incendiaries*, who, having no interest in *Heaven*, have called *Hell* to their assistance, . . . from Mr. Burr have nothing to *hope*. . . .

"Mr. Burr can be raised to the Presidency without any *insult* to the feelings of the Federalists, the friends of Government; . . . WITHOUT an *insult* to the *Memory* of *our* Washington; for it was not by Mr. *Burr*, nor was it by *his* friends, nor to *serve him that the great, the good, the immortal* Washington was charged with having, by his name, given a sanction to corruption, with being meanly jealous of the fame of even that contemptible wretch Tom Paine, with being an unprincipled Hypocrite and with being a foul murderer! a murderer under circumstances of such peculiar atrocity as to shock with horror the merciless savages, and to cause them indignantly to fly from his blood polluted banner!"

[1] "John Marshall . . . is the reputed author of a great part of the [rubbish] in the Washington Federalist." (Scots Correspondent [Callender] in *Richmond Examiner*, Feb. 24, 1801.) There is no proof of Callender's assertion; but some of the matter appearing in the *Washington Federalist* is characteristic of Marshall's style and opinions. See, for instance, the editorial on the prosecution of Theodore Dwight, denouncing "party spirit" (*Washington Federalist*, March 1, 1801). The *Aurora* of March 26, 1801, denounced " John Marshall's Federal Gazette at Washington."

[2] Monroe to Jefferson, Jan. 18, 1801; Monroe's *Writings:* Hamilton, iii, 256. An article signed "Horatius" in the *Washington Federalist* of Jan. 6, 1801, stated this position with great ability. The argument is able and convincing; and it is so perfectly in Marshall's method of

increased Republican alarm and fanned Republican anger. From Richmond came the first tidings of the spirit of popular resistance to "such a usurpation,"[1] even though it might result in the election of Marshall himself to the Presidency. If they could not elect Burr, said Jefferson, the Federalists planned to make Marshall or Jay the Chief Executive by a law to be passed by the expiring Federalist Congress.[2]

Monroe's son-in-law, George Hay, under the *nom de guerre* of "Hortensius," attacked Marshall in an open letter in the "Richmond Examiner," which was copied far and wide in the Republican press. Whether Congress will act on Marshall's opinion, says Hay, "is a question which has already diffused throughout America anxiety and alarm; a question on the decision of which depends not only the peace of the nation, but the existence of the Union." Hay recounts the many indications of the Federalists' purpose and says: "I understand that you, Sir, have not only examined the Constitution, but have given an opinion in exact conformity with the wishes of your party." He challenges Marshall to "come forward . . . and defend it." If a majority of the House choose Burr the people will submit, says Hay, because such an election, though contrary to their wishes,

reasoning and peculiar style of expression that his authorship would appear to be reasonably certain.

"Horatius's" opinion concluded that the power of Congress "is completely adequate . . . to provide by law for the vacancy that may happen by the removal of both President and Vice President on the 3d of March next, and the non-election of a successor in the manner prescribed by the constitution."

[1] Monroe to Jefferson, Jan. 18, 1801; Monroe's *Writings:* Hamilton, iii, 256.

[2] Jefferson to Madison, Dec. 26, 1800; *Works:* Ford, ix, 161–62.

would be constitutional. But if, disregarding the popular will and also violating the Constitution, Congress "shall elect a stranger to rule over us, peace and union are driven from the land. . . . The usurpation . . . will be instantly and firmly repelled. The government will be at an end." [1]

Although the "Washington Federalist" denounced as "a lie" [2] the opinion attributed to him, Marshall, personally, paid no attention to this bold and menacing challenge. But Jefferson did. After waiting a sufficient time to make sure that this open threat of armed revolt expressed the feeling of the country, he asserted that "we thought best to declare openly and firmly, one & all, that the day such an act passed, the Middle States would arm, & that no such usurpation, even for a single day, should be

[1] "Hortensius" to John Marshall, Secretary of State, in the *Richmond Examiner;* reprinted in the *Aurora,* Feb. 9, 1801. George Hay, the writer of this letter, was a lawyer in Richmond. Jefferson appointed him United States Attorney for the District of Virginia, and, as such, he conducted the prosecution of Aaron Burr for treason before John Marshall, who, as Chief Justice of the United States, presided at the trial. (See vol. III of this work.)

Marshall was again attacked in two open letters, signed "Lucius," in the *Richmond Examiner,* Feb. 10, 13, 1801. His reported opinion, said "Lucius," alarmed "the active friends of freedom"; Marshall was "the Idol of his party" and knew the influence of his views: unless he publicly disclaimed the one now attributed to him, "Lucius" proposed to "unveil" Marshall's "motives" and "expose" him "uncovered to the sight of the people" — his "depravity shall excite their odium," etc. "Lucius's" attacks ended with Jefferson's election.

[2] The paper criticized "the intemperate counsel of a certain *would be attorney-general* of the United States (George Hay, *Esq.* of the antient dominion) . . . under the signature of Hortensius, and addressed to General Marshall, in consequence of a lie fabricated against him relative to an opinion said to have been given by him upon the late presidential election, which the honorable attorney knew to be a lie as well as we did, but was fearful of being forgot, and despaired of getting a better opportunity to shew himself!!!" (*Washington Federalist,* Feb. 12, 1801.)

submitted to." [1] The Republicans determined not only to resist the "usurpation . . . by arms," but to set aside the Constitution entirely and call "a convention to reorganize and amend the government." [2]

The drums of civil war were beating. Between Washington and Richmond "a chain of expresses" was established, the messengers riding "day and night." [3] In Maryland and elsewhere, armed men, wrought up to the point of bloodshed, made ready to march on the rude Capital, sprawling among the Potomac hills and thickets. Threats were openly made that any man appointed President by act of Congress, pursuant to Marshall's reputed opinion, would be instantly assassinated. The Governor of Pennsylvania prepared to lead the militia into Washington by the 3d of March.[4]

To this militant attitude Jefferson ascribed the final decision of the Federalists to permit his election. But no evidence exists that they were intimidated in the least, or in any manner influenced, by the ravings of Jefferson's adherents. On the contrary, the Federalists defied and denounced the Republicans and met their threats of armed interference with declarations that they, too, would resort to the sword.[5]

[1] Jefferson to Monroe, Feb. 15, 1801; *Works:* Ford, ix, 178–79; and see Jefferson to McKean, March 9, 1801; *ib.,* 206.

[2] Jefferson to Madison, Feb. 18, 1801; *ib.,* 182.

[3] Monroe to Hoomes, Feb. 14, 1801; Monroe's *Writings:* Hamilton, iii, 259; and Monroe to Nicholas, Feb. 18, 1801; *ib.,* 260.

[4] For these incidents and reports see Gallatin to his wife, May 8, 1801; Adams: *Gallatin,* 249.

[5] Thus, for example, the *Washington Federalist* of Feb. 12, 1801, after the House had balloted "upwards of 30 times": —

"But say the bold and impetuous partisans of Mr. Jefferson, and

The proof is overwhelming and decisive that nothing but Burr's refusal to help the Federalists in his own behalf,[1] his rejection of their proposals,[2] and

that, too, *in the Teeth of the Assembled Congress of America* — 'Dare to designate any officer whatever, even temporarily, to administer the government in the event of a non-agreement on the part of the House of Representatives, and we will march and *dethrone him as an usurper. Dare (in fact)* to exercise the right of opinion, and place in the presidential chair any other than the philosopher of Monticello, and ten thousand republican *swords will instantly leap from their scabbards*, in defence of the violated rights of the *People!!!*

"Can our Countrymen be caught by so flimsy a pretext?

"Can it possibly interest either their feelings or their judgment?

"Are they, then, ripe for civil war, and ready to imbrue their hands in kindred blood?

"If the tumultuous meetings of a set of factious foreigners in Pennsylvania or a few *fighting* bacchanals of Virginia, mean the *people*, and are to dictate to the Congress of the United States whom to elect as President — if the constitutional rights of this body are so soon to become the prey of anarchy and faction — . . . it would be prudent to prepare for the contest: the woeful experiment if tried at all could never be tried at a more favorable conjuncture!

"With the militia of Massachusetts consisting of 70,000 (*regulars let us call them*) in arms — with those of New Hampshire and Connecticut united almost to a man, with half the number at least of the citizens of eleven other States ranged under the federal banner in support of the Constitution, what could Pennsylvania aided by Virginia — the militia of the latter untrained and farcically performing the manual exercise with *corn-stalks* instead of muskets — . . . What, may it be asked, would be the issue of the struggle?"

[1] "The means existed of electing Burr, but this required his co-operation. By deceiving one man (a great blockhead) and tempting two (not incorruptible) he might have secured a majority of the States." (Bayard to Hamilton, March 8, 1801; *Works:* Hamilton, vi, 522–24.)

"The Federalists were confident at first, they could debauch Col. B.[urr] . . . His conduct has been honorable and decisive, and greatly embarrasses them." (Jefferson to his daughter, Jan. 4, 1801; *Works:* Ford, ix, 166.)

[2] "I was enabled soon to discover that he [Burr] was determined not to shackle himself with federal principles. . . . When the experiment was fully made, and acknowledged upon all hands, . . . that Burr was resolved not to commit himself, . . . I came out . . . for Jefferson." (Bayard to Hamilton, March 8, 1801; *Works:* Hamilton, vi, 523.)

his determination, if chosen, to go in as a Republican untainted by any promises; [1] and, on the other hand, the assurances which Jefferson gave Federalists as to offices and the principal Federalist policies — Neutrality, the Finances, and the Navy [2] — only all of these circumstances combined finally made Jefferson president. Indeed, so stubborn was the opposition that, in spite of his bargain with the Federalists and Burr's repulsion of their advances, nearly all of them, through the long and thrillingly dramatic days and nights of balloting, [3] with the menace of physical violence hanging over them, voted against Jefferson and for Burr to the very end.

[1] The Federalist managers were disgusted with Burr because he refused to aid them in their plot to elect him. "Burr has acted a miserable paultry part," writes Bayard. "The election was in his power, but he was determined to come in as a Democrat. . . . We have been counteracted in the whole business by letters he has written to this place." (Bayard to Bassett, Feb. 16, 1801; *Bayard Papers: Donnan;* 126.)

Burr had not "used the least influence" to be elected. (Bayard's Deposition; Davis: *Burr,* ii, 127.)

"Had Burr done anything, for himself, he would, long ere this, have been President." (Cooper to Morris, Feb. 13, 1801; Davis: *Burr,* ii, 113.)

[2] Depositions of Bayard and Smith, in Gillespie *vs.* Smith; Randall, ii, 613–17; and Davis: *Burr,* ii, 135–37; also Baer to Bayard, April 19, 1830; *ib.,* 118; and see Bayard's account; Remarks in the Senate, Jan. 31, 1835; also, Bayard to McLane, Feb. 17, 1801; *Bayard Papers:* Donnan, 126 *et seq.*

In his "Anas" (*Works:* Ford, i, 392–93) Jefferson flatly denied his deal with the Federalists, and this, afterwards, provoked much controversy. It now is established that the bargain was made. See Professor McMaster's conclusion: "The price settled . . . the Republicans secured ten states." (McMaster, ii, 526.)

[3] For accounts by participants in this exciting and historic contest, see Gallatin's letters to his wife and to Nicholson from Feb. 5 to Feb. 19, 1801; Adams: *Gallatin,* 257–63; Dana to Wolcott, Feb. 11, 1801; Gibbs, ii, 489–90; Bayard to several friends, Feb. 22, 1801; *Bayard Papers, supra.*

The terms concluded with Jefferson, enough Federalists cast blank ballots[1] to permit his election; and so the curtain dropped on this comedy of shame.[2] "Thus has ended the most wicked and absurd attempt ever tried by the Federalists," said the innocent Gallatin.[3] So it came about that the party of Washington, as a dominant and governing force in the development of the American Nation, went down forever in a welter of passion, tawdry politics, and disgraceful intrigue. All was lost, including honor.

But no! All was not lost. The Judiciary remained. The newly elected House and President were Republican and in two years the Senate also would be "Jacobin"; but no Republican was as yet a member of the National Judiciary. Let that branch of the Government be extended; let new judgeships be created, and let new judges be made while Federalists could be appointed and confirmed, so that, by means, at least, of the National Courts, States' Rights might be opposed and retarded, and Nationalism defended and advanced — thus ran the thoughts and the plans of the Federalist leaders.

Adams, in the speech to Congress in December of the previous year, had urged the enactment of a law to this end as "indispensably necessary."[4] In the

[1] Jefferson to Madison, Feb. 18, 1801; *Works: Ford*, ix, 183.

[2] After Jefferson's election, for many days the *Washington Federalist* carried in italics at the head of its editorial columns a sentiment characteristic of Marshall: "*May he discharge its duties in such a manner as to merit and receive the blessings of all good men and without redding the cheek of the American Patriot with blushes for his country!!!*"

[3] Gallatin to his wife, Feb. 17, 1801; Adams: *Gallatin*, 262.

[4] Adams to Congress, Dec. 3, 1799; *Annals*, 6th Cong., 1st Sess.,

President's address to the expiring Federalist Congress on December 3, 1800, which Marshall wrote, the extension of the National Judiciary, as we have seen, was again insistently urged.[1] Upon that measure, at least, Adams and all Federalists agreed. "Permit me," wrote General Gunn to Hamilton, "to offer for your consideration, the policy of the federal party *extending the influence of our judiciary;* if neglected by the federalists the ground will be occupied by the enemy, the very next session of Congress, and, sir, we shall see —— and many other scoundrels placed on the seat of justice." [2]

Indeed, extension of the National Judiciary was now the most cherished purpose of Federalism.[3] A year earlier, after Adams's first recommendation of it, Wolcott narrates that "the steady men" in the Senate and House were bent upon it, because "there is no other way to combat the state opposition [to National action] but by an efficient and extended organization of judges." [4]

Two weeks after Congress convened, Roger Griswold of Connecticut reported the eventful bill to

187–88; and Richardson, i, 289. Yet at this period the business of the courts was actually decreasing. (See Brown: *Ellsworth*, 198.) But the measure was demanded by the bar generally and insisted upon by the Justices of the Supreme Court. (See Gibbs, ii, 486.)

[1] Adams to Congress, Dec. 3, 1799; as written by Marshall; Adams MSS.

[2] Gunn to Hamilton, Dec. 13, 1800; *Works:* Hamilton, vi, 483.

[3] The Federalist attitude is perfectly expressed in the following toast drunk at a banquet to Wolcott, attended by "the heads of departments" and the Justices of the Supreme Court: "*The Judiciary of the United States! Independent of party, independent of power and independent of popularity.*" (*Gazette of the United States,* Feb. 7, 1801.)

[4] Wolcott to Ames, Dec. 29, 1799; Gibbs, ii, 316.

carry out this Federalist plan.[1] It was carefully and ably drawn and greatly widened the practical effectiveness of the National Courts. The Supreme Court was reduced, after the next vacancy, to five members — to prevent, said the Republicans, the appointment of one of their party to the Nation's highest tribunal.[2] Many new judgeships were created. The Justices of the Supreme Court, who had sat as circuit judges, were relieved of this itinerant labor and three circuit judges for each circuit were to assume these duties. At first, even the watchful and suspicious Jefferson thought that "the judiciary system will not be pushed, as the appointments, if made, by the present administration, could not fall on those who create them."[3]

[1] *Annals*, 6th Cong., 1st Sess., Dec. 19, 837–38.
[2] *Richmond Examiner*, Feb. 6, 1801.
[3] Jefferson to Madison, Dec. 19, 1800; *Works:* Ford, ix, 159. The Republicans were chiefly alarmed because, in the extension of the National Judiciary, offices would be provided for Federalists. Even Jefferson then saw nothing but patronage in the Judiciary Act.

The "evident" purpose of the bill, said the *Aurora*, Feb. 4, 1801, was to "increase the influence of the present Executive and provide a *comfortable retreat* for some of those *good federalists* who have found it convenient to resign from their offices or been dismissed from them by the people."

In comparison to this objection little attention was paid to the more solid ground that the National Judiciary would be used to "force the introduction of the common law of England as a part of the law of the United States"; or even to the objection that, if the Judiciary was extended, it would "strengthen the system of terror by the increase of prosecutions under the Sedition law"; or to the increase of the "enormous influence" given the National Courts by the Bankruptcy Law.

The *Aurora*, March 18, 1801, sounded the alarm on these and other points in a clanging editorial, bidding *"the people beware,"* for "the hell hounds of persecution may be let loose . . . and the people be ROASTED into implicit acquiescence with every measure of the ' powers that be.'" But at this time it was the creation of offices that the Federalists would fill to which the Republicans chiefly objected.

But Jefferson underestimated the determination of the Federalists. Because they felt that the bill would "greatly extend the judiciary power and of course widen the basis of government," they were resolved, writes Rutledge, to "profit of our short-lived majority, and do as much good as we can before the end of this session" [1] by passing the Judiciary Bill.

In a single week Jefferson changed from confidence to alarm. After all, he reflected, Adams could fill the new judgeships, and these were life appointments. "I dread this above all the measures meditated, because appointments in the nature of freehold render it difficult to undo what is done," [2] was Jefferson's second thought.

The Republicans fought the measure, though not with the vigor or animosity justified by the political importance they afterwards attached to it. Among the many new districts created was an additional one in Virginia. The representatives from that State dissented; but, in the terms of that period, even their opposition was not strenuous. They said that, in Virginia, litigation was declining instead of increasing. "At the last term the docket was so completely cleared in . . . ten days . . . that the court . . . had actually decided on several [suits] returnable to the ensuing term." [3]

That, replied the Federalists, was because the courts were too far away from the citizens. As for the National revenues, they could be collected only

---

[1] Rutledge to Madison, Jan. 10, 1801; *Works:* Hamilton, vi, 511.

[2] Jefferson to Madison, Dec. 26, 1800; *Works:* Ford, ix, 161.

[3] *Annals*, 6th Cong., 1st Sess., 878.

through National tribunals; for this purpose,[1] two Federal Courts in Virginia, as provided by the bill, were essential. But, of course, sneered the Federalists, "Virginia would be well satisfied with one court in preference to two or with no court whatever in preference to one." [2]

But there was a defect in the bill, intimated the Virginia Republicans, that affected tenants and landowners of the Northern Neck. A clause of section thirteen gave the newly established National Court jurisdiction of all causes arising under the Constitution where original or exclusive jurisdiction was not conferred upon the Supreme Court or Admiralty Courts.[3] The National Court of the new Virginia District was to be held at Fredericksburg. Thus all suits for quitrents or other claims against those holding their lands under the Fairfax title could be brought in this near-by National Court, instead of in State Courts. This criticism was so attenuated and so plainly based on the assumption that the State Courts would not observe the law in such actions, that it was not pressed with ardor even by the impetuous and vindictive Giles.

But Nicholas went so far as to move that the jurisdiction of National Courts should be limited to causes exceeding five hundred dollars. This would cut out the great mass of claims which the present holders of the Fairfax title might lawfully have against tenants or owners. The Marshalls were the Fairfax assign-

[1] *Annals*, 6th Cong., 1st Sess., 879.

[2] *Ib.* The person who made this absurd speech is not named in the official report.

[3] *Ib.*, 896.

ees, as we have seen. No Republican, however, mentioned them in debate; but some one procured the insertion in the record of an insinuation which nobody made on the floor. In brackets, the "Annals," after the brief note of Nicholas's objection, states: "[It is understood that the present assignees of the claims of Lord Fairfax, are General Marshall, General Lee, and a third individual and that they maintain their claims under the British Treaty.]"[1]

For three weeks the debate in the House dragged along. Republican opposition, though united, was languid.[2] At last, without much Republican resistance, the bill passed the House on January 20, 1801, and reached the Senate the next day.[3] Two weeks later the Senate Republicans moved a substitute providing for fewer circuits, fewer judges, and a larger Supreme Court, the members of which were to act as circuit judges as formerly.[4] It was defeated by a vote of 17 to 13.[5] The next day the bill was passed by a vote of 16 to 11.[6]

When the debate began, the National Judiciary was without a head. Ellsworth, broken in health, had resigned. Adams turned to Jay, the first Chief Justice, and, without asking his consent, reappointed him. "I have nominated you to your old station,"[7]

---

[1] *Annals*, 6th Cong., 1st Sess., 897. This curious entry is, plainly, the work of some person who wished to injure Marshall and Lee. Nicholas's motion was lost, but only by the deciding vote of the Speaker. (*Ib.*) The bill, as finally passed, limited the jurisdiction of the National Courts to causes exceeding four hundred dollars. (*Ib.*)

[2] *Ib.*, 900, 901, 903, and 905.

[3] *Ib.*, 734.   [4] *Ib.*, 740–41.   [5] *Ib.*, 741.   [6] *Ib.*, 742.

[7] Adams to Jay, Dec. 19, 1800; *Works: Adams*, ix, 91.

wrote the President. "This is as independent of the inconstancy of the people, as it is of the will of a President." But Jay declined.[1] Some of the Federalist leaders were disgruntled at Jay's appointment. "Either Judge Paterson [of New Jersey] or General Pinckney ought to have been appointed; but both these worthies were your friends," [2] Gunn reported to Hamilton. The Republicans were relieved by Jay's nomination — they "were afraid of something worse." [3]

Then, on January 20, 1801, with no herald announcing the event, no trumpet sounding, suddenly, and without previous notification even to himself, John Marshall was nominated as Chief Justice of the United States a few weeks before the Federalists went out of power forever. His appointment was totally unexpected. It was generally thought that Judge Paterson was the logical successor to Ellsworth.[4] Marshall, indeed, had recommended his selection.[5] The letters of the Federalist leaders, who at this period were lynx-eyed for any office, do not so much as mention Marshall's name in connection with the position of Chief Justice.

Doubtless the President's choice of Marshall was influenced by the fact that his "new minister,

---

[1] Jay to Adams, Jan. 2, 1800; *Jay:* Johnston, iv, 284. Jay refused the reappointment because he believed the Supreme Court to be fatally lacking in power. See chap. I, vol. III, of this work.

[2] Gunn to Hamilton, Dec. 18, 1800; *Works:* Hamilton, vi, 492.

[3] Jefferson to Madison, Dec. 19, 1800; *Works:* Ford, ix, 159. It is impossible to imagine what this "something worse" was. It surely was not Marshall, who was in nobody's mind for the Chief Justiceship when Jay was named.

[4] Pickering to King, Jan. 12, 1801; King, iii, 367.

[5] Story, in Dillon, iii, 359.

Marshall, did all to " his " entire satisfaction." [1] Federalist politicians afterward caviled at this statement of Adams. It was quite the other way around, they declared. "Every one who knew that great man [Marshall] knew that he possessed to an extraordinary degree the faculty of putting his own ideas into the minds of others, unconsciously to them. The secret of Mr. Adams's satisfaction [with Marshall] was, that he obeyed his Secretary of State without suspecting it." [2]

The President gave Marshall's qualifications as the reason of his elevation. Boudinot reported to Adams that the New Jersey bar hailed with "the greatest pleasure" a rumor that "the office of Chief Justice . . . may be filled by" Adams himself "after the month of March next." The President, who admitted that he was flattered, answered: "I have already, by the nomination of a gentleman in the full vigor of middle age, in the full habits of business, and whose reading of the science is fresh in his head,[3] to this office, put it wholly out of my power as it never was in my hopes or wishes." [4]

Marshall's appointment as Chief Justice was not

[1] Adams to William Cunningham, Nov. 7, 1808; *Cunningham Letters*, no. xiv, 44; also mentioned in Gibbs, ii, 349.

[2] Gibbs, ii, 349, 350.

[3] As we have seen, Marshall's "reading of the science," "fresh" or stale, was extremely limited.

[4] Adams to Boudinot, Jan. 26, 1801; *Works: Adams*, ix, 93–94. Adams's description of Marshall's qualifications for the Chief Justiceship is by way of contrast to his own. "The office of Chief Justice is too important for any man to hold of sixty-five years of age who has wholly neglected the study of the law for six and twenty years." (*Ib.*) Boudinot's "rumor" presupposes an understanding between Jefferson and Adams.

greeted with applause from any quarter; there was even a hint of Federalist resentment because Paterson had not been chosen. "I see it denied in your paper that Mr. Marshall was nominated Chief Justice of the U.S. The fact is so and he will without doubt have the concurrence of the Senate, tho' some hesitation was at first expressed from respect for the pretensions of Mr. Paterson."[1] The Republican politicians were utterly indifferent; and the masses of both parties neither knew nor cared about Marshall's elevation.

The Republican press, of course, criticized the appointment, as it felt bound to attack any and every thing, good or bad, that the Federalists did. But its protests against Marshall were so mild that, in view of the recklessness of the period, this was a notable compliment. "The vacant Chief Justiceship is to be conferred on John Marshall, one time General, afterwards ambassador to X. Y. and Z., and for a short time incumbent of the office of Secretary of State. . . . Who is to receive the salary of the Secretary of State, after Mr. Marshall's resignation, we cannot foretell, because the wisdom of our wise men surpasseth understanding."[2] Some days later the "Aurora," in a long article, denounced the Judiciary Law as a device for furnishing defeated Federalist politicians with offices,[3]

[1] Bayard to Andrew Bayard, Jan. 26, 1801; *Bayard Papers:* Donnan, 122.

[2] *Aurora*, Jan. 22, 1801.

[3] It is worthy of repetition that practically all the emphasis in their attacks on this act was laid by the Republicans on the point that offices were provided for Federalists whose characters were bitterly assailed. The question of the law's enlargement of National power was, com-

and declared that the act would never be "carried
into execution, . . . unless" the Federalists still
meant to usurp the Presidency. But it goes on
to say: —

"We cannot permit ourselves to believe that *John
Marshall* has been called to the bench to foster such
a plot. . . . Still, how can we account for the strange
mutations which have passed before us — Marshall
for a few weeks Secretary of State ascends the bench
of the Chief Justice." [1] The principal objection of
the Republican newspapers to Marshall, however,
was that he, "before he left the office [of Secretary of
State], made provision for all the Federal printers to
the extent of his power. . . . He employed the *aristocratic presses alone* to publish laws . . . for . . . one
year." [2]

Only the dissipated and venomous Callender, from
his cell in prison, displayed that virulent hatred of
Marshall with which an increasing number of Jefferson's followers were now obsessed. "We are to have
that precious acquisition John Marshall as Chief
Justice. . . . The very sound of this man's name is
an insult upon truth and justice"; and the dissolute
scribbler then pours the contents of his ink-pot
over Marshall's X. Y. Z. dispatches, bespatters his
campaign for election to Congress, and continues
thus:—

"John Adams first appointed John Jay in the
room of Ellsworth. A strong suspicion exists that

paratively, but little mentioned; and the objections enlarged upon in
recent years were not noticed by the fierce partisans of the time.

[1] *Aurora*, Feb. 3, 1801.

[2] *Baltimore American;* reprinted in the *Aurora*, April 2, 1801.

John did this with the previous certainty that John Jay would refuse the nomination. It was then in view to name John Marshall: first, because President Jefferson will not be able to turn him out of office, unless by impeachment; and in the second place that the faction [Federalist Party] who burnt the war office might, with better grace, attempt, forsooth, to set him up as a sort of president himself. *Sus ad Minervam!*" [1]

That the voice of this depraved man, so soon to be turned against his patron Jefferson, who had not yet cast him off, was the only one raised against Marshall's appointment to the highest judicial office in the Nation, is a striking tribute, when we consider the extreme partisanship and unrestrained abuse common to the times.

Marshall himself, it appears, was none too eager to accept the position which Ellsworth had resigned and Jay refused; the Senate delayed the confirmation of his nomination; [2] and it was not until the last day of the month that his commission was executed.

On January 31, 1801, the President directed Dexter "to execute the office of Secretary of State so far as to affix the seal of the United States to the inclosed commission to the present Secretary of State, John Marshall, of Virginia, to be Chief Justice of the United States, and to certify in your own

---

[1] *Richmond Examiner*, Feb. 6, 1801.

[2] Marshall's nomination was confirmed January 27, 1801, a week after the Senate received it. Compare with the Senate's quick action on the nomination of Marshall as Secretary of State, May 12, 1800, confirmed May 13. (Executive Journal of the Senate, iii.)

name on the commission as executing the office of Secretary of State *pro hac vice*." [1]

It was almost a week before Marshall formally acknowledged and accepted the appointment. "I pray you to accept my grateful acknowledgments for the honor conferred on me in appointing me Chief Justice of the United States. This additional and flattering mark of your good opinion has made an impression on my mind which time will not efface. I shall enter immediately on the duties of the office, and hope never to give you occasion to regret having made this appointment." [2] Marshall's acceptance greatly relieved the President, who instantly acknowledged his letter: "I have this moment received your letter of this morning, and am happy in your acceptance of the office of Chief Justice." [3]

Who should be Secretary of State for the remaining fateful four weeks? Adams could think of no one but Marshall, who still held that office although he had been appointed, confirmed, and commissioned as Chief Justice. Therefore, wrote Adams, "the circumstances of the times . . . render it necessary that I should request and authorize you, as I do by this letter, to continue to discharge all the duties of Secretary of State until ulterior arrangements can be made." [4]

Thus Marshall was at the same time Chief Jus-

---

[1] Adams to Dexter, Jan. 31, 1801; *Works:* Adams, ix, 95-96.
[2] Marshall to Adams, Feb. 4, 1801; *ib.*, 96.
[3] Adams to Marshall, Feb. 4, 1801; *ib.*, 96.
[4] Same to same, Feb. 4, 1801; *ib.*, 96-97.

tice of the Supreme Court and Secretary of State. Never has there been another such combination in one man of these two highest appointive offices of the National Government. He drew but one salary, of course, during this period, that of Chief Justice,[1] the salary of Secretary of State remaining unpaid.

The President rapidly filled the newly created places on the Federal Bench. Marshall, it appears, was influential in deciding these appointments. "I wrote for you to Dexter, requesting him to show it to Marshall,"[2] was Ames's reassuring message to an aspirant to the Federal Bench. With astounding magnanimity or blindness, Adams bestowed one of these judicial positions upon Wolcott, and Marshall "transmits . . . the commission . . . with peculiar pleasure. Permit me," he adds, "to express my sincere wish that it may be acceptable to you." His anxiety to make peace between Adams and Wolcott suggests that he induced the President to make this appointment. For, says Marshall, "I will allow myself the hope that this high and public evidence, given by the President, of his respect for your services and character, will efface every unpleasant sensation respecting the past, and smooth the way to a perfect reconciliation."[3]

[1] Auditor's Files, Treasury Department, no. 12, 166. This fact is worthy of mention only because Marshall's implacable enemies intimated that he drew both salaries. He could have done so, as a legal matter, and would have been entirely justified in doing so for services actually rendered. But he refused to take the salary of Secretary of State.

[2] Ames to Smith, Feb. 16, 1801; *Works: Ames*, i, 292.

[3] Marshall to Wolcott, Feb. 24, 1801; Gibbs, ii, 495.

Wolcott "cordially thanks" Marshall for "the obliging expressions of" his "friendship." He accepts the office "with sentiments of gratitude and good will," and agrees to Marshall's wish for reconciliation with Adams, "not only without reluctance or reserve but with the highest satisfaction." [1] Thus did Marshall end one of the feuds which so embarrassed the Administration of John Adams. [2]

Until nine o'clock [3] of the night before Jefferson's inauguration, Adams continued to nominate officers, including judges, and the Senate to confirm them. Marshall, as Secretary of State, signed and sealed the commissions. Although Adams was legally within his rights, the only moral excuse for his conduct was that, if it was delayed, Jefferson would make the appointments, control the National Judiciary, and through it carry out his States' Rights doctrine which the Federalists believed would dissolve the

[1] Wolcott to Marshall, March 2, 1801; Gibbs, ii, 496.

[2] The irresponsible and scurrilous Callender, hard-pressed for some pretext to assail Marshall, complained of his having procured the appointment of relatives to the Judiciary establishment. "Mr. John Marshall has taken particular care of his family," writes Jefferson's newspaper hack, in a characteristically partisan attack upon Adams's judicial appointments. (Scots correspondent, in *Richmond Examiner*, March 13, 1801.)

Joseph Hamilton Davies, a brother-in-law of Marshall's, was appointed United States Attorney for the District of Kentucky; George Keith Taylor, another brother-in-law, was appointed United States Judge of the Fourth Circuit; and Marshall's brother, James M. Marshall, was appointed Assistant Judge of the Territory (District) of Columbia. These appointments were made, however, before the new Judiciary Act was passed. (Executive Journal of the Senate, i, 357, 381, 387.) Callender appears to have been the only person to criticize these appointments. Even Jefferson did not complain of them or blame Marshall for them. The three appointees were competent men, well fitted for the positions; and their appointment, it seems, was commended by all.

[3] Jefferson to Rush, March 24, 1801; *Works*: Ford, ix, 231.

Union; if Adams acted, the most the Republicans could do would be to oust his appointees by repealing the law.[1]

The angry but victorious Republicans denounced Adams's appointees as "midnight judges." It was a catchy and clever phrase. It flew from tongue to tongue, and, as it traveled, it gathered force and volume. Soon a story grew up around the expression. Levi Lincoln, the incoming Attorney-General, it was said, went, Jefferson's watch in his hand, to Marshall's room at midnight and found him signing and sealing commissions. Pointing to the timepiece, Lincoln told Marshall that, by the President's watch, the 4th of March had come, and bade him instantly lay down his nefarious pen; covered with humiliation, Marshall rose from his desk and departed.[2]

---

[1] The Republicans did so later. "This outrage on decency should not have its effect, except in life appointments [judges] which are irremovable." (Jefferson to Knox, March 27, 1801; *Works:* Ford, ix, 237.)

[2] Parton: *Jefferson,* 585–86. Parton relates this absurd tale on the authority of Jefferson's great-granddaughter. Yet this third-hand household gossip has been perpetuated by serious historians. The only contemporary reference is in the address of John Fowler of Kentucky to his constituents published in the *Aurora* of April 9, 1801: "This disgraceful abuse was continued to the latest hour of the President's holding his office." The "shameful abuse" was thus set forth: "It [Judiciary Law of 1801] creates a host of judges, marshalls, attorneys, clerks, &c, &c, and is calculated, if it could endure, to unhinge the state governments and render the state courts contemptible, while it places the courts of law in the hands of creatures of those who have lost the confidence of the people by their misconduct. The insidiousness of its design has been equalled only by the shameless manner of its being carried into execution. The Constitution disables any member of Congress from filling an office created during his period of service. The late President [Adams] removed persons from other branches of the Judiciary, to the offices created

This tale is, probably, a myth. Jefferson never spared an enemy, and Marshall was his especial aversion. Yet in his letters denouncing these appointments, while he savagely assails Adams, he does not mention Marshall.[1] Jefferson's "Anas," inspired by Marshall's "Life of Washington," omits no circumstance, no rumor, no second, third, or fourth hand tale that could reflect upon an enemy. Yet he never once refers to the imaginary part played by Marshall in the "midnight judges" legend.[2]

Jefferson asked Marshall to administer to him the presidential oath of office on the following day. Considering his curiously vindictive nature, it is unthinkable that Jefferson would have done this had he sent his newly appointed Attorney-General, at the hour of midnight, to stop Marshall's consummation of Adams's "indecent"[3] plot.

Indeed, in the flush of victory and the multitude of practical and weighty matters that immediately claimed his entire attention, it is probable that Jefferson never imagined that Marshall would prove to

by this law & then put members of Congress into the thus vacated offices. . . . This law can be considered in no other light than as providing pensions for the principals and adherents of a party [Federalist]. The evil however will not I trust be durable and as it was founded in fraud the return of a wiser system will release the country from the shame and imposition." (Fowler to his constituents in the *Aurora*, April 9, 1801.)

[1] Jefferson to Rush, March 24, 1801; *Works:* Ford, ix, 230–31; to Knox, March 27, 1801; *ib.*, 237; to Mrs. Adams, June 13, 1804; *ib.*, x, 85.

[2] Neither Randall nor Tucker, Jefferson's most complete and detailed biographers, both partisans of the great Republican, mentions the Lincoln-Marshall story, although, if it had even been current at the time they wrote, it is likely that they would have noticed it.

[3] Jefferson to Knox, *supra*.

be anything more than the learned but gentle Jay or the able but innocuous Ellsworth had been. Also, as yet, the Supreme Court was, comparatively, powerless, and the Republican President had little cause to fear from it that stern and effective resistance to his anti-national principles, which he was so soon to experience. Nor did the Federalists themselves suspect that the Virginia lawyer and politician would reveal on the Supreme Bench the determination, courage, and constructive genius which was presently to endow that great tribunal with life and strength and give to it the place it deserved in our scheme of government.

In the opinions of those who thought they knew him, both friend and foe, Marshall's character was well understood. All were agreed as to his extraordinary ability. No respectable person, even among his enemies, questioned his uprightness. The charm of his personality was admitted by everybody. But no one had, as yet, been impressed by the fact that commanding will and unyielding purpose were Marshall's chief characteristics. His agreeable qualities tended to conceal his masterfulness. Who could discern in this kindly person, with "lax, lounging manners," indolent, and fond of jokes, the heart that dared all things? And all overlooked the influence of Marshall's youth, his determinative army life, his experience during the disintegrating years after Independence was achieved and before the Constitution was adopted, the effect of the French Revolution on his naturally orderly mind, and the part he had taken and the ineffaceable impressions necessarily made upon him by the tremendous events of the first three Administrations of the National Government.

Thus it was that, unobtrusively and in modest guise, Marshall took that station which, as long as he lived, he was to make the chief of all among the high places in the Government of the American Nation.

END OF VOLUME II

APPENDIX

APPENDIX

I. LIST OF CASES

ARGUED BY MARSHALL BEFORE THE COURT OF APPEALS OF VIRGINIA

Case	Date	Reported
Joseph Cutchin v. William Wilkinson	Spring Term, 1797	1 Call, 1
William Fairclaim, lessee, v. Richard and Elizabeth Guthrie	Spring Term, 1797	1 Call, ‹5
Cabell et al. v. Hardwick	Fall Term, 1798	1 Call, 301
Hopkins v. Blane	Fall Term, 1798	1 Call, 315
Pryor v. Adams	Fall Term, 1798	1 Call, 332
Proudfit v. Murray	Fall Term, 1798	1 Call, 343
Harrison v. Harrison, et al.	Fall Term, 1798	1 Call, 364
Shaw et al. v. Clements	Fall Term, 1798	1 Call, 373
Graves v. Webb	Fall Term, 1798	1 Call, 385
Jones v. Jones	Fall Term, 1798	1 Call, 396
Auditor of Public Accounts v. Graham	Fall Term, 1798	1 Call, 411
Beverley v. Fogg	Spring Term, 1799	1 Call, 421
Rowe et al. v. Smith	Spring Term, 1799	1 Call, 423
Ritchie & Co. v. Lyne	Spring Term, 1799	1 Call, 425
Eckhols v. Graham, et al.	Spring Term, 1799	1 Call, 428
Noel v. Sale	Spring Term, 1799	1 Call, 431
Lee v. Love & Co.	Spring Term, 1799	1 Call, 432
Wilson v. Rucker	Spring Term, 1799	1 Call, 435
Garlington v. Clutton	Spring Term, 1799	1 Call, 452
Taliaferro v. Minor	Spring Term, 1799	1 Call, 456
Hacket v. Alcock	Spring Term, 1799	1 Call, 463
Rose v. Shore	Spring Term, 1799	1 Call, 469
Smith v. Dyer	Spring Term, 1799	1 Call, 488
Macon v. Crump	Spring Term, 1799	1 Call, 500
Flemings v. Willis et ux.	Fall Term, 1799	2 Call, 5
Eppes, Ex'r, v. DeMoville, Adm'r	Fall Term, 1799	2 Call, 19
Cooke v. Simms	Fall Term, 1799	2 Call, 33
Lawrason, Adm'r v. Davenport et al.	Fall Term, 1799	2 Call, 79
Price et al. v. Campbell	Fall Term, 1799	2 Call, 92
Eppes et al., Ex'rs, v. Randolph	Fall Term, 1799	2 Call, 103
Taliaferro v. Minor	Fall Term, 1799	2 Call, 156

Case	Date	Reported
Anderson *v.* Anderson............	Fall Term, 1799......	2 Call, 163
Crump *et al. v* Dudley *et ux*......	June, 1790...........	3 Call, 439
Beall *v.* Edmondson.............	June, 1790...........	3 Call, 446
Johnsons *v.* Meriwether.........	July, 1790...........	3 Call, 454
Barrett *et al. v.* Floyd *et al*.......	July, 1790...........	3 Call, 460
Syme *v.* Johnston..............	December, 1790......	3 Call, 482
Ross *v.* Pynes..................	December, 1790......	3 Call, 490
Rev. John Bracken *v.* The Visitors of William and Mary College...	December, 1790......	3 Call, 495
Hite *et al. v.* Fairfax *et al*........	May, 1786...........	4 Call, 42
Pickett *v.* Claiborne.............	October, 1787........	4 Call, 99
Beall *v.* Cockburn...............	July, 1790...........	4 Call, 162
Hamilton *v.* Maze...............	June, 1791...........	4 Call, 196
Calvert *v.* Bowdoin	June, 1791...........	4 Call, 217
Tabb *v.* Gregory................	April, 1792...........	4 Call, 225
Ross *v.* Gill *et ux*...............	April, 1794...........	4 Call, 250
White *v.* Jones.................	October, 1792........	4 Call, 253
Marshall *et al. v.* Clark..........	November, 1791......	4 Call, 268
Foushee *v.* Lea.................	April, 1795...........	4 Call, 279
Braxton *et al. v.* Winslow *et al*....	April, 1791...........	4 Call, 308
Commonwealth *v.* Cunningham & Co.........................	October, 1793........	4 Call, 331
Johnston *v.* Macon..............	December, 1790......	4 Call, 367
Hooe *v.* Marquess..............	October, 1798........	4 Call, 416
Chapman *v.* Chapman..........	April, 1799...........	4 Call, 430
Mayo *v.* Bentley................	October, 1800........	4 Call, 528
Turberville *v.* Self...............	April, 1795...........	4 Call, 580
Executors of William Hunter and the Executors of Herndon *v.* Alexander Spotswood.........	Fall Term, 1792.....	1 Wash. 145
Stevens *v.* Taliaferro, Adm'r......	Spring Term, 1793...	1 Wash. 155
Kennedy *v.* Baylor.............	Spring Term, 1793...	1 Wash. 162
Baird and Briggs *v.* Blaigove, Ex'r........................	Spring Term, 1793...	1 Wash. 170
Bannister's Ex'rs *v.* Shore........	Spring Term, 1793...	1 Wash. 173
Clayborn, Ex'r *v.* Hill..........	Spring Term, 1793...	1 Wash. 177
Anderson *v.* Bernard...........	Spring Term, 1793...	1 Wash. 186
Johnson *v.* Bourn..............	Spring Term, 1793...	1 Wash. 187
Eustace *v.* Gaskins, Ex'r.......	Spring Term, 1793...	1 Wash. 188
Wilson and McRae *v.* Keeling....	Fall Term, 1793.....	1 Wash. 195
Payne, Ex'r, *v.* Dudley, Ex'r.....	Fall Term, 1793.....	1 Wash. 196
Hawkins *v.* Berkley............	Fall Term, 1793.....	1 Wash. 204
Hooe & Harrison *et al. v.* Mason..	Fall Term, 1793.....	1 Wash. 207
Thweat & Hinton *v.* Finch.......	Fall Term, 1793.....	1 Wash. 217
Brown's Adm'r *v.* Garland *et al*...	Fall Term, 1793.....	1 Wash. 221
Jones *v.* Williams & Tomlinson...	Fall Term, 1793.....	1 Wash. 230

Case	Date	Reported
Coleman *v.* Dick & Pat.	Fall Term, 1793	1 Wash. 233
Taylor's Adm'rs *v.* Peyton's Adm'rs	Spring Term, 1794	1 Wash. 252
Smith and Moreton *v.* Wallace	Spring Term, 1794	1 Wash. 254
Carr *v.* Gooch	Spring Term, 1794	1 Wash. 260
Cole *v.* Clayborn	Spring Term, 1794	1 Wash. 262
Shermer *v.* Shermer	Fall Term, 1794	1 Wash. 266
Ward *v.* Webber *et ux.*	Fall Term, 1794	1 Wash. 274
Applebury *et al. v.* Anthony's Ex'rs	Fall Term, 1794	1 Wash. 287
Smallwood *v.* Mercer *et al.*	Fall Term, 1794	1 Wash. 290
Minnis Ex'r, *v.* Philip Aylett	Fall Term, 1794	1 Wash. 300
Brown's Ex'rs *v.* Putney	Fall Term, 1794	1 Wash. 302
Leftwitch *et ux. v.* Stovall	Fall Term, 1794	1 Wash. 303
Lee, Ex'r, *v.* Cooke	Fall Term, 1794	1 Wash. 306
Burnley *v.* Lambert	Fall Term, 1794	1 Wash. 308
Cooke *v.* Beale's Ex'rs	Fall Term, 1794	1 Wash. 313
Dandridge *v.* Harris	Fall Term, 1794	1 Wash. 326
Nicolas *v.* Fletcher	Fall Term, 1794	1 Wash. 330
Watson & Hartshorne *v.* Alexander	Fall Term, 1794	1 Wash. 340
Wroe *v.* Washington *et al.*	Fall Term, 1794	1 Wash. 357
Cosby, Ex'r, *v.* Hite	Fall Term, 1794	1 Wash. 365
Hewlett *v.* Chamberlayne	Fall Term, 1794	1 Wash. 367
Pendleton *v.* Vandevier	Fall Term, 1794	1 Wash. 381
Walden, Ex'r, *v.* Payne	Fall Term, 1794	2 Wash. 1
James Roy *et al. v.* Muscoe Garnett	Fall Term, 1794	2 Wash. 9
James Ferguson *et al. v.* Moore	Spring Term, 1795	2 Wash. 54
Currie *v.* Donald	Spring Term, 1795	2 Wash. 58
Shelton *v.* Barbour	Spring Term, 1795	2 Wash. 64
Brock *et al. v.* Philips	Spring Term, 1795	2 Wash. 68
Turner *v.* Moffett	Spring Term, 1795	2 Wash. 70
Turberville *v.* Self	Spring Term, 1795	2 Wash. 71
Brydie *v.* Langham	Spring Term, 1795	2 Wash. 72
Bernard *v.* Brewer	Fall Term, 1795	2 Wash. 76
Philip McRae *v.* Richard Woods	Fall Term, 1795	2 Wash. 80
Newell *v.* The Commonwealth	Fall Term, 1795	2 Wash. 88
White *v.* Atkinson	Fall Term, 1795	2 Wash. 94
Martin & William Picket *v.* James Dowdall	Fall Term, 1795	2 Wash. 106
Claiborne *v.* Parrish	Fall Term, 1795	2 Wash. 146
Brown *et al. v.* Adm'r, Thomas Brown, dec'd	Fall Term, 1795	2 Wash. 151
Harrison, Ex'r, *v.* Sampson	Fall Term, 1795	2 Wash. 155
Harvey *et ux. v.* Borden	Fall Term, 1795	2 Wash. 156
Lee *v.* Turberville	Fall Term, 1795	2 Wash. 162

II. GENERAL MARSHALL'S ANSWER TO AN ADDRESS OF THE CITIZENS OF RICHMOND, VIRGINIA

I WILL not, Gentlemen, attempt to describe the emotions of joy which my return to my native country, and particularly to this city, has excited in my mind; nor can I paint the sentiments of affection and gratitude towards you which my heart has ever felt, and which the kind and partial reception now given me by my fellow citizens cannot fail to increase. He only who has been . . . absent from a much loved country, and from friends greatly and deservedly esteemed — whose return is welcomed with expressions, which, di[rec]ted by friendship, surpass his merits or his ho[pes,] will judge of feelings to which I cannot do justice.

The situation in which the late Envoys from [the] United States to the *French Republic* found themselves in *Paris* was, indeed, attended with the unpleasant circumstances which you have traced. — Removed far from the councils of their country, and receiving no intelligence concerning it, the scene before them could not fail to produce the most anxious and disquieting sensations. Neither the ambition, the power, nor the hostile temper of *France*, was concealed from them; nor could they be unacquainted with the earnest and unceasing solicitude felt by the government and people of the *United States* for peace. But midst these difficulties, they possessed, as guides, clear and explicit instructions, a conviction of the firmness and magnanimity, as well as of the justice and pacific temper of their government, and a strong reliance on that patriotism and love of liberty, which can never cease to glow in the American bosom. With these guides, however thorny the path of duty might be, they could not mistake it. It was their duty, unmindful of personal considerations, to pursue peace with unabating zeal, through all the difficulties with which the pursuit was embarrassed by a haughty and victorious government, holding in perfect contempt the rights of others, but to repel, with unhesitating decision, any propositions, an acceptance of which would subvert the independence of the *United States*. — This they have endeavoured to do. I delight to believe that their endeavours have not dissatisfied their government or country, and it is most grateful to my mind to be assured that they receive the approbation of my fellow-citizens in *Richmond*, and its vicinity.

I rejoice that I was not mistaken in the opinion I had formed of my countrymen. I rejoice to find, though they know how to estimate, and therefore seek to avoid the horrors and dangers of war, yet they know also how to value the blessings of liberty and national independence: — They know that peace would be purchased at too high a price by bending beneath a foreign yoke, and that peace so purchased could be but of short duration. The nation thus submitting would be soon involved in the quarrels of its master, and would be compelled to exhaust its blood and its treasure, not for its own liberty, its own independence, or its own rights, but for the aggrandizement of its oppressor. The modern world unhappily exhibits but too plain a demonstration of this proposition. I pray heaven that *America* may never contribute its still further elucidation.

Terrible to her neighbors on the continent of *Europe*, as all must admit *France* to be, I believe that the *United States*, if indeed united, if awake to the impending danger, if capable of employing their whole, their undivided force — are so situated as to be able to preserve their independence. An immense ocean placed by a gracious Providence, which seems to watch over this rising empire, between us and the European world, opposes of itself such an obstacle to an invading ambition, must so diminish the force which can be brought to bear upon us, that our resources, if duly exerted, must be adequate to our protection, and we shall remain free if we do not deserve to be slaves.

You do me justice, gentlemen, when you suppose that consolation must be derived from a comparison of the Administration of the American Government, with that which I have lately witnessed. To a citizen of the *United States*, so familiarly habituated to the actual possession of liberty, that he almost considers it as the inseparable companion of man, a view of the despotism, which borrowing the garb and usurping the name of freedom, tyrannizes over so large and so fair a proportion of the earth, must teach the value which he ought to place on the solid safety and real security he enjoys at home. In support of these, all temporary difficulties, however great, ought to be encountered, and I agree with you that the loss of them would poison and embitter every other joy; and that deprived of them, men who aspire to the exalted character of freemen, would turn with loathing and disgust from every other comfort of life.

To me, gentlemen, the attachment you manifest to the government of your choice affords the most sincere satisfaction. Having no interests separate from or opposed to those of the people, being themselves subject in common with others, to the laws they make, being soon to return to that mass from which they are selected for a time in order to conduct the affairs of the nation, it is by no means probable that those who administer the government of the *United States* can be actuated by other motives than the sincere desire of promoting the real prosperity of those, whose destiny involves their own, and in whose ruin they must participate. Desirable as it is at all times, a due confidence in our government, it is peculiarly so in a moment of peril like the present, in a moment when the want of that confidence must impair the means of self defence, must increase a danger already but too great, and furnish, or at least give the appearance of furnishing, to a foreign real enemy, those weapons, which have so often been so successfully used.

Accept, gentlemen, my grateful acknowledgments for your kind expressions concerning myself, and do me the justice to believe, that your prosperity, and that of the city of *Richmond* and its vicinity, will ever be among the first wishes of my heart.

(From *Columbian Centinel*, Saturday, Sept. 22, 1798.)

III. FREEHOLDER'S QUESTIONS TO GENERAL MARSHALL

VIRGINIA. Fredericksburg, Oct. 2

POLITICAL QUESTIONS

Addressed to General MARSHALL *with his Answer thereto*
To J. MARSHALL, Esq.

RICHMOND, Sept. 12.

DEAR SIR,

Under a conviction that it will be of utility, should the answers to the following questions be such as I anticipate, I state them with a confidence of your readiness to give replies. They will, at all events, greatly satisfy my mind.

1st. Do you not in heart, and sentiment, profess yourself an American — attached to the genuine principles of the Constitution, as sanctioned by the will of the people, for their general liberty, prosperity and happiness?

2d. Do you conceive that the true interest and prosperity of *America*, is materially, or at all, dependent upon an alliance with any foreign nation? If you do, please state the causes, and a preference, if any exists, with the reasons for that preference.

3d. Are you in favor of an alliance, offensive and defensive, with *Great Britain?* In fine, are you disposed to advocate any other, or a closer connection with that nation, than exists at the ratification of the treaty of 1794? If so, please state your reasons.

4th. By what general principles, in your view, have the measures of our Administration and Government, in respect to *France*, been consistent with true policy or necessity? And could not the consequences have been avoided by a different line of conduct on our part?

5th. Are you an advocate for the Alien and Sedition Bills? Or, in the event of your election, will you use your influence to obtain a appeal of these laws?

A FREEHOLDER

(*Columbian Centinel*, Boston, Mass., Saturday, October 20, 1798.)

MARSHALL'S ANSWERS TO FREEHOLDER'S QUESTIONS

RICHMOND, Sept. 20, '98.

DEAR SIR: —

I have just received your letter of yesterday, [*sic*] and shall with equal candor and satisfaction, answer all your queries. Every citizen has a right to know the political sentiments of the man who is proposed as his representative; and mine have never been of a nature to shun examination. To those who think another gentleman more capable of serving the district than myself, it would be useless to explain my opinions because whatever my opinions may be, they will, and ought, to vote for that other; but I cannot help wishing that those who think differently, would know my real principles, and not attribute to me those I never possessed; and with which active calumny has been pleased to asperse me.

Answ. 1. In heart and sentiment, as well as by birth and interest, I am an American, attached to the genuine principles of the constitution, as sanctioned by the will of the people, for their general liberty, prosperity and happiness. I consider that constitution as the rock of our political salvation, which has preserved us from misery, division and civil wars; and which will yet preserve us if we value it rightly and support it firmly.

2. I do not think the interest and prosperity of America, at all dependent on the alliance with any foreign nation; nor does the man exist who would regret more than myself the formation of such an alliance. In truth, America has, in my opinion, no motive for forming such connection, and very powerful motives for avoiding them. Europe is eternally engaged in wars in which we have no interest; and with which the fondest policy forbids us to intermeddle.

We ought to avoid any compact which may endanger our being involved in them. My sentiments on this subject are detailed at large in the beginning of the memorial addressed by the late envoys from the United States to the minister of foreign affairs of the French Republic, where the neutrality of the United States is justified, and the reasons for that neutrality stated.

3rd. I am not in favor of an alliance offensive and defensive with Great Britain nor for closer connection with that nation than already exists. No man in existence is more decidedly opposed to such an alliance, or more fully convinced of the evils that would result from it. I never have, in thought, word, or deed, given the smallest reason to suspect I wished it; nor do I believe any man acquainted with me does suspect it. Those who originate and countenance such an idea, may (if they know me) design to impose on others, but they do not impose on themselves.

The whole of my politics respecting foreign nations are reducible to this single position. We ought to have commercial intercourse with all, but political ties with none. Let us buy cheap and sell as dear as possible. Let commerce go wherever individual, and consequently national interest, will carry it; but let us never connect ourselves politically with any nation whatever.

I have not a right to say, nor can I say positively, what are the opinions of those who administer the Government of the United States; but I believe firmly that neither the President, nor any one of those with whom he advises, would consent to form a close and permanent political connection with any nation upon earth.

Should France continue to wage an unprovoked war against us, while she is also at war with Britain, it would be madness and folly not to endeavor to make such temporary arrangements as would give us the aid of the British fleets to prevent our being invaded; but I would not, even to obtain so obvious a good, make such a sacrifice as I think we should make, by forming a permanent political connection with that, or any other nation on earth.

4th. The measures of the administration and government of the United States with respect to France have in my opinion been uniformly directed by a sincere and unequivocal desire to observe, faithfully, the treaties existing between the two nations and to preserve the neutrality and independence of our country. — Had it been possible to maintain peace with France without sacrificing those great objects, I am convinced that our government would have maintained it.

Unfortunately it has been impossible. I do not believe that any different line of conduct on our part, unless we would have relinquished the rights of self government, and have become the colonies of France, could have preserved peace with that nation. — But be assured that the primary object of France is and for a long time past has been, dominion over others. This is a truth only to be disbelieved by those who shut their eyes on the history and conduct of that nation.

The grand instruments by which they effect this end, to which all their measures tend, are immense armies on their part, and divisions, which a variety of circumstances have enabled them to create, among those whom they wish to subdue. Whenever France has exhibited a disposition to be just toward the United States, an accurate attention to facts now in possession of the public, will prove that this disposition was manifest in the hope of involving us in her wars, as a dependent and subordinate nation.

5th. I am not an advocate for the alien and sedition bills; had I been in Congress when they passed, I should, unless my judgment could have been changed, certainly have opposed them. Yet, I do not think them fraught with all those mischiefs which many gentlemen ascribe to them. I should have opposed them because I think them useless; and because they are calculated to create unnecessary discontents and jealousies at a time when our very existence, as a nation, may depend on our union —

I believe that these laws, had they been opposed on these principles by a man, not suspected of intending to destroy the government, or being hostile to it, would never have been enacted. With respect to their repeal, the effort will be made before I can become a member of Congress.

If it succeeds there will be an end of the business — if it fails, I shall on the question of renewing the effort, should I be chosen to represent the district, obey the voice of my constituents. My own private opinion is, that it will be unwise to renew it for this reason: the laws will expire of themselves, if I recollect rightly the time for which they are enacted, during the term of the ensuing Congress. I shall indisputably oppose their revival; and I believe that opposition will be more successful, if men's minds are not too much irritated by the struggle about a repeal of laws which will, at the time, be expiring of themselves.

J. MARSHALL.

(From *Times and Virginia Advertiser*, Alexandria, Va., Oct. 11, 1798.)

WORKS CITED IN THIS VOLUME

WORKS CITED IN THIS VOLUME

The material given in parentheses and following certain titles indicates the form in which those titles have been cited in the footnotes.

ADAMS, CHARLES FRANCIS, *editor. See* Adams, John. Works.

ADAMS, HENRY. The Life of Albert Gallatin. Philadelphia. 1879. (Adams: *Gallatin.*)
> *See also* Gallatin, Albert. Writings.

ADAMS, JOHN. Works. Edited by Charles Francis Adams. 10 vols. Boston. 1856. (*Works:* Adams.)

—— Old Family Letters. Copied from the originals for Alexander Biddle. Philadelphia. 1892. (*Old Family Letters.*)

—— Correspondence between the Honorable John Adams, late President of the United States, and the late William Cunningham. Boston. 1823. (*Cunningham Letters.*)
> *See also* Wood, John. History of Administration of John Adams.

ADAMS, JOHN QUINCY. Writings. Edited by Worthington Chauncey Ford. 5 vols. New York. 1913. (*Writings, J. Q. A.:* Ford.)

ALLEN, GARDNER WELD. Our Naval War with France. Boston. 1909. (Allen: *Our Naval War With France.*)

—— Our Navy and the Barbary Corsairs, Boston. 1905. (Allen: *Our Navy and the Barbary Corsairs.*)

AMBLER, CHARLES HENRY. Sectionalism in Virginia, from 1776 to 1861. Chicago. 1910. (Ambler.)

American Historical and Literary Curiosities. See Smith, John Jay, and Watson, John Fanning, *joint editors.*

American Historical Review. Managing editor, J. Franklin Jameson. Vols. 1–21. New York. 1896–1916. (*Amer. Hist. Rev.*)

American Remembrancer, The; or An Impartial Collection of Essays, Resolves, Speeches, &c., Relative, or Having Affinity to, the Treaty with Great Britain. 3 vols. Philadelphia. 1795. (*American Remembrancer.*)

American State Papers. Documents, Legislative and Executive, of Congress of the United States. Selected and

Edited under the Authority of Congress. 38 vols. Washington, D.C. 1832–61. [All citations in this work are
from Foreign Relations, Class I, unless otherwise stated
in the notes.] (*Am. St. Prs.*)

AMES, FISHER. Works, from his Speeches and Correspondence.
Edited by his son, Seth Ames. 2 vols. Boston. 1854.
(*Works:* Ames.)

ANDERSON, DICE ROBINS. William Branch Giles: A Study in
the Politics of Virginia and the Nation from 1790 to 1830.
Menasha, Wisconsin. 1914. (Anderson.)

AUSTIN, JAMES T. The Life of Elbridge Gerry, with Contemporary Letters. 2 vols. Boston. 1828–29. (Austin:
Gerry.)

AVERY, ELROY MCKENDREE. A History of the United States
and its people. 7 vols. Cleveland. 1904–10. (Avery.)

BASSETT, JOHN SPENCER. The Federalist System, 1789–1801.
[Volume 2 of The American Nation.] New York. 1906.
(Bassett.)

BAYARD, JAMES A. Papers, from 1796 to 1815. Edited by
Elizabeth Donnan. Washington. 1915. [Volume 2 of
Annual Report of the American Historical Association for
1913.] (*Bayard Papers:* Donnan.)

BEARD, CHARLES A. An Economic Interpretation of the Constitution of the United States. New York. 1913. (Beard:
Econ. I. C.)

—— Economic Origins of Jeffersonian Democracy. New
York. 1915. (Beard: *Econ. O. J. D.*)

BEAUMARCHAIS, PIERRE AUGUSTIN CARON DE. Beaumarchais
et son temps. *See* Loménie, Louis de.

BEE, THOMAS. Reports of Cases Decided in the District Court
of South Carolina and Cases Determined in Other Districts of the United States. Philadelphia. 1810. (Bee's
Reports.)

BENTON, THOMAS HART. *See* United States. Congress.
Abridgment of the Debates.

BINNEY, HORACE. Eulogy on John Marshall, reprinted. *See*
Dillon, John F.

BLENNERHASSETT, CHARLOTTE JULIA [VON LEYDEN], *Lady.*
Talleyrand. By Lady Blennerhassett (Gräfin Leyden).
Translated from the German by Frederick Clarke. 2 vols.
London. 1894. (Blennerhassett: *Talleyrand.*)

BONAPARTE, NAPOLEON. Life. *See* Sloane, William Milligan.
Also see Lanfrey, Pierre. History of Napoleon First.

BRACKENRIDGE, HENRY M. History of the Western Insurrection in Pennsylvania, commonly called the Whiskey Insurrection, 1794. Pittsburgh. 1859. (Brackenridge: *History of the Western Insurrection*.)

BRANCH, JOHN P. Historical Papers, issued by the Randolph-
Macon College, Ashland, Virginia. Richmond. 1901.
(*Branch Historical Papers*.)

BRISSOT DE WARVILLE, JEAN PIERRE. New Travels in the
United States of America, performed in 1788. Dublin.
1792. (De Warville.)

BROGLIE, *Duc* DE, *editor*. *See* Talleyrand, Prince de. Memoirs.

BROWN, WILLIAM GARROTT. The Life of Oliver Ellsworth.
New York. 1905. (Brown: *Ellsworth*.)

BURK, JOHN DALY. The History of Virginia, from its First Settlement to the Present Day. Continued by Skelton Jones
and Louis Hue Girardin. 4 vols. Richmond. 1804–16. (Burk.)

BURKE, EDMUND. Works, with a Memoir. 3 vols. New York.
1849. (*Works:* Burke.)

BURR, AARON. Memoirs. *See* Davis, Matthew L.
Also see Parton, James. Life and Times of Aaron Burr.

CABOT, GEORGE. *See* Lodge, Henry Cabot. Life and Letters
of George Cabot.

Calendar of Virginia State Papers and Other Manuscripts.
Preserved in the Capitol at Richmond. Vols. 1–11. Richmond. 1875–93. (*Cal. Va. St. Prs.*)

CALLENDER, JOHN THOMAS. The Prospect Before Us. Richmond. 1800. (Callender: *The Prospect Before Us*.)

CHANNING, EDWARD. A History of the United States. [Vols.
1–3.] New York. 1912–16. (Channing.)

CHASTELLUX, *Marquis* F. J. DE. Travels in North America in
the years 1780–81–82. New York. 1828. (Chastellux.)

CHRISTIAN, WILLIAM ASBURY. Richmond, Her Past and Present. Richmond. 1912. (Christian.)

COBBETT, WILLIAM. Porcupine's Works, 1783 to 1801. 12
vols. London. 1801. (Cobbett.)

CONWAY, MONCURE DANIEL. Omitted Chapters of History,
disclosed in the Life and Papers of Edmund Randolph.
New York. 1888. (Conway.)
—— *Also see* Paine, Thomas. Writings.

COXE, TENCH. An Examination of the Conduct of Great Britain Respecting Neutrals. Philadelphia. 1807. (Coxe: *An Examination of the Conduct of Great Britain Respecting Neutrals*.)

CUNNINGHAM, WILLIAM. *See* Adams, John. Correspondence.

DALLAS, A. J. *See* United States. Supreme Court Reports.

DAVIS, JOHN. Travels of Four Years and a half in the United States of America. 1798–1802. London. 1803. (Davis.)

DAVIS, MATTHEW L. Memoirs of Aaron Burr, with miscellaneous selections from his correspondence. 2 vols. New York. 1838. (Davis: *Burr*.)

Dedham [Mass.] Historical Register. Vols. 1–14. Dedham Historical Society, Dedham, Mass. 1890–1903. (*Dedham Historical Register*.)

DE WARVILLE. *See* Brissot de Warville, Jean Pierre.

DILLON, JOHN F., *compiler*. John Marshall, Life, Character, and Judicial Services. (Including the Classic Orations of Binney, Story, Phelps, Waite, and Rawle.) 3 vols. Chicago. 1903. (Story, in Dillon; and Binney, in Dillon.)

DODD, WILLIAM E. Statesmen of the Old South, or From Radicalism to Conservative Revolt. New York. 1911. (Dodd.)

DONNAN, ELIZABETH, *editor*. *See* Bayard, James A. Papers.

ECKENRODE, H. J. The Revolution in Virginia. Boston. 1916. (Eckenrode: *R. V.*)

—— Separation of Church and State in Virginia. A Study in the Development of the Revolution. Richmond. 1910. [Special Report of the Department of Archives and History of the Virginia State Library.] (Eckenrode: *S. of C. and S.*)

ELLSWORTH, *Chief Justice* OLIVER. Life. *See* Brown, William Garrott.

FINDLEY, WILLIAM. History of the Insurrection, in the Four Western Counties of Pennsylvania, in the year 1794. Philadelphia. 1796. (Findley: *History of the Western Insurrection*.)

FLANDERS, HENRY. The Lives and Times of the Chief Justices of the Supreme Court of the United States. 2 vols. Philadelphia. 1881. (Flanders.)

FORD, PAUL LEICESTER, *editor*. *See* Jefferson, Thomas. Works.
FORD, WORTHINGTON CHAUNCEY, *editor*. *See* Jefferson, Thomas.
   Correspondence.
   Also see Washington, George. Writings.
   And *see also* Adams, John Quincy. Writings.
   Also see Vans Murray, William. Letters.
FRENEAU, PHILIP. Poems of Philip Freneau. Edited by Fred
   Lewis Pattee. 3 vols. Princeton. 1902–07. (Freneau.)
FUNCK-BRENTANO, FRANTZ. Legends of the Bastille, trans-
   lated by George Maidment. London. 1899. (Funck-
   Brentano: *Legends of the Bastille*.)

GALLATIN, ALBERT. Writings. Edited by Henry Adams.
   3 vols. Philadelphia. 1879. (Gallatin's *Writings:* Adams.)
   See also Adams, Henry. Life of Albert Gallatin.
GARLAND, HUGH A. Life of John Randolph of Roanoke. 2 vols.
   New York. 1851. (Garland: *Randolph*.)
GAY, SYDNEY HOWARD. James Madison. [American States-
   men Series.] Boston. 1895.
GIBBS, GEORGE, *editor*. *See* Wolcott, Oliver. Memoirs of the
   Administrations of Washington and John Adams. (Gibbs.)
GILMAN, DANIEL C. James Monroe, in his Relations to the
   Public Service During Half a Century. 1776 to 1826.
   [American Statesmen Series.] Boston. 1895.
GILMER, FRANCIS WALKER. Sketches, Essays, and Transla-
   tions. Baltimore, 1828. (Gilmer.)
GRAYDON, ALEXANDER. Memoirs of His Own Time, with Remi-
   niscences of the Men and Events of the Revolution. Edited
   by John Stockton Littell. Philadelphia. 1846. (Graydon.)
Green Bag, The; an Entertaining Magazine for Lawyers.
   Edited by Horace W. Fuller. Vols. 1–26. Boston. 1889–
   1914. [After 1914 consolidated with *The Central Law
   Journal*.] (*Green Bag*.)
GRIGSBY, HUGH BLAIR. The History of the Virginia Federal
   Convention of 1788. Virginia Historical Society. Rich-
   mond. 1815. [Volume 1 is volume 9, new series. Volume
   2 is volume 10, new series.] (Grigsby.)

HAMILTON, ALEXANDER. Works. Edited by John C. Hamilton.
   7 vols. New York. 1851. (*Works:* Hamilton.)
—— Works. Edited by Henry Cabot Lodge. [Federal Edition.] 12 vols. New York. 1904. (*Works:* Lodge.)

HAMILTON, JOHN C., *editor*. History of the Republic of the United States, as traced in the Writings of Alexander Hamilton and his Contemporaries. 6 vols. New York. 1857–60. (Hamilton: *History of the Republic*.) *See also* Hamilton, Alexander. Works.

HAMILTON, STANISLAUS MURRAY, *editor*. *See* Monroe, James. Writings.

HAZEN, CHARLES DOWNER. Contemporary American Opinion of the French Revolution. Baltimore. 1897. (Hazen.)

HENING, WILLIAM WALLER. *See* Virginia. Laws.

HENRY, PATRICK. Life, Correspondence, and Speeches. Edited by William Wirt Henry. 3 vols. New York. 1891. (Henry.)
See also Wirt, William. Sketches of Life and Character of Patrick Henry.

HENRY, WILLIAM WIRT, *editor*. *See* Henry, Patrick. Life, Correspondence, and Speeches.

HILDRETH, RICHARD. History of the United States. 6 vols. New York. 1854–55. (Hildreth.)

Historical Magazine and Notes and Queries Concerning the Antiquities, History, and Biography of America. [1st Series.] Vols. 1–10. New York. 1857–75. (*Hist. Mag.*)

HOWE, HENRY. Historical Collections of Virginia. Charleston, S.C. 1845. (Howe.)

HUDSON, FREDERIC. Journalism in the United States from 1690 to 1872. New York. 1873. (Hudson: *Journalism in the United States*.)

HUNT, GAILLARD, *editor*. *See* Madison, James. Writings.

Interesting State Papers, from President Washington, M. Fauchet, and M. Adet, etc.; quoted by Edmund Randolph, Secretary of State, in his Defense of his Resignation of that Office. Philadelphia. 1796. (*Interesting State Papers*.)

IREDELL, JAMES. *See* McRee, Griffith J. Life and Correspondence of James Iredell.

JAY, JOHN. Correspondence and Public Papers. Edited by Henry P. Johnston. 4 vols. New York. 1890. (*Jay: Johnston*.)

JEFFERSON, THOMAS. Works. Edited by Paul Leicester Ford.

Federal Edition. 12 vols. New York. 1904. (*Works:*
Ford.)
  See Morse, John T. Thomas Jefferson.
  And see Randall, Henry S. Life of Thomas Jefferson.
  Also see Tucker, George. Life of Thomas Jefferson.
  And see Parton, James. Life of Thomas Jefferson.
JOHNSTON, HENRY P., *editor. See* Jay, John. Correspondence
and Public Papers.
JOHNSTON, MARY. Lewis Rand. Boston. 1908.
JONES, HUGH. The Present State of Virginia. London. 1724.
(Jones.)

KENNEDY, JOHN P. Memoirs of the Life of William Wirt. 2
vols. Philadelphia. 1860. (Kennedy.)
KING, CHARLES R., *editor. See* King, Rufus. Life and Corre-
spondence.
KING, RUFUS. Life and Correspondence. Edited by Charles
R. King. 6 vols. New York. 1894. (King.)

LANCASTER, ROBERT A., JR. Historic Virginia Homes and
Churches, with 316 Illustrations. Philadelphia. 1915.

LANFREY, PIERRE. The History of Napoleon the First. 4 vols.
London. 1871–79. (Lanfrey: *Napoleon.*)
LA ROCHEFOUCAULD-LIANCOURT, FRANÇOIS ALEXANDRE
FRÉDÉRIC, *Duc* DE. Travels through the United States of
North America. 4 vols. London. 1800. (La Rochefoucauld.)
Lippincott's Monthly Magazine. A Popular Journal of General
Literature. [1st Series.] Vols. 1–62. Philadelphia. 1868–
98. (*Lippincott's Magazine.*)
LODGE, HENRY CABOT. Life and Letters of George Cabot.
Boston. 1878. (Lodge: *Cabot.*)
—— George Washington. 2 vols. Boston. 1889. [American
Statesmen.] (Lodge: *Washington.*)
  See also Hamilton, Alexander. Works.
LOLIÉE, FRÉDÉRIC. Prince Talleyrand and His Times.
Adapted by Bryan O'Donnell. London. 1911. (Loliée:
Talleyrand and His Times.)
LOMÉNIE, LOUIS DE. Beaumarchais et son temps. 2 vols.
Paris. 1856. (Loménie: *Beaumarchais et son temps.*)
LORING, JAMES SPEAR. The Hundred Boston Orators. Boston.
1855. (Loring: *Hundred Boston Orators.*)

Louisiana Law Journal. Edited by Gustavus Schmidt. [1 vol.] New Orleans. 1841–42.

LYMAN, THEODORE, JR. The Diplomacy of the United States. 2 vols. Boston. 1828. (Lyman: *Diplomacy of the United States.*)

MACCABE, JOSEPH. Talleyrand, A Biographical Study. London. 1906. (MacCabe: *Talleyrand.*)

MCHENRY, JAMES. Life and Correspondence. *See* Steiner, Bernard C.

MCMASTER, JOHN BACH. A History of the People of the United States. 8 vols. New York. 1914. (McMaster.)

MCREE, GRIFFITH, J. Life and Correspondence of James Iredell. 2 vols. New York. 1857. (McRee.)

MADISON, JAMES. Writings. Edited by Gaillard Hunt. 9 vols. New York. 1900. (*Writings:* Hunt.)
  See also Rives, William C. History of Life and Times.
  And see Gay, Sydney Howard. James Madison.

MARSHALL, HUMPHREY. The History of Kentucky. 2 vols. Frankfort. 1824. (Humphrey Marshall.)

MARSHALL, JOHN. Autobiography. *See* Smith, John Jay *and* Watson, John Fanning, *joint editors.* American Historical and Literary Curiosities. (*Autobiography.*)

—— Same. In National Portrait Gallery of Eminent Americans. Paintings by Alonzo Chappel, and Biographical and Historical Narratives by Evert A. Duyckinck. 2 vols. New York. 1862.

—— Same, reprinted. *See* Dillon, John F.

—— Life of George Washington. [1st Edition.] 5 vols. Philadelphia. 1805. [2d Edition.] 2 vols. Philadelphia. 1840. [The 2d Edition is cited in this work unless otherwise stated in the notes.] (Marshall.)
  See also Thayer, James Bradley. John Marshall.
  And see Flanders, Henry. Lives of the Chief Justices.
  Also see Van Santvoord, George. Sketches of the Lives of the Chief-Justices.

MASON, GEORGE. Life. *See* Rowland, Kate Mason.

Massachusetts Historical Society. Collections. [Series vii.] Vols. 1–10. Boston. 1792–1915. (Mass. Hist. Soc. Coll.)

MEADE, *Bishop* WILLIAM. Old Churches, Ministers, and Families of Virginia. 2 vols. Richmond. 1910. (Meade.)

MONROE, JAMES. Writings. Edited by Stanislaus Murray Hamilton. 7 vols. [Unfinished work.] New York. 1898–1903. (Monroe's *Writings:* Hamilton.)

MOORE, FRANK. American Eloquence, A Collection of Speeches and Addresses by the most Eminent Orators of America. 2 vols. New York. 1857. (Moore: *American Eloquence.*)

MORDECAI, SAMUEL. Richmond in By-Gone Days, Being Reminiscences of An Old Citizen. Richmond. 1856. (Mordecai.)

MORISON, SAMUEL ELIOT. The Life and Letters of Harrison Gray Otis, Federalist, 1765–1848. 2 vols. Boston. 1913. (Morison.)

MORRIS, GOUVERNEUR. Diary and Letters. Edited by Anne Cary Morris. 2 vols. London. 1889. (Morris.)

MORRIS, ROBERT. *See* Oberholtzer, Ellis Paxton. Robert Morris.

MORSE, JOHN T. Thomas Jefferson. Boston. 1795. [American Statesmen.] (Morse.)

MUNFORD, GEORGE WYTHE. The Two Parsons; Cupid's Sports; The Dream; and the Jewels of Virginia. Richmond. 1884. (Munford.)

New Jersey Historical Society. Proceedings. Vols. 1–10. Newark. 1847–1905. (*Proc.,* N.J. Hist. Soc.)

North American Review. Vols. 1–202. Boston. 1815–1915.

OBERHOLTZER, ELLIS PAXTON. Robert Morris, Patriot and Financier. New York. 1903. (Oberholtzer.)

OTIS, HARRISON GRAY. Life and Letters. *See* Morison, Samuel Eliot.

PAINE, ROBERT TREAT, JR. Works, in Verse and Prose, with Sketches of His Life, Character, and Writings. Boston. 1812. (*Works of Robert Treat Paine.*)

PAINE, THOMAS. Writings. Edited by Moncure Daniel Conway. 4 vols. New York. 1894–96. (*Writings:* Conway.)

PARTON, JAMES. The Life and Times of Aaron Burr. [Fourteenth Edition.] New York. 1861. (Parton: *Burr.*)

—— Life of Thomas Jefferson. Boston. 1874.

PAULDING, JAMES K. A Life of Washington. 2 vols. 1835. [Harper's Family Library. Stereotype Edition, 1836.] (Paulding.)

PAXTON, WILLIAM M. The Marshall Family, or a Genealogical Chart of the Descendants of John Marshall and Elizabeth Markham. Cincinnati. 1885. (Paxton.)

PECQUET DU BELLET, LOUISE. Some Prominent Virginia Families. 4 vols. Lynchburg, Va. 1909. (Pecquet du Bellet.)

Pennsylvania Magazine of History and Biography. Published by the Historical Society of Pennsylvania. Vols. 1–40. Philadelphia. 1877–1916. (*Pa. Mag. Hist. and Biog.*)

PERKINS, JAMES BRECK. France in the American Revolution. Boston. 1911. (Perkins: *France in the American Revolution.*)

PICKERING, OCTAVIUS. Life of Timothy Pickering, by his son and continued by Charles W. Upham. 4 vols. Boston. 1867–73. (Pickering: *Pickering.*)

PICKERING, TIMOTHY. Life. *See* Pickering, Octavius.

RANDALL, HENRY S. Life of Thomas Jefferson. 3 vols. New York. 1858. (Randall.)

RANDOLPH, EDMUND. Life and Papers. *See* Conway, Moncure Daniel.

RANDOLPH, JOHN. Life. *See* Garland, Hugh A.

RICHARDSON, JAMES D. A Compilation of the Messages and Papers of the Presidents. 1789–1897. 10 vols. Washington, D.C. 1896–99. (Richardson.)

RIVES, WILLIAM C. The History of the Life and Times of James Madison. 3 vols. Boston. 1859. (Rives.)

ROWLAND, KATE MASON. Life of George Mason. 2 vols. New York. 1892. (Rowland.)

SCHMIDT, GUSTAVUS, editor. *See* Louisiana Law Journal.

SCHOEPF, JOHANN DAVID. Travels in the Confederation, 1783–1784. Translated and edited by Alfred J. Morrison. 2 vols. Philadelphia. 1911. (Schoepf.)

SCHOULER, JAMES. History of the United States of America under the Constitution. 1783–1877. 7 vols. Washington, D.C. 1895–1913. (Schouler.)

SCOTT, JOHN, of Fauquier County, Va. The Lost Principle. By "Barbarossa" [*pseud.*]. Richmond. 1860. (Scott.)

SLOANE, WILLIAM MILLIGAN. Life of Napoleon Bonaparte. 4 vols. New York. 1796–1897. (Sloane: *Life of Napoleon.*)

SMITH, JOHN JAY, *and* WATSON, JOHN FANNING, *joint editors.*
American Historical and Literary Curiosities. New York.
1852. (*Am. Hist. and Lit. Curiosities.*)
Southern Literary Messenger. Vols. 1–38. New York and
Washington. 1834–64.
SPARKS, JARED. Correspondence of the American Revolution
[being letters' of eminent men to George Washington].
4 vols. Boston. 1853. (*Cor. Rev.*: Sparks.)
     See also Washington, George. Writings.
STEINER, BERNARD C. The Life and Correspondence of James
McHenry. Cleveland. 1907. (Steiner.)
STORY, JOSEPH. Discourse on John Marshall, reprinted.
     See Dillon, John F.
     Also see Story, William Wirt.
STORY, WILLIAM WIRT. Life and Letters of Joseph Story. 2
vols. Boston. 1851. (Story.)

TALLEYRAND-PÉRIGORD, CHARLES MAURICE DE, *Prince* DE
BÉNÉVENT. Memoirs. Edited by the' Duc de Broglie.
5 vols. New York. 1891. (*Memoirs of Talleyrand:* Bro-
glie's Ed.)
—— Memoirs. [Edited] by [—— Stewarton] the author of the
Revolutionary Plutarch. 2 vols. London. 1805. (*Me-
moirs of Talleyrand:* Stewarton.)
     See Loliée, Frédéric. Talleyrand and His Times.
     Also see Blennerhassett, Charlotte Julia, *Lady.* Talley-
rand.
     And see MacCabe, Joseph. Life.
THAYER, JAMES BRADLEY. John Marshall. Boston. 1904.
[Riverside Biographical Series, No. 9.] (Thayer.)
THOMPSON, JOHN, *of* Petersburg, Virginia. The Letters of
Curtius. Richmond. 1804. (Thompson: *Letters of Cur-
tius.*)
TICKNOR, ANNA, *and* HILLARD, GEORGE S. *joint editors.* *See*
Ticknor, George. Life, Letters, and Journals.
TICKNOR, GEORGE. Life, Letters, and Journals. Edited by
Anna Ticknor and George S. Hillard. 2 vols. Boston.
1876. (Ticknor.)
TUCKER, GEORGE. Life of Thomas Jefferson. 2 vols. Phila-
delphia. 1837. (Tucker.)

United States. Congress. Debates and Proceedings in the Congress of the United States. [1st Congress, 1st Session, to 18th Congress, 1st Session; Mar. 3, 1789 to May 27, 1824.] 41 vols. Washington, D.C. 1834–56.

—— Benton, Thomas Hart. Abridgment of the Debates of Congress from 1789 to 1856. 16 vols. New York. 1857–61.

UNITED STATES. State Trials. State Trials of the United States during the Administrations of Washington and Adams. By Francis Wharton. Philadelphia. 1849. (Wharton: *State Trials.*)

UNITED STATES. Supreme Court Reports. Dallas, A. J. Reports of the Cases Ruled and Adjudged in the Courts of Pennsylvania before and since the Revolution. Philadelphia. 4 vols. 1806–07.

VAN SANTVOORD, GEORGE. Sketches of the Lives and Judicial Services of the Chief-Justices of the Supreme Court of United States. New York. 1854. (Van Santvoord.)

VAN TYNE, CLAUDE HALSTEAD. The Loyalists in the American Revolution. New York. 1902.

VANS MURRAY, WILLIAM. Letters to John Quincy Adams, 1797–1803. Edited by Worthington Chauncey Ford. [Reprinted from the *Annual Report of the American Historical Association* for 1912, pp. 341–715.] Washington. 1914. (*Letters:* Ford.)

VIRGINIA. House of Delegates. Journal of the Virginia House of Delegates. 1776–1916. Now in the Archives of the Virginia State Library. (Journal, H.D.)

VIRGINIA. Laws. Hening, William Waller. The Statutes at Large. Being a Collection of the Laws of Virginia from 1619 to 1808. 13 vols. New York. 1819–23. (Hening.)

VIRGINIA. Laws. Revised Code, of the Laws of Virginia, being a Collection of all such Acts of the General Assembly. [By William Waller Hening.] 2 vols. Richmond. 1819. (Laws of Virginia, Revised Code, 1819.)

VIRGINIA. Law Reports. Call, Daniel. Reports of Cases Argued and Adjudged in the Court of Appeals of Virginia. 6 vols. Richmond. 1824–33. (Call.)

VIRGINIA. Law Reports. Washington, Bushrod. Reports of Cases Argued and Determined in the Court of Appeals of Virginia. 2 vols. Richmond. 1798–99.

Virginia Magazine of History and Biography. Published by the Virginia Historical Society. Vols. 1–24. Richmond. 1893–1916. (*Va. Mag. Hist. and Biog.*)

VON HOLST, H. The Constitutional and Political History of the United States, by Dr. H. von Holst. [Translated from the German by John J. Lalor, and Alfred B. Mason.] 7 vols. Chicago. 1876. (Von Holst: *Constitutional History of the United States.*)

WARVILLE. *See* Brissot de Warville.

WASHINGTON, BUSHROD. *See* Virginia. Law Reports.

WASHINGTON, GEORGE. Diary from 1789 to 1791. Edited by Benson J. Lossing. New York. 1860. (Washington's *Diary:* Lossing.)

—— Writings. Edited by Worthington Chauncey Ford. 14 vols. New York. 1889–93. (*Writings:* Ford.)

—— Writings. Edited by Jared Sparks. 12 vols. Boston. 1834–37. (*Writings:* Sparks.)

  And Lodge, Henry Cabot. George Washington.

  Also Marshall, John. Life of George Washington.

  Also see Paulding, James K. Life of Washington.

WASHINGTON, H. A., *editor. See* Jefferson, Thomas. Writings.

WATSON, JOHN FANNING. Annals of Philadelphia and Pennsylvania, In the Olden Time. 3 vols. Philadelphia. 1877–79. (Watson: *Annals of Philadelphia.*)

WELD, ISAAC. Travels Through the States of North America, and the Provinces of Upper and Lower Canada During the Years 1795, 1796, and 1797. [3d Edition.] 2 vols. London. 1800. (Weld.)

WHARTON, FRANCIS. *See* United States. State Trials.

WIRT, WILLIAM. The Letters of the British Spy. [9th Edition.] Baltimore. 1831. (Wirt: *British Spy.*)

—— Sketches of the Life and Character of Patrick Henry. Philadelphia. 1818. (Wirt.)

  See Kennedy, John P. Memoirs of William Wirt.

WISE, JOHN SERGEANT. The End of An Era. Boston. 1899. (Wise: *The End of An Era.*)

WOLCOTT, OLIVER. Memoirs of the Administrations of Washington and John Adams. Edited from the papers of Oliver Wolcott, by George Gibbs. 2 vols. New York. 1846. (Gibbs.)

WOOD, JOHN. History of Administration of John Adams, Esq. Late President of the United States. New York. 1802. (Wood.)

𝕮𝖍𝖊 𝕽𝖎𝖛𝖊𝖗𝖘𝖎𝖉𝖊 𝕻𝖗𝖊𝖘𝖘

CAMBRIDGE . MASSACHUSETTS

U . S . A